W9-BPJ-496

TABLE OF CONTENTS

PART 1— HOW TO RAISE A CAT WHEN
NOBODY'S HOME

PART 2— THE NOBODY'S HOME
CAT GROWS UP

PART 3— PENNY PINCHING HOME
HEALTH CARE

This book was inspired by
and dedicated to my husband Jim
and our cat-loving family

With appreciation to
Juanita Riedel
Lisa Climer-Harding
Marian W. Koppler

Preface

Dear Readers,

In this book I have tried to share with you the joy and companionship our family has shared with our cats and the rewards of having well-trained, fun-loving feline friends.

I designed the book to be read from cover to cover in just a few evenings. Along with training suggestions there are also stories to instruct and entertain you.

Once you have read this easy-to-use guide to successful cat rearing, you will wish to refer to it frequently as you encounter discipline problems with your growing kitten. In fact, the reason I am asking you to read the book through at once, is because many times the solutions given in one area of training may also be used successfully in other situations.

I hope all of you from eight to eighty enjoy raising a healthy, happy, loving cat to maturity and old age with the help of this book.

Jerry Climer

How To Raise
A Cat
When
Nobody's Home

Training and Fun
For You and
The Family Cat

SECOND EDITION
Written by Jerry Climer
Illustrated by Robert R. Hetzer

Excerpts from this book previously appeared
in *Cat Fancy Magazine* columns, *One Cat Lover.*

How To Raise A Cat When Nobody's Home
Copyright 1983-1992, by Jerry Climer

Second Edition, completely revised and expanded.
All rights reserved. Reproduction prohibited
without permission.

Set in typeface designed for easy reading.
Printed in the United States of America.
Library of Congress Cataloging in Publication Data
International Standard Book Number 0911793-04-6

Penny Dreadful Publishers
315 South Bowen St
P. O. Box 364
Jackson, Michigan 49204

PART 4— MAN AND CAT LIVING,
      LOVING, COPING

PART 5— QUESTIONS AND ANSWERS

PART 1

How To Raise
A Cat
When Nobody's
Home

The Capricious Feline

There is one word that truly describes a domestic feline—capricious. It is defined in my *Webster's New World Dictionary* as "sudden, impulsive, apparently unmotivated turn of the mind or emotion, subject to caprices; tending to change abruptly and without apparent reason, erratic; flighty, fanciful, fickle, and whimsical."

As far back as I can remember, this aptly describes every cat that I have ever owned, or more appropriately, owned me. In fact, twenty years ago, one of my favorite cats was named Caprice. She devoted her entire life living up to her moniker.

Why do cats take minutes settling into a comfortable position in a chair, only to get up a short time later and race furiously around the house? I have never seen a cat that didn't perform this apparently spontaneous act, which seems to come at any time with no previous thought or motive.

Why do cats meow plaintively for food, seemingly on the verge of death from starvation if not fed immediately, and when given the food, take one sniff, and walk disdainfully away? I can only assume that our capricious dears have abruptly changed their minds in a flicker of flighty, fanciful whimsy.

There are other definitions for the word capricious. They include addle-brained, giddy, scatter-brained, and crazy; but regardless of how others feel, I prefer to think of my cats as loving, free spirits who express their feelings in a sudden flight of fancy.

Convenient Pets for Today's Busy People

Many young couples today share comfortable incomes which provide not only necessities, but a variety of luxuries as well. They have lots of friends and usually are involved in a variety of weekend social events. The parents of these young adults, now alone after years of child rearing, also want to feel free to participate in social and cultural activities and to travel without being tied down.

Though life for these childless families is good, there's still a desire for some loving companion to come home to. So what do they do? In the highly populated metropolitan areas, as well as in the suburbs, they lavish their money and affection on the cat, the easiest-to-care-for of all house pets.

Cat ownership has steadily expanded over the last few years with an increasing number of Americans deciding every day that felines are their kind of pet. Now more than ever before, because of our changing social trends, both mixed breed and pedigreed cats have the chance to live in the lap of luxury. Cat food captures a growing share of the retail market, and cat care supplies—dishes, climbing trees, toys, grooming aids, books—are a major market in a fluctuating national economy.

In large cities, it's common to find two-career families choosing cats as the most suitable companions for apartment living. If they desire a classy exotic breed, there is a large selection; and of course, mixed breeds are available at all animal shelters. Once neutered, the cats can be brought home and quickly litter-trained. The owners then have clean-living, attractive, loving companions waiting each evening for their return. Cats don't have to be walked. In fact, for their entire lives, they may never go out of doors except to visit the vet. Cats are easily groomed, can cuddle up with you in bed; and best of all, cats may be occasionally left alone overnight since generous amounts of both dry and semi-moist foods can be safely left in the cat's dish. Given a good supply of water and a clean litter box, the kitty can do quite well by himself for a day or so. Of course, it's always comforting if a neighbor drops in to give the cat a little companionship.

Felines are so convenient to live with that a growing number of single men, once scorning cats with grim macho disdain, are now finding that the companionship of a cat relieves loneliness without altering their lifestyles.

While cats can be demanding and sometimes naughty, they require very little energy and care, compared to other household pets. In return they offer love and friendship. Their most endearing quality is their need for affection.

Cats make ideal playmates for children. They teach responsibility, are noncritical and happily greet the child coming into an empty home after school. Unlike the adults who control a child's life, cats don't give orders and require little attention.

Giving a Cat as a Present

Along with America's changing patterns of living, customs of gift-giving vary according to the new lifestyle. Once considered irresponsible, giving a cat as a present is

now considered a delightful and innovative surprise for adults living alone or with older children. Of course, any time a pet is given as a gift, the giver must be assured that the pet is wanted and will be cared for and loved. When giving a cat as a gift, advance preparation is the key to success.

The gift of a cat must fit the owner's needs, and sometimes on-the-spot changes must be coped with. We learned a good lesson when we gave a cat to our oldest daughter. She was about 13 years old at the time and desperately wanted a Siamese kitten. On Christmas Day, because of the presence of younger children and all the excitement, Linda received a beautifully wrapped, stuffed Siamese cat with a note assuring her that we would take her to the cattery and allow her to select the kitten she liked best. After a few days of excited anticipation, we went to visit the kittens and allowed Linda to make her selection.

On seeing the litter, we immediately fell in love with each kitten that crawled over our laps and batted at our shoelaces. Linda, delighted with all, finally selected an adorable female kitten and we prepared to leave, giving the breeder repeated assurances that we would follow his instructions. As we opened the door, a half-grown, cross-eyed, male Siamese, shunned by all buyers, dashed into the room, talking all the way. Need I tell you that our daughter immediately changed her mind, opting to adopt the reject, named Charlie. We shared our lives and love with that mouthy, charming boy for more than 10 years.

We learned with our daughter that it's human nature to talk about pets we have always wanted, but our wishes can change in just a moment. If you are confident that a gift of a cat will be well received, giving a stuffed toy beforehand and allowing the receiver to make the final selection makes good sense.

Over the years I have often given a much desired cat as a gift by first presenting the stuffed animal on Christmas night, then when all the noise and excitement has abated, brought home the live kitten with the necessities for its care. However you decide to give it, a loving cat makes every home a little brighter and every heart a little warmer.

Pets—A Family Commitment

The decision to bring a new pet into your heart and home calls for a definite commitment by the family. Caring for a pet is a learning experience for your child but in reality everyone concerned must at times share in the responsibility. Whether you acquire a kitten or an older cat, all work involved should be delegated among family members.

Consider these questions before your family makes the selection. Do you plan to raise an indoor/outdoor cat, or will you keep him confined inside all of the time? Would you enjoy a long-haired kitten? They are beautiful, but require many hours of brushing. If you teach your kitten to enjoy being groomed while he is young, you may find fussing over him in the evening while you watch television allows you to do three activities at once. You will keep your hands busy, which most people like to do; you will enjoy your favorite T. V. show; and you will share attention and affection with your cat. Do not expect a child to take complete care of a long-haired cat's grooming needs. Everyone in the family, at one time or another should help.

Certainly few cat owners would allow a valuable pedigreed cat to roam outside and possibly get injured or stolen, and statistics prove that indoor cats live longer since they are continually cared for and protected.

It is easy to decide that your small kitten will never be allowed outside but when you take a stray cat into your family, many times this decision is made by the cat, who will yell for days if not allowed outside. This is often frustrating for the patient owners and most of the time both cat and his new family will be happier when the stray is allowed to establish his/her own routine. It is a comfort to remember that your cat knows how to survive outside.

Bringing Up Baby

When you bring a new kitten into your home, all responsibility for protection and development instantly shifts from the mother cat to you. While raising her family, the mother cat nipped, patted and growled at her kittens to teach them proper behavior. It will be necessary for you to continue a

similar parental pattern if you wish to raise a loving, well-behaved kitten.

Since cats are creatures of habit and enjoy living in an orderly environment, it is not difficult to establish proper behavior if training begins early and is consistent. The feline brain develops just as rapidly as the feline body; the kitten's physical and intellectual growth are nearly complete by the time he is five or six months old.

It's easy to see why early training is so important. Most of your training should be done before the cat is six months old. The habits of an older cat can be changed, but why wait? It will be much harder on both you and the cat.

Cats are independent and dependent at the same time. They are also the most social and antisocial of all household pets—and the bossiest and lovingest of all animals. These contradictory characteristics are two of the reasons we love our cats. We do not want nor would they allow us to destroy or alter these traits in the training process. All kitten training should be done with gentle discipline and lots of love.

Before you bring a kitten into your home, set aside a small area, cage or room in which to isolate the kitten when you cannot or do not wish to watch him. This will keep him out of mischief, and prevent the development of bad habits when he is left alone. Ideally, it should be in a light, airy room with a window through which the kitten can view the world. If you have a small laundry or bathroom, it can easily be made cat-proof and safe for the kitten. It does provide more stretching space than a cage.

Do not keep your cat in a basement or garage. Basements are dull, dark, and lead to boredom, uncleanliness and poor behavior. Garages are either too hot or too cold.

Wherever you confine your kitten, be sure to have a dish of water, a little dry food, a clean litterbox and a few safe toys. Our little Simon has a small cat bed, but it is not necessary. A rug or blanket will do.

Regardless of where you put the kitten's food dish, always feed in the same place. Even snacks should be carried to the dish while the kitten is still young. By establishing one feeding place, you will discourage your cat from walking the kitchen counter in search of food as he matures. When there are also dogs living in the same home, it will be necessary to find a kitchen shelf or desk to feed the cat upon. If not, you will have a fat dog and a skinny cat. I have never known a dog that wouldn't eat all available cat food.

Cats enjoy nibbling and should be allowed to work out their own feeding schedule unless it becomes too demanding. Skipping a meal once a week, once the cat has matured, will help keep the cat's appetite sharp and prevent a fussy eater.

Until the kitten is four or five months old, working owners should arrange for someone to visit him at lunch-time. A little freedom to roam the house after eating, and of course some loving attention, will help him through those long, lonely days. Toys are important, too. They help develop a fun-loving disposition and insure strong muscular coordination through playful leaping, twisting, and turning.

Kittens need a great deal of sleep. Even when the family is home, allow the kit to sleep whenever he wishes. The waking hours will then be fun for both the kitten and the family.

Since everyone loves to hold a kitten, teach the children to sit on the floor to hold their pet. If you insist on this, you will never have him injured by jumping from someone's arms.

Now: Relax, keep your sense of humor, and enjoy the delightful antics and diversions your kitten will think up. No other animal is as innovative and playful as the graceful feline.

A Schedule for Busy Families

Busy families today must be well organized to insure that all household pets are well cared for AND taught to behave correctly when left alone. A schedule of the cat's daily food and activities taped to the refrigerator door is by far the most efficient method I have found. Your schedule should provide the following information, and any other comments you wish to add.

Time	Activity	Responsibility
Morning 7:00 to 8:00	Breakfast-1/2c cat food, check water dish. Put cat in his own room.	Child's, as he is the last to leave home.

Noon 12:00 to 1:00	Feed kitten again, give some love and attention. Put cat back in own room.	Any family member who comes home for lunch.
After school 3:00 to 4:00	Allow kitten out of room. Play and take care of him until the family comes home.	Child.
Evening dinner 5:00 to 6:00	Evening meal.	Any family member.

During the evening hours, your kitten will need a generous amount of "quality time" with the family. This will compensate both you and your cat for the daytime hours spent apart. You must do this, or your little friend will not build the bonds of affection, nor build good habits which will make it such a loving pet.

Since your "nobody's home" cat rests and sleeps through the day, nighttime will also be a challenge. To keep your cat active and playful, use a feather to tantalize, a ball on a rubberband to tease, or a friendly game of chase. With a little understanding and effort, by bedtime both you and your cat will be able to snuggle together in happy harmony and sleep peacefully until morning. (See Insomniac Cats)

With family's busy evening activities, it's easy to forget to take care of the cat. Your child may need a reminder to check kitty's sleeping area. The litter box must be cleaned

and fresh water and food provided. If possible, the cat and child should be allowed to sleep together.

Along with the cat's daily schedule, you will find it convenient to tape another sheet on the refrigerator with kitten's "Do's" and "Don'ts."

DON'T ALLOW THE cat in Mom and Dad's bedroom. Please keep the door closed.

TAKE THE CAT outside with you when you have the time to stay with him. He cannot stay out alone.

DO NOT LET the cat scratch the furniture. Chase him away with a newspaper or give him a gentle shake.

BE SURE THE cat is locked in his room if you are the last person to leave the house.

14

BE CAREFUL THAT the cat doesn't slip out of the open door when you enter or leave.

FEED THE CAT if you come home and he seems hungry. No one is perfect and the responsible person has either forgotten or been delayed.

Once you have established the schedule and assigned the task, the parents must insist that the routine be followed. You'll be amazed at the responsibility your child will assume when he/she has the schedule to follow, and of course, a few gentle reminders from Mom or Dad.

Teaching Your Cat To Be A Loving Family Member

Nearly all cats enjoy and crave attention and affection, if they are lovingly handled from birth. Lack of time to give each kitten enough handling while young is a common problem both breeders and eventual owners of kittens face today. We must realize, however, that each kitten differs in personality and intelligence, and each requires careful training to help him adjust to a new home and environment.

Often the same litter will produce a few kits so wild and peppy they climb the curtains and destroy the furniture, while their brothers and sisters are so shy they run and hide at the slightest noise. Whatever the temperament, each kit must be handled and taught to enjoy the companionship of his new owner. The wild kitten must learn to become tame and controlled and the shy one must be helped to overcome

15

his fears. Our two cats, Eleanor and Heathcliff, are good examples of differing intelligence and disposition. Eleanor, at three months of age, was one of those shy, quiet kittens, easy to have around, but not very receptive to training. The poor little kit also lacked personality and was rarely playful. Heathcliff, a half-grown stray, part Siamese, lived in our garage for a week before I could get near enough to touch him. Once in the house, he became wild and excitable—a whirlwind of mistrust and fury.

Fortunately, our family had enough experience and interest to help each cat overcome its individual problems.

The Shy Kitten

Eleanor was the easiest to train. As the two cats grew older, she also enjoyed her relationship with Heathcliff, as well as with the family. Fortunately Eleanor was a patient cat, as it was her destiny to always give way when Heathcliff, her impetuous playmate, demanded.

I began Eleanor's training by confining her to the smallest room in the house, so the elusive kitten could not escape under the furniture. I sat on the floor to prevent injury, should she jump from my arms.

Knowing that cats are frightened if held cradled on their backs like babies, I calmly picked up the kitten and positioned her rear hips and legs under my left elbow. Bringing my left hand forward under the cat's chest, I held her front legs comfortably separated by my fingers, so the kitten's body was secure and controlled. The right hand, still free, could be used for discipline, should the kitten bite, or for smoothing, petting and calming her fears.

I scratched Eleanor's ears, talked quietly, and insisted she remain agreeable. Sometimes she would rebel and try to bite my finger. A quiet "no," together with a gentle tap on the nose, stopped her small resistance. As soon as she once again became docile, I praised the kitten and gave her some butter to lick from my finger. *I always reinforce my cats' good behavior with petting and praise.* An occasional treat of food is also very effective.

Since Eleanor was such a young kitten, she quickly learned to behave and even enjoyed being handled. The more affection our family showered on her, the more people-oriented, loving and demonstrative Eleanor became. The cat's behavior reinforced our feeling that all family pets need discipline as well as love, in order to become accept-able, well-adjusted members. In return, the family respected the kitten's occasional need for privacy and allowed her to view the world from her window seat, undisturbed for hours on end.

The Strong-Willed Cat

Heathcliff, frightened and fearful from unknown past experiences, ate our food, but hissed and glowered at any-one who came too close. He had lived in our house for over a week, spending most of his time on the seat of a chair under the dining room table. Each time we extended a hand, we were met with slashing claws and a frightened retreat. Clearly we could not allow him to live in such fear.

When I began Heathcliff's training, I wore leather ski gloves which neither tooth nor claw could penetrate. Twice a day, morning and night, week after week, I held my frightened cat, using the same technique that I had found so successful when training Eleanor. But what a difference. Heathcliff, with all his feline fury, growled, writhed and threw his body in vain attempts to escape my grasp. When escape was impossible, Heathcliff literally tried to bite the hand that fed him.

It took many weeks to win Heathcliff's confidence and at first many sessions were a failure. It became evident that a few disciplinary taps, snaps and pinches were required to teach the cat to have a soft bite and velvet paws. Every few days some small progress would be evident as a little reward for my effort. Before long, Heathcliff would walk around the kitchen as he shared Eleanor's enthusiasm for snatching forbidden treats. Eventually, he learned to enjoy the family's attention and affection.

A year later, Heathcliff, along with Eleanor, now rubs against my legs to purr with love and satisfaction. Occasionally he will even jump into a family member's lap to spend a quiet hour or so. There are still a few indications of the stress Heathcliff suffered during the early months before we knew and loved him; but who knows, perhaps over the years, the past will blur as the cat's future becomes more and more secure.

18

I am proud of Heathcliff's progress and hope that by sharing his story, others will be encouraged to give their cats discipline and training along with love and attention.

Developing Your Cat's Personality

Standing at the kitchen sink, peeling potatoes in preparation for the evening meal, I suddenly became alert. That eerie feeling of someone watching was slowly interrupting my thoughts." Oh no," I suddenly realized." It's Charlie again." Whirling about to look for my cat in his favorite spot on top of the refrigerator, I barely had time to yell, "No!" before the soft bundle of fur hurled through space into my quickly outstretched arms.

"Very funny, Charlie," I said sarcastically, while hugging the spoiled beast.

"Good catch, Ma," he replied by rubbing his furry chin against mine.

This is one of Charlie's best and least endearing tricks. As a full-grown boy, he is now a heavy catch. If I had tried to teach him such an advanced trick, he would have rebelled. He thought up this performance on his own while a small kitten, and "Ma" didn't discourage him. She did, in fact, encourage him, so the habit has persisted into adulthood.

Charlie was a funny, loving, impetuous Siamese kitten who wallowed in the love and attention of a family of parents, children, dogs, fish and gerbils. Now, as an adult, he is far from the perfect cat, but has a personality all his own.

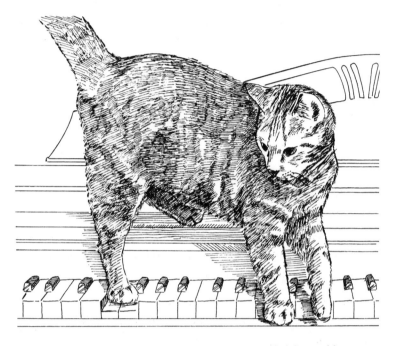

How do you raise a cat to be loving, sociable and have an interesting personality? It isn't difficult. With the proper upbringing, every cat can be personable—even today, when so many are necessarily left alone while their families are at work.

If your cats were raised in the wild, like their cousins, the pumas, cougars and lions, they would spend most of their lives dozing in the sun. In fact, they would sleep or doze, on and off, 15 to 20 hours out of every 24. This is one of the reasons domestic cats make such good pets for busy people. Household cats, as well as their wild relatives, don't mind being left alone for long periods of time. Once past their exuberant kittenish stage, most cats seem perfectly content to sleep the day away, as long as food, water and litter pan are readily available.

Anyone can raise a boring, uninteresting and uninterested cat by simply providing for their needs and otherwise ignoring them. *Cats like all living creatures need lots of attention to develop into fun-loving companions with personalities of their own.*

Cats raised exclusively indoors are usually more sociable than those who spend most of their time outside. A cat allowed outside spends comparatively little time in close contact with family members. When he does come inside, he's usually too tired for anything but sleep. Of course, given the choice, the cat will never be around when strangers call.

The indoor cat, on the other hand, will be well-rested, happy and mentally alert when the family comes home in the evening. Since his entire life is focused on the household activities, he will be eager for play and companionship.

Most cat owners enjoy interacting with their pets. As a child, I remember visiting the local "cat lady," a kind, somewhat eccentric old woman who lived for the pleasure and companionship of her 15 or so cats. She spent most of her day wearing a colorful housedress under an old, full-length bathrobe that flowed along as she walked. As she moved around her house, cats appeared from all directions to stalk, pounce upon, ambush and attack her trailing robe.

In imitation of my friend, as I grew older, I frequently entertained both cats and family by tying a sash to my waist and playfully dashed about the house with the cats in hot pursuit. As I became busier or less energetic (or perhaps smarter), I found it was much simpler to attach a sash to a doorknob, tie a knot at the other end, and allow my cats endless hours of fun and exercise. Eventually I learned to make this entertainment even more enjoyable by adding a few embellishments.

Making a Doorknob Toy

I did this by cutting a sash or cord into three unequal lengths, tying them together at one end and fastening them to the doorknob. I then took three pingpong balls and marked spots on two opposite sides of each one. Small holes were cut at each of the marked places. One piece of the hanging sash or cord was threaded through the holes of each ball. A very large knot was firmly tied at the end of the material, so that it could not possibly come loose. This setup allows your cats to chase the bouncing balls with no risk of losing them under the furniture.

Since cats are playful and imaginative by nature, it doesn't take expensive toys to entertain them. A small ball or piece of paper placed in the bathtub will amuse a cat for hours. An empty spool, cork or catnip mouse will stretch your feline hunter's imagination and provide the exercise needed for a firm, healthy body. An empty bag, box or newspaper on the floor is a delightful find for a curious cat.

Don't be surprised if your cat becomes very attached to a special toy. My son-in-law David laughed as he told me his story of Fozzie Bear and the mouse.

Last Christmas our daughter Carrie made and gave each cat in our family a catnip felt mouse. This gift soon became Fozzie's favorite toy. He took the mouse to his bed, outside, and back in again. It soon became the most bedraggled of all his possessions. By this time, Linda was throwing the mouse outside each time she found it on the carpet. No sooner out, than Fozzie brought it in.

Finally David took the mouse to the garage and threw it into a garbage bag for disposal. Two days later, Fozzie brought it back into the house. Again David threw the mouse away in the bag. Again Fozzie dove to the bottom of the huge bag to retrieve his much prized toy.

No one knows how long David and Fozzie Bear would have kept up the game because Linda put an end to it by mending and patching Fozzie's mouse and thereafter allowed the felt rodent to reside in the house with Fozzie and his family.

Build Good Playtime Behavior

Most of the time, you can give your cat attention with barely a pause in your own activity. Talking to your pet, a most important stimulant for developing an imaginative and affectionate personality, can be done while fixing a meal, making a bed or writing a book. It's not what you say that counts, but the way you say it. I have read checkbooks, letters and invoices to my cats. These were received with the same great enthusiasm given my most spirited rendition of a favorite song. The important thing is a soft, enthusiastic tone; the affection you are communicating is much more basic than words.

As you can see, helping your cat to develop a pleasing personality is not difficult. You must remember, though, that along with the fun, your cat must learn acceptable behavior. Many times, behavior that is delightful in a kitten is totally unacceptable in an adult cat. For example, allowing your kitten to ambush and pounce upon your foot or ankle may be funny when the claws are small and teeth harmless, but you'll find yourself resenting those attacks as the cat gets older. Wagging fingers or wiggling toes for your kitten to attack is also encouraging behavior you won't appreciate when he is grown.

On the positive side, we all enjoy playing on a bed with our cats. Placing our hands under the blanket and tempting the cat to attack is good fun and can be permitted into adulthood. No one gets hurt, and the cat doesn't associate the attack with bare skin, since the blanket is always between tooth and hand.

Helping your cat to develop a happy, outgoing personality will bring its own reward. Your loving companion will continue to amuse, delight, surprise and fascinate you for many hours.

Touching—A Hand and Paw Communication

As I pushed the key into the lock and hurriedly flung the back door open, I realized how late it had become. Rushing into the house, I dumped my packages on the dining room table and immediately went to the kitchen hoping to start dinner before the family arrived.

When I finally paused in front of the open cupboard door to make a selection, I felt the soft fur of our half-grown cat, Teddy, rub against my leg. Of course, the affectionate rub was accompanied by his usual conversation. Paying little attention to the kitten, I said the usual, "I'm glad to see you, too, Teddy," as I turned my back to continue my preparations.

I immediately forgot the cat as my mind flitted over a dozen more important concerns. With enough done in the kitchen, I walked into the living room and started up the stairs. As I passed the large, flat newel post at the bottom of the steps, I felt a swat on my arm. I had taken another two steps before I realized that what I had felt was not just a pat. Indeed, it was a rather hard smack!

Surprised, I paused to look, then stepped back to stand eye to eye with my usually good natured cat.

Teddy, pulling himself upright, full of dignity and indignation, started to bawl me out. The kitten was obviously distraught and trying to tell me something. I stood there absolutely dumbfounded.

After a few moments, the disgust and antagonism disappeared from the kitten's voice and it became lower and

softer. He finally stopped talking and sat looking sad and alone. Teddy had been obviously upset and I had callously disregarded his small request. Feeling guilty, I put my face close to him to say how sorry I was and promised we would look into his problem. Soon we were nose touching nose, a position Teddy always favored when carrying on a conversation. We murmured a few more words to each other and then I felt his gentle forgiving paw softly caress my cheek.

Of all household pets, none enjoys touching more than the cat. Physical contact to him is absolutely necessary for sound mental and emotional health. Like other animals, felines have areas of the body which are more sensitive to touch than others.

Picture your cat as it curls up asleep on your lap. The underpart of the body is next to you, and the ears, neck, back and tail are exposed, inviting your touch. Cats enjoy head petting, ear scratching, back rubbing and tail stretching. The skin sensors in these areas produce mostly pleasurable sensations. Touch the pads of your pet's feet, though, and the immediate reaction is withdrawal. The "oh, so sensitive" foot pads are not to be touched.

The rough, thick skin covering the cat's feet contain the body's sweat glands and layers of fat which cushion the tough outer surface. Though the pads of his feet are tough, they are extremely sensitive to touch and temperature. Almost every object a cat encounters is touched, patted and finally batted by the paw, as kitty determines the desirability of the contact.

The hairless areas of the cat's body also include the nose, which is padded up to 75 times thicker than other parts of the body. Each cat's nose is ridged in a pattern so individual that a feline nose print is as distinctive as the human fingerprint. His nose has pigment for color, nerve fibers and very sensitive sensory receptors, which respond to pressure and temperature.

You usually get a mixed reaction when rubbing your pet's stomach. At times he will relax, roll about and enjoy. Other times the claws flash out and you are reminded to keep your hands off this often touchy area. The stomach is one of the most vulnerable parts of a cat's body. It is also sensitive to touch. It takes a cat that lives in harmony with himself to allow his stomach to be rubbed. With gentle stroking, the cat's muscles relax, and the heart rate decreases, allowing the body systems to slow down.

Bonding Builds Love

Touching, if it is started while the cat is young, binds you and your pet for life. In fact, many times an orphan cat will not thrive because he lacks physical contact with his mother. Since cats are socially dependent animals,deprivation of affection is damaging to a kitten's emotional and physical development.

The best example of bonding is between mother and offspring. When a parent cat licks and grooms its offspring, the digestive tract is activated and circulation improves, producing healthy alert youngsters.

The hair over most of a cat's body is lubricated with oily secretions from the sebaceous glands. These help to water-proof the coat and give it a healthy shine. The sebaceous glands also secrete cholesterol, which is converted to vita-min D by sunlight. As the cat grooms, it ingests this valuable nutrient.

Fear of being touched is often the result of poor handling during kittenhood, or lack of human contact during the early formative weeks of life. This early contact between animal and human is a strong and necessary bond.

When you hold and stroke your pet, a general feeling of well-being is shared. Bonding builds a trusting, secure relationship between individuals. In some cases, such as

when a stray cat "adopts" a new owner, bonding is insti-
gated by the cat. Bonding can also occur between two cats
or between a dog and a cat.

All cat lovers know that as each kitten grows, he develops
an individual personality and assumes his own quirks of
behavior. This is what makes each of our cats so endearing
to us. We should remember, however, that no matter how
dissimilar our cats are in looks, behavior and attitude, it is a
fact that there are certain patterns to which all cats conform.

Touching is the most noticeable and certainly the most
enjoyable form of cat communication. It can also transmit
other emotions: anger, jealousy and fear, for instance. This

was demonstrated by my cat, Teddy, when he finally lost all patience with me and gave me a sharp swat to gain the attention he needed.

When I put my face against Teddy's soft forehead, my touch communicated an inner feeling to him. I said, "I'm sorry. All will be well soon."

As Teddy's paw caressed my cheek, I received his inner communication." I forgive you and everything is fine again."

Teaching "Come" When Called

Bonding will instill in your kitten the desire to be with you. Since all love and care is provided by his family, naturally all fun and satisfaction comes when the cat is near the people he loves. There is no need to teach your kitten to "come" when called if he has developed a strong individual identification through your loving bond. In fact, at least half of the time, you may not be able to get him out from underfoot.

You are defeating yourself when you call "Here kitty, kitty." Your cat may answer, but usually only if he is hungry or wishes to come in the house.

Teach your cat his name and use repeatedly. While holding, petting and playing, talk to him saying his name frequently. Within a short time, you'll be amazed to find that your cat will come each time you call him correctly.

You never hear dog owners call their dog with "Here doggie, doggie." The reason they use their dog's name is because the pet associates better with his own identification.

Cats respond to their own identifying name in the same way. Being taught and called by his individual name builds a sense of pride and a bonding relationship within the family.

Scratching—A Necessary Ritual

Daily scratching is a self-grooming ritual for cats. It is as necessary and normal to a feline as eating and sleeping. Scratching is not only a vital activity in a cat's life, it is also enjoyable. Each time your cat carries out this instinctive ritual, he enjoys a good stretch and at the same time gives himself a pedicure.

The old lore that cats sharpen their claws by scratching is only partially true. We now know that the claws of domestic cats are covered by a sheath. This thin tissue, much like our own fingernails, continually grows. As the cat scratches, this outer sheath falls away leaving a new sharp claw.

When our cats scratch in the litter box, on the floor around the food dish, or on the scratching post, we take little notice. Not so when we see them dig their claws into the upholstery of a favorite chair or the living room drapes! Our tempers flare as we imagine dollar bills floating by in a flurry of shredded fabric. Certainly these rambunctious felines must be taught where they may and may not scratch. What's more, the lesson must begin immediately.

Since cats, especially indoor cats, are going to scratch somewhere, the first step toward a well-behaved animal is to provide acceptable toys and scratching places. Why toys? Because if you give them adequate areas for exercise and diversified entertainment, it is unlikely that your pets will become obsessed with any one activity, such as excessive scratching or soiling. Destructive behavior is often the result of boredom and loneliness.

As for providing acceptable scratching places, there are many kinds of scratching posts—from simple homemade pad to the elaborate floor-to-ceiling cat trees that are commercially available. Whichever type you choose, you may find that you have to teach your cat to use it. Rub a little catnip into the material to get kitty's interest and rub its paws up and down on the surface several times to show what you expect.

Material for Scratching Post

Most felines enjoy scratching on carpeting, burlap, or denim materials if a good tree trunk isn't available. You can make your own scratching post by nailing one of these fabrics on to a sturdy post—perhaps even a stairway post— or a flat surface. I lightly pad a 36-inch square board, cover it with my pet's favorite fabric and nail it to a door or wall near the cat's sleeping area. *Cats love to stretch and scratch after a nap.*

Remember, too, that cats will naturally be attracted to furniture covered in burlap and denim fabrics. When buying, avoid open weaves and rough textures. As a further deterrent, place your furniture so it doesn't become part of his pathway. Watch him to see where he likes to sit or nap. If he finds it convenient to climb up the leather sofa to get to the window ledge, you are asking for trouble. You can make life easier for both yourself and your cat if you provide a cat perch with a small ladder and move the sofa.

Moving the sofa may be an easy solution to the climbing problem, but what if your cat has decided to use that same sofa arm for his daily scratching? In this case you have two alternatives: Either learn to live with shredded furniture which many cat owners do, or insist that your pet stop the destruction immediately and permanently. *It's really not hard if you remember that you are smarter than your cat and you set the rules.*

Gentle Early Training

Let's start with training the younger cat since this will avoid more severe discipline in later years. Decide beforehand which areas will be off-limits for your pet. Of course, he will pick his favorite spots, and he should be allowed to do so whenever possible, but you have the power to veto his decisions and the ability to make those places so uncomfortable that your cat will "decide" that he doesn't really like them after all.

From three months on, kittens become a whirlwind of activity. They are feisty, hard to catch, and will disappear at the first sign of disagreement. It is, therefore, necessary to confine the kitten when you cannot or do not wish to supervise his activities. Allow your pet out of this restricted area only when you have the time to train and play with him.

When you are ready, release the kitten and give him some much-needed attention. Being a normal cat, he will probably be full of energy after spending most of his day napping. Before long, he will approach the forbidden furniture. When he does, walk quickly to the kitten, pick him up, give him a little shake, say "no" firmly, and take your kitten to the scratching post. Show him the proper place to scratch by gently rubbing his paws up and down on the post while speaking soothingly.

If you start teaching your kitten while he is young and follow through by punishing each forbidden act, your reward will be a loving, nondestructive adult cat. But if he missed this kind of kitten training, the gentle discipline described here will probably not work now. If he has been scratching the furniture and getting away with it for months, or even years, stronger measures are in order.

Nail Clipping

As a first deterrent to household destruction, I always keep my cat's claws clipped and filed to prevent snagging. Clipping is not difficult if you plan ahead. Choose a time when your cat has just eaten and is taking one of his frequent naps. If you work fast, you can usually clip the nails before your pet is fully awake and ready to resist. I use a guillotine-type clipper that allows me to insert the nail tip through a hole and snip off only the end.

Of course, early training makes this task easier. If you clip kitty's claws from the time you bring him into your home, the task will soon become routine. When necessary, wrap your little friend in a towel or large net bag, confining all but the paw you are working on. This will allow you to continue without risking bodily injury.

PART 2

The
Nobody's Home
Cat Grows Up

Massage—A New Concept in Veterinary Care

For thousands of years, healers have used touch in various ways to diagnose sickness and relieve suffering. Today, this touching is called massage. This laying on of hands, a new concept in veterinary medicine, is thought of as a binding touch in which animals become emotionally attached to their owners through close physical contact.

Therapeutic massage is not the same as the pats of affection we have always given our pets. Rather, it is the direct application of pressure to the surface of the skin. This will help prevent sickness and promote good physical and mental health. When used during illness or stress, it can stimulate self-healing.

Massage may also be used to speed convalescence, to add mobility in old age, and to ease the pain of sprains or sore muscles. It always communicates love and feelings of well-being to your pet.

When you consider that cats and humans have similar and sometimes identical disorders, such as diabetes and glaucoma, arthritis and hip joint pain, isn't it logical that many human massage techniques developed over the centuries can be just as helpful to animals?

As we watch our cats wash and touch each other, and sometimes in their enthusiasm lick our skin with contentment and joy, could there be any doubt that a "hands-on" approach will bind our pet to us?

THE HEALING TOUCH: Begin your cat's massage with gentle, flat palm strokes, reassuring your pet all the while that this will be fun. If you begin with this relaxation stage, you and your cat will both become calm and receptive.

Gradually increase the pressure of the strokes as you proceed. Continue across the gentle slope of the shoulders and down the front legs to the feet. Finish the body with smooth, firm strokes along the back, including the hips and hind legs.

Return to the head and massage the head and neck, finishing with a gentle rub to relax the muscles of the face and jaw.

To finish the session with your cat, reach down and give the chest and abdomen areas a thorough rubbing. The hips and hind legs should then be raised slightly, stretched and given a stimulating massage.

DIAGNOSTIC MASSAGE: After your cat's general rubdown, you may wish to try a fingertip massage. Diagnostic or fingertip massage helps you to seek out physical problems which can be solved more quickly if detected early.

Using fingertips to gently probe and feel for sore or touchy areas is the most effective stroke in animal massage. Fingertip massage is done with two or three fingers extended and held together. The skin is rubbed in a circular pattern, sliding from one area to another without losing contact with the skin.

While the cat will love the flat rub massage, it may not be too receptive at first when you use the more probing fingertips. Take as much time as necessary to help your cat relax and enjoy the massage. Younger cats are easier to train, of course, but be patient, any cat will benefit greatly from the touching experience.

As you massage, use the "feel-see" method to find and examine each pain point and watch for swelling and tenderness.

Some of the cat's troublesome pain points that you should watch carefully are:

EARS—for ear mites or painful ear canal infections.

TEETH—for abscess or gum infection.

ANAL GLANDS—found at the base of each side of the tail. They can get impacted. Usually found by fingertips or feces odor.

HIPS, KNEES, ELBOWS—for arthritis and pulled muscles.

PAWS—for foreign objects, cuts and bruises.

After you have completed a general and diagnostic massage, ruffle your cat's hair and rub the skin between the thumb and fingers to check for tumors, fleas, and other external parasites. If you find redness from scratching, dandruff or hair loss, you will be able to discover the cause early and avoid expensive treatment later.

A daily "flat hand pat and rub" roughhouse with your cat when you arrive home will help to increase the pet's circulation. This allows energy to course from organ to organ. It brings renewed life and balance, harmonizing the mind and body. You will then have a perky, happy companion to share your evening.

Kitchen Manners For Your Cat

Many cat owners are convinced their pets cannot be trained. In fact, they believe their cats have the right to indulge themselves, behaving as they please.

I find no objection to this thinking as long as an owner has the time and patience to cater to his or her cat's every whim. I have found, however, during 20 years of raising, living with and loving cats, that too much indulgence and too little expectation on the owner's part lead to poor behavior from the cats and eventual unhappiness for the patient, but exhausted, owner.

While it is certainly true that cats are nonconformists by nature, they can be easily trained—if you teach a lesson your cat wishes to learn.

As I sit watching Fancy, our new kitten, dart across the kitchen floor in pursuit of a small ball of cellophane, I remember a lesson taught to our first Siamese kitten many years ago.

While working in the kitchen one evening, I tripped over Charlie, our talkative, cross-eyed Siamese. As he demanded equal rights to an immediate dinner, his companion cat, Thomasina, a quiet calico, flitted about the floor searching for crumbs. Busily carrying a pot of hot soup from stove to table, the thought struck me that I could have easily tripped over either pet and hurt both the cats and myself. I resolved henceforth to lock the cats out of the kitchen during meal time.

While I paused, thinking over my problem, I happened to glance at our two family dogs, each sitting on her allotted rug, patiently watching the now familiar evening scene. I had taught the dogs "go to your rugs" and "stay" to keep them out from underfoot while I worked in the kitchen. Why not, I reasoned, teach the cats acceptable kitchen manners? Teaching them was so easy that over the years, I have taught the same trick to every cat our family has owned. I think both you and your cat will be delighted if he learns this "good cat" trick called "go to your place."

When a kitten is four to six months old, he is able to jump up on chairs, tables and countertops. In fact, cats much prefer to view the world while looking down.

Realizing this, I knew our cats would never accept sitting on a floor rug like the dogs. I chose, instead, a pair of wooden stools. When not in use, they were pushed side by side under the kitchen table. Any desk or shelf will work as well, as long as the cats are close enough to feel that they can get your attention.

For the first lesson, which was held before dinner when the cats were hungry, I pulled the stools out and slightly away from the table. I then patted the hard, wood surface to make a drumming sound as I called the cats.

Of course, the reluctant felines sat a few feet away ignoring me. I immediately walked over, squatted down and dangled a piece of meat by each of their noses, patting the stools again as I lured the cats to jump up on the chosen seats. For the first two lessons, each cat went as far as the stools, but balked at jumping on the seats. No fuss! I just refused to give them the treat and stopped the lesson.

The third day both cats jumped up on their stools and, once properly seated, were instantly rewarded with the enticing tidbits they were eagerly trying to snatch from my hands. Along with their rewards, the pets were also given lavish praise for their outstanding performances.

From that day until our cats learned to jump up on the stools whenever I patted them, we served all food, including meals, on the stools. Each time food was given, the stools were patted to teach the cats to associate the sound with food and where they must go to get it.

During the training period, every time the cats took their places on their stools, they were rewarded with a small treat.

It didn't take our glutton, Charlie, long to figure out the whole show. He became devoted to sitting on his stool and carrying on conversations with anyone who walked by. Thomasina, always the lady, sat and looked primly sweet, only occasionally murmuring a request for her share of attention.

If at any time during the training period the cats chose to be disagreeable, and continued to sit at my feet meowing, they were ignored. Between the tidbits and their regular meals, it didn't take the pets long to run into the kitchen at the first sound of meal preparations. They would immediately jump up on their stools, and being safely out from underfoot, wait patiently for their expected treat.

Classy Cat Tricks

"Mom, come quick!" Lisa yelled as I hurried into the kitchen. I was surprised to see her flat on her stomach watching her kitten, Thomasina, daintily dip her paw into the glass of milk, gracefully hold the paw above her nose and, with superb cat manners, lick the milk off her paw.

Lisa, now grown and married, called a few days ago to tell us about the abandoned, half-grown kitten her husband Phil had found and brought home from work." You'll never guess what I just taught him," laughed Lisa.

"Bet I can," I replied." Hasn't everyone in our family taught each kitten the same paw-in-the-glass trick?"

It's fun to teach tricks to your cat, and many enjoy the attention they receive when performing. Most cats are

natural actors already, and some are real hams, so it's not hard to teach them tricks if you use the right approach.

I always enjoyed watching our two cats, Thomasina and Charlie, come into the kitchen, jump up on stools that sat side by side and wait patiently for their snacks.

After I taught the cats to sit on their own stools, I taught them to "speak." Teaching Charlie to talk was easy since he was an outgoing, totally charming Siamese. Thomasina had an entirely different personality; she was quiet, calm and inclined to allow Charlie to speak for them both.

Teaching Thomasina to meow was the hardest part of the routine. I had to hold Thom's front paws on the stool and tantalize her to speak by dangling a piece of meat in front of her nose. She wanted to sit up and bat at the food, but I refused to allow her to do so. Finally, in desperation, she would meow. I immediately gave her the food and lots of praise. Of course, I always used the key word, "speak," for this trick.

"Sit up" was the last part of the series of tricks I wanted the cats to perform while they sat on their stools. This was easy. I held a tasty tidbit over their heads, and the cats quickly learned to sit up while trying to snatch the food. I never allowed them to get the morsel by grabbing it, then disappearing. This would have defeated the purpose, as they would have refused to perform, if they could have snatched and run. Our friends were very impressed (especially the so-called cat haters) when the cats ran into the kitchen, jumped up on their stools, sat up and meowed for their treats.

After I taught our pets to jump up on their stools when I patted the seat, I found that they agreed to jump up on any surface I tapped. This was an added pleasure for family members who needed only to pat the cushion they were sitting on to have one or both cats join them immediately. Naturally, they received lots of affection to reward their performances.

The best time to teach a cat most tricks is when he is hungry, but "roll over" is best taught when he is just waking up from a good rest. Kitty will be both relaxed and a little hungry as he stretches out on the floor. Kneeling beside him, dangle food enticingly near his nose and encourage him to roll from one side to the other as you make a half circle with the food. You may have to use your other hand to push him from one side to the other. It won't take kitty long to realize that rolling about takes little time and effort and the rewards are great.

With repeated training, your pet will follow your hand with or without food in it. Each time he performs, repeat the command, "roll over," so the words become part of his vocabulary.

Another accepted method of teaching the "roll over" trick is with a gentle tickle on the reclining cat's stomach. If he isn't too ticklish, he will usually roll over. Many of my cats have playfully attacked my hand instead of rolling over, so I prefer using food as a stimulant to encourage them to perform. Perhaps a combination of the two may work well for you and your pet.

I enjoy teaching our cats to jump over a stick. This trick is easy to teach and fun to watch. It is best taught when your pet is in a playful mood and hungry enough to follow food used as a lure. Use a rod or stick that is rigid,but lightweight and comfortable to hold. Starting at floor level, lure the cat back and forth across the stick with a treat. After a little practice to assure him that the stick is harmless, raise it off the floor slightly. Gradually increase the height of the stick in subsequent sessions. As long as the cat can walk over the stick, you'll have no problems.

When the stick gets high enough that he must jump over to get the treat, you will have to proceed slowly, and at times go back to a lower level. If he is familiar with walking on a leash, this is a perfect time to encourage kitty, with gentle tugs, to jump over the hurdle.

Be patient. Work at each height for awhile and do not push him to go too high too soon. I prefer to teach this trick in a narrow hallway so he cannot conveniently walk around the stick to obtain the treat.

Finally, to borrow a phrase, you can teach an old cat new tricks—at least some of the less strenuous ones. You'll be surprised how much both you and your cat will enjoy the compliments.

Jealousy Over New Baby

A new baby in the home threatens a cat which has monopolized all of his owner's love and attention. The ugly horns of jealousy rise and the senior pet retaliates. What better way to pay you back than misbehave under the guise of innocence.

Household pets are masters of retaliation. Many times their jealousy is demonstrated by scratching on forbidden furniture, nipping, refusing to eat, or ignoring previously obeyed commands. When you bring a baby into your home, advanced preparations are necessary to help your cat accept the new family member. Let's look at this situation from your cat's point of view.

For several months your pet cat sensed an air of excitement and expectation in the house. He has been annoyed by the occasional changes in routine, but enjoyed playing with the interesting packages wrapped in gay, crinkly paper. Exploring the newly decorated nursery and playing on the ladder left during decorating was great entertainment. All told, life has been stimulating and fascinating for this fun-loving feline.

Suddenly the household changes. The excitement is gone, the rooms empty and quiet. Though the food dish is full, life has become dull and lonely because his best friend has disappeared—but not for long.

Soon the cat's loved ones come home bringing a new family member wrapped in a soft, warm blanket. The cat is naturally curious and eagerly jumps upon the bed where the infant is lying.

Your reaction during this introduction is important to the future happiness of your whole family. Allow the cat to smell the baby he is going to watch grow up.

Over the next few months, the cat will react to baby in his own way. With every new sound, at each feeding and bath, he will be around to investigate. He may become devoted to this new and interesting toy, or perhaps find the whole routine boring and merely observe from a distance. If the cat shows signs of jealousy, you can easily give him extra attention when baby sleeps.

Every owner knows that cats love to be warm. They will take naps on top of furnaces and registers, snuggle up to hot lamp shades, and nap in the clothes dryer if given a chance.

When a cat is looking for a warm, comfortable place to sleep, what could be more soft and inviting than sharing a bed with baby? The bed is in an area where a cat can catch a few winks in peace and baby is warm and cuddly to lie against.

I have raised babies and cats together for many years and I'm sure that cats will not deliberately harm an infant, but since newborn babies are so helpless it's better to be safe and keep felines and babies apart when you cannot supervise their activities.

Helpful Safety Suggestions

If your new baby sleeps in a small bassinet, it is especially important to keep your cat out of the room. If a large feline jumps and hangs on the side of a lightweight bassinet, baby, bed and cat may come tumbling. Even when using a full size crib you'll need to keep your cat out of the sleeping area for a few months.

Since most parents are uncomfortable with the door to the nursery closed, remove the wood door and replace it with a screen door. This will keep your pet out, but allow you to hear every sound coming from the room.

Allow your cat to share in family activities. When you feed the baby, offer your pet dinner or a treat at the same time. You will also find that many of your happiest hours will be spent playing on the bed or floor with baby and the cat.

As your child grows, teach him or her to protect and be gentle with animals. A child must learn to control all affectionate exuberance, for the cat's sake. Just as your cat will not harm the baby deliberately, your child does not mean to harm the family's much loved pets. *Both child and cat must be carefully guarded and trained during their early years while learning to live together.*

Repelling the Attack

Almost all cat owners will agree that an attacking cat is merely behaving in an instinctive way. That is, though the cat lives in harmony with humans, he still retains the inherited hunting traits—stalking and attacking—of his wild ancestors.

It's also reasonable to assume that an attacking cat has either been allowed to develop an undesirable attacking habit, or is living in such a stressful situation that he has reverted to fighting back as a defense. There is a reason when a normal, loving cat becomes aggressive. If you can find and eliminate that reason, he can be retrained much easier.

Begin by ruling out disease, infection or other physical disorders. Have your cat thoroughly checked by a veterinarian. If he is physically healthy, you should search for emotional disturbances.

Rough handling, loud noises and family fighting are just a few causes of severe stress and emotional trauma for a cat. Some felines react to these situations by becoming listless, withdrawn and depressed. Others may become unmanageable, wild and hysterical.

Poor behavior may also occur when a cat has been mistreated, refused affection or handled violently during his growing years. In extreme cases, even love, understanding and patient care will not erase the deep inner hurt, or completely relieve the anxiety such a cat must live with constantly.

In many cases, undesirable attacking behavior is simply a case of improper training. Every cat owner knows the amusement of watching an impish kitten, body crouched, ears flattened and tail low, stealthily pursuing its prey. And we've all smiled as he wiggles his hips, swishes his tail and leaps to the attack. What fun for the kitten as the owner flashes a hand to tempt this behavior. Before the owner has time to notice, though, the kitten has modified the rules and perfected his strategy. He now attacks unsuspecting feet, as well. It doesn't matter—those little claws and baby teeth cause no pain.

But too soon he grows up. An adult cat who plays the game of ambush and attack is no longer amusing. He attacks his owners and many times the owner's guests. How sad that he was allowed to grow up thinking this was acceptable behavior.

The cat is now confused and cannot understand why he is being punished for something that he was once encouraged to do. Fortunately, with patience and diligence, an owner can correct this behavior.

While the cat's harmful playing must be stopped, kicking and hitting him with a paper or your hand is not the way to retrain. This abuse could even make the situation worse by forcing the pet to retaliate.

Now is the time to use creative strategy since the cat thinks the attacking behavior is a fun game. When he is in an attacking mood, draw a peacock feather, scarf, or ball tied to a cord across the floor. Sometimes this simple distraction works quite effectively, especially with a younger cat. Still, it may take awhile until he prefers the distraction to your feet or hands, so be patient.

Strategy Stops Stalk-and-Strike Game

If a simple distraction doesn't work, try a combination of tempting the cat with a toy along with firm discipline to repel the attack. What else can be done to convince all but the most die-hard attacker that hands and feet are no longer fun to play with?

In addition to your distraction toy, arm yourself with a plastic spray bottle (available at any hardware or grocery store). Fill it with water, and if necessary, you may add a teaspoonful of cider vinegar to the water to make it more distasteful to the cat. Now, keeping the bottle in your hand but hidden from the cat's view, walk by and tempt him once again with your scarf or ball.

If the cat attacks the toy, great. This is exactly what you want. Play for a short time and praise your good pet. If, however, he attacks your feet as you walk by, say a firm "no" and immediately use the water spray. Kitty will react as all cats do by sulking, refusing food and maybe slashing out at you. Be kind to him otherwise, but continue your discipline each time he attacks the wrong object—you. Most cats find that stalking and attacking hands and feet are no longer fun after a few days of consistent discipline. If he resumes these attacks at some time in the future, you must immediately stop the game, or you'll be right back where you started. If you can't stop the cat's attack before he latches onto your tender skin, or if he is a die-hard assailant who stalks and strikes with deadly earnest, sterner measures are in order. You may have to buy or borrow heavy gloves. With your hands protected, you will be able to grab the determined aggressor by the scruff of the neck and snap his nose with your thumb and forefinger to get him to release his grip. Then, hold him away from you, give him a good shake and a firm "no."

Once you have decided with firm determination that your cat must be brought under control, you may have to wear gloves each time you pet or pick him up. He will probably not like this situation, but if you remain calm, speak quietly, bribe him with favorite tidbits from your hand, and refuse to allow your ferocious feline to gain control again, you can win the battle.

In the end, if you impress upon your pet that he cannot always get his own way, you'll find the cat will calm down and both of you will start enjoying life together.

Walking on a Leash

As a young bride, I brought my long-haired Persian, Muffie, to live with Jim and me in a city perched on the shores of beautiful Lake Michigan. Being a country cat, Muffie adjusted to the beach and rolling sand hills immediately and seemed to feel at home wherever her loved ones chose to live.

Muffie and I were constant companions, walking the beach, chasing crabs in the shallow pools and gazing into the water for hours on end. I think we would both have enjoyed living our lives out together in this most perfect spot. But like the wilting of a perfect flower, our serenity vanished as the cool fall days turned into winter's harsh disillusionment.

Since our cottage was only a summer residence, Jim and I decided to move into an apartment in the city. Muffie, of course, would come along. We thought she would become a city cat just as easily as she had accustomed herself to life by the water.

A few hours after we moved into our small apartment, Muffie and I had our first real disagreement. Being an outside cat, the stubborn feline refused to use her new litter box and insisted at the top of her lungs, that she be allowed to roam out of doors as she had always done.

I was shocked! This bossy loudmouth was a different cat than I had ever known. On top of that, the landlady who had reluctantly allowed us to house our cat, complained bitterly about every sound. Believing there was no other recourse,

I put the cat outside and prayed she would find friends among the neighborhood cats and dogs. Most of all, I worried about the traffic on the busy streets surrounding us.

It didn't work. The dogs in the neighborhood clustered in groups as they roamed, belligerently terrifying every cat they could find. To make matters worse, since we lived on the second floor and our windows were inaccessible, Muffie took to sitting on the outside ledge of the landlady's kitchen window. Muffie yowled, the landlady screamed, and I was in a panic.

What should I do? What could I do? To give my beloved cat away was totally unacceptable.

I finally decided that even though the cat had never worn a collar, and was three years old, she would have to learn to walk on a leash. I could then protect her from the dogs and she and I would once again enjoy the long companionable walks we both relished so much.

I began Muffie's training by placing a lightweight piece of cord around her neck to help her accept the collar that was to come. Although she occasionally caught her claws in the cord while scratching her neck, she seemed indifferent to the small hindrance.

Within a few days, I removed the twine from Muffie's neck and replaced it with a narrow leather collar. The next step was to get the cat accustomed to moving with the pull of the collar.

First, I tied a short cord to Muff's collar and allowed her to drag it about the rooms until she got used to the feel of the new leash. Hooray! This was easily accomplished and the lessons proceeded.

Till now, I had not used food to help Muffie learn her lessons, but NOW was the time. The next step was to teach her to accept a person at the other end of the leash. I began by placing some butter on my finger and sitting on the floor. Then I tugged on my cat's leash, urging her to come to me. She resisted and I insisted. When she finally was pulled to my side, the tempting treat was offered.

After a week of outright bribery, I continued giving Muff her treat, along with extravagant praise for her good work. The next few days, I tapered off the food and increased my insistence that she walk where I wanted. Twice daily after our jaunts around the apartment, I gave the obedient cat her favorite morsel along with lavish praise.

Since Muffie refused to use her litter box, I had been taking her out doors three or four times a day. She had a favorite patch of dirt which she quickly used, then she was whisked back inside.

Two weeks of fairly successful indoor training finally gave me the courage to take Muffie outside to play. Oh glorious day! I had tied a long cord on the cat's collar and we sat on the sweet smelling grass, watching autumn's final show of color as the last golden leaves fluttered down from the trees.

Muffie, flitting about chasing leaves and spying bugs, was unconcerned when she reached the end of the rope. I sat with my back against a tree, relaxed, and occasionally murmured approval when my companion made an exceptional catch. Life was good that day.

Although Muffie was doing well, both in the apartment and in the yard, it became increasingly apparent that however her collar was put on, the cat could slip out of it, if she wanted. Obviously, the only answer was a strong light-weight harness which would be more comfortable and equalize the pressure from the pull of the leash.

That night I wound a cord around Muffie's chest behind the front legs, to her back and tied a knot. I then brought the cord up to her neck between the shoulders, to the collar and tied it securely. It was a secure, lightweight and comfortable harness.

The cat didn't react to the change, so I tied a leash to the makeshift harness and walked her around the apartment, once again encouraging her with soothing words of satisfaction.

Within a short time, Muffie was wearing a ready-made cat harness. It was a handsome ensemble. Even the landlady grudgingly admitted that my lovely grey cat looked stylish while wearing her red jeweled leather harness with matching leash.

Oh yes, Muffie and I had a few ups and downs, and more than one disagreement over who was leading whom; but while each of us won or lost a few, we eventually learned to become a team.

The lessons were well worth the effort. Once again my beautiful Muff and I roamed the streets and parks, talking to each other, and discovering together that a city can also be a fascinating place to explore.

Riding in the Car

For many years our family has taught all our pets to ride in the car and enjoy every moment. It all started when we purchased our first Siamese cat many years ago. He was a handsome, cross-eyed, outspoken fellow who lived for six months as a country cat. Charlie was his name, and for the rest of his life, he adamantly refused to respond to any other.

Charlie loved riding in automobiles. He would sneak into any four-wheeled vehicle that moved—milk and bread trucks, repair vans and neighbor's cars. Since our family took frequent trips to a cottage at the lake, Charlie settled easily into the family routine.

Thomasina, a shy, quiet calico cat, joined our family a few years later. She and Charlie shared similar likes and dislikes, except Charlie's love for riding. Motor vehicles terrified Thomasina. Since we knew we would have to include Thom on the family visits to the lake, we opted to try teaching the reluctant feline to tolerate car rides.

I have since taught all our family cats, as well as friend's and neighbor's household pets to ride in a car and even to enjoy occasional trips. Here is how I did it.

Thomasina, being a quiet feline, was not as receptive to training as Charlie had been. I have found over the years that cats like Thomasina are often indifferent to all training and must have gentle, but firm discipline, while still young. I began Thom's training by sitting on the floor and holding her a few minutes at a time. I scratched her ear and talked soothingly, but insisted that she remain agreeable. If she began to fight back, I would slap her paws lightly or shake her gently to teach her to control her temper. As soon as she stopped her bad behavior, I immediately resumed the petting to reinforce her good attitude.

Since she was just a young kitten, she quickly learned to behave when she was handled. In return, the family respected her occasional need for privacy, and the cat training—for all of us, including Thomasina—progressed agreeably.

Teaching Thom to enjoy the family automobile was the next step. For training sessions, we tried to choose a time when the cat was in a quiet, contented mood. We picked her up, cuddled her, and quickly carried her out to the car. We sat quietly inside with the door open.

During the first week of training, Thom would almost immediately jump from our arms and leave the car; however, she did seem to enjoy walking over the soft seat to make her exit. She did not appear to be frightened, just alert in a strange area. We continued her training a few minutes at a time until she accepted staying in the car with no fear. Before long, Thom could not resist the spacious front seat and would sometimes leave our laps and sprawl across the seat cushion.

Amazing happenings occur when you teach your cat proper behavior. Thomasina became more loving, people-oriented, and demonstrative. Our family, especially the children, learned that all family pets need discipline as well as love. We also discovered that since training was done only a few minutes at a time, it did not disrupt our daily schedule as much as we had feared. Every family member participated in the training and we enjoyed discussing Thomasina's progress.

Once she accepted the car and relaxed while walking about in the enclosure, we began to introduce the mechanical noises from the motor and the occasional buzzing seat belt that cats often find so frightening. We had once thoughtlessly allowed a cat to become terrified by the noise of the seat belt, and she never forgot the experience, although she did eventually become a quiet but reluctant car passenger.

As it turned out, the motor was not a problem. Thomasina seemed to ignore the soft, idling sound. Accelerator and brake noises were also accepted with relative ease.

Food as Training Aid

Up to this time, we had not used food to help Thom adjust to the car. Now was the time to introduce enticing tidbits. At the next sitting, I was prepared with a small jar of pureed meat. Placing some meat on my finger, I offered Thomasina the treat as I released the seat belt and allowed it to buzz for only a second. Thom jumped at the sound, but greedily resumed licking her treat. I repeated the noise at short intervals, three times the first day and for several days thereafter. Before long, she could tolerate the buzz, even without food as a reinforcement.

I used baby food meat as an aid in Thomasina's training for two reasons. It was a great treat to her; and all my earlier cats had enjoyed licking meat or butter from my finger. Most of the time they continued to lick long after the treat was gone. From feline mother, to brothers and sisters, to pseudo-human parents, cats enjoy and learn by licking. Thomasina, as she licked and smelled my finger, began to identify this smell with security, love and discipline. Animals have an intense desire to see where they are going. With Thomasina, it was easy to allow her to ride on the back of the front passenger seat since soft fabric upholstery was used in those days. With today's automobile, vinyl is a popular seat covering and it can easily become ruined by cat claws. While Thom and Charlie frequently rode on the seat back, or on a rug across the rear window, we have since found it more convenient, and much safer, if a car seat or cat perch is provided.

An Innovative Car Seat

Had I known with Thom and Charlie what I figured out a little later with another cat, I would have trained all my cats from the very beginning to sit in a car seat. In fact, a few years ago, I found an old bicycle basket in the garage. We cleaned and repaired it, and a clever neighbor fitted the basket with hooks taken from a baby car bed. The basket was then hung facing forward over the passenger seat back. It became an ideal, attractive and safe cat car seat.

Several years and a few cats after that experience, I learned the ultimate secret in training a cat to enjoy using a car seat. Long before I began any training, I taught them to sleep in one as a bed inside the house. This became their favorite sleeping place, and when the bed was moved into the car, the training was the easiest I had ever done.

Once the cat was accustomed to the car noises as well as the seat or perch, we drove the car up and down the driveway. This training will be much easier if you have someone to act as chauffeur.

With Thomasina, each trip was lengthened until all the noises became common sounds. Finally, the day came when Thom was content to share her companion Charlie's greatest joy—riding with the family in a moving four-wheel vehicle.

Discipline for Older Cats

Older cats will not respond to the gentle training used with kittens. This is especially true if your pet has been scratching the furniture and getting away with it. You have been defeating yourself if you have allowed your cat access to forbidden scratching areas while you were away from home, then scolded or hit him for the same behavior when you returned.

These conflicting signals cause the cat to become confused, sneaky and withdrawn. It's better to have the battle in the open and get it over with. Then, both you and your pet can retreat, lick your wounds, and begin to rebuild your relationship, this time based on mutual respect, as well as affection. As a mature cat owner, you should be able to take a few huffy snubs from your feline pet and realize that they won't last forever.

If you have already fallen into the trap of disciplining him only some of the time, don't despair. There is still hope, but you will have to make up your mind with absolutely no exceptions that this naughtiness must stop.

You will have to isolate your cat in a cage or room, away from furniture he can scratch, when you are not able to supervise his activities. If you do this consistently, it won't be long before you will once again be able to give your pet freedom in the house at all times. What's more, after a day of work or play, you will be able to return home without shuddering at the thought of the damage he may have done while you were away.

Effective Evening Training

After-dinner training sessions will be more effective if you establish a routine for the evening hours. It's probably already your practice to come home after work, let your pet loose and feed and play with him.

Don't forget how important it is to talk to your cat. Felines love verbal communication and will respond to familiar words. Talking is also the easiest way to give a pet attention when your hands are busy doing something else.

Later in the evening, take your cat into the area where the forbidden scratching has occurred. Make yourself comfortable and ignore him while you read or watch television. But stay alert and observe his movements out of the corner of your eye. When he starts to scratch, stop this misbehavior by using one of the following methods.

Spray the cat with water. A forceful stream of water from a spray bottle is one of the most common and successful methods of discipline used by cat owners. When the cat misbehaves and is caught in the act, give him a good squirt and accompany it with the verbal command "no." If your cat is one of the few who does not seem to mind being sprayed with plain water, add a small amount of cider vinegar as a little extra incentive. The vinegar will sting enough to make him uncomfortable, but will do no lasting damage. *As soon as the cat stops scratching, praise his good behavior.*

Spray the cat with air. This is an effective, but less severe (and less messy), means of discipline. The water spray works well if you are spraying it on material that will not be damaged; but the air spray has an obvious advantage if your cat is scratching a delicate fabric that will stain. You can purchase canisters of air at any photographic store. Some of the air cans have adjustable spray nozzles. Others have more, or less, air pressure depending on the brand. There is one air spray made of soft plastic that is squeezed like a bulb. This releases only a slight amount of air per squeeze.

I discovered this gentle method of discipline when I purchased a can of air to use when cleaning my camera. While using the air, I accidentally sprayed one of my cats. His reaction was astounding. He hissed and jumped into the air, then sat back down and acted as if nothing happened. Since the cat didn't associate the source of irritation with me, he didn't even move away!

A week later, I used the same air spray on the same cat to discourage him from jumping onto the table. I hid under the table to make the discipline a complete surprise. After only three attempts, he decided to sit on the chair instead. I tend to believe that he associated the air spray with a hiss.

Remember, as with the water spray, to accompany the air spray with the verbal command "no" and follow it with lots of affection when the bad behavior stops.

Above all, keep yourself cheerfully determined to consistently discipline your cat. When you cannot supervise him, see that he is in an area where he cannot do damage. This isolation is not punishment for your cat, it is a deterrent to further damage to your home and a means of keeping the pet from developing or reinforcing a bad habit.

With this in mind, remember to give your little friend lots of love and affection when you release him from his confined area. *With a combination of love and consistent discipline, you can have loving cats and a lovely home.*

Insomniac Cats

At one time or another, all kittens have problems with nighttime wakefulness. By this I mean both cat and owner are awake, but on the owner's part, it is not by choice.

Kittens and cats have a tremendous amount of energy. They also express a wide range of emotions: affection,rage, indifference, sadness and happiness. They are all demonstrated at one time or another. Sometimes the cat's energy level is accelerated by anxiety and stress, which often makes him restless and prevents good sleeping habits.

All cats, when left alone, will sleep the greater part of the day and be awake and playful in the evening. It's easy to change his pattern of eat-sleep-play if we are at home during the day and take the time to reinforce a daytime-play, nighttime-sleep schedule.

Many of us, busy or away during the day, don't notice what bad habits our cats are falling into until we are awakened in the middle of the night with kitty nibbling on our ears, punching us in the stomach, or playfully digging under the blankets.

We, in return, push the cat away while mumbling dire predictions about his future health—only to encounter a fresh assault because the cat naturally assumes that we are also playing! From here on, the battle becomes stronger as we try to convince the playful darling that we are not amused and don't wish to play at 3:00 A. M. Isolating the cat in another room is successful only for the few owners who can sleep through any yowl, or who own houses large enough to remove the pet to some place out of earshot.

While a cat is one of the easiest pets to have around, all living creatures do require some time and attention. If your schedule forces you to be away for many hours, leaving the cat to sleep during your absence, you will need to teach him to adjust to your living habits.

Of course, cats do resist change, but this is not a change, it's merely an adjustment which should not cause any stress-induced temperamental outbursts. In fact, you are the

one feeling the stress, so you have an added incentive for finding the time to reverse your pet's sleep pattern.

Remember, your cat will be happiest if you establish and follow a set routine. If you are more than a few minutes late with your cat's regularly scheduled meal, be prepared to get a good bawling out before he condescends to eat your offering. On such occasions, I have found that apologizing at the top of my voice as I enter the kitchen and quickly prepare the cat's meal leaves my feline too surprised to be angry.

Since cats doze anywhere from 18 to 20 hours a day, you will need to offer some daytime entertainment to help him remain alert during your hours away from home. A window for your pet to view the world is the easiest entertainment available. Since he is naturally curious, viewing the outside world is a great delight.

Provide a few toys which he enjoys and change the playthings once or twice a week to keep your cat from becoming bored. A strong scratching post with a toy swinging from it will amuse him for quite a while. A paper bag left on the floor with a ping-pong ball inside is sheer delight for any playful feline.

Once you have set the new household schedule and decide to follow it conscientiously, you should return home each evening, reasonably close to dinner time. Once home, take a few minutes to give your pet the attention he has been waiting for. Talking, petting and scratching the ears and tummy help to soothe him and put him in a playful mood.

Your actions during the early evening hours will mean the difference in whether your cat sleeps all night or wakes up refreshed and ready to play before morning's light. There is no other way to keep his schedule the same as yours, except to keep kitty awake for at least two hours before bedtime. This is not as difficult as it may seem. With a little planning, your new schedule will be established within a short time.

Exercise—Inside/Outside

Although the cat that never goes outside alone is safe, he will need more of your attention to help him work off excess energy. During nice weather, you might try taking him outside on a harness and lengthy lightweight cord. With your cat confined in a harness, you can sit in the yard and allow him to sniff, roll and play safely while you doze or read. Playing fetch with a piece of crumpled paper can also be done outside. This provides strenuous exercise for the pet, but requires little effort on your part.

Living in an apartment can be an exciting life for any cat, if you schedule a daily walk through the halls, down to the laundry room, or to visit a neighbor in the same building. Kitty will always find new and interesting sights, sounds and objects, even if the same route is covered each evening.

Evening play for the household feline is also a pleasure for you, the owner. After all, you own a cat for your enjoyment and your cat feels he owns you for his enjoyment—so enjoy! Play chase with a sash, ribbon or cord. Urge him to fetch with any round soft ball. Cut a hole in a large grocery bag and after the cat runs into the bag, dangle your fingers or a cord through the hole for him to snatch.

Hold and play with your cat. Satisfy his boundless energy. You will both be tired as bedtime approaches, and I guarantee that you and your pet will get a good night's rest.

Daytime/Nighttime Schedule

Assuming that you work in the daytime, try this system on Friday evening and see if you can get a good schedule started by Monday morning.

Feed your cats Friday morning before leaving for work and upon returning in the evening. From this day on, feed your cats their regular meals in the morning and at night. After this have snacks available at all times. If the cats become hungry between meals they can nibble on the snacks. Dry tidbits are adequate.

During the evening hours keep the cats awake by playing, petting and entertaining them. You will get tired, but don't allow the cats to sleep until you go to bed. If they wish to go out-of-doors during the early evening, or if you think it's a good time for their outside exercise, put the cats outside and ignore their pleas to come back inside until you think it's time. You are now establishing a comfortable routine for both you and your cats.

During your sleeping hours, put your cats in an area as far away from your bedroom as possible. Be sure they have their snacks, water, and litter box with them. Now begins the battle of endurance. Since you have given in to your cats so often, they will undoubtedly yell and scratch at the door. Cats rather enjoy this type of battle and can show amazing determination. You, on the other hand, will soon become tired, and wish to give up the battle. **Don't do it!** Your cats are fed, warm and have all they need for a comfortable night. It will not take too many nights before they give up and sleep. In the morning, feed and play with them before you leave the house. Of course they will sleep while you are gone. It's too bad you will not be able to do the same. If the cats have a window to watch the world's activities, they might stay awake a little more, but don't count on it.

Here are a few added suggestions:

Never feed your cats except at their morning and evening meal time and continue providing the nutritious snacks. Do not, under any circumstances, get up in the night for the cats unless you have to use discipline. They must learn to leave you alone to sleep. A few months from now, if the cats have adjusted to their new schedule, you may allow them to sleep with you, but only if the cats follow your rules. During retraining when the cats yell and scratch so much you are a wreck, open the door and spray or pour water on them. At the same time say "no!" and immediately close the door.

If you really stick to this routine—and it will be hard for you—your cats will eventually adjust. Soon you and your feline pals will start a new and loving relationship, based on mutual respect.

Christmas Safety

Each holiday it's fun to find suggestions for seasonal gifts. I offer an assortment of ideas for seasonal gifts to make for cats. It also makes me feel better when I include some holiday home safety suggestions. I don't want you to think that these ideas come from some divine revelation, or like a bolt out of the blue. The truth is, they come from years of learning about cats the hard way—through trial and error.

Our family has owned cats that disdainfully ignored our Christmas trees. We have even owned a few cats that

angelically sat before the decorated tree, watching the blinking lights while patiently waiting for their gifts. Most of our curious felines, however, have to our dismay, climbed our beautifully decorated trees, and cats and trees came tumbling down.

Finally through the years, we've worked out a sure-fire system which insures both a house safe from cat damage, and most importantly, a cat having fun while enjoying a safe holiday season.

Securing the Tree

Each year before we place our Christmas tree in front of the living room window, one of the family members climbs a ladder and screws two small metal eyes into the top surface of the window frame. We put the eyes about a foot to each side of where the center of the tree will stand. From each eye, a strong thin wire is secured, then brought forward and tied to the upper trunk of the tree. The metal eyes in the molding and the wires to the tree are virtually impossible to see once the tree is decorated. If we have a smaller tree, we adjust the wires until satisfied that the tree will remain upright—even if our latest cat decides to climb the inviting new toy.

Once our Christmas tree is secured in its floor holder and fastened with wires from above, the strings of electric lights are brought from the attic. The lights are then laid out around the living room floor and checked for burned out bulbs and dangerously exposed wiring. While the lights are strung around the room, I walk about and place dabs of Tabasco sauce on portions of the wires, particularly the bit of wire that runs along the floor between the last light bulb and the wall outlet. Tabasco sauce will not harm animals, but its hot taste will discourage cats from chewing on the dangerous wires.

After all the preliminary work is done, the fun begins as we start decorating the tree. Years ago we decided it was sensible to place the precious older family bulbs, as well as any edible decorations, in the upper half of the branches. Along the very lowest branches are hung playful, attractive plastic toys, harmless to sniffs and swats from our curious feline companions.

When the tree is finally decorated, our last job is to fill the water pan beneath the tree. After the tree is watered, the festive tree skirt is tightly tied to the trunk of the tree above the water. To reinforce the skirt ties, a bit of wire is also wound around the tree trunk over the skirt ties. This prevents household pets from drinking the tainted water.

At the same time we were working out all the necessities to ensure our family and cats a safe holiday, we discovered a delightful toy to keep our cats occupied during the festivities. Quite by accident we found that a box containing a catnip mouse can become a source of entertainment.

Two weeks before Christmas, one of our children, with childish delight, wrapped a box containing a catnip mouse in gay holiday paper and placed the present under the tree. The cats were excited. The smell of delicious catnip was enticingly out of reach inside the box. The rattle of cellophane within the lightweight parcel piqued their curiosity. The gift became an amusing favorite toy before it was opened! The cats pushed, tossed and fought playfully until the grand opening on Christmas Eve. Each year we have continued to present this gift, and all our cats have found hours of amusement from one child's loving thoughtfulness.

Gifts Children Can Make

All children enjoy making gifts long before their small fingers can manipulate scissors and tools. Since cats enjoy playing in paper bags, here is a simple, inexpensive present to make for grandmother's or uncle's favorite cat.

Purchase some wide colored tape for sealing packages. If you cannot find a color, wide brown masking tape will work just as well. Using the largest and strongest grocery bag you can find, help your child cut a three-inch square hole in the center of one of the wide sides. Reinforce the edge of the hole and all folds of the bag with the colored tape. Also reinforce the top edge of the bag to help the paper resist tearing. You now have a colorful bag in which any cat will love to hide. The hole in the side of the bag will entice your pet to reach out to catch your fingers when you play with him.

The bag may be further decorated any way your imaginative child wishes. My young son simply used red tape on the brown bag and blocked in red felt pen, the words "CAT HOLE" with an arrow pointing to the spot. This toy was attractive and both relatives and cats loved the gift.

Ping-pong balls are a cat's delight—lightweight, durable and as full of bounce as the pet that plays with them. Most important of all, ping-pong balls make creative, inexpensive gifts. Give your child some scissors, scraps of material, felt, colored markers or crayons, and let his or her imagination soar to the heights. Ask your child, "What do you see when you hold the round white ball? "Glue on two ears, draw eyes, a nose and whiskers—why it's a cat! "Can you make a mouse? I'm sure Tabby will love it as much as Grandma will."

Wicker baskets for pet beds are an "in" item this season. They are attractive and comfortable, but expensive. Since all young animals will chew on wicker, before you give a wicker bed as a gift, or if you have received or bought a wicker bed, I hope you'll take a few minutes to insure your pet's safety with these inexpensive precautions.

Wash and dry a pair of old nylon stockings. Tie one stocking leg neatly at the corner of the basket opening. Spread the nylon out as you wrap the material in, out, and around the wicker opening. When one stocking comes to an end, overlap another nylon, secure it and keep wrapping until the wicker is covered. Nylon stockings are also effective when used to wrap plastic or vinyl cat beds.

Take some extra time and follow these safety procedures. It's better to be safe than sorry.

Peacock Feather—A Popular Tickler

Usually the first thing you see when you enter a building where a cat show is being held are rows of tables filled with products to help you care for and delight your cats. There are all kinds of climbing trees carpeted in various fabrics, litter boxes of every description (and, of course, a selection of litter materials for filling them), health items, foods, vitamins, toys, and a library of books and pamphlets telling you how best to use all these products.

While the products displayed vary with each show, it's a rare assortment that doesn't include at least one tall jar holding peacock feathers. These are usually prominently displayed so that the soft down of each feather undulates hypnotically as the customers circulate about the tables making their selections.

Why peacock feathers at a cat show? The idea is perfectly simple. They make beautiful, enjoyable toys that will amuse both you and your cats for hours, even years. They are also widely used during the exhibitions in the show ring.

As the judging begins, each cat is brought from one of the cages behind the judging table. The cat is examined, displayed, discussed and finally returned to its cage. Most of the cats are docile and agreeable while being examined. Because of this relaxed attitude, he may not display the alert, attentive expression that tells the judge so much about the cat's beauty and personality.

To obtain this desired expression, after all the cats in each category have been examined and returned to their cages, some judges walk along the cages flicking a peacock feather invitingly across the bars. As the iridescent feathers ripple before them, the cats leap forward, each with one paw raised to catch the wispy plume. At that moment, the cat's ears become erect, his eyes blaze with concentration and his whole being becomes alert. For just a few seconds, the cat shows off his beauty to the fullest. That's what the judge wants to see.

While cat shows are interesting and a great spectator sport for any cat lover, it's not necessary to attend one to enjoy your own cat's reaction to this delightful toy. In fact, peacock feathers are available in most pet supply stores and pet departments of the larger chain stores. If you have an attic, you may even find one free, attached to one of

Grandma's old hats. They make reasonably-priced, unusual gifts for anyone who owns and loves felines.

Cats love to play the game of "chase the feather." Of course, other feathers may be used, but no other feather has the pliable strength and playful flow of the peacock feather. One sniff of the plumage stirs in the cat an instinct of ancestral hunters in days long gone by.

As you hold the stalk and ripple the downy plume across the floor, every muscle and all his senses leap to attention. With total concentration few humans ever experience, he stalks, parries and attacks, only to fall back and prepare for yet another assault. The rules of the game vary with each sweep of the feather, and both cat and player can become obsessed with devising complicated strategies calculated to surprise and outdo the opponent.

For any special occasion, why not gather a few peacock feathers, tie them together with a pretty bow to make an attractive bouquet and give it to one of your cat-loving friends? The blue-green plumage is lovely when displayed alone, or used in a bouquet of winter flowers. Even the most lackluster arrangement comes alive with the addition of a peacock feather or two. Your friends will be delighted with this unusual gift and you will have spent little time, money or effort spreading that joy.

PART 3

Penny Pinching Home Health Care

Looking Good—Grooming

Your cat's fur is made for outdoor living. It protects the skin from sun rays, extreme cold, dampness, and helps to regulate the cat's body temperature. The double (under and outer) fur coat provides the insulation which helps the feline's body adjust to extremes in temperature with ease and comfort. In fact, your cat's coat is his health barometer.

While outdoor cats shed seasonally, those kept indoors shed year-round. It's easy to see when your long-haired pet is shedding. The loose hair quickly covers furniture, rugs and clothing. Short haired cats shed just as much as those with long hair, but unless the color of your furniture and carpets contrast with his hair color, you may not notice.

Since most feline's sweat glands are in the feet, the skin does not secrete moisture to keep the coat in good condition. When a cat grooms himself, nature provides the moisture necessary for a healthy coat.

There are several reasons for helping our pets with grooming chores. If a cat, especially a long-haired one, does all his own grooming, he can swallow an excessive amount of hair. The hair then forms a ball in the stomach that becomes a dangerous obstruction, interfering with his digestive system.

The Tongue—A Feline Hairbrush

As a grooming tool, a cat's tongue has no equal. It becomes a brush for keeping feline hair smooth and in place. It is a nail file for grooming the claws and pads, and it works as a stimulating massage for internal organs.

There are times, though, when the best tool becomes the worst. A cat's tongue is a good example. The loose hair it removes so effectively is often swallowed, particularly by long-haired cats. After licking the coat, the swallowed hairs, if not passed through the digestive system, adhere to the stomach and form a tubular mass that is difficult for the cat to eliminate.

On occasion, your cat may cough up a dark mass. This is usually hair, and you should give the pet some help in passing further hairballs, or it may develop a blockage in the digestive tract.

First Aid for Hairballs

Oil from canned fish is an easily digested lubricant for the digestive tract. Wheat germ, mineral or vegetable oils are all excellent and may be mixed with any food. Commercial products, such as Petromalt purchased in any pet shop, are very effective. When giving Petromalt or a similar product, just squeeze the paste onto your index finger and rub it behind the cat's lower front teeth. It is unlikely that he will be able to spit out the medicine, because it sticks to the roof of his mouth.

Though the tongue is an effective cleaning instrument, it cannot help where it cannot reach—behind and under the ears. As the cat licks its paw to reach around and clean the outer surface of the ear-cup, only the surface hair is washed.

If your cat has long hair, you need to brush and comb deep under the outer hair and remove all mats, or the surrounding skin will inflame and become very painful.

Grooming Techniques

If dandruff is a persistent problem, dry air is probably the cause. Adding moisture to the air in your home will help prevent dry hair, flaking dandruff, and hair loss. It will also minimize the static electricity that often causes both you and your cat to itch. An occasional application of one of the protein coat conditioners available for felines will also keep the coat sweet smelling and healthy.

Most cats enjoy being brushed, if grooming is started while they're kittens and is made a pleasant routine. A grooming session can be a special time that allows both you and your kit to have fun together and show one another affection.

If your adult cat does not enjoy being brushed, you can still do this by wrapping him in a towel or putting him into a mesh bag that allows you to expose only the area of the body that you are brushing.

Placing a harness on your cat while brushing is a gentle yet effective way of keeping the pet under control. If you have used the harness when walking, it won't disturb kitty at all. It is particularly effective to hold the cat up on its hind legs with the harness in one hand, while brushing the stomach and inside legs with the other.

Preventing medical and physical disorders is an added advantage to grooming your cat. While brushing and combing, run your hands inquisitively over the feline body. Look and feel for lumps, sores, rashes, matted hair, abnormal hair loss, and fleas or other parasites. Most of these problems can be cared for at home, if noticed quickly. If you run across a major disorder, even if you must make a trip to the veterinarian, your pet will still have a good chance for recovery, since early diagnosis is always preferable. Cats love their daily brushing and consider it affection and attention. *After all, the cat's mother washed the kit for many hours—you are only continuing this loving touch.*

Removing Tangles—Grooming Tools

Every long-haired cat occasionally gets mats and tangles. To help with these problems, you may wish to try a commercially prepared detangler product. If you don't have one on hand when you need it, here's a simple home remedy that has always worked well for our pets.

Begin by rubbing mineral, cooking or wheat germ oil into the tangles. Allow the oil to set for a short time and carefully work the tangles free with your fingers. Finish by combing the area with first a wide-tooth then a fine-tooth comb. Once the mats and tangles are gone, shampoo the spot and rinse carefully. Your cat may get a little feisty before you finish this treatment, but most will submit without a battle if only a small area is involved.

A spot shampoo, followed by a thorough rinse with a wet towel, is also an effective and easy way to keep the hair around the ears and tail free from oil. After rinsing the spot, rub the cat's entire coat with the clean wet towel. Finish with a good brushing to leave the coat tangle-free, clean and shiny.

A few years ago, I found another grooming aid that I use on both cats and dogs. It seemed that the hair around the pets' outer ears was often oily and messy looking because of the cleanser I used to keep their inner ears clean and free of parasites. Now I prefer an acne pad or commercial feline ear solution to treat their inner ears leaving the surface hair clean and free of oil.

Good-quality tools make grooming easier and more comfortable for both you and your cat. Natural bristle brushes cost a little more, but they are far superior to nylon. Wash them often to remove oil. Medium-width steel combs with round, smooth teeth protect a fine coat and won't hurt sensitive skin. A soft toothbrush makes removing dark eye stains easy, and a soft shoe polish brush is great on the cat's face, around the ears, and between toes.

Attachments for animal care, now available with some vacuum cleaners, are new and useful grooming tools. These provide a wonderful way to remove loose hair from both cats and dogs; but you have to accustom your pets to the noise and suction while they are still young.

Pick a time when your kitten is content and sleepy to hold him and rub the vacuum nozzle attachment, power off, over his body. Repeat this often till your pet is familiar with the feel of the nozzle.

Next, turn on the vacuum motor, but keep it far away from the kitten at first, giving him time to become familiar with the noise. Gradually move it closer. If you take your time, the cat will eventually become comfortable with the vacuum noise and find pleasure in the gentle rubbing on his coat.

I have trained all my pets to enjoy being vacuumed. My family and pets both recommend this marvelous and comfortable grooming aid.

Care of the Ears

All cats scratch their ears occasionally, but when you see them scratch continually, you'll know they have a problem. It could be a simple case of fleas, or in the autumn, scratching may be caused by allergies.

The most common reason for scratching among household pets is a small invisible mite called otodectes cynotis, or the common ear mite. This mite causes discomfort, restlessness and often severe pain.

Ear mites are easily detected by dark discharge, reddened skin and the obvious discomfort of your cat. Mites are constant travelers and one of the few parasites that cat and dog transmit to each other. In fact, kittens are often infected soon after birth by the mother cat. When you find ear mites on one household pet you should check all others and begin treatment on the infected animals.

Ear mites will not go away without treatment. The mite will breed more larvae and inflame and damage the surrounding inner ear tissue. The infection will become worse as the tormented pet scratches and further bruises the tender skin.

If you have not encountered mites before, take your cat to the vet for a proper diagnoses. He or she will check a sample under a microscope for white specks which move. They are about the size of the head of a pin.

Do not attempt any treatment until you have a proper diagnosis. Once you have treated ear mites, you will have no trouble identifying them. When you are certain the cat is infected by mites again, you can then ask the vet for the medicine without an office call.

How to Apply Ear Medicine

Most ear medicine comes in long-nozzled tubes, which are inserted into the ear canal before releasing the medicine. Wrap your cat in a towel or have a partner hold him tight while medicating so the tip will not damage the delicate skin of the inner ear. Squeeze the medicine into the ear and gently rub the outer surface to help the liquid work deep into the ear canal. Massage the broad, lower part of the ear near the head until you hear a squishy sound. You will then know the application has been effectively completed.

Claw or Declaw

Your cat's claws are one of the most important parts of his body. They are unique in their construction. Claws are utilized as fighting tools and grooming aids. They give your cat a feeling of well-being when used for kneading. They are truly indispensable for your cat's very existence if he lives out-of-doors.

When your cat stretches his claws and scratches, his feeling of self-esteem and contentment rises. If his claws are clipped, he is still able to extend and retract them, and is not affected by the loss of a small amount of nail.

Many owners of cats that never go outside clip their pets nails as a weekly ritual. This along with adequate scratching posts and toys for the cat's pleasure and entertainment, will usually prevent destructive scratching in the home.

It's common for young cats to occasionally scratch on forbidden furniture. An air, or water spray usually stops this destruction after a few disciplinary sessions. But what do you do with a cat that is truly destructive? After all discipline has been used consistently and every effort made to halt the damage, you may decide to have your cat declawed.

Declawing your cat is a major decision and should not be taken lightly. Once the cat's claws are removed, he must be protected for the rest of his life. If allowed to slip outside, your cat will be in constant danger and almost defenseless. Declawing is a drastic step to take, however most felines survive the operation and live long lives. If it comes to getting rid of your cat or having him declawed, I would recommend you have the cat declawed.

Does Your Cat Have Fleas?

Skin infection and hair loss are two symptoms commonly associated with flea infestation. Usually, the pet's neck, stomach and lower back are the easiest places to spot the insect. If you do not see fleas in these areas, you might instead find small, black specks. These may be bits of your cat's blood already digested by the flea's system. To determine whether the specks are caused by fleas or are just dirt, place the specks on a sheet of white paper and add a drop or two of water to them. If the specks become red in color, they are caused by fleas.

Did you know that one little flea will bite your cat on the average of 25 times in one hour? Two fleas mean twice the discomfort, and you can just imagine the havoc a whole family of fleas can wreak in just a short time upon your unsuspecting feline.

The flea's constant movement and biting cause itching and irritation that can make your cat so uncomfortable, he will be unable to rest. In addition, flea bites and the scratching they prompt can cause infections that require expensive treatment.

Since the flea lives on blood, a severe flea infestation can cause a pet to suffer from anemia, and cause weight loss and generally deteriorating health.

If fleas weren't such dangerous and irritating little critters, one could almost admire their ability to survive. Fleas breed anywhere and everywhere. They love carpets and can survive and breed in the deep pile all year round. Outside, the yard and garden are also perfect breeding spots. Even if you never allow your pets outside, fleas will find their way to them. They can travel inside on your clothing or simply invade your home through open doors and screened windows. In warmer climates, fleas are a constant problem, while only the hardiest of fleas can survive the cold weather in the northern states. Regardless of where you live, after only a few weeks of warm weather, the flea population literally explodes. That's why flea control should start early in the summer and continue through the warm fall months, even in the cold winter states.

Effective flea control includes removing the insects from both the animal and his environment. In fact, it's cruel to allow your household pets out of doors in the summer without adequate protection from flea infestation.

Spraying gardens and adjacent property with a good yard and kennel spray and repeating the treatment as often as directed on the container, is one effective flea control method. But one weapon alone will not win the war. It's also necessary to use either a flea spray or flea powder routinely, or put a flea collar on your cat. If you have more than one pet, each must be treated simultaneously, since fleas can easily jump from one pet to the other.

You can increase the effectiveness of a spray or powder by wrapping your pet in a large blanket or towel for about 20 minutes after applying the insecticide. This cover will insure that the fleas don't jump off the animal before the poison has a chance to work. Do take care, however, to protect the pet's nose and eyes from the insecticide and keep his or her face open to fresh air during the treatment. When you remove the wrapping, you may be surprised at the number of dead fleas you'll find on the cover and on the animal's fur.

It's almost impossible to control fleas in most areas without the help of insecticides; but if you treat the environment—spray the yard, the carpets and furniture in your home—you may be able to avoid using these chemicals directly on the pet. Regular use of a flea comb maybe all the extra protection your friend will need. A few pet owners have reported some success with the use of brewer's yeast, or tablets containing brewer's yeast, as a means of repelling fleas. Frequent vacuuming, paying particular attention to corners and areas along the baseboards, is another nonpoisonous method of flea control. Be sure to discard the dust bag frequently to keep it from becoming just another breeding ground for these hardy pests.

Commercial Flea Collars

Certainly, the most popular method of flea control is the flea collar. Collars are convenient, comparatively inexpensive and effective when used correctly; but there are a few potential dangers you should guard against.

The flea collar is damp when the package is first opened. Leave the collar in the opened package until it's dry—usually two days. Avoid touching the damp collar.

Once the collar is dry, wipe the excess powder off the collar before placing it around the cat's neck and be sure to wash your hands after handling it.

The collar should be loose enough to allow you to slide two fingers between it and the pet's neck, but not so loose that the cat can slide it up and into his mouth. (This can happen and usually results in a very sick pet!)

Check the cat's skin underneath the collar periodically for any signs of skin irritation. If any redness or rash appears, remove the collar at once and consult your veterinarian.

Cut off the extra length of collar. If your pet chews on the dangling end, he may show signs of poisoning, such as vomiting, diarrhea and convulsions.

Do not wrap a collar around your cat's neck more than once even if it is long enough to allow this.

Do not put a flea collar on a very young pet. Kittens and puppies should be at least 12 weeks old before wearing a flea collar.

Do not use a dog flea collar on a cat. Use only collars made specifically for cats.

Do not use a flea collar in combination with other insecticides, such as shampoos, dips or powders—unless the procedure is recommended by your veterinarian.

Avoid touching the collar to your skin when you handle the cat. Human skin may sometimes react to the insecticide, producing a rash that can last up to 90 days.

Hopefully, these suggestions will help both you and your pets enjoy a happy, flea-free, healthy summer.

Nature's Best Flea Collar

When your cat has an already existing skin problem, the best trial and error method of finding products that your delicate cat can live with comfortably starts with gentle but effective herbs.

Herbs used in flea collars are suggested by Ray Jacobs, D. V. M., who combines his veterinary skills with herbal medications. He recommends using these flea-repellent herbs: eucalyptus, pennyroyal, citronella and garlic. They can all be purchased in a variety of forms at your local health food store. I prefer to use the oils of these herbs.

You may want to add a few crushed leaves of other herbs for a more pleasant smell. Eucalyptus, citronella and garlic all have rather pungent odors! You may want to use lemon juice, instead of garlic.

An herbal collar can be made of several different materials, but I like to use an old nylon stocking because its mesh is very fine. Many other fine-woven nylon net materials are available, and some are colorful, attractive, and a little easier to work with than the softer nylon stocking.

Measure your cat's neck with tape or string, and add two inches to the length to allow for the end seams. Cut the strip of material about one and one-half inches wide by the length you measured. If you prefer, leave a generous amount of material at the ends so you can tie the collar in an attractive bow.

Stitch one seam the length of the fabric, closing the long opening, unless you wish to leave extra length to tie a bow. Leave the bow strings unstitched. Turn the collar inside out.

Fill the collar with the crushed herbal leaves, or you may spread the oil sparingly on cotton balls or soft fabric.

Try the collar around your cat's neck to check for comfort and fit. Add or remove herbs as necessary. Tuck in the end seams, stitch the seams closed, and add the fastener. With heavier materials, use snap fasteners, Velcro tabs, or a button to fasten the ends.

If you wish, you can decorate the collar with small bows or buttons after you fill it. The bows are especially pretty with nylon net. Thin ribbon wrapped at intervals and stitched to the fabric gives a pretty striped effect and does not deter the herb's effectiveness in an attractive and protective collar for your feline companion.

Yeast and Garlic Flea Control

Lions and tigers protect their fur from fleas and other parasites through natural means, such as rolling in weeds or dust. Dust baths clog the respiratory systems of the itchy intruders, causing them to suffocate and die.

Internal supplements can also help in the control of fleas. Each day, try adding up to one-quarter teaspoon of brewer's yeast into the cat's food, or sprinkle the yeast directly onto and into the fur. You may also feed your pet fresh garlic, or open a 50-milligram garlic capsule and add to the daily ration. Many owners include a little clove or chopped parsley along with garlic to help remove the strong odor. If you try garlic or yeast, though, be alert to possible gastric upsets. Some cats develop excessive gas or diarrhea from these products.

Comfrey—Nature's Soothing Herb

Recipes for the use of comfrey have been handed down by herbalists for centuries. Of all the ancient herbs, this seems to be the favorite. When given to either human or animal, comfrey fortifies the inner system and skeletal hair and skin, depending on how it is used.

If your cat suffers from skin rashes, allergic reaction to flea bites, or in general seems to itch much of the time, try a gentle, soothing herbal rinse with comfrey.

Add a teaspoon of comfrey to two cups of boiling water and steep. When it is cooled and diluted to pale brown and sponged into the cat's fur, the tea will bring delightfully soothing relief.

Add some of the solution to your own bath water, or have a cup of comfrey tea and both you and your cat will smell and feel marvelous. It's great for both cat and owner.

COMFREY POULTICE: Comfrey may be taken internally, but it is most effective when made into a poultice for relief of itching and pain caused by sores, insect bites, rashes, infections, arthritic pain, or joint stiffness. Try putting a warm comfrey poultice on the distressed area as you hold and cuddle your pet. This treatment should bring comfort to your little feline, as the gentle heat of comfrey penetrates and soothes the body.

The best fabric for a poultice is flannel or old toweling. Fold the material in half and cut it to fit the area you wish to cover. Soak the material in warm comfrey tea and wring it out. Spread a few teaspoonfuls of the drained tea leaves onto half of the material, fold and place on the distressed area for fifteen minutes or more.

Catnip—A Feline Love Potion

Cats love catnip. It is nature's gift to felines. No doubt, cats were rolling in catnip gardens 2,000 years ago, as Roman cooks and doctors were using the herb for food and medicine. For centuries, humans prepared and consumed warm, minty catnip tea for relief from various ailments of the throat and stomach.

While man was growing catnip through the centuries, their beloved cats were nipping at it in every accessible yard and garden. As early as 1754, according to Rodale's *Illustrated Encyclopedia of Herbs*, the British horticulturist Philip Miller wrote a thoroughly exasperated description of cats rolling on a patch until it was absolutely flat, a serious loss in days when catnip was sold for tea or medicine.

In 1796, catnip came to North America along with immigrants who brought it with other necessities. It soon escaped cultivation and spread throughout the new world.

Catnip is as easy to grow as it is to buy in a store. Using well-established plants certainly is the easiest method of growing this herb. Once started, the plants are sturdy, fast-growing, pleasant smelling and wholesome for cats.

The plant may be recognized as a coarse-leafed, grey-green perennial with a strong odor of mint. The flowers have white petals sprinkled with purple-pink spots. The sign of the mint family, a square stem, will help you find the herb.

Of course, there is no easier method of growing catnip than digging up a plant from the countryside or a friend's yard, and planting it in a generous patch of sun. With an occasional watering, it will continue to grow for many years. Catnip can also be grown in any pot. However, you may need to find a farm feed and supply store to buy plants or seeds. Plant your herb in a large pot with room for proper rooting and watering when needed. Cut while the stems and leaves are young and still tender.

Hang a portion of the catnip upside down in a dry area for winter use. The leaves and small stems may also be washed, dried, and frozen in zip-lock bags. When thawed in the winter, chop fine and add to your cat's dinner. If you look at it from your feline's point of view, it's as good as fish and chips.

Felines have a wonderful sense of smell and enjoy the aroma of catnip most of all. At times, when you observe your cat biting the catnip leaf, she is usually breaking the leaf to release more aroma of mint. Regardless of how often your feline plays with this delicious herb, it is the essence of happiness.

Sprouting Herbs

Wheat, barley and alfalfa sprouts are fun to grow and become a delicious gourmet treat for a cat. If your cat is lethargic or if its diet is low in roughage, the answer may be as simple as adding sprouts to its food. The seeds are inexpensive and can be grown easily in a flower pot or a flat container, such as a cake pan. They will sprout within a few days.

To grow sprouts for your cat, put about an inch of soil in your potting pan or fill a flower pot about three-quarters full, sprinkle the seeds on top, and cover them with a small amount of additional soil. Keep the soil moist for a few days. Within a week, your cat will be happily nibbling on its new treat.

"We always cut our sprouts when they are about 3 or 4 inches high," says Veterinarian Dr. Ray Jacobs." That's when the plants are loaded with vitamins, minerals and chlorophyll. As the sprouts continue to mature, most of their energy is pulled from the stalk and leaves into the grain that is forming at the top. To obtain every available nutrient from the sprouts, keep trimming them as they grow."

Shopping for a Veterinarian

Most cat owners are as genuinely concerned about choosing a good veterinarian as they are about choosing a good family practitioner. It's wise to start your pet with a veterinarian while he is very young because your pet should receive all necessary inoculations and at least one checkup each year.

How should you choose a veterinarian? What makes one vet better than another? Is a good personality important?

Here are some practical tips for pet owners:

The easiest and most direct method of finding the best vet for you is to talk about it with friends and acquaintances. You may also write to your State Veterinarian Medical Association for a list of animal doctors in your area.

Most reputable veterinarians are members of their state association and can take advantage of the educational courses offered. This helps them keep up to date with the latest developments in their field.

Once you have chosen a vet, make a visit to the office. One visit will tell many things. Are the facilities and staff clean? Is everyone helpful and kind in handling your cat? Do they really listen to what you have to say and honestly try to answer your questions? Is someone available day and night for an emergency? Are they willing to discuss the cost of specific services such as worming, neutering and shots?

Animal doctors may specialize in large and small animals, which would include horses and cows, or they may provide service to only small animals. Some vets specialize in a particular medical field such as dermatology, radiology or ophthalmology. Fortunately we now have many veterinary hospitals and clinics which specialize in felines only.

Any reputable veterinarian will send clients to a specialist when necessary. In return, you should also feel free to consult another doctor if you are uncomfortable with the diagnosis or treatment of your pet. Please have the courtesy of talking your concern over with your vet before going to another doctor.

Occasionally you may be upset about the treatment, or worse, the death of your pet. If you feel that your veterinarian has behaved in an unethical or unscrupulous manner, you may inform your State Board of Veterinary Medicine which will investigate the situation. This is a serious step and should not be taken lightly. You should give yourself time to calm down, get over your grief and once again talk to your vet before considering such a measure.

Happily with proper exercise, good nutrition and loving care, most pets live long lives and maintain good health with only a yearly visit to a veterinarian.

Timing Crucial for Calling Vet

Knowing when to take your cat to the veterinarian is one of the most perplexing problems for the average owner.

If I take my pet to the doctor at the beginning of an illness, I am usually told that it's a little early to tell.

If I wait and take the cat when he is really sick, I'm told that I just made it, but with a little luck and a great deal of skill he might survive.

Tiring of this type of hit or miss diagnosis, I have developed a list of "hurry to the vet" symptoms that I have found useful:

BREATHING DIFFICULTY: If the cat has been exercising vigorously, labored breathing is normal. If the cat frequently gasps for breath or pants after a short exertion, you should be concerned. Your pet might have foreign matter in the lungs, an allergy or respiratory disease. Shortness of breath may be a result of insufficient oxygen to the heart. Distemper, severe anemia or broken ribs all create a demand for more air. Don't wait! Take your cat to the vet immediately.

RUNNY EYES: If this is the only symptom the cat has, wash out his eyes twice a day with cotton balls and sterile water. Unless the eyes become bloodshot or have pus in the corners, I don't worry about the cat; the eyes usually clear in a few days. If pus or other signs of illness develop with the eye problem, of course you must find out what the trouble is.

COUGHING: This is always serious enough to stay alert. If a cough persists for more than two days you must get the cat to a vet immediately. Coughing is nature's way of clearing the respiratory passage of obstruction. A cough could be a symptom of an allergy, pneumonia, hairballs or an obstruction in the throat. Coughing should never be ignored.

VOMITING: Many people are so disgusted and angry with this unpleasant act that they forget that vomiting is a symptom of intestinal disorder. A light cold, eating spoiled food, or a stomach obstruction are among reasons the stomach rejects food. I usually stop all food for 24 hours if one of my cats has a stomach upset. After 24 hours I give a very light meal and see if the cat retains the food. If he vomits again it is best to call the vet and discuss the problem.

SNEEZING: When sneezing is the only symptom I observe, I usually assume my cat has run into something she is allergic to. Unless the sneezing continues for more than a day, I ignore the whole thing. If the reaction is severe, you should get some medicine for the cat's relief.

ACCIDENTS: Any time my cat is hit by a car, even if he gets up and seems to feel fine, I have him checked by the veterinarian. Internal injuries do not always develop immediately.

DIARRHEA: This is such a common complaint that we may overlook the fact that it is dangerous, especially in kittens, if not checked. Diarrhea can result from something as simple as a change in diet or an emotional upset. It can also be the symptom of serious illness, such as internal parasites, poisoning or infection. It may even precede the common cold. Whatever the cause, help must be found as soon as possible. If the stools do not return to normal after two days of a bland diet, take the cat to a veterinarian.

FEVER: A warm, dry nose is not a sign of fever. The only accurate way to find out if your cat has a fever is to take its temperature. A normal reading for a cat is about 101 to 102.5 degrees Fahrenheit. Watch for further signs of illness, and consult your veterinarian.

BAD BREATH: This is a common complaint, especially with older cats who are having problems with teeth. You should periodically check the cat's teeth and gums thoroughly. If they appear healthy, you need to look elsewhere for the solution.

Quite often, mouth odor originates in the stomach or intestinal tract. The problem could be simple indigestion, and a change of food could stop the odor. If the odor

persists, I usually give my cat a little charcoal, available in pet stores. It is supposed to aid digestion. Many times, bad breath is hard to diagnose. If you cannot find the answer within a reasonable time, take your cat to the veterinarian for a good checkup.

CONVULSIONS: These frightening episodes are always a symptom of some problem. They could be caused by something as simple as an ear infection or as severe as poisoning, distemper, brain damage or heart trouble. A call to the vet is in order.

As a whole, common sense tells us when to go to the veterinarian and when to try a few simple home remedies. When in doubt, a call to the veterinarian may save hours of needless worry.

How to Give Medicine

Since even the bravest cat owner quakes at the thought of giving their reluctant feline medicine, here are some methods you may try until you find the easiest and most effective application for both you and your cat.

The quick push: Place the cat on your lap and calmly pet and sooth him while you place your hand on his head, with your fingers pointing forward. With the palm of your hand against the back of his head, quickly wrap your fingers around until you press the joints at the corners of the cat's mouth. With the thumb and index finger, open the mouth. As it is forced open, elevate his head and tighten your hold.

With the other hand, push the pill as far down the cat's throat as possible. After inserting the pill, hold the mouth closed and slightly tilt the cat's head until he swallows. Stroking the throat downward or blowing gently into the nose will hasten the pill's descent.

When you use the "quick push," you must work fast. It takes a little practice to complete the action before your cat has time to resist. Many people use this method with great success, but it is best accomplished when the cat is in a relaxed mood and the pill is injected quickly.

There is a commercial pill pusher available in pet supply stores. It works well, once you become accustomed to using it. The pusher looks like a large plastic syringe and the action is the same as an injection. The tip, which goes into the cat's mouth, is soft and the unit in non-breakable. You may find, upon trying, this inexpensive method of pill pushing is convenient for you and non-irritating to your cat.

Crushing the pill and adding the contents to your cat's favorite food is a simple task, but most felines with their persnickety taste and fantastic sense of smell, refuse to touch it.

Giving liquid medicine with a plastic eye dropper is by far the most comfortable for both you and your cat. Find a time when he is sleepy and content then gently pull the skin at the side of his lower jaw out far enough to insert the dropper tip and release the medication into the side of the cheek. Tilt the cat's head back so the liquid will flow down the throat. If you do this quickly, the cat will hardly notice.

Since many cats accept liquid medication with fewer battles, ask your veterinarian if the medicine your pet needs is available in liquid form. If not, find out if the pill may be crushed and added to a liquid without altering the effectiveness.

Correct Finicky Eater's Habits

All cats should have healthy appetites and eat a well-balanced diet. When there is more than one animal in the family, you usually have no problem; however, a cat raised alone may get spoiled. If you have a fussy eater, you can stop all of that nonsense and change your pet into a happy eager eater with the following system.

Check with your veterinarian to be sure that your cat has no internal parasites. If he is in good health, find a convenient food that contains nutritious ingredients and is pleasant tasting.

Now the hard part—you must forbid your cat all food for twenty-four hours. Not even a scrap should be given. This system may be hard on you if you have children in the family giving the cat snacks, but you are doing this for his health, so you must be firm.

After twenty-four hours have passed, put one-fourth of your cat's normal amount of food in a dish, put it down and leave the room. Twenty or thirty minutes later, return and remove the dish whether your cat has eaten the food or not. Until the food is completely eaten, continue this schedule.

When the cat eagerly eats up the food, you may increase the amount by another quarter at the next feeding. It may take only a few days or as long as a week or two before the cat is ready for a larger amount of food. Don't be discouraged, he will eventually eat. In fact, you may have been overfeeding the pet, so increase by quarter amounts only when he has completely eaten the last meal. Remember, don't feed your cat between meals until his appetite has improved.

Many catterys feed their cats a well-balanced dry kibble. It's convenient and less expensive to serve dry kibbles, and if your cat prefers, the food may be moistened with meat broth, milk, or water. Chewing dry food aids in keeping your cat's teeth clean and provides all necessary nutrition.

When your cat is eagerly eating its food, reduce one-half of one meal, once a week. This system of refusing food may sound extreme, but remember, you will have a happy eater because you loved your cat enough to be concerned about its health.

Quick Appetizers For Your Pet

Once your cat is eating well and may occasionally be rewarded with a treat, try our family pets' favorite crunchy munchy cookies. This healthy snack is so easy to make that even a pre-teenager can manage alone. The recipe is sufficient for a cat or a small dog. I double or triple the ingredients for gift giving.

CRUNCHY MUNCHIES FOR CATS AND DOGS

Mix a three and one-half ounce jar of strained meat baby food, four heaping teaspoons of powdered non-fat milk, and six heaping teaspoons of wheat germ.

Shape the dough into small balls, roll in wheat germ or flour and flatten slightly with a fork. If you find the ingredients too dry to handle comfortably, add a little meat broth or water.

Bake on a greased cookie sheet until brown and dry, in a 350 degree oven. This takes about 30 minutes. If you double the recipe and make larger cookies, increase the baking time according to the size.

Crunchy munchies are dry, hard, and excellent for keeping your pet's teeth clean. They also make great gifts when given in a decorative, air tight container, with a bow on top.

Balanced Diet for Fat or Thin

If your cat is so plump that his ribs cannot be felt through the fat, it's time to put your friend on a diet. Overweight cats tend to have shorter lives and more problems with their health. The most common ailments fat cats suffer are heart disease, arthritis, and respiratory illness.

Growing kittens under one year of age, need twice the amount of protein that adult cats require. To keep your pet slim, trim, and healthy, you should feed your older cat fewer calories as he ages.

If your cat is fed an all meat diet, whether fresh, frozen, or canned, he is probably getting too much fat. Although cats do need protein in some form, they do not require meat for a well-balanced daily ration.

There are many canned cat foods on the market which have supplements to provide the added nutrients needed for a balanced diet. If you insist on canned meat for your cat, read the labels until you find a food with the proper proportions of protein, carbohydrates, and fat.

Vegetable protein soy products are a valuable low-fat diet supplement for cats with special nutrition requirements. If you feel your cat needs a special, or low-fat diet, consult your veterinarian.

The individual meal size packets of food, now available in all flavors to suit the most fastidious taste, are certainly convenient. They do not require refrigeration and are so handy that I usually switch all my family pets to these carefree packets when we travel. Individual packets of food vary in content and flavor, so shop around for the best quality at a reasonable price. High priced foods don't seem expensive when you have a single pet, but both canned and individual packets of food can become high priced when you have more than one family pet.

A normal cat that does not need a special diet will grow and stay healthy when fed a well-balanced dry commercial food. You may serve kibbles either moistened with milk, canned meats, or with added table scraps. My cats enjoy eating kibbles as they come from the bag with nothing added. Of course there is a large bowl of water beside the food at all times.

Dry kibbles not only provide a complete diet, they also help to prevent dental tartar and promote healthy teeth and gums.

When you feed your cat, allow him 20 to 30 minutes to eat and then remove the dish. This is plenty of time for your eager eater to finish the meal. Throw away any food left in the dish and do not feed your cat again until the next scheduled meal.

Any cat that needs to lose weight must have his daily calories reduced. This is easily accomplished by cutting the amount of food offered by one-fourth. The reduced amount of food may be given twice a day to help your cat escape hunger pains.

Give your cat only low calorie snacks while he is on a diet. You are being tough because you want your beloved pet to live a long and healthy life.

Litter Box Care

Cleanliness is a vital concern to all cat owners, and good litter box habits are necessary for a happy home. Provide your kitten with a litter box large enough to be comfortable and contains space for the kitten to do a little wild scratching. All cat owners soon learn that cats occasionally get into their litter boxes just to scratch up a storm. Excess energy? Only your cat knows. Regardless, you must be prepared for litter all over the floor if the box is not large enough for your cat's antics. Besides scratching, many cats enjoy sleeping in their litter boxes instead of the beautiful beds we provide. I usually try to discourage this, but with cats you can't win all the time. Most cats, luxury lovers that they are, will eventually seek a softer bed.

Your cat may refuse to use his box because the litter is not changed often enough. The strong odor of urine ammonia discourages him, and in desperation he will use the floor.

If you line the litter pan with two thick layers of newspaper, the papers will absorb much of the urine and the litter will remain dry. You may also use one of the new padded liners available in your pet supply section. Add about 4 inches of litter on top of the papers, and when the top layer gets wet, slip it out and throw it away. This will keep the litter dry and odor-free longer.

When cleaning the litter box, remove the urine-soiled newspapers and place them in a plastic garbage bag together with the soiled litter. Tie up the bag and you have a water-proof, easy-to-handle parcel ready for trash pickup.

Placement and Cleaning

Give some thought to the placement of the litter box. Many cats require privacy. If there is too much traffic where the litter box is located, the cat may decide it is safer to go elsewhere. Some cats like the covered litter boxes for this reason, but because odors may be emphasized inside covered boxes, you will have to be especially careful to keep these boxes clean.

Many cat owners do not realize that the cleaning materials they use to cleanse and deodorize the litter box might also repel the cat. Some cleaning products may even be dangerous to your cat's health. No matter what you use, rinse the pan thoroughly. To get rid of any offensive chlorine or ammonia odors that may be left behind, add baking soda to the rinse water and allow it to remain in the litter box for a few minutes.

Litter Box Fillers

There is a wide selection of litter box fillers on the market; experiment to find the one that best fits your needs. Clay litters are the most popular, but some cat owners prefer to use sand, and one breeder I know swears that shredded newspaper, changed daily, is the most efficient. Occasionally you will find a cat that prefers only one kind of litter and refuses to use any other. Indulge him and just be happy he uses the box.

You don't really have to train a cat to use a litter box. Indoor cats are naturally clean, and with a little guidance they will accept and use their litter pan with no problems. This is especially true if the kitten was raised by a conscientious mother. Burying their feces is instinctive for cats. It's a trait carried over from their wild ancestors who used this technique to help hide their dens from predators.

It's a good idea to keep the litter box close to the kitten's sleeping area for at least the first few weeks. During this training period, it is also helpful if you place a small amount of soiled litter back in the clean box to remind the kitten what the box is used for. But always keep the litter box clean. Even as a youngster, a cat is fastidious and may refuse to use badly soiled litter. An offensive litter box can cause a kitten to develop poor bathroom habits as he matures.

PART 4

Man and Cat
Living, Loving, Coping

Two Owners—One Cat—A Shared Experience

Owning pets in today's world is not easy. In fact, there are many pet lovers who long to own a cat, but their business and social lives are not compatible with animal care.

There is a solution to this problem—shared pet ownership. It really does work, if proper planning is done before the kitten is introduced into its two homes.

Duo-ownership can be a wonderful option for working singles or couples who travel frequently.

Business travelers and retirees can have the best of both worlds while away from home, knowing their little pet is lovingly cared for during their absence.

It's not even necessary that the owners be close friends. In fact, I have seen two strangers with a common love for animals become partners as they successfully co-owned a pet.

I had shared two of my cats with a relative for many years before I realized that any two compatible adults can achieve the same results.

CONCERN FOR YOUR PET: Sharing one cat can solve many problems. You will no longer feel guilty about leaving your pet in a kennel. You will no longer need to worry about the anxiety your pet feels when left alone too long. You will not be constantly trying to compensate your cat with quality time when you know deep inside, a short amount of time spent with your cat, whether quality or not, is not enough.

FOOD: Once the kitten for duo-ownership is decided upon, a schedule must be worked out between the owners. It should include simple food which is easily purchased near each home. It is important that the pet is fed the same food and the same quantity at approximately the same time in both homes.

The owners must agree to be careful when giving snacks, since no one needs a fat cat.

EXERCISE AND SLEEP: Schedules for play and sleep should be determined by the owners, so consistent habits are established in both homes. This may mean rearranging your schedule for the time your kitty is with you, but don't forget, your responsibilities will change as your partner takes over the care.

DISCIPLINE: It must be clearly understood by each participant that training and discipline are vital to the success of your arrangement. There are pet consultants who can work up a simple chart for training the cat, if necessary. All you need do is decide between yourselves how it is to be accomplished.

CASES AND CAGES: I have always trained my cats that their carrying case is their private property. It is a place for storing much loved toys and, of course, a comfortable place to sleep. Most dogs and cats love their own room and will go in frequently during the day to hide a toy or take a nap. At night in either home, no matter where it is placed, the case is always your pet's good old home.

The carrying case is a perfect arrangement for transporting small to middle-sized pets. It will fit into almost any car back seat, can be taken on a train, and generally is a great convenience for the owners. Should you find you must board your cat occasionally, many boarding kennels will allow pets to bring their small cages with them so they feel comfortable in their home away from home.

HEALTH RECORDS: A medical record must be kept and if possible attached to the top of the carrying case so the information is with the pet at all times. Your veterinarian will be happy to help you keep the cat's health record up to date. Of course, the feline must visit the same doctor each time for consistency and the convenience of both pet and partners. Since you will be sharing the medical bills, each partner will be well-acquainted with the kitty's health.

WHEN THE UNEXPECTED HAPPENS: It is important from the start that each of the co-owners must remain flexible and realize that emergencies and other situations will arise which could not have been anticipated. These occasions must be dealt with at the moment by whomever is available. When both parties are aware of this, common sense and mutual affection for your pet should help you both reach the right decisions.

Felines on the Move

Americans are always on the move. Either we change jobs, which involves moving to a new home, vacation frequently, or visit relatives and friends near and far.

Without a doubt, during the average feline life span, your cat will accompany you to many new homes and make frequent short trips. Its first trip will almost certainly be a visit to the veterinarian. Even a short ride in the car, especially with no advanced preparation, can be stressful. The cat must endure confinement in a strange vehicle, disorientation while enroute, and exposure to new people.

To avoid these problems, if you love your cat and also wish him to remain healthy, take a little time to train your pet to enjoy using a cage, wearing a harness, and traveling in any kind of vehicle. After learning to tolerate these restraints, even though your cat may never enjoy them, at least he will learn to accept traveling. (See Chapters: Car Riding and Walking on a Leash.)

There are many perks and pitfalls when taking your pet with you on a vacation. Regardless, the majority of cat owners who communicate with me talk about the joy of not worrying about a pet left at home. Cat owners camp in tents with their cats, travel in recreation vehicles and trucks, or stay in the classiest hotels and enjoy every minute of it.

Their felines, on the other hand, experience unusual situations, but eventually learn to enjoy riding in a vehicle.

MEDICAL PREPARATIONS BEFORE LEAVING: When leaving for more than a few days, your cat should have a medical check-up, vaccination boosters, health certificate, and vaccination records from his veterinarian. I like to put the records in a zip-lock plastic bag and tape it to the outer top of the cage. Then cat, case, and records with name, address, and the phone number of either your pet's doctor or a close relative of the family are available in case of emergency.

Most veterinarians recommend that cat owners avoid giving tranquilizers to their cats before a trip, because the medicine may leave your pet's system sluggish and less able to cope with the stress of travel. If you do decide to try tranquilizers, give one to your cat a week before you leave and watch the results. You can then make the best decision.

MAKE TRAVELING FUN: While you are preparing for your trip, let your pets know how great it will be. Talk to them while you make preparations, and even though life gets a little hectic while packing, try to relax and anticipate being a happy, carefree road warrior with a furry crew.

Pack a picnic lunch for yourself and your pet for the first day. Include favorite cat snacks, bottled drinking water, paper bowls, or heavy pottery if your cat prefers it. Stash a bag of litter, litter box, cat bed, toys, and a box of plastic garbage bags for neat disposal of litter. You may prefer to use shredded newspaper as a liner for the cat cage. It can be quickly changed in case of accident.

DO'S AND DONT'S WHILE TRAVELING:

DO isolate your cat in a room while you are packing the car. Animals can sense when changes are coming and disappear quickly. When all is ready to depart, put the cat in his cage or carrier and leave.

DO try to work out a way to weave the seat belt through the cage. I usually find that a metal cage can be held down with the belt through the base. Use seat belts whenever possible, so you don't have to worry if you stop suddenly.

DO give everyone in the car proper ventilation, but use the air conditioner. Never roll down the window, unless your pet is in a harness tied with a leash.

DON'T feed your cat before you leave. It should eat at least two or three hours before the trip to prevent stomach upset from excitement while traveling.

DON'T ever leave a cat in the car during extreme heat or chill. The interior temperature can increase drastically on a hot day, even in the shade.

DO talk, sing, and have fun with your pet during a trip. He will enjoy the ride more and you will find that you are also keeping yourself in a positively happy mood.

Changing Environment May Cause Stress

I don't remember ever moving to another city without toting at least two cats along with the family. Those were the good ol' days, when cat owners simply got along as well as they could, trying earnestly to help their felines adjust to their new territory. Many cats, lacking the freedom to choose their environment when moved, disappeared at the first opportunity and became strays, or found new homes.

Fortunately today we have the opportunity to understand our cat's emotions and the resulting stress involved when they are forced to change their surroundings. By understanding, we have the ability to help our felines adjust to the new environment, without prolonged separation anxiety.

Indoor cats usually find adapting their daily routine to new surroundings much easier than outdoor cats. Of course, those living indoors must re-route their daily exercise pattern along a new household path; but they can keep their eating and grooming habits intact.

Outdoor cats when relocated face as many new situations as a new kid in the neighborhood. Hostile strangers and unfamiliar territory can certainly disturb and frighten the normally easy-going feline. Panicked by the forced change, the cat may become nervous, fearful, and finally anti-social.

Cats, of all domestic animals, are without a doubt the most rigid about their routines. No red-blooded feline would put up with the casual schedules forced upon dogs by their owners. Upon coming home exhausted and late from an important appointment, we are promptly punished for our cat's delayed dinner by being snubbed or yelled at.

Dogs, on the other hand, greet us cheerfully, thankful that we show up at all. *It is easy to see that dogs, the most people-oriented of all household pets, adjust to new surroundings more easily than cats, the most self-oriented of all family pets.*

There are many "if possible" activities that you, the owner, can do to ease your pet into a new home and territory.

If possible:

Train your cat to ride in the car before you take him on the long trip to your new home.

Take your cat with you to visit your new living quarters several times before the actual move. He will probably enjoy sniffing around the empty rooms. When the permanent move is made, he will remember the territory and relax.

Arrange the furniture in your new home the same as in the old house. Your cat may then follow many of the rituals he has set for his daily routine without too much interference. After a few months, the furniture may be moved; but as expected, he will either love or hate the new arrangement.

Put the cat's food, litter box and other accouterments in approximately the same place in your new living areas.

Since smelling is our cat's most important method of identification, bringing the everyday smells of the old home into the new home can help. The same personal odors that pervade the bedroom, bath, kitchen and living room can easily be distributed through the new home with little difficulty. In fact, to prevent future litter box problems, check the flooring in your new home for old urine stains, and clean the area thoroughly with a strong deodorizer.

On the day, it's important to keep your cat confined. Both indoor and outdoor cats should be kept in the house for several days before the move. A cat can sense when change

128

is in the air; and if allowed outside, he may depart to hide. If you keep kitty in the house, you'll know he will be there when you look for him. Give him extra love and reassurance when you can. Try to stay calm during this stressful time.

On moving day don't carry the cat in your arms out to the car. A sudden noise can panic even the calmest feline, provoking a quick jump from your arms. Put him on his leash or in a secure box. Once inside the car, keep him close to you to pat and assure him that all is well.

When you have arrived at your new dwelling, lock your cat in a room to prevent him from slipping outside while the doors are open. Place his litter box and dishes in the same room and allow him to relax while he explores this part of his new home.

An outdoor cat should be kept indoors for at least one week after moving. During this time, he becomes familiar with the new neighborhood as he watches the activities through the windows. Daily walks on a harness and leash will help your pet to get acquainted with the neighbors and live in harmony with both humans and animals.

Introducing Second Cat Is Touchy

Much to my surprise, a friend who had found a stray cat at a local market, walked into my house and set the cat down. Fortunately for all involved, the cat immediately seemed at ease with our household pets. They, though

curious, did nothing worse than run into the kitchen to guard their food.

Baby, as we called him, leaving a proper name to the future owner, turned out to be a gentle, loving boy, apparently about 5 months old. He had big paws and a large bone structure, indicating that he was destined to become a very impressive adult. We enjoyed having the cat around us and he had such winning ways we were sorely tempted to add him to our menagerie. Fortunately the next day we received a telephone call for help that established Baby's future home.

Paul and Judy were having discipline problems with their one-year-old Siamese male, named Sammy. He had always been temperamental and high-strung, but as he got older, he became snippy, and at times downright mean.

His over-indulgent owners had tried once before to bring a small kitten into their home as a companion for Sammy. Their effort had failed, partly because the meeting was not well-planned and partly because they had introduced a young defenseless kitten to a large, strong-willed dictator. The kitten was soon rescued and given another home.

Paul and Judy, reluctant to go through another nerve wracking encounter, had asked me to help them find a proper companion for Sammy to work off some of his excess energy. Meanwhile, at my suggestion, Sammy was being neutered.

Baby was certainly the perfect size and had the right disposition to adjust to their temperamental cat; but I knew that Sammy would not accept another feline in his home without thoughtful advance preparation.

Since Sammy had definitely established territorial rights to every room in his home, I decided that we should introduce the cats in neutral territory. Our home seemed the only sensible place, so we arranged an evening for the meeting. I have helped introduce a second cat quite a few times, and it is always a touchy situation. Often you do not have a second chance once the territorial cat rejects the invader.

In preparation for the cats' meeting, I asked my son to wipe Sammy down with a solution of apple cider vinegar and water. After drying, he had to be sprinkled with baby powder. Baby received the same treatment at our home.

With this precaution, both cats would lose their specific body odors and smell familiarly alike.

On the appointed evening, I placed our other household pets in a comfortable upstairs bedroom so they could not complicate matters.

As Sammy came through the door in his owner's arms, he was yelling his Siamese disapproval. When placed on the floor, he became mollified and sniffed the carpet and furniture. Advancing halfway across the living room, Sammy was suddenly confronted by Baby, casually entering through the kitchen doorway.

One look and Sam dropped to a crouch, each hair on his body soaring to attention. As Sammy bellied threateningly across the floor toward the kitten, Baby circled in the opposite direction, each approaching the other from the rear.

Once within nose reach, Sammy stretched his neck to smell his rival. Baby backed away each time Sam's nose came near. Persistently, Sammy tried to smell Baby's tail until finally our good-natured boy, tired of retreating, smacked Sammy, ran across the room and jumped upon the seat of a chair. Sammy's hair slowly flattened as he stood up, walked to the chair and batted Baby's draping tail. Since there was no offensive odor and no difference in smell, the cats began a hesitantly playful chase around the room.

The cats' first encounter lasted for two hours. Each was cautious while playing, never really trusting the other. Sammy, confused and fearful, had behaved better than we had hoped; but he was a long way from accepting Baby as a lasting friend.

Paul and Judy were encouraged by Sammy's less aggressive behavior and carefully followed our plan. For the next two evenings, both cats were wiped all over with the vinegar and water mixture followed by powder, and reunited.

During the cats' second meeting, Sammy was excited and eager to find Baby as he jumped from his owner's arms and sashayed across the room. Baby, delighted to see his new friend, smacked Sammy across the head. The chase was on.

That evening and the following night were very different from the cats' first meeting. Now they romped, bit and scratched each other, playing gently but more aggressively each time they met. While they rested between bouts, we could hear them talking to each other in soft guttural purrs.

On the fourth night, it was decided that the cats were ready to live together. Sammy had used Baby's litter box occasionally while he was visiting, and he had even eaten out of Baby's food dish. In other words, Sammy had established himself as top cat and Baby seemed agreeable to the arrangement most of the time.

As our daughter-in-law related later, there was little sleep for either humans or cats that first night at home. Sammy had always shared his king-size bed with his owners; but he spent half the night chasing Baby away. Baby, though not as clever as Sam, was just as persistent and kept coming back for more. By 4:00 in the morning, both cats, too exhausted to continue, curled up with Paul and Judy and fell asleep.

During the next few weeks, Sammy, Baby and their owners slowly adjusted to their new living arrangement.

Whenever the cats got huffy with each other, potential battles were avoided by powdering both cats again.

Sammy has a long way to go before he relaxes completely with another cat in the house. Maybe he will always be high strung and excitable. At least, we know Sam is happier sharing his lonely hours with Baby than being alone and Paul and Judy no longer feel guilty leaving their cats at home while they work or take a day for pleasure.

Most of all, although no one thought of it but me, my Baby had a wonderful, loving home. That's my reward.

Spraying—A Territorial Instinct

Cats spray urine to mark their territory. The scent left by spraying informs other felines of their territorial possessions. Upon smelling the odor, other cats do not appear frightened or intimidated, merely informed.

Tom cats spray a heavy scent that everyone recognizes immediately by the overpowering urine odor. Occasionally a female or neutered male will also spray, but usually they mark territory by scratching or by rubbing their chins, foreheads or tails, which contain scent glands, over an object leaving a mild odor on it. Often, when the marking scent produces a mild or inoffensive odor, a second cat, after careful investigation, will aggressively superimpose his own scent over the area, thus claiming it for his own.

Outdoors territorial marking, even in a small area, becomes clearly defined by all the felines living in a neighborhood. If the area is very small, the instinctive need for territorial marking adjusts to the situation, allowing the various cats to coexist peacefully. Of course, arguments do occur, but cats become so sophisticated in marking, that often the same territory belongs to different felines at varying times of the day. That is, a well-worn path may be one cat's territory in the morning, a second cat's territory in the afternoon, and a third cat's exclusive property at night.

Indoor pets instinctively use the same procedure as their outdoor cousins. Observe your felines. One cat will sun himself in a specific place each morning. Another one will have afternoon privileges in the same desired location with no argument from the first occupant. Pathways through the house are also marked by each cat. Specific trails, which make no sense to the observing human, are carefully followed each time the cat moves about the area. Up, down, around and through, the animals follow invisible trails and markings in a pattern, which cat's owners, if not knowledgeable, might consider weird and unexplainable.

Indoor Spraying

An indoor cat, especially if confined in a small area, may occasionally try to expand his realm. Many times, this desire for realignment of boundary lines happens after several years of seemingly happy coexistence with companion cats. Of course, sparks fly and tempers explode as his territorial drive tortures his owners. Vocalizing, hair raising, slapping and chasing, all become armaments in the battle for territory. The companion cats, unable to defend themselves from this domination and finding it difficult to escape, may resort to soiling or shying away, and if not helped may even become reclusive. Yesterday's happy household suddenly becomes today's battleground.

The owners of these felines are mystified to find themselves in the middle of all this turmoil. They have not observed the subtle, overt signs of scrimmages to come. Loving each cat, they are torn at being forced to take sides in each unacceptable attack. To top it off, the same cats that used to be so clean are now soiling all over the house.

To realign his boundaries, an unneutered, or possibly a neutered male, sprays urine in seemingly random spots over the area. The companion cats, exhausted, nervous, unhappy and unable to cope with the situation, cry for help by refusing to use the litter box and soiling the rugs.

Isolation for Spray Training

What do you do with your cats when this situation occurs in your home? Your immediate recourse is to isolate the spraying cat. Discipline will not help; the animal's actions are dictated by nature. You are dealing with 2,000 years of instinctive behavior that your cats could not change if they wanted to. Isolating the offending male will solve some of your immediate problems. You will be able to clean and thoroughly deodorize your home. The other cats will be able to relax and hopefully resume their normal routine.

136

Many times, isolating the male in a small room or cage for several weeks helps him to forget, but this will usually help only if the male has been neutered. It is important that he be isolated continuously for several weeks. You can go into his area to feed, change the litter box and give the cat some affection, but don't allow him into the rest of the house.

Before you allow your cats to meet again, wipe each one with a solution of vinegar and water. Saturate their coats well to remove any offensive odors that might prompt renewed battles.

The first week when you bring the male cat into the family area, isolate the other cats for the few hours he is with you. It will be enough for him to readjust to the area alone without the other cats around. While playing with him and allowing him to roam about, you should have available a

137

spray bottle filled with vinegar and water. Hopefully, the previously soiled areas are now odorless and the cat will ignore them. If by chance, he starts to soil, you must be ready to give him a spray of water in the face, together with a firm "No!" command.

Over the next few weeks, you can continue allowing your aggressive boy access to the household areas frequently and for longer intervals. Take your time with this retraining, and you may succeed once and for all. Reintroduce his former companions when you feel all cats are ready to meet. If you are doing well, but the disciplined cat suddenly relapses into his previously bad behavior, isolate him again and start over. Don't be discouraged; it shouldn't take as long the second time around.

Many times veterinarians prescribe hormones to try to alleviate the spraying problem. Sometimes hormone injections are successful, but often the medication doesn't work. If your retraining efforts don't obtain the desired results, consult your vet.

Emotionally Disturbed Stray Cats

A week ago a stray cat was dumped off at my door. It's not the first time this has occurred. Maybe he was meant for one of the neighbors, or maybe someone just dumped him and hoped he would find a good home. Worst of all, some child may be crying for this well-cared-for, affectionate half-grown cat. I tried in every way I knew to find the cat's home and owners.

138

Frustrated, I decided to talk to my young cat-loving neighbor down the street. I met Cheryl Hoyle a few years ago when I walked by her old stately farmhouse located right in the middle of a city block. The large yard, not beautiful by people standards but neat and clean, has lots of grass and a few very old oak trees that shed their abundant large leaves early in the fall. I was first attracted to Cheryl's home on a day in late autumn when I saw a half-dozen cats playfully diving under the dry leaves. The cats seemed carefree and fun-loving until I tried to approach them, but dashed for cover as I drew near.

Cheryl, a mathematics teacher in a local high school and a very independent lady, came out and talked about her cats. As a collector of stray cats, she ranks among the best because her cats cannot be placed with a family. They live in a special world of fear and uncertainty." You must make stray cats adopt you," confides Cheryl." Many times it takes months and often the cat that has been too neglected or misused can never become confident of your affection."

As Cheryl continued, I tried to see into one of the two wooden cat houses which stood side by side on the front porch." That's Arthur," said Cheryl." He is a truly quirky cat. When he came here most of his bottom teeth were gone, one eye had cornea damage and was all cloudy and no one could get near him. He was a fighter and all of the other cats ran from him. I fed him," she continued, "for six months before I could get a good look at him. He needed medical care and it's hard to stay calm and wait, but there is little else you can do.

"I put food out for Arthur every morning and evening. He was always waiting and would come and sit at a distance, until I had put the food down and gone back inside of the house. Each feeding, poor Arthur would eat and then run away to hide. But I had to wait for my stray cat to adopt me," she exclaimed again as she leaned down and stretched a loving hand to scratch Arthur." It was a year before I could touch this boy and gain his trust. He still will not live in the house or with the other cats, but the fire is gone and he is enjoying old age."

Strays Must Find Water

Few people realize that cats need drinking water and many times cannot find it. Most stray cats will not eat snow and suffer continually from lack of their most basic necessity—water. Cheryl puts buckets of warm water near the back door year-round. Warm water many times helps comfort the stray, plus warm water will remain free of ice longer. In cold weather, she also heats the milk given daily to the strays.

When a stray shows up in the Hoyle yard, Cheryl puts extra food and water in a secluded area to tempt the cat to eat. Since much of the stress a stray cat feels is "where is my next meal coming from," this first communication with food is the most important contact. Along with the stress of finding food, Cheryl knows that the cat is thinking, "can I trust anyone?"

Jud came into the Hoyle yard one day and stayed. Since he was an agreeable cat, Cheryl easily caught him and went to the vet to have him neutered as soon as she could. Jud came home, well and happy and immediately disappeared. Six months later he showed up at her door again. He still shows up occasionally but obviously has other homes." You just take a stray cat on its terms," sighed Cheryl." You can't bathe them or fuss over them. Many times it takes weeks just to get near enough to take care of the noticeable wounds they have. Of course, I always try to catch the strays and have them neutered, but sometimes even that is impossible. The rewards are there though," she said." Even though it's not necessary, once in a while one of my cats stops fighting the world, and turns to lick the hand that feeds it. I treasure those moments."

What should you do when you notice a stray cat in your yard? Your first objective is to offer food and water to the cat. If at all possible, look the cat over without touching and see whether it needs medical help. After the cat has eaten, provide a bed in a secluded area such as a garage or tool shed. *Don't bring the stray into the house among your household pets until it is examined by a veterinarian.* The cat may be sick or infected with parasites, which can be transmitted to your home and inhabitants.

Don't try to touch the cat if it is frightened. You must let the stray develop confidence in you at its own pace. Never rush at a stray cat or it may leave your area. As time passes, watch the cat for indications of trust. When you feel the time is right, offer some tasty food from your hand. As your hand feeding progresses, you will eventually find the proper time to reach out and carefully pet your little friend.

Since eating and sleeping are a cat's main occupation, do as Cheryl suggests and give your stray a variety of foods. Dry kibbles which take longer to eat are desirable, with alternate meals of semi-moist and canned food. Milk is optional, but most stray cats enjoy this treat. Always keep fresh water near the sleeping area.

What are the stresses that control a stray cat's life?

TRUSTING—Can I trust anyone? If I do will they suddenly turn on me?

FOOD AND SHELTER—Will it always be available and safe?

EXTERNAL ENEMIES—Must I be careful of other cats, dogs, cars and people?

ILLNESS—Where can I safely hide when I am sick and hurt?

How much easier it is to be patient with the homeless cat when we are aware of its problems. It is also easier to understand why many stray cats, even though they are well cared-for, pace about the house crying for no apparent reason. Many of them remain restless for the remainder of their lives.

How To Place A Stray Cat

Certainly a neutered cat is more easily placed in a new home. If you find the cost prohibitive, contact your local animal shelter or humane society. They may have help for homeless pets and their owners. Most potential owners find having a neutered pet offered is far more desirable than assuming the cost themselves.

Have confidence in the potential owner of your stray cat and tell him/her of any daily problems which might reoccur. Most cat lovers can handle the cat's stress if prepared ahead.

Many laundromats, cleaners and corner stores will place a small announcement to help you find a new owner. If you include a picture of the cat, you may get a faster response.

A cleverly worded, short ad in the local newspaper is worth the money. Spreading the news through friends and acquaintances is also helpful. Meanwhile, until you find a home which will be beneficial for your stray cat, continue your loving care. He trusts you.

Growing Old—Feeling Good

Old age comes all too soon for our beloved family pets, Yet of the three stages of life—youth, maturity and old age—the last can be the most rewarding.

By the time a cat is ten years old, signs of aging appear. The once sparkling eyes lose their luster; hair becomes thinner and lacks the shine that constant grooming makes possible. Your old tiger is no longer jumping, playing and demanding attention as he did in his prime.

Your cat's golden years can and should be a wonderful experience for both of you. While it is necessary to stay alert for signs of physical and psychological complications, a majority of healthy, well-cared-for felines proceed through their teen years with good health and an astonishing amount of vigor. It's best to continue with your cat's daily routine as he ages, unless you notice changes that indicate discomfort or irritability.

He is now content to spend his time sleeping and taking short walks around the house and yard. The cat accepts and enjoys the attention you give, then lounges away the hours in his favorite spot watching the rest of the world whirl around.

Litter Box Disorders—Older Cats

Many times your senior citizen will show physical or mental stress by refusing to use his litter pan, or worse, insulting you by soiling right beside it. If this happens after years of cleanliness, you should look for the source of your cat's problem. Few cats will indiscriminately soil without justifiable cause. Of course, you and your pet may have a differing definition of "justifiable cause," especially in this frustrating situation.

Many times, the most simple motive is the explanation: **Has your daily** routine been changed, thus causing your cat emotional stress? A good example of this is a change from daytime to nighttime work among the family members. Have you accepted a job requiring long hours away from home, when your cat has always had your daily companionship? You can overcome these problems; but you must remember your old cat loves a never-changing schedule. Perhaps you can give your pet a little more affection when you come home and during your after-work activities. With these small efforts, the cat will eventually re-adjust his schedule and return to his former cleanliness. During this adjustment period, you should express your disapproval over his litter box behavior.

Did you move your cat's litter box to a different area? If so, put it back and slowly move the box a little each day until you have the litter where you want it. If kitty objects,you'll have to figure out a compromise, if possible. At least, there is one simple solution: move the box back to its original place. Then, thank your lucky stars your cat is once again clean.

Do you have a new tenant in your home? Be it man, woman, dog, baby or another cat, your old boy will not share your enthusiasm for the intruder. Proper introduction to the stranger will help; but you, the one your cat focuses his affection on, must take the time to help your distressed senior citizen to adjust.

Many feline owners, out of affection for their old friend, bring a kitten into the home thinking their cat will be happier. This is a misconception and should not be believed. Even though life seems boring for the elderly pet, he is content with his routine and should be allowed to monopolize your attention as long as possible. Of course, there are changes in your lifestyle that he must accept; but unless the older cat adopts another kitten or cat of his own free will, you will both be happier leaving your home life as it is.

Did a member of the family leave home? The death or departure of a companion causes great stress in the elderly cat. He must learn to adjust; but you can help by giving more attention and affection to your old buddy during this difficult period.

Are physical reasons preventing your cat from using his litter box? Is he having pain during urination? Is he straining when he attempts to evacuate? He may be telling you of his distress by bringing attention to his litter box misbehavior. A trip to the veterinarian for a diagnosis should be made as soon as possible.

Is your cat feeling discomfort when going up and down the stairs? This could be a simple answer, if you have always put the litter box in the basement, or in an upstairs bath or bedroom. Perhaps your cat has painful arthritis and no longer wants to climb as he used to. Putting the litter box, along with his food dishes and bed in the living area he shares with you, may bring peace and cleanliness once more.

If you notice stiffness or pain when your cat moves, you can add to his comfort by placing a stool, ladder or chair under the high areas he has always enjoyed. Aging bones may not respond to jumping to the high places that were accessible when he was young. These aids will allow your old boy to continue, with dignity, to enjoy the daily pleasures he relishes so dearly.

Preventive Medicine for Elderly Cats

Preventive medicine is most important for assuring your cat a comfortable, healthy old age. Yearly checkups should be stressed as the feline ages and all booster shots should be scheduled when necessary.

Older cats do not require as much food as they did in younger days; and being overweight is a serious drawback to good health. As the elderly, less active cat gains weight, the fat stored in his system requires more energy to make the vital organs function. This causes an additional burden to the heart, kidneys and digestive system. The most common geriatric problems are kidney disorders, tumors, arthritis and heart conditions. Obesity can be a major contributor in most of these problems.

Loss of appetite is a frequent occurrence at one time or another as your cat ages. Certainly the sense of smell and taste are decreasing over the years. Many times stronger flavoring added to your pet's food will stimulate the appetite. Garlic, onion and fish flavorings are especially enticing to a fussy feline and, of course, mixed meat, vegetables, butter and fats encourage lagging appetites.

Along with the declining appetite, tartar build-up on your cat's teeth may cause eating discomfort. It may be directly related to loss of appetite, since excessive tartar can cause gum infections. This results in loose, and eventually, lost teeth. Eating then becomes very painful. You should inspect your cat's teeth occasionally for tartar and receding gums.

A weekly routine of wiping the teeth with a piece of rough toweling will help. If the condition becomes severe, a veterinarian will have to put your cat temporarily to sleep and give his teeth a thorough scraping. Fortunately, tartar removal doesn't need to be repeated very often.

Good grooming or looking good surely must be the first requirement for admittance into cat heaven. This must be true since all healthy felines spend hours each day washing their coats to shining perfection. A well-groomed coat is the

148

sign of a healthy cat. Grooming gives him exercise, a feeling of well-being, and helps to work off excess energy.

Mutual grooming is the ultimate affection shown by companion cats. For aging cats, grooming can become an overwhelming burden. Even though they try to maintain their coats, the extra energy required is not there. If this happens to your old pal, it's time for you to step in and help with this daily chore. When you groom your cat, you are showing affection and re-establishing his feeling of well-being. This is important to the feline's mental health. All experts agree that helping your pet look and feel well-groomed increases his life expectancy.

Occasionally the aging cat must have a bath. Frequent spot washing around his face, ears and tail will help maintain cleanliness, but there does come a time when a warm water bath must be given to make the cat smell nice again. If you are hesitant about bathing him, many grooming shops now include this as an added service.

When spot washing and brushing your pet, watch for lumps, warts and beginning mats. Malignant lumps or tumors can be successfully treated, if discovered early. Mats found when they are just forming can be easily sprayed with "mat and tangle remover" or oil and gently pulled apart by your fingers with no discomfort to your pet.

Death and Dying

Death and dying eventually come to all living creatures, but your aged cat will suffer less than you. The decision to

149

put an end to your pet's suffering is made with knowledge and love. You need not make this difficult decision alone. Your veterinarian will be most helpful in consultation about the health of your family pet.

The decision to put him to sleep is not a single problem. It must be discussed with the entire family and ultimately decided by all involved. Although painful for the family, the final act of love—relieving your old friend of pain and suffering—is the merciful decision you must inevitably make. Many owners of aging cats delay this difficult step too long. When the proper time arrives, euthanasia is suggested.

If you feel, however, that your pet is still enjoying life relatively free from pain, take each day as it comes and delay the end by giving him good care and affection. If you love your pet, show the strength necessary to consider him first.

PART 5

Questions and Answers

Questions & A

Video Memories

While watching the festivities at a wedding reception, I noticed the bride's attractive cat, brushed and be-ribboned for the occasion, warily approach the bride's bouquet, which had been left on a chair. As the cat drew near, I motioned to the bride to look at her cat." Oh, how cute," she remarked and immediately signaled the video photographer to catch the action on film. At just the right moment, the brave feline stood on his hind legs to obtain a closer look at the bouquet. From that moment on, I was aware of the value of filming the many important events we share with the pets in our lives.

A letter from Melodie A. Blair of Pigeon Forge, Tennessee, confirmed my thoughts on the value of the video recorder to pet owners. She wrote to tell me about the events surrounding the death of her dear Siamese, Mi-Mi.

"Last November, Mi-Mi became quite ill with a kidney disease, but by January she was back to normal. That rough November made me face the fact that my time with Mi-Mi was limited.

"I had owned a VCR for about a year, and Mi-Mi's illness had started me thinking that, while she was still healthy, I should make a tape of her. A friend was kind enough to lend me her video camera and to tape Mi-Mi and me together.

"She even left the camera for me to use, so I had the opportunity to catch Mi-Mi doing her little feline things. On several occasions, I propped the camera up and sneaked into the picture with Mi-Mi. We took footage of the two of us cuddling and watching TV together and even captured an unplanned series of three kitty sneezes." Near the end of April, Mi-Mi began losing interest in food again and later died peacefully in my arms at the veterinary clinic. I was so thankful for the extra months we had together, and I was truly comforted during her final illness knowing I had a bit of Mi-Mi on tape. It may take me a while before I can watch it, but I still have a bit of my cat.

"Please suggest to others that they could rent a video camera, even a VCR to play back on, if they don't have one. It is such a comfort to capture this memory and relive the pleasant experiences with a beloved pet."

Older Cat—New Kitten Adjustment

Q.   I just got a new kitten and my older cat refuses to like him. I have heard and read that cats should learn to coexist with each other in a week or less. Well, it's been more than a week and now whenever the kitten or I get near the adult cat, she scratches us. Do you have any suggestions to help get rid of this situation?

A.   Your adult cat feels that you and the kitten are leaving her out of all the fun. I know it's hard to ignore a kitten, but that's what you're going to have to do for awhile. When you ignore the kitten and pay more attention to the adult cat, the cats will work out a living arrangement together. Without your attention, the kitten will turn to the older cat for companionship. Once your older cat becomes friendly with the kitten, it will be up to you to see that they both get an equal amount of attention. In fact, the older cat will probably demand, and get, a bigger share, and little brother won't even notice.

Deaf Cat Becomes Neurotic

Q. For the last year, my neutered, male, white Persian, who is deaf, has been acting mean, hissing for no reason and running off scared. He is six years old and I've had him since he was a baby.

Last October I brought home a nine-week-old female sealpoint Himalayan kitten. After a year the two tolerate each other, but that's about all. I keep them separate at night when we are not home and give them each their own dish and litter box.

Last March they both had tapeworm and the Persian could not get enough to eat. They were both treated and started gaining weight. Now he weighs 13 pounds and has an obsession with food. The only time he is friendly any more is when I'm eating and he wants some.

Lately he will be sitting calmly by himself and all of a sudden his ears go back and he looks around as if scared, he'll hiss, run off and cower. He did this four times in a row the other day, while I was at the kitchen table eating. Nobody bothered him to cause this, not even the Hima-

layan. I'd appreciate any advice you could give me. He doesn't act sick and I hate to get rid of him.

A.   After much thought and worry about your problem, I consulted a few of my cat associates, and they confirmed my opinion. You have a problem which you cannot solve.

Apparently your older, deaf Persian cannot adjust to sharing his home and loved ones. He is becoming extremely neurotic, and the only answer, for your peace of mind, is to find a good home for one of the cats. Since you assure me that the cats have no physical problems, you must assume that your deaf cat will not change and proceed from there. Good luck.

Old Odor on Carpet

Q.   We have just moved into a nice home in Illinois. The only problem that we have is a smelly carpet from the previous owner's cat. How can we remove the odor without paying for professional services?

A.   Cat urine does seem to smell stronger with age and the odor is both unpleasant and frustrating to get rid of. The best method I have ever used to remove both stains and odor takes little time, effort or money. It is very effective.

You will need a large bottle of soda water (as in scotch and soda) and a large number of paper towels, paper napkins or facial tissues. Pour one cup of soda water on each soiled area, soaking it well. Let the soda water stand for 20 to 30 minutes. If the spot is old or very soiled, rub the area well with a rough sponge or brush. Blot the carpet dry with the absorbent paper. It is very important that you keep changing the blotting paper until all moisture is absorbed. You will then be sure that you have removed all of the dirt and odor broken down by the soda water. Repeat this process if necessary after the rug has completely dried. If you have brought another pet into the home, sprinkle pepper on the dry rug to discourage any further use. As an added precaution, spray the previously soiled area with a good deodorizer, such as Nilodor.

Soggy Rugs

Q. I have five cats that stay indoors since we live by a busy street. My problem with three of them is they urinate on throw rugs, but not the laid carpet. I can't put any rug down without them leaving their mark. The cats are male neuters. Are they just lazy cats, or are they telling me something with their behavior? Can anything be done to stop this behavior?

A.   Your cats' poor behavior may result from boredom, a dirty litter box, or simply one cat started soiling and the rest followed suit. I'm sure you have thought of all these reasons and have provided toys, scratching post, etc. to entertain your felines. What many cat owners do not realize is that once a pet soils a rug, the odor goes deep into the carpet, the padding, and even the flooring below. The smell will lure the cat back to the same spot. Washing the rug is not enough. Remove the throw rugs you've been using, and either throw them away or wash and deodorize them and put them aside for a few months.

Don't be surprised if your cats still insist on soiling the same areas, even though the rugs have been removed. After you have removed the rugs, it will be necessary to thoroughly clean and deodorize the floor beneath. There are many good products on the market made especially to remove urine odor, or you can use your own household cleaner. With wood flooring, be particularly careful to clean the cracks. During the next two months, clean the floor several times to permanently remove the odor. As an extra deterrent, you can place a chair or any piece of furniture upside down over each previously used spot to prevent the cats from soiling again during the cleanup process. You really will have no trouble correcting this situation if you deodorize carefully.

As a final precaution, I like to put a little pepper, vinegar or Tabasco sauce on the forbidden spots. It's also good to use the repellents on the rugs when they are placed on the floor again.

Hospital Odors Confuse Companion Cats

Q. Recently, I had a battle of dominance between my two cats. Both are city apartment cats who live with me alone in a small apartment with no access to the out-of-doors.

My 15-year-old female Siamese, Thai, underwent dental surgery and came home the same day, weak and groggy. Over the next three days, my four-year-old male hybrid, Tigger, showed the most bizarre and unaccustomed behavior. He repeatedly attacked Thai, growling and bristling. No damage was done, but she was alarmed and frightened, and so was I.

My vet suggested that the cats were fighting for the position of "top cat" in the household. I was advised to let my younger cat know his behavior was unacceptable. It took about a week before he finally returned to his old, sweet self, and the problem has not recurred. It was almost impossible for me to separate them, so I never did.

My problem is that Thai, although in relatively good health, will probably continue to have health problems as she ages. What do I do about protecting her and solving the dominance problem? Will Tigger get more aggressive as she weakens? I would appreciate your advice and wonder what others do in such a situation.

A. In multi-cat households, it is usually true that there is one cat who is dominant over the household or some particular area within the household. This dominance varies from absolute tyranny to benevolent dictatorship. Usually the oldest or first resident becomes dominant, regardless of sex. The bizarre behavior displayed by your younger cat doesn't necessarily mean he was battling for control over your older cat. In fact, your young cat would have a hard time getting the upper hand on any healthy 15-year-old.

159

From a strong-willed, people-loving Siamese, like your Thai, it would be almost impossible.

There is no question that Tigger was upset and confused when he attacked his old friend Thai with what, to you, seemed little or no provocation. I'm pretty sure what actually happened was that poor old Thai came home smelling like a veterinary hospital and Tigger couldn't believe that any cat smelling like an animal hospital could be his old roommate. He then acted as he would toward any strange cat that invaded his home.

After a few days in the apartment, Thai had washed and rubbed off most of the obnoxious odor (which she hated as much as Tigger) and all was well again. Tigger realized his mistake when Thai began smelling like the pal he knew and loved, and peace reigned again in your home.

Many cat owners fail to understand that felines, whether living in the wild or in a home, use their sense of smell over all other senses. Feline olfactory systems are highly developed and rarely fail to identify individual scents. Since hospital odors such as antiseptics are pungent and remain in animal hair for several days, pet owners upon bringing their pets home, should neutralize all odor in the fur by giving their pet a bath. Many times a firm rub with a towel soaked in vinegar/water solution will be more acceptable to the animal and also prevent chilling if the pet is aged or ill.

As to future problems with your aging cat, it is best to just face each problem as it comes. As the years go by give Thai protection, if necessary, lots of love and preventive health care. Since your cats are usually loving with each other, I doubt that Tigger will attack again if you wash Thai's fur after each hospital visit. In fact it's not a bad idea to wash down both cats so they will smell alike.

Surprisingly, while most pet owners are not familiar with this problem, cat breeders encounter this hostility between their cats frequently. At the last show, one breeder told me, "When I notice my cats starting to bicker and fuss, I usually powder them all down with a little baby powder. It's a simple system, but the cats seem to settle down and enjoy each other again."

Medicate for Anxiety Attacks

Q. We have a beautiful, 2-year-old male cat which we acquired as a stray. We love him dearly, except for one annoying habit we cannot seem to break him of: biting. Whenever we pet him, he will sit for a few seconds and then begin to bite—hard. We had him neutered, hoping that would help, but it didn't. We know he was abused before he came to us. Could this have anything to do with it? Do you have any suggestions?

A. Your cat was certainly lucky to find such understanding owners, because he is going to need all of the help your loving family can give him. There is no doubt that your cat is suffering from anxiety and stress. Cats who have been abused or who have lacked affection while they grew cannot help but suffer later in life. It will take patience on your part to help your cat establish a good self-image and learn to relax and enjoy life.

For a while, resist the temptation to pick up the cat except when necessary. If he jumps on your lap, talk to him, but don't pet or scratch him. Talk to your cat as often as you can. Use his name and speak lovingly and quietly. If you wish, lean down and pet his head or scratch his ears, but only for a moment at a time. When your cat does lie down with you, stay calm, take deep breaths and allow him to feel how relaxed you are. This will relieve some of his anxiety. If you study the cat's behavior, you will find there are certain body movements that precede each attack. When you see or feel your cat tense for the attack, get up and leave before the cat carries out the action.

I think your cat would also benefit from a mild tranquilizer given daily for a few months. As his anxieties lessen, you can taper off the medication. Talk to your veterinarian about this and start as soon as possible. Your cat is young and will no doubt be the delight of your life as soon as his problems are solved.

Hitting—Ineffective Discipline

Q. I have a two-and-a-half-year-old, female, half-tabby and half-Siamese cat. She is not an affectionate cat and seldom enjoys being held. My problem is this: When I try to pet her, she will either respond by rolling on her back, or she will bite me viciously. On other occasions she attacks and bites my ankles. I say no and she'll do it again, harder and harder. I will then hit her on the rear and she will viciously bite me as hard as she possibly can and walk away. In the same situation, I will put her out of the room and close the door. After a few minutes she will cry and I'll open the door. Generally, her biting will cease.

Help. I can't stand her biting. I'm all scarred up. How can I stop her vicious attacks?

A.   I am firmly convinced that hitting a cat on the back end is ineffective and leads to retaliation. In other words, the cat will find some way of paying you back. I suggest that you carry a spray bottle of water around with you and when the silent stalker attacks, shoot a full spray of water in her face. As soon as the cat stops biting, lean down and pet her to reinforce her good behavior.

A cat will often bite or grab the hand that scratches her tummy, as she rolls around on her back. Many times the biting is from pleasure instead of anger. Regardless of the reason, it is painful and the cat must cease. A snap on the cat's nose will shock the cat and stop the attack. Once again, always give affection for good behavior.

Stop Cat Digging

Q.   I have a cat that is a year old. She is declawed because she is an inside cat and she plays with my dog all the time.

I go to school. My mother works during the day, and so does my father. Every day when I get home, my mother's plants are all dug up. Even when I go on vacation she digs up all our plants. I scold her, but she keeps on doing it. Why does she do it? Is there anything I can do to stop her?

A. Your cat sounds normal and very nice, except for her digging problem. If you and I can figure out how to stop your cat's bad habit, all will be happy in your house again. Try this! Ask mom to buy some Tabasco sauce at the grocery store. Tabasco, a hot sauce to put into chili or Mexican dishes tastes hot, but it will not hurt your cat. Put dabs of Tabasco on the rim of the flower pots and some on the dirt. Your mother can help if you need it. Another good repellent is red or black pepper sprinkled in the dirt.

While you are keeping the cat away from the plants, remember that she is probably digging out of boredom. Be sure to give your cat some toys to play with while you are away.

Traffic Danger to Outdoor Cat

Q. *We live in a suburban town in New Jersey. Our alley cat named Suzie was a healthy indoor-outdoor cat. She was six years old in March when she died. We think she was hit by a car. Suzie's spinal cord was broken, and we had to have her put to sleep. It was very sad. We would like to get another cat and train it not to go into the street. I think cats have a right to go in and out as they please, but I would like to train the cat to protect itself. Thank you for your help.*

A. Sorry, I wish I could find a magic solution to this impossible problem, but there is none.

Cats can learn a great deal through patient training by their handlers and owners; but I have never heard of a cat successfully trained to avoid streets. Cats also learn from experience, but often the price they pay for their experience is too high. Pet ownership always involves a certain amount of worry and concern, but allowing a cat to roam freely near busy streets is inviting disaster. Cats can live long, healthy and happy lives indoors. Perhaps you can train yourself to accept that lifestyle for your cat!

Disoriented Cat

Q. We moved into a new mobile home recently. Our six-year-old cat suddenly refused to use his litter box and started using the register in the dining room. Needless to say, we are not happy with the old boy's behavior. Can you help us figure him out?

A. Your old boy is probably suffering from displacement shock. Cats don't like to have their life patterns changed. First, try giving the cat lots of affection. At the same time, clean the heating duct and thoroughly deodorize the whole area. You can probably find a cake deodorant, made for toilets, that will hang below the register grill (inaccessible to the cat) and act as a repellent. Now fix a nice, clean litter box far away from the dining room and watch the cat for a few days to be sure he understands that he must follow the house rules. Good luck!

Shy Cat May Be Happy

Q. I have a shy cat two and a half years old. My Angela has progressed but I would like some more ideas on how to help her.

If I am alone, Angela will come to me and curl up in my lap to be petted and loved, but even the presence of another family member makes her hide and refuse to make an appearance. Sometimes I have wondered if the agony she lives with of being frightened all of the time is worth it for her. Yet, when we are alone, it is hard to believe she is the same cat. Do you or any readers have ideas on how I can help her out of her shyness and the misery of confronting other people?

A. Angela does sound unusually shy, and possibly a little disturbed. However, you have been working on her problems for two and a half years with some results. Certainly, you are doing everything possible to make life comfortable and easy for your cat; so I think you should relax, accept and enjoy your devoted friend. It sounds as if you are fighting basic instincts which are sometimes impossible to battle.

Many cats live in isolation with ill or handicapped people for years and are absolutely content. In fact, our family also owned a shy cat that spent all of her time in a bedroom, unless her owner (my daughter) was at home. Looking back, I still believe that our "shy cat" was simply a one-person feline and lived a perfectly happy life.

INDEX

The riders came close, their shaggy onagers panting steam and frost, and rode in a circle around her. She aimed her bow at one muffled rider, then another. They moved too quickly to get a proper bead.

Then they stopped and Sekmé could have picked off any one of them she chose, but she hesitated. The riders were silent and anonymous. All she could see were their bright red eyes, like smoldering coals, peering through the thick fur lining their parkas, eyes shaped like wau-weh eyes, narrow at the corners. She became confused and let her bow go slack.

"*What* are you?"

One of the riders, a bit taller than the others and more heavily built in the chest and shoulders, pushed back his hood with his white gloved hand. Sekmé gasped. He was beautiful, ageless—a man with long, loose white hair whose inhuman eyes in his ice-pale, unlined face were full of a sadness and pity that seemed thousands of years old. He spurred his mount a few steps toward her and Sekmé reraised her bow.

"I don't want to hurt you," she said sincerely, "but I will if I have to."

T H E

DIVIDED

KATIE WAITMAN

DEL
REY

THE BALLANTINE PUBLISHING GROUP

NEW YORK

A Del Rey® Book
Published by The Ballantine Publishing Group

Copyright © 1999 by Katharine L. Waitman

All rights reserved under International and Pan-American Copyright Conventions. Published in the United States by The Ballantine Publishing Group, a division of Random House, Inc., New York, and simultaneously in Canada by Random House of Canada Limited, Toronto.

Del Rey and colophon are registered trademarks of Random House, Inc.

http://www.randomhouse.com/delrey/

Library of Congress Cataloging-in-Publication Data
Waitman, Katie.
    The divided / Katie Waitman. — 1st ed.
  ISBN 0-345-41437-3 (alk. paper)
  I. Title.
  PS3573.A4124   S24   1999
  813'.54—dc21   98-26229
                                                                        CIP

Manufactured in the United States of America

Text design by Ann Gold
Cover design by Heather Kern
Cover illustration by Cliff Nielsen

First Edition: February 1999

10   9   8   7   6   5   4   3   2   1

FOR MY MOM——THE ORIGINAL JO——
AND MY DAD, WHO LOVES HER

I will rest my head in the sands of Sa'Har.
　　　　—Anonymous Tel-mari poet

PART ONE

THE
GREAT
DIVISION

CHAPTER 1

ODDS OR EVEΠS

I n Maurhet, the firstborn inherited war and its symbol: the family weapon. Sekmé's weapon, a classic oil-cartridge flare rifle, had seen so much service over the centuries and undergone so many repairs, upgrades, and modifications that nothing of the original piece remained except the decorative electrum inlay on its thornwood stock. The weapon represented history, although at the moment, it was less meaningful than a cheap hand sling picked up for three paners at a Tel-mari "slip-slap" dealer's: the damned thing couldn't fire.

Sekmé tried to unjam it. Every few minutes or so she'd halt her desperate, scrambling flight through the rain-drenched night streets of the Hives, Eshna's massive tangle of downtown slums, yank back the bolt, and peer into the ignitory capsule only to be interrupted by a spray of sniper fire that stripped away the ragged edges of the paving stones beneath her boots or ripped a line out of the masonry just a hand's breadth above her head. A sharp hiss followed these close calls, and corrosives wept down the stone, wounding it with uneven grooves. The Tel-mari insurgents meant business: they had gotten hold of some acid shells. There'd be no prisoners to ransom this time.

The rifle, slung over Sekmé's shoulder, beat against her back while her dun-colored fatigues, baggy at the best of times, now

sopping with rain and mud, slapped her knees and thighs, impeding her escape. She'd been running for hours and, battered and burdened this way, couldn't keep it up much longer. She had to find shelter.

But where? She had the terrible feeling she'd been running in circles. Not only did all the streets and alleys look alike—higgledy-piggledy jumbles of rock, plaster, tar, and tin hastily piled one on top of the other like deformed barnacles—they also smelled alike, like grmysh, the rank Tel-mari stew of fried goat organs and fermented cabbage.

She kept running and the rifle kept banging, broadening her bruises, until she turned a corner she didn't quite remember and entered a blind alley. No way out.

"You're cornered or covered, Sekmé," she gasped to herself. "Make the choice."

The first three doors wouldn't budge and had probably been bolted for years. The fourth had a warped jamb and stuck, but with a good shove squeaked open and revealed a damp, chilly slice of airless, windowless darkness as thick as oil gum. In no mood to be fussy, Sekmé slipped inside and pushed the door to.

Out of the noise and wet, she heaved a sigh and passed her hands over the short dark hair plastered against her skull then flicked the water from her nose and sharp, squarish jaw. She'd always been lean but had gotten even thinner lately, the leanness of battle. Her stomach made a small, halfhearted growl. It had learned not to expect much relief.

A small rustle in the corner seemed to answer and the rifle dropped off her shoulder into her hands and was cocked before she remembered it couldn't fire. However, whatever had made the rustle held still, fortuitously unaware of that fact.

Sekmé cradled the weapon in her right arm, fished in a deep hip pocket for her oilstone, and struck it against the rough wall of the room. The petroleum-impregnated black stone sparked and a benign yellow flame wavered on its tip, illuminating the

room, apparently at one time a dry goods storeroom, and its other inhabitant.

"Odds or evens!" he cried, shaking something that clinked metallically in his cupped hands.

"What?"

The man's accent startled her more than the inappropriateness of his words. She'd never met a Tel-mari who spoke such excellent Maurheti.

"Odds or evens!" he repeated with a manic grin, and shook his hands again. He seemed a fairly typical Tel-mari, perhaps in his mid-thirties, short and dark with a full black beard, slightly tilted black eyes, strongly aquiline nose, a long, heavy goat's-wool robe, matching long vest, and miserably broken leather boots. He was filthy, of course, and smelled like cabbage, but his teeth were sound, his body broad and powerful, and his accent . . . incongruous.

"*What* odds?" Sekmé set the oilstone on a large overturned basket that had a long rent in its side, but she kept her weapon trained on the Tel-mari.

"Odds you kill me, evens you don't."

"What makes you think I'd honor the outcome?"

"Nothing at all!" The Tel-mari's grin widened. "It's a risk, I admit, but you haven't killed me yet so the chance is worth it, don't you think?" He tossed the silver coins he'd been shaking—there were four of them—into the air and let them land with a small puff of dust on the dirt floor.

"Two birds, two feathers!" he cried triumphantly. "Evens!" He quickly scooped up the coins and hid them in his robe. "Too bad, my dear. You've played the round and I certainly do hope you *will* honor its outcome, although your lot obviously knows little about it."

"Is that so?"

"It stands to reason," the man said with a worldly shrug. "Honor? From people who allow a *girl* to fight as a soldier?"

Sekmé thrust her weapon forward until the triple tip of her bayonet poked into the man's beard. He watched closely as she slowly combed the bayonet through the coarse hair, catching it once or twice on a snarl, but he didn't flinch.

"This 'girl' is a very *good* soldier," she said softly, "and she has a rifle."

"Then why are you running?"

"Why are you hiding?"

"Apparently, we share a common impetus."

Sekmé twisted a smile and shook her head. Wherever, however this Tel-mari had learned her language, listening to it was as entertaining as listening to a trained kelamang play the thetl—a circus act.

"Do you think you've outrun them?" he asked.

"Perhaps." Without taking her eyes from him, she put her ear to the door and listened. There was gunfire, but it was distant and seemed to be moving away.

The man sat on the floor, crossed his legs, and leaned back against the wall, hands clasped casually in his lap.

"You desert locusts certainly have made a mess of things," he said. "A market day attack! Women and children everywhere. What fiend from the nether bowels of the world came up with that idea? Kill the babies to lure out the men . . . then bomb them again." Briefly overcome, he gazed off into the shadow-blackened corner farthest from the oilstone as if the ghosts of the massacred were watching him from its darkness. "The Evil One is brilliant, yes. Brilliant without heat. Or light."

Sekmé kept her ear pressed to the door. She didn't want to talk about this.

"I guess you don't have children," the man continued. "No mother, I don't care from where, could have witnessed such a thing—as I suspect you did—and remained sane, let alone unmoved. No children and no husband, I'll wager. Maybe what they say is true: the Maurheti cut off more than the hair of their girl soldiers."

"You talk too much," Sekmé said flatly. "I can't hear what's happening outside."

"It's *raining*, my dear."

"*Shut up.*"

The man rolled his eyes, sighed, and removed from his sleeve— Sekmé raised her rifle again—an egg. Sekmé hadn't eaten in five days and her body tensed with desperate, animal need.

"Give that to me," she said.

"It's my dinner," the man replied.

Sekmé skewered his beard again. He hesitated just long enough to show her he wasn't in any particular hurry even with a rifle in his face, then reluctantly handed over the egg. Sekmé quickly cracked it open on the wall . . . and its contents plopped to the ground in one slimy splat.

"It's raw!" she cried in disgust.

"Oh, now isn't that just like a Maurheti?" the man sneered. "He takes away what others have by force, then doesn't know how to appreciate what he's stolen. Pitiful. You must not be as hungry as you think."

Before Sekmé could react, he pulled another egg from his sleeve, cracked it gently, expertly on his knee, tilted his head back, and broke the egg over his mouth. The raw protein slid into his throat and he swallowed it.

"It's not polite to stare," he said.

"Do—do you have another?"

The man slapped his thigh and laughed bitterly.

"You must think I'm *made* of eggs! No, I don't have another. God above!" He quickly kissed his fingertips then held up his palm to salute the divine. "The market is *gone*, remember? Real evil hurts everyone, including those who call it forth." He straightened his hood and smoothed his mustache. "What a fool you are to be here."

"It's my *business* to be here! We're putting down the insurgents in the Hives—"

The man snorted.

"—but *you*. Why are *you* still here when everyone else has run off? You're obviously no sniper, you're too cowardly to be an insurgent yourself—"

"I beg your pardon!"

"—and if you had any money, you'd buy better boots. Explain yourself."

The Tel-mari blinked slowly and cocked his head at her as though idly studying a spider too far away to see clearly.

"Why should I explain myself?" he murmured. "I *live* here."

"It's not safe!"

The man leered at her.

"Now . . . whose fault is that?"

"I'm beginning to regret not killing you," Sekmé growled.

"Then do it!" The man threw open his arms and Sekmé caught a glimpse of a new light in his eyes: not irony or grief or anger, but ecstasy. The ecstasy of despair. "At least I'll die in my own land and enter a heaven full of women and babies."

Sekmé uncocked the rifle and let the barrel drop.

"Was your family in the marketplace?" she asked.

The Tel-mari's cheek twitched and he began to giggle.

"Not mine! I don't have one." The giggle opened into an onager-like bray. "Just everyone else's!"

Sekmé spat on the floor.

"Madder than a wau-weh in heat—"

"Must be the scent of the bitch," he retorted.

"Better than the piss in your beard, you rancid he-goat!"

"Desert whore!"

"Bog beast!"

There was laughter in the alley, abruptly ending their argument. Sekmé returned to the door to listen.

"Scavengers," she whispered. "They're drunk."

"How many?"

"At least three."

"Four is luckier."

Sekmé scowled at him.

"For *them*," he explained. "Scavengers are as superstitious as they are wicked."

"Harsh judgment coming from a countryman." Sekmé began unscrewing the triple-bladed bayonet from her rifle.

"I disown them." The man's heavy brows knit. "What are you doing?"

"You don't think I'm going to discharge a firearm in such close quarters with all this flammable rubbish around, do you? It'll be hand-to-hand."

"They may not stop here."

Sekmé shook her head.

"They're drunk, it's still raining, and this is the only unlocked door in the alley."

The Tel-mari grunted, got to his feet, and began to limber up his hands by cracking his knuckles.

"What are *you* doing?"

"I'm going to fight with you. If I don't, you haven't a chance and they'll kill me, too. Together, we've better odds. Or evens."

"I appreciate your altruism," Sekmé said sourly, and she blew out the oilstone.

The rain had eased and they could clearly hear the men's approach. The Tel-mari had been right: Sekmé heard four distinct voices now, a bit garbled with intoxication, but exhilarated and high key, a hair trigger away from violence. They'd had a successful day.

"Did you see the old man run? Looked like a crippled mire rat. God's fart! They should shoot 'em before they get that old."

"Ha-ha! Better hold still, then . . ."

"Shit . . . I'm soaked to the bone."

"Must be someplace we can dry off."

"Sure! Up your ass! It's the only dried-up spot in Tel-mari!"

"Shh! You're making too much noise."

"Ain't nobody to listen—Hey! This one's open."

"Black as a Maurheti heart in there."

"Dry, though. Come on."

"Where'd I put the oilstone?"

"Just get in! I've got snails in my boots . . ."

They entered in darkness and Sekmé kicked the door shut behind them.

In the middle of the ensuing chaos, Sekmé actually took a moment to think, *Now I know what it's like for Set when we wrestle,* although, in many ways, this fight was the opposite of every tussle she'd ever had with her brother. Those had been an excuse for closeness; this was a struggle for murder.

The scavengers may have been drunk, but the surprise of the invisible attack sobered them up instantly and they fought viciously, tooth and claw, and even injured each other. Sekmé clutched someone's beard and was about to wring his neck when she recognized—how, she wasn't sure—the Tel-mari refugee of the four coins, her supposed ally in the fray. She could have, perhaps should have, killed him anyway since she owed him nothing, but his inexplicably fine Maurheti and ironic grin flashed in her memory and she let him go.

Someone tripped her and fell on her back and they rolled over in the dust and crashed into a stack of boxes of coarsely ground meal that tumbled down on them. One of the boxes burst open and the grit pressed into Sekmé's mouth and skin as she continued to thrash about with her assailant. Then, quite suddenly, the man released her. She heard a short gasp, a muffled crack, as though a log at the bottom of a small kitchen fire had shifted, and a heavy thump she assumed was another box or sack of something dense and loose falling from its perch.

Now it was silent. Sekmé sat up, a little dizzy, and waited for the tinnitus to fade before crawling about in search of the oilstone. She found one body, dead certainly, a big man with his head turned almost completely around backward. The second body may have been merely unconscious, but it was wet with something warmer than rainwater nearly everywhere she touched. He wouldn't last long, but he had an oilstone in his pocket. She struck it on her boot. The flame sputtered then jumped high

and lit up all four bodies arranged about the room in almost comically twisted attitudes.

The Tel-mari of the coins, face and beard streaked with bloody dust, leaned against the door with Sekmé's flare rifle in his hands. He pulled back the bolt.

"H'm, so *that's* the problem." He caught her astonished stare. "You're quite ferocious in the clinch, my dear—" He wiggled his finger into the firing chamber. "—an excellent, and remarkably dirty, fighter, but it still would have been more efficient to shoot them when they opened the door."

He squinted down the barrel then pulled a slender dirk from his ruined left boot and poked it into the various workings of the weapon, scraping and bending.

"I'm sure you would have repaired this yourself if you'd had the time, but it's difficult to employ the finer motor skills when one is dodging sniper fire."

He slid the bolt to with a smart and proper-sounding snap and Sekmé realized she was now in the same room with an armed enemy.

But the Tel-mari did not take aim. He offered her his hand.

"Get up, my dear. It's foul there among the dead."

When Sekmé was on her feet, the Tel-mari handed her the rifle.

"Test it," he said. "I'm a superb mechanic but it's been a few years since I tinkered with such a classic."

"I'll bet you rigged it to explode in my hands," Sekmé said as she shoved the door open with her shoulder. The rain had stopped and a rare break in the clouds let a pale gray predawn light into the alley.

"Perhaps." The Tel-mari's voice was as ironic as before, but he wasn't smiling.

Sekmé aimed her weapon at the distant remains of a balcony and, cursing herself for her foolhardiness, pulled the trigger. An oil cartridge hissed out of the rifle, made a clean arc over the gutted tenements behind the warehouses, struck the balcony,

and exploded in a tight orange ball. The balcony dropped away in a small, ragged avalanche of stone chips.

Sekmé lowered her weapon. The Tel-mari smiled wistfully.

"I wonder what it would be like without all this," he said.

"Without all what?"

"This." He made a sweeping gesture with his arm that seemed to take in the entire city. "Without this destruction." His eyes met hers. "What would it be like to live without fighting each other?"

She blinked at him.

"You *are* crazy."

"Oh, I know, but . . . just imagine. For once."

"It's impossible. You're not of God."

The Tel-mari glanced at the sky, slowly drew his hood up, and shrugged.

"You'd better get out of the Hives before other survivors find you," he said.

"You're a very strange man."

He nodded and began to walk away down the alley. Sekmé watched him, an anonymous shadow on the brief pearly shine of the wet pavement, until he turned the corner and was gone.

CHAPTER 2

THE DESERT PROPHET

The man striding purposefully across the peach-colored dunes at midday was ninety years old and naked except for a water skin, a shoulder pack of woven onager hair, and a thornwood staff, but his nearly coal black skin, although loose in places commensurate with his advanced age, was as sleek and shiny as a young boy's. He had many nicknames and titles, but his unusually youthful skin in such a harsh climate had earned him his most common epithet: Wepanu ul-Bahf, or Wepanu the Youth. As if to reinforce the name, he had never been circumcised. He was the only uncut male of the nomadic Denneshur tribes.

He came to the top of a rocky rise and paused in his journey to sniff the heat, heavy as the blazing foot of God pressing one's body into the sand, and to scan the horizon. Behind him to the east were the barren, rugged, but softly hued Hills of Whispers, their streaks and waves of gold, yellow, white, lavender, green, rust, pink, and black marking the veins of different minerals thrust up from the underworld by ancient volcanoes and recent quakes. One could wander their parched valleys for many days and not meet another living creature, not even a spider, then suddenly come upon a great camp of Denneshur, their onagers and oryx, perhaps fifty people and two hundred animals, drawn

by a small grove of thornwood trees and the hidden spring below their long roots. With the great patience of all peoples who lived in open places, the Denneshur slowly chipped a deep hole through the hard rocky soil to the bed of limestone underneath, which they cracked open with an iron ax. If they were lucky, the brown, mineral-rich water would gush out like a geyser, soon filling the new well. If not, they calmly refilled the wound in the desert and moved on.

At night, the Denneshur slept with their animals, in caves or in low, brightly patterned tents. The wind through the wadis and ravines would whisper from the rocks about things forgotten and not yet known and the yellow wau-wehs would scratch their sharp ears, gather up their pups, and trot out of their dens to hunt for lizards or to sit on the rocks under the stars and yip and yowl to their mates.

Farther east, beyond the Hills of Whispers, lay a vast grassland plateau where the Denneshur snared most of their onagers. Here there were seasonal lakes that dried into cracked mudflats full of stinging black flies as the rains, their sources farther inland, retreated every second year.

Beyond the grassland plateau lay the subjugated country of Tel-mari and its woodlands and waterfalls, bogs and marshes, and densely populated villages and capital city of Eshna.

And beyond Tel-mari? The swamp, of course, and the high moors, then the uncharted, unexplored wastes of the White Mountains, frozen teeth few desert dwellers had ever visited and no Tel-mari dared.

Wepanu shifted his shoulder pack from right to left, took a squeeze from his water skin, meditatively swished it through his strong, yellow teeth, then let it slip down his throat. The world was much wider than the Tel-mari suspected or the Maurheti had time for. The jo had told him so, not in words, because they rarely resorted to such crude forms of communication, but through scent and light, dream and the prickling of his skin. When they did speak, the jo spoke in a thousand different voices,

and he paid them homage every day with a blood offering for allowing him to understand. This morning: an oryx kid's intestines, a very special and lavish offering. He'd stretched the rest of its flesh and skin to dry on a rack hung from a high branch of a thornwood tree so the wau-wehs couldn't get at it, taken up his staff, and begun his journey.

Below him, to the west, peach-colored sand shifted over the desert valley, its surface shivering in the heat as though preserving the ghost of the sea that once covered it. South, about halfway between his left shoulder and the horizon, lay the silver white ribbon of the Nawset Highway, which ran all the way from the eastern swamp to the western sea cliff, passing through both Eshna and its Maurhet equivalent, the desert city-state of Kemphor. A highway of many uses and personalities, the Nawset curled and twisted like an eel in Tel-mari to skirt lakes and negotiate wood and mountain, but here, in the desert, it ran straight and flat, like nothing in nature but like many things in a dull and practical man's mind.

Wepanu frowned. He could not consider the Maurheti, who had built the road, dull or practical although their creations attested to a belief in regularity. Several smaller, perpendicular roads, tributaries if you would, led off the highway, one to each of the holdings, the great walled-in plantations of the wealthy, each a little city in itself with a centrally located residential complex of white stone surrounded by servants' quarters, livestock barns, storehouses, and mews, and the orderly progression of inner kitchen gardens to grazing leas, fruit trees, and grainfields to the backlands stocked with game animals. Everything in a holding, including the backlands, was well tended, lush, perennial— and imported. Even the water in the irrigation canals came from outside: a half dozen desalination plants sat at the base of the sea cliffs churning brine through their purifiers.

The holdings were impressive, monuments to the Maurheti need to control the land and make it give beyond its limited desert ecology, and they were extremely successful, but they

wilted in comparison to Kemphor itself. Not even Wepanu knew of another settlement in the world conceived on a grander scale. Four million people lived in Kemphor and transformed the raw materials from the interior into clothing, furniture, utensils, coins, art, fertilizer, paper, weapons—everything they needed. From spices to disguise the heavy, oily flavor of locally netted sea snakes, to oilstones and petroleum for light and fuel, to fine marbles and gold for their temples and gemstones to adorn their bodies, the Maurheti worked their technological cleverness—and pumped their wastes back into the sea and skies. Literate, healthy, and aggressive, they believed in a God of light and infinite power who fought a never-ending and yet ultimately triumphant battle against the forces of chaos and darkness. From the towers of its massive encircling wall and the lanterns of its gold-plated domes, brown uniformed sentries watched the desert and strolled casually, their weapons across their shoulders like yokes, hands hung loosely over stocks and barrels, daydreaming as the light changed on the city's spires topped with ornamental lightning rods in the shape of twisted oryx horns, the symbol of God. City watch was easy duty, much preferable to a tour in Tel-mari.

Wepanu squatted in the dirt to defecate then kicked sand over his leavings. The ages-long hostility between the Maurheti and Tel-mari did not concern him personally. He couldn't care less who slaughtered whom in which skirmish in what bog or misty fell, but the jo cared and had given him a message for Roon XXII. He was on his way to that dusty, haze-shrouded concentration of noise, ambition, passion, pollution, and folly to deliver it.

"Let the Divine guide me," he prayed. "In myself I am nothing, but in the hands of my Master I am the Voice of the Future."

CHAPTER 3

LOKAR

In the command hut of the Maurhet Anti-Insurgency Forces in the wooded dale just south of Eshna, the nearly constant rain drummed its muffled fingers on the oiled canvas roof, a dull and subtle sound, easy to ignore if one was occupied, dismayingly percussive if one wasn't. Field General Am was always occupied, but depressed all the same. He had the entire square hut to himself, fully four times as much space as he needed considering his files were stored on magnetic strips in another hut, but he still felt closed in. The damp, the dark, and the deep sleep of the massive trees outside oppressed him. He missed the clear bright air of Maurhet, the dry light breezes, and the good sharp burn of the sun on his skin. He'd been in Tel-mari continuously, give or take the odd month or two of leave, for thirty-five years. He'd never gotten used to it.

Recently, he'd noticed a slight doubling of his vision, as if the aerial to a surveillance tower had been bent in a storm, and his hair, deep blue black all his life and a mild source of vanity, now sported a handful of pure white threads. The possibilities of ocular implants and dyes notwithstanding, he couldn't deny he was getting old. His firstborn, a somewhat dim young man with a bullying style of command, was a second officer now. Perhaps he should give him the family weapon, a flame dart

pistol with a 700-year-old silver and shell holster, and retire to his modest holdings a day's drive south of Kemphor in the relatively wild and rustic Pen Foothills.

He sat back from his wide steel desk buried in a paper snowfall of orders, forms, requisitions, reports, and complaints, and took a moment to indulge in this daydream.

He saw himself on the western terrace in a loose, pale blue dressing robe, the sun setting over the sea. He imagined he'd gained back the weight he'd lost in Tel-mari and looked a good ten years younger, sunburned and smiling as his lovely wife, Mu, in saffron—no, rose—glided out barefoot, a string of tiny silver coins tinkling about her ankle, to join him. She smiled and a cool sea wind blew back her platinum hair as he gently embraced the warm, dear form of the woman who would always, always be his lover.

A halfhearted gargle of remote thunder returned him to the present and his depression, especially acute due to recent events. Defeats were inevitable, he supposed, given war's perpetual place in the world order, but they were always unpleasant and this one, coming so close on the heels of an unusually clever success, was especially dismal—and probably completely unnecessary.

Am got up from his desk, strolled to the door of the hut, and peered out its small window—a rough circle cut, at his request, in the wooden panel and fitted with a filmy piece of plasticoat—to see what the men were doing. A poor idea. Even if he could have made out anything in this weather, the men were undoubtedly keeping to their own quarters and their own thoughts. If he wanted to check on morale, he'd have to go for a slog in the mud.

He returned to his desk. Actually, he already had a pretty good idea how the men felt. Not only had they lost a hundred of their comrades in that ill-starred mop-up patrol, they'd lost their commander, their Iron Virgin, and that could be considered almost an equal blow, at least psychologically.

He smiled bitterly to himself. What an odd case she'd been!

Few firstborn females chose combat positions—they weren't required or expected to—and those who did, especially those
trained as officers, were mercilessly harassed by the men until
they decided life behind a desk, for all its tedium, would be
more productive and less a danger to their sanity.

But Sekmé had been different. Maybe it was because she'd
grown up surrounded by male relatives, but she seemed imper-
vious to insult and when the harassment became physical, she
proved perfectly willing to fight back and was quite good at it.

Then came the series of semiamphibious raids into the nearby
woods to flush out an entrenched group of hamjis, Tel-mari insurgents who specialized in assassination. Am still didn't understand how given the treacherous terrain and an appalling lack of
appropriate supplies and information—the young officer had
never led that kind of attack before and her immediate super-
visors, many of whom were her worst detractors, hadn't deemed
it necessary to advise her—Sekmé nevertheless managed to kill
or capture over 170 of the hamjis without losing a single one of
her own men. The rank and file didn't care to understand. Soldiers were superstitious; it functioned as a kind of psychological
counterpoise to the grim realities of their profession. The men
promptly determined the young female officer was "lucky" and
the harassment ceased.

Remarkably, whether she really *was* lucky or this lack of in-
subordination suddenly made her job much easier, Sekmé continued to lead a charmed battle existence, taking on larger and
more complex assignments and succeeding with the lowest casualty rate in the force. She rose through the ranks with near
meteoric speed until, at the unheard-of age of twenty-four,
she'd attained full commander.

But, it seems her luck finally ran out, Am mused. I suppose
it was inevitable. Those who rise fastest, fall soonest . . . or
something like that. Poor girl! A life reduced to an academic
truism.

Someone grabbed his hair, pulled back his head, and pressed

a knife against his throat under his chin. He smelled wet, rank cloth and musky, distressed flesh.

"Where . . . were . . . my . . . reinforcements?" she hissed.

In spite of his awkward position, Am's heart gave a skip and an embarrassing joy heated his limbs.

"Commander!" he gasped. "Bless God!"

She leaned over him and presented an upside-down view of her matted hair, pale features, and bloodshot eyes.

"We called for help *repeatedly*," she whispered.

"I don't know," he said. "Honestly, I don't. We never got those transmissions."

"What?"

"By the time we knew you needed help, it was too late. The pontoon bridge had washed away and we couldn't get through."

She released his hair and removed the knife.

"You're lying," Sekmé said, but didn't sound as if she believed the accusation.

She walked around the desk and Am got a good look at what was left of his "lucky" officer. Her fatigues were rags. Leaves and twigs stuck out of her hair and the tops of her boots. Both knees were bloody, and slime ran freely out of the barrel of her flare rifle, which she clutched so tightly the knucklebones seemed to have split the skin; she must have swum a bog with it. Even so, Sekmé seemed whole and her fury gave her tremendous vitality. The air fairly crackled around her.

"No . . . truly. We heard nothing," Am said, wondering how she'd managed to sneak into camp and into his hut. There were guards everywhere.

"Seven transmissions and you heard *nothing*?"

"I'm sorry, Commander. The storm must have shorted our receiver."

Sekmé made a sound somewhere between a groan and a snarl and, with nothing better to do in her frustration, began to pace back and forth before Am's desk.

"I went in with minimum force. We thought we'd cleaned them out and the roads were so bad—"

"Yes, yes. I know. It was brilliant, Commander. A fabulous victory. You're a hero now, thank God, and not a martyr."

"—but we were ambushed, Field General! Some—some pod of them had escaped and—and the bodies—they were—"

She was very agitated now, eyes blazing on some remembered horror and not on the gloomy space of the mildewy hut. Am had seen that look too many times.

"Commander? Commander!"

Sekmé stopped pacing and stared at him.

"It's over, Commander. Finished. Your men have been enfolded by God."

Sekmé cocked her head as if having trouble understanding him.

"Come down, Commander. It's war. You fought well. What happened merely proves that we must continue. Darkness is relentless."

Sekmé's body sagged and she rolled her head as if working a knot out of her neck.

"What do I tell their families?" she asked softly.

"I'll take care of that if you wish. Commander, there's no shame."

"Not outside, maybe, but inside . . ."

Her eyes fell wide on him. Strange that in his five years as her superior, five years of guilty fascination with this serious young woman, he'd always thought her eyes were dark, but they were really gray green. A sea color. Such an expression! She'd definitely seen something terrible.

"Commander, I've been a soldier a long time, longer than you've been alive, and I know what you're going through. This is your first real taste of the Not-God's power. Anyone serious about their service goes through it at some point, that brush with pure evil that weights the soul and sinks it into despair. You can't let it defeat you. In a strange way, it actually proves

your potential for greatness. Simple combat wasn't enough to frighten you, Commander, and it forced the Not-God's hand, made it pay attention."

Am smiled with what he hoped was paternal warmth and not the more suspect heat he still felt at seeing her safe and whole.

"It hurts terribly, I know, and you'll have nightmares from this for the rest of your life, but you're young, Commander. In time, the nightmares will ease and become more abstract."

Sekmé yawned.

"You need rest, Commander."

She shrugged and cracked open the rifle.

"What a mess," she mumbled.

"I can give you a month or so with your family. Be nice to see that brother of yours again, wouldn't it?"

She was shaking more slime out of her rifle.

"Set?"

"That's right. He's the poet, isn't he?"

Sekmé snapped the rifle together then unceremoniously tossed it onto the field general's camp bed. She turned to him, her hands on her hips.

"Who was in command of communications that night, Field General?"

This was exactly what he'd feared she would ask and he waffled.

"Well, there were a number of stations operative and—"

"And one officer in command," she cut in. "Who was it?"

"Let me check the roster and I'll—"

"You know who it was!" she cried, and Am heard as much pain as anger in her voice.

"There's nothing you can do about it, Commander. There won't be any proof."

The tension eased out of her brow and her mouth curled slightly in a bitter smile.

"Lokar," she said.

"Let it go, Commander."

"He'll never forgive me for being promoted before him."

"He's a clever mind, but a petty spirit. Don't waste your wrath on him."

"But he's responsible!"

"I know!" Am banged his fists on his desk, which, snowed under as it was, replied with a very unsatisfactory soft thump. "I guess I'll have to repeat myself, won't I? *There is nothing to be done!* Do I make myself clear?"

Sekmé scowled but retracted her claws. In a way, Am was sorry. Her rage was damned arousing.

"Yes. Sir."

"Good." Field General Am clasped his hands behind his head and looked his officer over one more time. He shook his head. Oh, to be young again! "I'll get you that leave. Give you a chance to dry out."

"Thank you."

Not one to stand on protocol when she was upset, Sekmé didn't wait to be dismissed but sauntered wearily over to the camp bed to retrieve her rifle. However, she stopped just as she was about to pick it up and slowly straightened her body.

"Commander? Are you all right?"

"Perfectly," she said with deliberate calm. "There is, of course, the traditional way of settling disputes."

Am started, then broke into a grin.

"Why, yes. There is. However, are you in any condition for it?"

"I'm angry enough."

After smoothing back her hair and shaking off the organic debris she'd picked up in the process, Sekmé took a deep breath and marched back out into the rain. Am scrambled around his desk and jogged after her. He wouldn't miss this for the world.

Outside, the wet-weather dusk was the same as it had been

all day since dawn, but the camp timekeeper had announced supper and the men had set up their braziers under the awnings of their four-person tents to cook their dinners: defrosted oryx steaks, tuber slices, and local greens. The smoke hung low in the rain, reducing the men to silhouettes in the braziers' glow. When Sekmé appeared in the murk, stamping across the muddy inner court of the camp, Am saw the silhouettes jump to their feet and several braziers were overturned.

"It's the lucky commander! She's alive!"

"*Un*lucky, you mean. She's the only one."

"That woman's tough as a Denneshur assassin."

"Pig shit! No Denneshur could stand this rain. It rots your bones."

"She looks upset."

"Uh-huh, like a wau-weh whose pups have been drowned."

"Better keep your distance. Something ugly is going to happen, I can tell."

Sekmé planted herself in the soggy center of the camp court and faced Lokar's dark tent. Even though no brazier was set, she could sense he was inside.

"Lokar! Drag your miserable sack-of-dung carcass out here and face me!"

The men hooted and immediately doused their braziers so the smoke wouldn't obscure their view. Many of them nipped inside their tents and brought out their portable storm lamps, tempered glass cylinders with fixed wicks of cut oilstone, and soon the wet dusk brightened with jaundiced light.

Lokar, who'd been napping, snapped open his yellow eyes. Sekmé? Couldn't be, unless nightmares could cross the threshold and put on substance.

"Lokar!"

God . . . it *was* her. He sat up slowly and stretched his long arms and back. What an extraordinarily unpleasant development.

"What do you want?" he called back, as if he didn't know.

He pulled on his boots and slid his dagger into the left one's ankle sheath.

"You suppressed my transmissions calling for reinforcements! You made sure my men would die!"

Lokar heard scattered low cries of surprise and the mutters of outrage. So much for an impartial hearing. Oh, the dreariness of life with enlisted men!

"Prove it!" He slipped on his jacket. How had she gotten out of Tel-mari? What kind of demon was helping her? Twenty-four and already a commander. A girl commander, and apparently an indestructible one.

"You know I can't prove it! But it's true and I intend to crush your balls into the mud for it!"

The men whooped again; a few cheered. Lokar was not particularly popular and he knew it. However, he deeply resented its being made the source of public celebration. He stepped out of his tent and crossed his arms over his chest. He was two heads taller than Sekmé, and she was exhausted from fighting her way back from Eshna without food or supplies. Even so, he secretly shuddered. Most women downplayed their brains for the sake of flirtation or underhanded manipulation, and Lokar, who'd begun his military career as a spy, admired them for that. He understood this behavior given women's generally smaller physiques and, therefore, greater need for self-preservation. This one, however, never played the game and it left her vulnerable to the fire of male ego. Foolish, and yet she'd proven equal to it. She didn't use guile to command her men and submitted to everything they underwent, no matter how vile or lethal. She never asked for special treatment, never used her gender as an excuse for anything, and never asked for her burden to be lighter than a man's although she had the right. Lokar thought her unnatural but the men respected her, even liked her. When drunk, they made ridiculously puerile toasts to her mother's breasts, as if *that* gained them any credit with anyone!

Still, Lokar thought as he faced this little girl who'd been promoted ahead of him, guile *can* undermine even the purest of spirits.

The men probably believed his guilt. No matter. He'd have his revenge in spite of the consequences and, in all likelihood, squeak out of them as well.

"You're not really worth the effort—" He yawned and tossed back his lank hair. "—but come on. Let's have our little game."

It surprised him utterly when the bedraggled commander cleared the muddy ground between them in one leap and landed both feet in his chest, knocking him down, windless.

Sekmé skipped back and waited for him to get to his feet. How irksome! She was fighting fair, which would only drag this ordeal out further.

The men erupted into full holiday rowdiness. Contraband flasks of Tel-mari damnation ale came out of hiding and were passed around openly.

"Do it again, Commander!"

"H'm, not bad, but she's a little off her form."

"Well, she *has* been puddle jumping for almost a week."

"What would you follow with?"

"A close combination."

Sekmé did. She suddenly rushed around to Lokar's left, jabbed his ear, and kneed his kidney before his own punch whiffed past her sleeve.

"Predictable."

"She's just warming up."

"Five paners says it's another combination."

"No. A clean kick."

"You're on."

Sekmé whirled around and her boot heel cracked up into Lokar's chin.

"Ha! You owe me."

On his knees in the rain, gasping, Lokar was getting very tired of these assessments of his nemesis's technique, as if he were

a sand-filled sparring dummy. Nevertheless, his dignity was used to bowing before a greater cause. He just hoped he could hold out long enough against this fiendishly quick opponent to turn the tables.

Sekmé stepped back and rubbed her cheek pensively. The men yelled out suggestions.

"Slam him, Commander!"

"Use the plucking combination!"

"Hey, I'm rusty! Demonstrate the desert dust storm so I can take notes!"

But Lokar's mouth was bleeding, his left eye was swollen shut, and he wheezed as though she'd broken, or at least bruised, his ribs. She didn't mean to kill him, just vent her anger and take some of the unearned swagger out of his posture. The weariness reclaiming her joints told her the adrenaline charge was nearly spent.

She walked up to Lokar, knelt before him, and tenderly cupped his battered face in her hands. He actually leered at her, as if expecting a kiss, but she spit in his yellow eyes instead and shoved him facedown in the mud. Then she stood up and walked away.

The men laughed and whistled, clapped each other on the back, and exchanged their pocket change to settle their bets. Field General Am, who hadn't made a wager, stood quietly apart. He'd enjoyed the fight; he *always* enjoyed a good fight. After all, he was a traditionally raised Maurheti male. And yet it had disturbed him because Sekmé, who also came from a very old, respected, tradition-soaked family, had not. His Warrior Witch, as some of the higher ranking officers called her—never to her face—was more spent by her ordeal than he'd thought. He'd send her out of Tel-mari first thing in the morning. He couldn't afford to lose her.

It was while Sekmé was crossing the court back to Am's hut to retrieve her weapon that Lokar suddenly revived and slipped his fingers into the top of his left boot.

"Sekmé!" Am cried, and Lokar flung his knife directly at the commander's back.

He missed. Sekmé dropped to the mud the same time Am called her name, as if she knew her danger before he did, and the knife zipped past her and nipped Am's right hip before sinking up to the handle in the damp-softened wood wall of the hut.

The field general yelped and six of the duty guards jumped Lokar, clubbed him a few times each with their flare rifles, and yanked him to his feet.

Am gingerly put his hand to his hip and frowned at the crimson that collected on his fingers.

"You, sir," he said to the nearly unconscious Lokar, "can consider yourself a dead man. This will be one of the fastest court-martials and executions in history. I guarantee it."

Meanwhile, Sekmé, completely coated in mud as though the muck had given birth to her in parody of the First Creation, had gotten to her feet. She looked without expression at Lokar, a bloody pulp in the guards' huge arms, and limped to one of the tents where five young men had been sitting on camp stools under the awning and sharing damnation ale. They quickly stowed their flasks and jumped to attention. Sekmé waved her hand at them wearily.

"At rest, at rest . . ."

Their stiffness eased, but they did not sit back down.

"Subcom Dek?"

The youngest of the quintet, a rawboned, heavily freckled teenager with light brown hair and eyes, gulped and blinked nervously.

"Yes, Commander?"

"Do you have any plans for this evening?"

Dek couldn't hide his dismay. His shoulders drooped.

"Well, um, Commander, that is . . ."

"Relax, Subcom. This is a voluntary chore I'm asking."

"Oh. Well, yes, you see, I—"

"It'll take all night," Sekmé interrupted. "I need someone to keep a frequency open to Maurhet for me. I have a lot of families to contact."

Dek reddened and glanced at his comrades, who lowered their eyes. He straightened his back.

"Yes, Commander," he said briskly. "Of course I'll help you."

Sekmé nodded then turned to the other officers, calmly extended her hand, and cleared her throat. Sheepishly, the officer with the flask, a fleshy, baby-faced young man, handed it to her.

"Sorry, Commander, but . . . you know."

Sekmé didn't reply, but efficiently twisted off the cap and tossed back a healthy draft of the nearly lethal beverage before recapping the flask and tossing it to the stunned young officer. She nodded to Dek.

"This way, Subcom." She resumed her original route toward Am's tent. "First things first. I need to clean my weapon."

Injected with painkillers and sedatives, Lokar was placed in the infirmary tent. He lay very still on his hard hospital cot, and the guard set to watch him grew drowsy staring at his unconscious charge. He assumed the battered back stabber wouldn't wake for hours and, displaying a gift common to Maurheti soldiers, fell asleep standing up. Am ripped into him the next morning when Lokar was found missing.

"You were supposed to *watch* him!" he cried.

"But, sir! He was unconscious."

"Idiot! Lokar's been an addict for fifteen years. That dose wouldn't have brought a yawn, let alone knocked him out!"

Although they searched the camp and surrounding woods, they found no trace of Lokar.

As for Sekmé, after a sleepless night of terrible calls to fathers, mothers, wives, and children who cursed her, wept, begged, laughed bitterly, denied all reality, and, in general, hurled their

fully loaded grief at her exhausted soul, she fell asleep on the shoulder of the driver of an empty troop transport vehicle heading to the southern air base. For the entire trip, the driver kept glancing at her nervously, wanting to wake her up because his arm had fallen asleep and his bladder was full, unwilling to do so because it had been months since he'd been this physically close to a young woman, and afraid to do so because she was his superior and might resent being wakened, or, worse, misinterpret his *not* waking her. Paralyzed by parallel disasters, he bit his lip and bounced his balloon-tired vehicle smartly through the woods, partly to get to the base more quickly, partly in the hope the commander would be jolted awake.

But Sekmé was in a dream. She thought she saw her brother playing his thetl and reciting the *Hit-har Battle Epic* in a vast dome-shaped room to an audience of forty otherworldly beautiful men and women. These men and women were peculiarly somber given the rousing patriotism of the stanzas and the fact that each one of them sat unconsumed in a spear of deep scarlet flame.

CHAPTER 4

THE PROPHECY
FOR ROON

When the coal black naked man approached the east-ern gate of Kemphor, the young guard half dozing on the tower above snapped alert then trotted down the tower's winding staircase to arrest the old lunatic for public indecency. However, when he got there, Wepanu gave him a prophecy.

"You are a fortunate young man!" he cried with a grin, right hand raised in respectful welcome. "Your curly-haired wife car-ries not one child, but two, a boy and a girl."

As a result of this stunning news, the guard did not arrest Wepanu per se, but escorted him to his commanding officer, who in turn drove him in a fat-tired dune rover through the busy traffic of a smoky, oilstone-polluted late afternoon and the throngs of restless but well-dressed and well-fed people, to the great domed palace. There the officer turned Wepanu over to a court chamberlain, a tall, broad young man whose grim authority seemed more appropriate to a bodyguard—but what, after all, did Wepanu know of guards and chamberlains?

I'm only a desert wanderer, he reflected with an internal tweak of self-irony that made him smile.

He followed the chamberlain quietly through long halls lined with carved panels of russet-colored hardwood from the forests of Tel-mari. In these echoey outer corridors, the reliefs were

abstract variations of the stylized lightning bolt that symbolized God, but inside the Dome, the heart of the palace, everything changed.

The outside of the Dome, a smooth demiglobe coated with nearly pure hammered gold, reminded the world, especially in the blinding reflection of sunset, of the outward forms of Maurheti power: its wealth, industry, and military strength virtually sunlike in their influence. Inside, the vast hollow cavern represented the Maurheti soul, its national and religious purpose. Here, the friezes were of colored marble from the desert mountains carved in narrative bands depicting the creation—and ultimate end— of the universe. Moving in and around the petrified figures of warriors, angelic hosts, and demons, embroidering them together with silver and gold inlaid arabesques, were excerpts from the Book of Division, the Maurheti holy scriptures. The deep stone hearth in the very center of the polished basalt floor held an eternal fire whose light flashed and flickered from one quote to another as though directing the reader to regard each passage as equal, simultaneous in time to all others, eternal and unending as the round contours of the Dome itself. The story of First Creation and Final Destruction met seamlessly over the heavy, but plain, armchair that functioned as Roon XXII's throne.

Wepanu frowned at the carefully interlaced calligraphy. He couldn't read. Not that that was much of a problem. If he needed to know what the words said, the jo would tell him. In fact, one of the bright little effluxes of divinity was flitting about the ceiling at this very moment. Wepanu looked back over his shoulder at the chamberlain. The young giant, hands clasped behind his back, casually admired the friezes as though warmly familiar with every nook and cranny and hopeful this desert wildman was suitably awestruck.

Wepanu sighed. Sometimes it got lonely being a medium between the physical world and the beyond. Once again, he was the only one who could see or hear the jo . . . and she was giggling.

At least, she seemed female, although one could never be

sure. Wepanu had seen jo change gender and shape so many times and with such caprice that he knew to avoid personalizing them with misplaced assumptions.

"Ah, my pity on these foolish men of flesh!" she whispered in his head although her tiny bright body was at a very great height. "Here are shown their concepts of Beginning and Ending, and how narrow they do conceive them!"

"What do the words say?" Wepanu asked silently. The one and only time he'd spoken aloud to the jo, his family had tied him up and beaten him in an effort to cure his madness.

The jo looked down at him, all three of her round red eyes, like carbuncles, lit up from within with spiritual fire.

"Patience, little boy, and I'll tell you."

The jo shot across the space of the Dome to the friezes directly above the throne.

"Before All Time, or so it claims here," she said, pointing a very long sharp finger at the arabesques set into the wall, "everything was confounded together in a lightless soup, a miasma of all that was, is, or ever would be, jumbled up indiscriminately. A real mess."

The jo put her hands on what Wepanu guessed would be her hips and shook her head. Her weightless, transparent body was improbably thin, almost a figure drawn with a wand.

"Out of this stew," she continued, "God pulled His bits together and caused the Great Division."

"The Great Division?" Wepanu asked.

"I told you they were fools! They believe their God separated that which was light and good and of Him from that which was dark and foul and not of Him."

Wepanu smiled. This much he'd already learned in his wanderings.

"My little boy," the jo said, suddenly serious, "do you see the damage in this? The danger of such a belief?"

Wepanu didn't answer. Better to play the dutiful pupil and wait for his supernatural teacher to provide it.

The jo turned back to the frieze.

"The Spirit of Not-God resented being so cast aside and watched jealously as God invented the living creatures, including the Maurheti who worshiped him. In a fury, the Spirit of Not-God retaliated by creating manlike creatures of its own, beings who did *not* worship God. Thus was born the Eternal Conflict, the War between the Forces of God and the Forces of Not-God, which shall not be resolved until the end of Time itself when God will draw into Himself all of His creations and annihilate those of the Spirit of Not-God."

The jo spun around, rolled her three eyes, and snarled in extreme exasperation.

"Puny creatures!" the minuscule figure snapped. "Even a child knows the flame and the shadow do not contend. They enhance!" She looked over the Dome. "They don't even see the truth of their own creations."

Wepanu shrugged.

"They are a strange people," he replied.

"They're *dangerous*," she said. "Be careful how you address this Roon man of theirs. A direct answer to his question may not be prudent."

Wepanu nodded and scratched his scrotum thoughtfully. This very problem had been nagging him ever since he'd set out on his journey.

The jo giggled again.

"Even the most ludicrous morsel of the flesh itches, does it?" She quickly dug her fingertips into her face and pulled and prodded its features and shoved out its snout until her attenuated body had the canine head of a wau-weh—a wau-weh with an extra eye perched like an inflamed boil on the tip of its nose.

Wepanu tried not to show any reaction whatsoever. If he laughed, she might be insulted and inflict him with stinging warts on that bit of flesh she found so funny.

"See you mind your manners, little boy," she barked, and her bright form snuffed out in a shower of sparks.

None too soon. From another corridor perpendicular to the one Wepanu and the chamberlain had used, Roon XXII strode into the Dome. An active man in his mid-fifties, the monarch had a military officer's efficiency of movement and a veteran politician's charisma. When he smiled at Wepanu, the desert prophet noticed that nothing above the man's nose moved or changed in any way. His dark eyes remained hard and steady.

"So, you are the one they call Wepanu ul-Bahf," he said in a pleasant baritone. "Wepanu the Youth, Wepanu the, uh—" He glanced at the tribesman's exposed organ. "—uncircumcised."

"Yes, great king."

"They say you know many things and can see into the future."

"I know and see nothing but what the jo give me."

The corners of Roon's mouth lifted ever so slightly.

"The jo, eh?"

"The great king does not believe in the jo."

"The great king is merely circumspect," Roon said. He walked over to the plain throne, sat down, got a clay pipe and a pouch of cured seaweed out of his pocket, and proceeded to prepare himself a nice smoke.

Wepanu wasn't fooled by Roon's studied casualness and refined cordiality. He could smell the carefully hidden contempt, a sour funk in the air. To get away from it, and to rest his own ninety-year-old bones, he sat cross-legged on the cold black floor next to the central hearth, but off to one side so Roon could still see him around the fire.

"When did you first become aware, Wepanu, that you could see the jo?"

"There was never a time when I couldn't, great king, but they kept their secrets to themselves until I was of age."

"Of age? But, I understand that, among the Denneshur, one is not of age until one is cut."

The wanderer raised an ironic eyebrow.

"It happens whether one is cut or not, great king," he said.

"Call me what they will, I have not been a child since the night I ran away into the desert, the night I *would* have been cut had the jo not entered my body and taken over my will like a great temblor splitting the mountains."

"Tell me about it." Roon held the pipe in his teeth, puffed calmly, and steepled his fingers. "I have heard of others—a rare and strange brotherhood to be sure—who claim a similar experience."

"I was transformed. They ran me over the burning sands for forty days and yet I did not tire. I never hungered, never felt thirst. My skin roasted to a powdery crust that on the fortieth day sloughed away like the skin of a snake, leaving me smooth and black, the color of mystery."

"The color of evil."

"Not so!" Wepanu said with some heat. "I have seen into the void and it marked me. This mark protects me. I can face the sun at midday, look it in the eye, and not be blinded. I pass between both light and darkness."

The king seemed pensive. Until this point, he'd appeared more absorbed in his pipe than Wepanu's story, but now his attention to the former waned. He no longer puffed and the pipe seemed in danger of going out.

"What . . . else?" he asked slowly.

"On that day, the jo released my body, but not my soul. Whether I welcome them or not, they speak to me. My will is no longer mine."

"You're a slave then?"

Wepanu grinned, exposing his straight, strong, stained yellow teeth.

"We are all slaves to something," he said, "but, compared to you, great king, I am freer than the songbirds in your gardens or the wau-wehs calling in the hills. *I*, at least, am a slave of the divine. *You* are a slave of the world and the flesh."

These disrespectful words alarmed the chamberlain, who

marched threateningly across the floor to Wepanu until Roon raised his hand and stopped him.

"Easy, Kerz," he said. "A desert prophet spends his time among rocks and lizards. We can't expect him to know the finer points of polite behavior." He lowered his hand. "You came here with a purpose, Wepanu. You asked, demanded rather, to see me."

Wepanu turned to look at the eternal fire.

Now it comes, he thought. Now I must be prudent.

"First, great king, tell me what this fire means. It's in the heart of this man-built cave." He swept his arm up to take in the Dome and saw the jo, still dog-faced, hovering at the apex. "This fire . . . is significant."

"Yes," said Roon. "It symbolizes the Maurheti mission."

"A people can have a mission?" Wepanu blinked with counterfeit innocence. "I thought only single persons could have missions."

Roon removed his pipe, chuckled gently as though charmed by a child, and stood up.

"You're a bit naive after your years alone," he said. "Our people serve the most important mission of all: the eternal struggle against ungodliness, against darkness."

"So you subjugate the Tel-mari."

"We tried to convert them—" Roon began to stroll in a slow circle around the fire. "—but they are truly not of God. They resisted. They will *always* resist. All we can do is control them the way one controls a herd of unruly oryx. When one takes off and tries to butt, you have to lasso him." He stopped strolling and gave Wepanu a surprisingly genuine expression of long suffering and pity.

"The Tel-mari can't help what they are," he said. "It's in their nature. The Rebel Darkness created them. It grieves me that a people so similar to us in so many ways can, nevertheless, be beyond redemption until that great day when all will be purified. Their creator is the most cruel force in the universe."

Wepanu returned his attention to the fire. He was in grave danger in this man's company, but the jo were relentless.

"Great king," he began softly, "to make a fire, one needs three things: heat, fuel, and air. Take any one of them away, and there is no fire."

Roon's eyes narrowed, but he remained composed, patient.

"One way to kill a flame," Wepanu continued, "is to introduce another flame in its path. When they meet, they consume all air and fuel . . . and extinguish each other."

"Well, of course. That's why vigilance—"

"Such a flame will soon burn into the path of this Maurheti fire and your world will be changed."

Roon blanched and the jo in the Dome giggled maliciously.

"He believes in the End Time!" she shrieked. "You grasp his soul in your fist, little boy!"

"What do you mean?" Roon asked. "A new insurgent? A terrorist?"

"No, great king." Wepanu raised his eyes to Roon's, and the monarch involuntarily took a step back at the sight of their reddish glow.

"This violence is of your own tribe," Wepanu said, "a hound from your own kennel."

Silence descended heavily in the Dome. Heavily for everyone but Wepanu who heard the piercing shrieklike laughter of the jo in the ceiling. She was still laughing when Roon curtly told the chamberlain to "take him away," and the big man escorted Wepanu, with periodic bad-tempered shoves into his bony shoulder, out of the Dome and out of the palace.

Alone with the king, the jo dropped onto his shoulder and toyed with the dark hair over his ears. He felt nothing.

"You still doubt, but you are disturbed," she cooed. "Will this be enough proof? Here comes interesting news."

The captain of the palace guard suddenly appeared at the doorway and saluted Roon by placing his right palm on his heart and bowing his head.

"What is it?" Roon asked impatiently.

"A tower guard, Officer Benu, has asked for a day's leave, Your Majesty. His wife has delivered."

"No need to bring that to me, Captain. You can grant him leave yourself."

"I realize that, Your Majesty. I am here merely to give information since I understand you gave audience to Wepanu the desert seer. The old man was right."

"In what way?"

"He predicted twins and that is what Benu's wife had."

"Any good midwife can predict twins!" Roon cried, surprising himself with the extent of his own irritability. He immediately curbed his voice. "Wepanu could have heard something."

"But can they predict the *sex*, Majesty?"

"Of course not."

"Wepanu did. We heard him. He stood there naked as a corpse and predicted a boy and a girl."

"That's one in a million, Captain." Roon smiled. "Maurheti women do not have mixed-gender twins."

"Benu's wife did."

The jo stuck out her tongue, twice as long as herself, and poked it into Roon's ear, straight through his skull, and out the other side. She wriggled with delight.

"H'm," Roon said. "Excuse me, Captain, but I suddenly have a terrible headache and must lie down."

"Of course, Your Majesty. God protect your health."

The captain saluted again and departed.

Roon stamped his boot on the floor, then, because the jolt intensified the pain in his head, rubbed his temples.

On the heels of a fine victory, he thought, temporarily setting aside the memory of the subsequent defeat—which hardly mattered anyway—comes this. Prophets bring nothing but gloom and doom. Maybe I should have Wepanu murdered—

His headache leapt up and he nearly vomited.

—Not now, though. I need rest.

CHAPTER 5

HOME

S ekmé was surprised how easy it was to climb back into the cockpit of a Needle and engage the vertical thrust. She'd expected some residual psychological disturbance, vertigo perhaps or a quick flash of panic, but apparently none of her inner confusion was connected to the aircraft itself. Its source lay deeper.

The long, thin silver craft lifted slowly straight up through the trees and, once clear, Sekmé angled the nose, ignited the forward thrust, and shot into the clouds. Within seconds, clear sky broke overhead and Tel-mari was gone, buried beneath its wet atmospheric blanket. She leveled the nose and set the Needle to cruise.

Field General Am had given her three months' leave, twice the usual furlough. She'd protested but Am had countered with a question that, to her chagrin, she could not answer.

"When was your last leave?"

She'd had no idea.

"I'll tell you." Am flipped open his dog-eared personnel roster. "Five years ago at least. You haven't had a leave since I took command here, and my predecessor, may God hold him close, stopped keeping records near the end."

"But, sir," she said, "he wrote in his records all the time."

"Gibberish. His mind was gone. In any case, it doesn't change the fact that you haven't been home in a very long time."

So, she was going home. Home to her father's . . . no, *her* holdings outside Kemphor. She still had difficulty thinking of them as hers although her father had been dead a dozen years. True, she'd appointed her mother overmaine, but she, Sekmé, was the mistress, the baronne.

"Some landowner," she scoffed as she tipped the short narrow port wing down and veered away from a massively towering cumulonimbus. "A scrawny mud rat with the deaths of a hundred of her own on her hands."

Even so, as the miles passed, much of her depression slipped away. The cloud floor thinned and the stark, dry points and ripples of the Hills of Whispers came into view. A deep wave of pleasant pain rose through her chest. Was this homesickness? She wasn't sure, but she found herself dropping the Needle's nose so she could skim along closer to those pink and gold and copper green peaks.

On the ground, just outside the Northern Maurhet Air Base, Sekmé's cousins, all fifteen of them, all male, watched the sky and quieted their restless onagers. All but one wore loose-fitting riding shirts and breeches of fine white muslin, red boots, double silver spurs, and silver belts. The eldest, underofficer to the base general, wore dun fatigues as befitted the firstborn.

When the Needle flashed over the hills, its scream several seconds behind it, the dark-haired young men and boys waved their arms and shouted, and sure enough, the Needle rolled once, swung a wide loop out over the dunes and the sea cliff, and stopped to hover over the base. A moment later, it began a stately vertical descent.

Sekmé's cousins mounted their onagers, shook out the colored tassels on the reins, and spurred the animals' dusty chestnut flanks. By the time the crystal bubble over Sekmé's cockpit slid back with a soft gasp, a band of shrieking desert riders with

wildly flapping sleeves was headed her way. An older man, a bareheaded officer with long white locks, was already on the tarmac, waiting for her.

"Are those yours, Commander?" the base general asked with a nod to the horde as Sekmé climbed down from the Needle.

"I'm afraid so, General." She grinned.

"Is that my underofficer in front bouncing like an under-cooked pudding?"

"Go easy on him, sir. Bahé's only a boy."

"He's three years older than you are."

"You know what I mean."

At about the same time, a small group of dust-covered lumps just outside the steel-thorned fire-wire fence of the base suddenly threw back their hoods, shook the desert from their dark robes, and held out armloads and baskets of trinkets, embroidery, and colored stones. They called out in happy, rough-accented Maurheti to the riders and officers. "Look! Look! Such lovely things! All authentic! Very reasonable! Denneshur crafts-manship for your women . . . or lovers."

The last was added for Sekmé's benefit and she smiled wryly. Maurheti considered the dark brown desert tribesmen parasites even though an ancient monarch had declared them of God, undoubtedly because, heretical tenets and the occasional con notwithstanding, they were basically harmless and often use-ful. They were "wild children" under Maurheti protection al-though they didn't acknowledge it. Sekmé preferred to think of them as a clever category of man all their own, and as she moved through the eager grimaces and overly familiar bejew-eled fingers to meet her cousins, she kept one hand on the flare rifle slung over her shoulder and the other in her pocket on her purse.

The tribesmen wouldn't let up even as she tried to talk to Bahé.

"Sekmé!" her eldest cousin cried. "It's commander now, isn't it? You're pale as a sheet."

"Look! Look! Desert spices! Very fragrant . . ."

"And you're fat as a buffalo, cousin."

"Fine gems and crystals you can't find anywhere else! Just make me an offer . . ."

"Nonsense! It's all muscle, believe me!"

Sekmé was skeptical. Maybe some of his weight was muscle, but enough of it was fat to affect his gait. His swagger was a bit wide, splayfooted.

"Why isn't Set with you, Bahé?"

"Have you seen our beaten copper pots? The best in the world! All hand finished . . ."

"Something about composing a special poem for you. Did he tell you he's going to give a recitation for the king?"

"No! The devil! He's going to have to explain—"

"Look! Mountain vulpé fur!"

This last tribesman pushed a small pelt right into Sekmé's nose. She nearly sneezed on the fur then brushed it away.

"Get that thing out of my face!"

"But, look! Look! See how soft! Touch it, mistress."

She sighed, resigned to her fate, and looked at the pelt. It certainly was unusual, blazingly pure white, not even a freckle of any other color, fur so thick and soft her hand sank out of sight before she even felt it.

"Remarkable," she said. "What animal did you say this was from?"

"Mountain vulpé," the tribesman smirked, tongue lashing over his lips with the foretaste of a lucrative sale, "from the White Mountains."

"Bat shit," Sekmé scoffed, although the fur intrigued her. No *local* animal wore such thick insulation.

"It's true! On my sister's virtue! I bought it from a man who traded with the White Riders themselves! Paid twelve soolis for it."

"I'll give you three." The White Riders were a fanciful legend, but perhaps Set would enjoy the pelt.

"Ah, you stab my soul," the tribesman whined, and rolled his

sun-reddened eyes. "I must recover my outlay. I can't let it go for less than fifteen and still make a profit."

"The wau-weh piss on your campfire." Sekmé began to walk away.

"Be fair, pretty mistress!"

Sekmé chuckled to herself. When the tribesmen began to flirt, the bargaining was well under way.

"Five," she said. "No more."

"Twelve and a kiss and I'll consider it even."

Sekmé made a show of great revulsion, and her cousins and the base general guffawed.

"I'd rather kiss a goat's testicles!"

"Eleven, mistress! You've broken my heart! I'm losing money just to please you."

"Forget it."

"Nine."

"Six."

The tribesman dropped to the sand and scuffled along on his knobby knees after her. Sekmé frowned. Fun was fun, but this was getting tawdry.

"I am dying! How can an angel be so cruel? Eight! It will kill me, but I must have your love!"

He began to weep and, while waving the pelt with one hand, rubbed his eyes and nose with the other.

"I can't go on!"

Sekmé didn't even look at him.

"Seven."

The tribesman underwent a miraculous transformation and hopped to his feet as agile as a cricket, suddenly all business.

"Done," he said, and snapped his fingers for the money. "Seven soolis."

"You haven't lost your touch," Bahé said admiringly as Sekmé handed over the coins and secreted the pelt in the deep pocket of her fatigues.

"The Tel-mari are even worse," she said, but the comment

brought up a vision of the Eshna marketplace and her throat clenched on sudden nausea. She shuddered.

"Are you all right, cousin?"

"Just hungry, Bahé. Correction: *starving*. Something I'm sure you can relate to."

"Excellent! Your mother's putting on a banquet tonight in your honor."

"Whatever for?"

"Don't be ridiculous! You're a hero, Sekmé."

"A *hero*?! Oh, for the love of God, Bahé!" She turned to the base general for help, but the senior officer was laughing.

"Over half of your fellow former cadets will be there," he said, "not to mention a good helping of the High Command."

Sekmé groaned.

"This is a disaster! Maybe I should get back in the Needle and get lost in the desert."

"Oh, no, you don't!" Bahé cried, whistling to his brothers, who grabbed Sekmé and nearly threw her, kicking and cursing, onto an onager.

"General!"

"Sorry, Commander!" He saluted as the startled beast took off at a gallop almost before Sekmé could get her boots in the stirrups. "This is a family matter. I have no authority."

Finally secure in the saddle, Sekmé snatched up the reins and wheeled the onager around only to see her cousins on their mounts giving chase. The challenge proved irresistible and she turned the onager's head and spurred her in the direction of Kemphor. The compact little jenny squealed and shot off over the dunes like a whirlwind.

You're a slave to your passions, Sekmé thought as her heart gave itself up to the thrill of the race. They think you're the great stone soldier, but there's nothing like the desert wind and a pounding ride on the dunes to blow away all your discipline.

She looked back. Her cousins must have resigned themselves to defeat, because they'd slowed their gallop to stand on their

saddles, reins in their teeth, in tribute. Even the youngest, a boy of seven, had scrambled up and was bobbing serenely, standing on the back of his cantering mount.

Sekmé whooped then let out a long, wavering traditional cavalry wail something like the howl of a wau-weh, and like a howl, it ran up against the Hills of Whispers and bounced back at her—and shocked her into cutting it short.

Her cousins were laughing behind her and trying to knock each other into the sand. They must not have heard what she heard—which was just as well. Not only had her cry failed to sound triumphant, it hadn't sounded human.

All in all, it seemed much too early to celebrate her "heroism."

Sekmé's family holdings, although larger than many, were laid out in traditional fashion. From the Nawset Highway, the private road ran at a nearly perfect right angle due north for over a league before it reached the gates in the high red limestone wall that surrounded the holdings, protecting them from the sea and desert winds and the sand. Between the gate and the buildings lay the formal park. Thick carpets of contrasting inland grasses wound patterns between hedges of tiny, sweet-scented white perennials and carefully shaped fruit trees of many varieties: from mang, with their broad green leaves and heavy oval yellow fruit whose soft white flesh was used in pastries and sweetened cheese, to bin-balek whose startled crown of spiky leaves tipped with tight knobs of musky red flowers produced a netlike pouch full of soft black berries best served raw with crystallized sugar, to the yarprin, a kind of tree vine without leaves at all but, instead, millions of flat, fleshy green polyps that functioned both as leaf *and* fruit, a sour, acid fruit refreshing in drinks and prized as a special ingredient in sauces for meats.

There were nut trees, too, and these attracted the small, bright turquoise and orange Maurheti desert parrots who found the nuts easier pickings than the spiky-husked fruit of the native thornwoods.

Small white oryx grazed in the park and made especially good holiday eating themselves. There would be plenty of oryx dishes at Sekmé's welcome-home banquet.

Around the main house and outbuildings curved flower gardens spilling over with blossoms of maroon, scarlet, canary, periwinkle, lavender, blush, cream, white—even black. These last, the drooping, bell-shaped ebon ladies, not only offset the other, brighter blooms, but often accompanied tearstained letters from young heartsick lovers to the aloof objects of their desires.

In Tel-mari, the same flowers were called fen widows and were used in cemeteries.

Outside the kitchen, the low multi-hued greens of the herb and vegetable garden ran almost all the way to the servants' housing and the mews.

Farther north, beyond the buildings, the lake garden with its network of ornamental ponds, streams, and fountains and accompanying water plants, reeds, lilies, rushes, and stilt-rooted exotic swamp trees successfully hid its other function as the reclamation and recirculation center of the holdings' vast irrigation system. One of the older servants, a gardener whose arthritic hands were no longer flexible enough to tend to flowers, had introduced a small selection of imported waterfowl, mostly inland teals and a couple large, bright yellow marsh herons, and had had respectable success breeding them. The small black or olive green babies either swam or scooted in nervous lines after their parents.

Beyond the lake garden, the rest of the holdings were backlands, a deliberately overgrown wild area of artificially built-up hills and strategically deepened dales randomly planted with conifers, shade trees, and shrubs, grasses, and ferns that grew wild inland but were carefully tended here by greenkeepers who not only knew every font of the disguised irrigation network but made sure the stock of "wild" game animals remained healthy.

From the air, the holdings looked like huge square islands of

brilliant color sharply, and abruptly, cut off from the much greater expanses of golden peach sand. From the ground, they were secret mini-kingdoms, self-contained and remote, hermetically sealed behind their dull red walls. The very air changed when you passed through the gates from sharp, dry, and mildly sea-salty, to cool, sweet, and moist.

Sekmé took a deep breath of that air as her onager trotted through the gate, her retinue of mounted cousins in a clattering bunch behind her.

How lovely! she thought. But, also, how strange. She assumed it had to do with her long absence—cold memory could only partially reproduce sensation—but still wondered if she'd changed. Most of these plants grew in Tel-mari although they looked very different there, larger or smaller or more unkempt, and she experienced an unsettling overlap of her childhood and the war. When the breath of these fruits and flowers first greeted her, it was as if she'd suddenly met a complete stranger who nevertheless looked uncannily like her.

Sekmé dismounted halfway to the main house, slapped her jenny on the rump, and the onager cantered cheerfully into the formal garden.

"Is that wise, Commander?" Bahé asked, also dismounting. "She'll eat the flowers."

"Let her," Sekmé said, "and, please, call me Sekmé. You're kin and we're on family ground."

Her big cousin smiled brightly.

"When you're free," he said, "I want to discuss possible choices for family weapon. I'm an officer now—"

"Yes, I know."

"—and, being firstborn of a second son, well . . ."

"Yes, yes," she said, a bit distractedly. "We'll discuss it."

Sekmé had not yet seen her brother and she wouldn't put it past him to spring on her unexpectedly from the trees—but she could detect no trace of him.

Her mother and uncle and a contingent of servants waited

on the broad stair to the grand receiving hall. All of the delicate latticework wall screens had been removed, opening the hall into a columned extension of the garden, where more servants were laying out the rugs and cushions for the evening's festivities.

Sekmé suddenly felt shy in the role of returning mistress, but gamely greeted the servants, most of whom she remembered by name as they clasped her hand and touched it to their foreheads—even the arthritic gardener who'd known her father since the day the late officer was born.

Sekmé's mother, Hatula, was nowhere near as staid and formal as the servants. It was all she could do to wait properly in place without bouncing up and down in an excess of maternal enthusiasm. When finally face-to-face with her daughter, she flung her arms around her, burying her in brightly painted silk gauze, sweet perfume, row upon row of stone-encrusted bangles, and billows and cascades of slightly sticky, dyed, fluffed, and lacquered black hair. Anyone else might have been overcome by the layers of art coating her mother's body, but Sekmé instinctively sought out the warm softness underneath, picked out its true scent from the perfume, and heard its excited voice and heartbeat at its source.

"Sekmé!" Hatula cried in her permanently husky contralto. "My dear warrior child is here in one piece! Oh, let me look at you!"

She held Sekmé at arm's length and danced her small, bright, widely spaced eyes over her daughter and grinned, the laugh lines wrinkling up her sun-darkened cheeks until they resembled thornwood bark. She embraced Sekmé again.

"Moom," Sekmé said, not just a babyhood pet name for Hatula, but the only sound she could muster with her face crushed in her mother's soft breasts.

"Hatula, really!" Sekmé's uncle Atto laughed. "High Command will be very upset if you suffocate their soldier of the hour."

Hatula reluctantly released her daughter, and Sekmé clasped

her uncle's forearm in a bone-crushingly hearty handshake. Except for the passage of years, Atto, father to all those hooligans laughing and wrestling each other at the foot of the stair, looked a great deal like her own father: tall, black bearded, naturally athletic with a broad-boned sturdy build, big feet, and huge, powerful hands. His voice was similar as well, deep, slow, and rolling, but the mischief in his gray eyes was unique. Sekmé's father had shouldered all the cares of the firstborn and his eyes had always been steadier, more melancholy. As the younger son, Atto had grown up with a lighter, more reckless personality.

He gave her a hard but playful slap on the shoulder.

"You look good, lassie! A little pale, perhaps, but as dangerous as always. When I heard what you'd cooked up to crush those Hive insurgents, and that you'd actually gotten out of it alive . . . well! I said, 'That's my girl, all right! No one else could do that.' "

"Um . . . thank you, Uncle. I was lucky."

"Lucky? Nonsense! Bahé!" he called to his son, and the officer jumped up from where he had pinned his two youngest brothers in a double hammerlock. "While Sekmé is on leave, learn as much from her as you can." He turned back to Sekmé and shook his head. "He needs some direction. Some discipline. Maybe you can work that gut off of him."

As Atto led the way into the house, Sekmé saw him casually take Hatula's hand in his, not an unusual gesture since she was his sister-in-law, but Hatula responded by caressing his great, engulfing fingers with open and exceptional tenderness. Sekmé raised her eyebrows, which Hatula saw, and wonder of wonders, the older woman blushed, deeply. Sekmé looked questioningly at Atto—and *he* blushed, too.

"We—we weren't sure how to tell you, Sekmé," he rumbled awkwardly, "but we thought you'd have no objection and anyway—"

"You couldn't *tell* me?" Sekmé cried in mock fury, and she

shoved Atto in the chest. "You marry my mother and keep it to yourself? What's the matter with you?"

Sheepish embarrassment looked exceedingly silly on a big man like Atto, and Sekmé's theatrical ire quivered, spluttered, and fell apart.

"I'll bet that's why Set didn't meet me at the base," she laughed. "He never could keep a secret from me." She squeezed her mother's arm. "Where is he, Moom? I have to beat him up."

"I don't know, my love. You know how well he can hide."

Sekmé's jaw set and her eyes flashed with a hunter's pleasure. "Not for long."

She dashed across the rugs, leapt over the crouching servants, and disappeared into the maze of chambers and stairways, closets, corridors, anterooms, balconies, porticoes, and workrooms that made up her family home.

She searched through the guest chambers, where servants were setting out linens and flowers and bottles of bathing oils for the expected deluge of young men. No Set. She poked through the cupboards and cold pantries of the enormous kitchen where ten cooks fought at high decibels over vats of steaming sauces, racked spits of marinated sides of oryx, crates of tubers and bowls of cut fruit, huge hogsheads of honey liquor, tubs of giant sea eels as long as five men and as thick as tree trunks, their black and white scaled skins flashing like chain mail, and an entire side pantry full of soft, edible flowers.

No Set.

Repair shop, hunters' room, library, bath chambers, offices, music room, game parlor, storerooms, prayer room—no Set. Sekmé sighed with disappointment, then shrugged.

"He'll show up," she told herself, and headed into her own bedchamber.

She could have claimed the larger, master's chamber with its incomparable view of the distant city, but she'd already decided to let her mother and uncle keep it. She much preferred the

more modest room she'd slept in as a girl with its balconied window that looked east past the gardens to the desert and the Hills of Whispers, which were just beginning to turn gold in the late afternoon sun. Soon they'd begin the silent, stately show she'd watched many times with her brother at her side, describing to him in detail the shift from gold to rose to lavender to blue and the slow appearance of the stars in the deepening evening sky, the first being Rahin, God's Eye, the brightest star in the hilt of the constellation of God's Spear, a double-curved shape that referred to lightning.

Sekmé stepped onto the balcony, leaned her elbows on the rail, and stared at the hills. It suddenly struck her that she'd successfully lived off the land many times in Tel-mari, but would be hard-pressed to survive in the desert of her own land. Oh, she knew how to find water and had often camped out in the hills with her brother and cousins. That wasn't the point. It was a question of psychological tolerance. She loved the desert, but had been trained to endure wet and cold without thinking about it. Heat and dryness, on the other hand, remained personal, too laden with emotion and memory. Undoubtedly, should she ever find herself abandoned in the sand, it would cut through the armor of her indifference, fill her with sensations superfluous to survival, distract her will, and, eventually, her energy.

Sekmé straightened up, her brow furrowed with confusion.

Was this really true? she wondered. It had always been her experience that nostalgia, tenderness, and, yes, love were fatal in the field. They had to be set aside for the sake of the greater victory, which was why soldiers wept so much at ceremonies honoring valor or made love so violently with prostitutes. These set-aside feelings had to be released in safety or they would explode in battle and bring on the madness Sekmé had seen far too many times.

Perhaps she could release the roiling mixture of emotions she felt over her Eshna Hives campaign at the banquet tonight.

It was the appropriate venue, after all: a ritual feast and wake in the drunken arms of comrades who would know exactly what she felt without her needing to tell them.

"No," she said suddenly. "They can't know. They didn't see it."

"Then tell *me*," came a familiar clear bright voice behind her. "I've seen everything."

Sekmé stepped back quickly into her bedchamber, her heart so lightened it seemed to be winging about her neck and face. She stopped to crouch at wrestling ready, her grin wide, almost painful.

Her brother, Set, framed across the room in the doorway, cocked his head slightly and matched her crouch.

"Oh, ho!" he said. "Someone wants revenge for not being let in on a secret."

Sekmé began to move cautiously in his direction, humming softly. Set evaded her with a quick step sideways along the wall.

"Don't hum!" he said. "I don't want you to make it easy for me."

Set had been born without eyes, the genetic result of his father's exposure to an experimental, and since banned, exfoliant. Ocular surgeons had replaced the benign but useless pockets of pink jelly that filled his sockets with quite beautiful, soft-bodied artificial eyes that matched his sister's sea green ones. They'd even fused them to the orbital muscles so he could move them like real eyes. Even so, they did not function.

On the other hand, as was often the case with the blind-from-birth, Set had developed extraordinary senses of hearing, touch, and smell. An especially handsome young man who looked enough like his sister to be her twin and had a similar lithe physique—slippery, Atto called it when he was teaching them to wrestle—Set moved gracefully about the world as if guided by sonar. Quite a few of his friends had known him for years before they realized he was sightless.

Brother and sister sized one another up like sparring mantises, a feint to the left, another to the right, before diving into

each other. Set hooked his leg around Sekmé's knee and they tumbled to the floor and rolled, nearly crashing into the antique whale-ivory armoire. Sekmé surprised herself with a giggle, a sound she almost didn't recognize, then twisted her brother's shoulders and tried to force him down, but he arched his back, deflected her, and sprang back up to his feet. Sekmé flung her entire body at his waist and they tumbled back in the other direction right up onto her low bed of woven mats, furs, comforters, and teal-feather pillows. Sekmé quickly tangled him in the bedclothes and pushed him flat, her knee on his chest.

"I won," she whispered.

"You cheated," he whispered back.

Sekmé tweaked his nose then pulled the vulpé pelt from her pocket and pressed it into his hands. Set's features melted into ecstasy and he crushed the fur to his cheek.

"Ooooh! Marvelous . . ."

Sekmé left her sensory-drunk brother and returned to the balcony. The hills had turned a misty blue violet.

"Is this from the White Mountains?" Set cooed.

"How did you know?"

"Not even a Tel-mari marmot needs such luxurious warmth."

Sekmé bit her lip.

"I—I have to tell you something, Set. Something that happened in Tel-mari."

Set put aside the pelt, undid himself from her bedclothes, and sat up.

"Sit next to me."

She did.

"Now, when you tell me," he said, brow and eyelids shaping concern around his ersatz sight organs, "don't forget the colors."

Sekmé smiled softly. Years ago, when they were very young, she'd taught him the colors by comparing them to things and sensations he understood. He'd been fascinated by the concept of light in hues, and his first poem had explored the idea, pitting the colors against his own experience of nonsight, which

wasn't even darkness, he'd explained, but nothing, a void. Still, it was not evil. Rather a page for stories. He'd won a prize for the poem.

"I'll try not to," Sekmé said, "although there were very *few* colors. Eshna is a dull and gray city, cluttered. Perhaps tipped with the flat green of mold."

"Gray and dying green," Set whispered to himself. "Decay. Wet. Smell of disease."

"Exactly," Sekmé said, briefly unsettled by the accuracy of her brother's interpretation. "But, every eight days, even in the most overcrowded, wretched part of Eshna known as the Hives—"

"Drone. Legs. Bodies crawling over each other."

"—they hold an outdoor market where they sell many kinds of fresh fruit and vegetables—reds and oranges and yellows—as well as spices and incense, meats and poultry."

"Sweet juice of the fruit and green bite of vegetable on the tongue, a heat to their juice in the raw. Nostril tightens at the spice—too much, too dense—which will be used very sparse and delicate in the meats. Iron, blood smell, bitter and sweet. Cold metal tang of fresh. Corrupt, oily stink of rot. Feces. Rats in the corners."

Sekmé shuddered. Set "saw" the market almost too well.

"The women and children, all in black—"

"Color of void and selflessness."

"—do the shopping, stocking up for the days ahead. Thousands of women. Children clinging to their robes, slung on their backs, tied to their breasts."

"Sticky hands, soft round faces. Little voices asking, asking . . ."

Sekmé pressed her finger over Set's lips. This was more commentary than she could bear.

"Please . . . not so . . ."

"Yes. I understand."

"It's just that I—"

"I understand."

Sekmé dropped her hand and stared at her brother's waiting face. Five years had refined his features, chipped away at the last of his baby flesh and yet left his mouth intact, a slight child's pout in the tuck of the full lower lip, which pushed the upper one slightly forward. An erotic mouth. One for kissing and sucking in secret places. For one brief caesura, Sekmé forgot what she was talking about and wondered if her brother had found anyone yet to be intimate with.

"The market, Sekmé?"

"Yes. The market." Sekmé rubbed her forehead. "I led an air strike on the market in order to draw out the men, the insurgents, who were hidden in the houses. We gel-bombed them."

"Gel-bombed?"

"A gel bomb is a thin metal sphere filled with galca, the gel you get out of oilstone when you subject it to high compression. It's extremely unstable. Catches fire on impact and explodes then leaves a thick, sticky, caustic tar behind called burn."

"So . . . you gel-bombed the market."

"Yes." Sekmé began to tap Set's knee with her finger. She didn't look in his face. "One pass of three Needles. It was very successful. The market went up like thorn tinder and the men in the houses panicked. They ran out after their burning women and babies, and we made another pass."

She rested her palm on his thigh and was silent a moment.

"Ten thousand dead, maybe," she said at last. "I'm not sure. One of their between-season storms came up soon after and we were grounded. The weather was so bad our follow-up contingent couldn't get in for five days."

"You led them?"

"Yes. There were only a hundred of us. We were sure . . . all the signs seemed to point to extensive destruction of insurgent forces. No enemy transmissions, no unusual refugee shift, nothing. We encountered no resistance at all until—"

She broke off. Set curled his long fingers around her chin

and cheeks and tilted her face up, as if he were looking in her eyes, but actually to better feel the tension of her expression.

"Until?"

"The center of the Hives, where they hold the market, is a square surrounded by narrow, tightly packed together four-story buildings. I think they were guild halls once. Something mercantile. The square is not a safe place."

"No. It wouldn't be."

"But, it was silent when we entered it, as if the entire city had been abandoned, but . . . someone, or ones, it would have had to be many . . . all the bodies . . ."

"What? What about the bodies, Sekmé?"

He saw it. She knew he could. Liquid pooled around his artificial eyes; his tear ducts had always been intact and functional.

"Someone had gathered up every single body, every burned man, woman, child, even the animals, and laid them out in rows, perfect rows, like ranks of soldiers. Every last one of them with a right hand or paw or hoof, even if it had broken off, placed on what was left of their nose or snout—*cursing* me."

Set shuddered.

"*Thousands* of them, Set. The square was covered with them end to end, all with that same obscene gesture."

Set's hands slipped limply from Sekmé's face and his expression became blank with shock, exactly the way Sekmé knew *she* had looked when first confronted with this grisly monument to her cruelty.

"We . . . I . . . didn't know what to do. I've seen terrible things, Set. I've seen the corpses of women and babies fused together by the heat of the burn. I've seen men cut off pieces of live prisoners for souvenirs. I've been able to look right at some of the ugliest manifestations of evil you can imagine and not flinch, but this . . ." She shook her head slowly. "My soldiers broke ranks and wandered over the dead like automatons. What could I say? They wouldn't have heard me. Scattered about the

square like that, we were easy targets when the surviving insurgents in the fourth-story windows opened fire."

"But, what about reinforcements?"

Sekmé's brow clouded over like a sudden winter thunderstorm.

"Lokar," she snarled, and Set nodded. He already knew about the officer who'd loudly decried his sister's promotion in spite of her stellar military record. Sekmé had sent a finger-card letter telling him all about it. "He tried to stab me in the back but cut the field general instead. They would have court-martialed him, but he escaped."

Set smiled.

"Well, he escaped into Tel-mari, right?"

"What do you mean?"

"He's not as gifted as you are, Sekmé. The bog monitors will eat him."

Sekmé laughed bitterly.

"Poor dumb lizards! They'll get indigestion."

Set folded his arms around Sekmé, and the close warmth of his calm, familiar form, the shift of muscle as he tightened his grip, broke through the last of her composure. With a heavy groan, she wilted into sobs.

"My poor sister," Set said tenderly. "Somehow, you'll have to save your grief for later."

"How? I dream those bodies over and over, cracked and black as mummies, and they all say, 'Damn you, Sekmé! Rub your nose in shit!' "

"I know, I know, but you need to gather yourself together for your guests."

"Ha! As if I could entertain anyone just now . . ."

Set kissed her brow and smiled at her.

"Listen, Sekmé, I've composed a new kind of poem."

"New?" She used the corner of a sleeve to wipe her eyes.

"Yes, I think so. Very new. I wanted you to be the first to hear it. That's why I was hiding. I was practicing."

Sekmé grew sly.

"What do you think of Atto and Moom, eh?" she asked.

"We'll talk about that later. First, the poem."

He sat back and, because he'd learned it was a common behavior among the sighted, closed his eyes while he searched his memory and put all the new lines in order. It didn't take long. Then he looked up—a little too high. His eyes seemed focused on a spot above and behind Sekmé's head.

"In the lake, a teal.
I think he heard my laughter
When you leapt and tore your sleeve."

Sekmé waited, watching her brother closely. He often used long pauses in his recitations to excellent effect, but, after several moments, she realized he was finished.

"Is that all?"

"Yes. What do you think?"

Sekmé pursed her lips.

"Well, it's a nice beginning . . ."

"That's the entire poem."

Her puzzlement grew.

"Are you sure? It's very short."

"I'm sure."

"It's not an epic or an ode."

"No. As I said, it's new."

Sekmé had to think about this. A bit of nature, two people, probably lovers, a minor accident. It was nothing very specific . . . just potential.

"What happens next?" she asked.

"I don't know."

"What do you mean you don't know?!" she cried. "*You're* the poet! Does she push him in the lake? Do they make love? Does the teal bite him on the ass?"

Set laughed and clapped his hands.

"I don't know! Isn't it wonderful?"

"It's crazy! There's no story at all!"

"Who said there had to be a story?" Set asked. "That's what's so wonderful about it. It just *is*! Every answer and no answer fits because all we get is the question. We'll never know!"

"It makes me uncomfortable," Sekmé said.

"It's supposed to."

"It's sexy."

Set's eyes opened wide in ingenuous surprise.

"It is?"

For an answer, Sekmé gave her brother's shoulder a hard shove and he toppled off the low bed onto the floor with a mild thump.

"I don't know!" she said, and began to pull off her boots. "Do you want to scrub my feet?"

"*I've* already bathed," Set replied haughtily. He got up, straightened his clothing, and felt about for the vulpé pelt, which he slipped fur-side-in down the front of his loose shirt.

"I'll let the chamber servant know you'd like extra of everything." He ambled out of the room.

Sekmé still felt the Tel-mari damp, a sense that there was mold in her bones, and she drew a bath so scalding that it fogged in the tiled bath chamber. She winced and instantly turned crimson as she lowered herself slowly into the square, herb-scented pool, settling on the submerged stone perch where the water lapped against her collarbone.

"Congratulations," she chuckled to herself. "Parboiled to perfection."

A servant quietly entered the chamber and began to set out an extra bottle of oil and more towels, fulfilling Set's unnecessary instructions. It was a bit difficult to pick out the servant's features in the fog, and like all chamber help, he kept his eyes lowered in the presence of employer undress, but Sekmé saw immediately that he was not the usual kind of person assigned these tasks. He was very tall and impressively, she dared to think

magnificently, muscular—a truly splendid male specimen. His hands were as strong and lovely as the hands on a marble sculpture of a hero.

Sekmé felt a bit at a loss. She wasn't self-conscious about her nudity per se, but she was vain enough to regret her scars: a shiny pink stripe over her left breast where an acid pellet had grazed her flesh, too close for humor, and a purplish dent in her right thigh, a shrapnel souvenir. Still, this striking young man was worth a few words.

"Good evening," she said.

"Good evening, mistress."

Oh, fine tone! A lovely, rich tenor from the chest.

"I don't believe I've seen you before. Are you new on the staff?"

"About a year, mistress. The lady your mother purchased my services when the grand mistress Wemal's estate was liquidated."

Wemal had been the last of her line, having lost all her brothers and her husband in Tel-mari skirmishes. She'd never remarried and never had children.

"But, Wemal didn't use you as a chamber servant, did she, uh? . . ."

"Haru, mistress. No. I was her master baker and sous-chef."

"And Hatula made you a chamber servant?"

"You already have a master baker, mistress."

"Well—" Sekmé shifted forward, the better to see Haru. "—in my opinion, you can't have too many master bakers."

"The mistress has never worked in a kitchen, has she?"

"No, you have me there . . ." She sucked in her lower lip. "It's difficult to talk to a man without seeing his face. Please. Look at me."

Hesitantly at first, then boldly, Haru raised his eyes and confronted her. The water had cooled somewhat and the fog thinned so Sekmé could see the large, dark blue eyes that went so well with his jet-black curls. Curiously, his beauty saddened her, almost to the point of tears.

"Who in your family serves, Haru?"

"My elder sister and an aunt," he said.

"Of course. Administrative staff."

"You chose combat, mistress."

Sekmé lifted her foot from the water and studied her red-dened toes with apparent absorption when, in reality, she didn't want this beautiful, healthy young man to read her turmoil in her eyes.

"I did. It's what I always wanted."

"Why?"

She looked up in surprise. This kind of question, its bold curiosity, was rare coming from a servant. It sounded almost confrontational, but, when she met his gaze, she realized his concern was genuine. He exhibited no guile whatsoever. This made her even sadder. He was a creature of another reality, one she hadn't been part of in a dozen years.

"Because I wanted to kill," she said. "Are you shocked?"

Haru picked up a towel, shook it out, and began to fold it, a needless activity considering it had already been a perfect component of a perfect, squarish stack.

"I don't know," he said cautiously. "You're firstborn."

"You think killing comes naturally just because I was born first? What about your aunt and sister?"

Haru turned away.

"That's not what I meant, mistress."

Sekmé didn't want his discomfort. She wanted him to look at her again.

"Actually, it may *be* natural," she said gently and, she hoped, apologetically. "They say the need to defend oneself is natural to all creatures and that war is the highest expression of that need since we're the highest of God's creations."

She sat up a bit higher in the bath and felt a slight chill cross her breasts.

"I—I've been wondering about that though. I mean, we've all seen animals fight—there's nothing more desperately vicious

than a dune marmot trying to beat off a pack of wau-wehs, and onagers fight over females all the time—but war . . ." She sighed and shook her head. "I don't want to eat or mate the Tel-mari, I just want to kill them, pure and simple. I used to think it was because they killed my father and this was revenge, but the women and babies didn't kill him, did they? I didn't go out hunting for his assassins, I kill total strangers. Is that natural? Is that what man does as one of God's creatures?"

Haru finally looked at her again and, very subtly, straightened his back and squared his heavy shoulders, effectively erasing his subservient manner. Sekmé's chest tightened with a peculiar excitement somewhere between frost and scorch and she suddenly wished she could curl up inside him and let his unpolluted vitality squeeze the war out of her.

"Maybe you're thinking this way because you've become a bit strange," he said.

"Strange?"

"You've been apart from people a long time, perhaps too long."

Haru picked up a bottle of green oil and approached the bath.

"But, my men—"

"All right, yes—" He nodded slightly and tipped a short stream of the oil into the water. "—you've been with your men, but you outrank them. Are they really friends? Can you talk to them?"

Sekmé stared at his hands, those exceptional baker's hands, and felt the onset of tears sting her eyes.

"I could use a friend, Haru," she whispered. "The things I've seen and done are getting heavy."

She shifted her stare to his eyes and wondered if he understood what she wanted. She only half understood it herself since she'd never paid it much attention until now. It had always seemed unimportant, unnecessary, but now . . .

"I'm sick of dead people, Haru."

His dark blue eyes narrowed and the tremble in her chest

dropped to her belly. She slipped back into the bath until only her head was exposed. The water lapped her chin.

"I'm sorry. I . . . never . . ."

Haru had restoppered the oil and was gathering up Sekmé's mist-sogged fatigues from where she'd dropped them on the wet tile floor.

"I—I can speak to the master baker," she stammered. "Maybe I can get you into the kitchen."

"As you wish, mistress," he said stiffly.

"No, no . . . as *you* wish. Your—your hands were made for kneading dough."

He glanced at her once—a curious, unsure expression—then left the bath chamber.

Sekmé closed her eyes, and without warning, her mind flashed on the hands of the Tel-mari refugee who had repaired her rifle. It was as though she was allowing him to share her bath with her and she shook her head sharply to dispel this distasteful image.

"I need rest," she muttered, "months of it."

Too bad she had a banquet to attend. Still, she had time for a quick nap and it was rude for the guest of honor to show up early.

CHAPTER 6

THE BANQUET

From the head of the stairs, Atto watched the arrival of the young officers. It was dark now, a velvety black night full of stars. The crescent moon had risen with its closer, considerably smaller oblong moonlet—the Calf—crossing its curve in a formation known as the Drawn Bow. In the formal garden, tiny lights winked in the fruit trees, a special touch Hatula had devised for her daughter.

"She loves little lights," she'd said. "Always has. Candle flames, oilstones—a single lamp on the balcony outside her window could ease her fussing when she was a baby and put her to sleep."

Atto sighed and sipped his flute of honey liquor. Legally, he remained Sekmé's uncle but, unofficially, and for some years, he'd functioned as a stepfather. What was one more when he was already father to fifteen? Still, he needed to think things through. In the five years since Sekmé's last leave, Atto had seen his circumstances change, subtly at first, but undeniably.

Three balloon-tired transport vehicles, their canvas roofs folded back, bounced up the drive and disgorged a mob of boisterous young men in brown, half of them already "bee-bit and besotted." Laughing, they picked themselves up and trooped up the stairs. Bahé came running out of the reception hall and brushed past his father.

"I thought you dune rats had crashed in the desert and were spending the night humping wau-wehs or something!"

"We, ah, urp! We were delayed."

One of the officers staggered over to a bush and, rather elegantly, with a look of poetic melancholy, vomited.

"So I see," Bahé said. "Now, get inside, you miserable bastards. Sekmé's going to set the place on fire if this thing doesn't start soon."

They reeled into the reception hall. Most of them completely ignored Atto, although a few of the less inebriated said, "Hello, sir," as they passed and even saluted awkwardly in spite of the fact Atto had never served in any military capacity other than hand-to-hand trainer to the cadets, officially a civilian post.

Once Bahé and his colleagues were safely inside, Atto returned his contemplation to the garden just as a low, dark government vehicle purred up to the stair. Its hatch door lifted up like the wing of a beetle—Atto heard the soft sigh of the vehicle's air-chill system—and Dand Ubit, the royal household secretary, climbed out.

Atto nodded as the short, bull-bodied official teetered delicately up the stairs on abnormally tiny feet, an inconvenient, but hardly debilitating, birth defect. Some junior officials mistook this peculiarity as sign of a weak, easily malleable disposition, but Atto, a district representative in the Common Council, knew better. Dand Ubit was a viper.

"God protect you, Secretary."

"Atto. Good to see you." The secretary's voice, as usual, hummed at a dispassionate monotone.

"What brings the household 'underking' to a private party in the holdings?" Atto took another sip of his drink. "I thought you disliked military functions."

"Special circumstances," Dand Ubit hummed. "We need to speak privately, Atto."

"Then a turn in the garden is in order." Atto pulled a small

parchment bag of green selt kernels from his pocket. "Sometimes I like to give the oryx a little treat. It's very relaxing."

Dand Ubit grunted enigmatically and they descended the stair into the twinkling garden. Atto led the way across the grass and almost immediately two white oryx trotted up for a palmful of crunchy kernels. The two men were alone and the sounds of celebration in the brightly lit house, although close, seemed worlds away.

"Your niece is a very aggressive and thorough officer, Atto."

"Thank you, Secretary."

A hornless juvenile gamboled up and nuzzled Atto's buttock. He gave it some kernels.

"And remarkably fortunate in battle," Dand Ubit continued. "All the more remarkable when you consider her gender."

Atto didn't reply. The secretary was circling his point, but would strike soon.

"If her career continues on this same course, I'd be willing to wager she'll make field general before she's thirty and might crack into High Command soon after that."

Dand Ubit gestured for some of the kernels himself. Atto obliged, and he gave them to a pregnant female and stroked her head.

"In fact, Atto, given time, Sekmé could eradicate the opposition in Tel-mari."

Atto chuckled gently.

"My, my, Secretary! You've just cast my niece in the role of Deliverer, the Bringer of the Golden Age!"

Dand Ubit's calm did not change and he continued to feed the pregnant oryx, but Atto knew something was not right.

"Do you understand the true nature of the Great Division?" the secretary asked quietly.

"It's the separation of good and evil."

"There's more to it."

"Well, of course, but I was unaware you desired a sectarian

debate, Secretary." Atto smiled. "Had I known, I would have brushed up on my knowledge of the Book of All Things."

"Don't make light of it," Dand Ubit said without even a trace of irony. "This is very serious."

He gave the oryx a pat and she trotted away. There was enough reflected light from the house and the twinkling trees to illuminate her round white belly long after her black legs melted into the shadows.

"The Great Division's true nature is struggle," the secretary said. "All of life, all of existence, is a struggle between that which would preserve and that which would destroy, although it's not always clear which is which. That which preserves one thing, annihilates another. As long as the essential balance is maintained, life goes on."

"I don't see what this has to do with Sekmé."

"Don't you? There is a finite amount of evil in the world, Atto. When times seem especially bad, it's because we are unable to understand the real purpose of much we believe is evil. Something painful may, in actuality, be necessary to reachieve balance. Something we think evil may, in fact, be good."

Atto was getting impatient. Dand Ubit's tone reminded him of his boyhood tutor's, a slow lilt appropriate for addressing children, but irritating and frankly disrespectful when used with an adult.

"Conversely," the secretary continued, "something we think good may actually be evil."

"You think Sekmé is evil, Secretary?"

Dand Ubit raised his brows as if unwilling to commit to an assessment of Atto's niece one way or the other.

"Who can see such things? However, the king received a disturbing prophecy the other day."

"Really? I didn't think Roon consulted fortune-tellers."

"This one is more than a fortune-teller." Dand frowned. "Wepanu's a seer and he predicted one of our soldiers—a 'hound from our own tribe'—would put an end to our sacred mission, changing our world forever."

"And that's supposed to be Sekmé?" Atto scoffed. "Don't tell me you read something *specific* in that charlatan's pious rubbish?"

"Not at first, but I've done some calculations. Imagine, for a moment, what would happen if your niece decimated an entire generation of would-be insurgents."

"You're joking—"

"It's already begun. The figures from the Hives massacre are in. At first we assumed the low trickle of refugees out of Eshna represented Tel-mari stubbornness, a will to remain in spite of hopeless odds, but further research proved us wrong. Central Eshna is virtually empty—a ghost town—the result of a single day's activity. Magnify that over your niece's career . . . H'm, she's twenty-four now. She could serve another thirty years or more if she's lucky."

"Secretary, please!" Atto said irritably, tossing the remainder of his kernels in the grass. A mother teal and her babies, hidden in the shadow of a hedge until that moment, scooted out and rapidly pecked up the windfall before the oryx got to it. "The Tel-mari breed like rats. We'll never run out of insurgents—or are you suggesting she pick off a few of *our* boys to keep the scales even?"

"You know as well as I do, Atto, the higher the casualties, the greater the resistance, the more people become insurgents rather than workers. Naturally, the greater the resistance, the greater the response, the higher the casualties on both sides, and so on." Dand Ubit sighed. "It's true there are more Tel-mari than Maurheti, but, eventually, this kind of escalation takes a toll."

Atto was silent. A war of attrition.

"The Eternal Conflict is about balance, Atto. Without balance, we lose everything, in particular that conveniently cheap Tel-mari labor force in the occupied districts. What, then, would happen to these beautiful holdings of yours? Excuse me, your niece's?"

That was nasty. Atto could not control a shudder.

"We depend on this war, Atto. It supports our life."

Dand Ubit's moon-shaped face and heavy-lidded eyes turned up toward Atto.

"Your niece is deadly. For all of us."

"Assuming what you say is true," Atto replied, a little clipped, "what can we possibly do about it?"

"Oh, we've had to curb this kind of thing before." Dand Ubit shrugged. "It's part of the good that masquerades as evil."

"Indeed? Who?"

"Your brother, of course."

This was the first Atto had heard of it, and the mix of emotions that came over him effectively choked off all response and left him blank. He didn't know whether to be furious . . . or grateful.

"Why are you telling me this?" Atto whispered. "I'm kin. Aren't you betraying your interests?"

"I don't think so," Dand said with a small smile, like a scar on a summer melon. "I believe you're exactly the man to share such a confidence with."

"I'm insulted, Secretary."

"Perhaps—" Dand Ubit girded up his heavy loins and stepped carefully back across the grass to the idling vehicle. "—but only a little."

Atto waited for the vehicle to leave—and his anger to cool—before he went into the banquet. It took a long time. When he finally arrived, the rugs were lined with plates and platters piled high with the ruins of the meal. Several decanters of honey liquor had spilled and the hunting hounds, inexplicably freed from their kennels behind the mews, were licking up the sticky amber fluid and trying, halfheartedly, to initiate fights or disoriented mating. Atto groaned. The beasts would be sick for days, cruelly thirsty, and completely useless to hunt with.

In the middle of the room, a couple dozen officers, unbuttoned in more ways than one, linked arms and danced riotously over one another's feet, voices raised high in six different keys of

four different songs. Meanwhile, Sekmé, arm resting across her brother's shoulders, lounged in the corner and listened as other young men from the camp outside Eshna related to their base-bound colleagues the story of her fight with Lokar.

". . . then Lokar, seething like a sow in heat—"

"Ooh! Slander on a poor piggy!"

"—leaps up with his knife and flings it at the commander's back."

"What a cowardly thing to do!"

"And a serious military crime," Bahé added between monstrous bites of glazed oryx liver, "grounds for court-martial and twenty years' imprisonment."

"Oh, but the worst, or best depending on your point of view," the storyteller continued after a gulp of liquor, "is that our slippery-slick commander here—"

"Slippery!" Sekmé cried in false indignation to the great amusement of the men. The word had recently taken on a salacious meaning in the camp brothel. "I'm not slippery!" She lowered her voice suggestively. "I'm positively slimy."

Their mirth doubled. Sekmé's celibacy was well known and the source of considerable confusion and dark rumors. The commander herself egged on the jokes as a way of countering this poison.

"Anyway, our *agile* commander drops to the mud and zing! The knife bites the general in the hip."

The heretofore uninitiated "oohed!" and gave each other knowing sideways glances.

"Precisely." The storyteller nodded. "Lokar was a dead man, but damned if he didn't trick the infirmary guard and get away."

"May he rot in the bog!" Bahé said.

"Hear, hear!" The others clicked their glasses together before a communal shot.

Atto watched his niece closely. He knew her as well as anyone and could see that, in spite of her disheveled camaraderie,

she was cold sober. The plate of food at her side was untouched and the arm around Set was tense as if to prevent his escape. She was not enjoying herself.

Weird lassie, Atto thought. No one had to tell him she was dangerous. He'd known it for years, ever since he'd begun teaching her at the age of twelve the fine arts of self-defense and she'd broken his wrist the very first lesson.

He looked at Set, amazed for the millionth time by how effectively the young man simulated sighted behavior. Set looked from speaker to speaker, leading with a very natural swiveling of his artificial eyes, and widened and blinked his lids at appropriate moments.

Atto did not believe Set's blindness was the fallout of chemical warfare. Contrary to all sense, even his own, he blamed Sekmé and it had led him to be even more demonstrably affectionate to his niece than necessary.

He knew this absurd belief stemmed from the fact that his wife, after bearing fifteen healthy sons, bled to death while delivering a stillborn sixteenth child, a daughter. He cursed that hapless child and, when Set was born, translated his own misfortune into the conclusion that Sekmé, by being a girl and born first, had somehow sucked the life force from Hatula's womb so that all she could bear was a sightless son . . . and nothing since.

Now Atto looked at Bahé and watched his overweight son's body shake as he laughed at some puerile soldier's joke. Untried, practically unweaned, this was *his* firstborn. What were *his* prospects, military or otherwise? If the fool got himself killed, which was very likely, it was very *un*likely he'd leave proper instructions for a fair division of the holdings among his fourteen brothers.

Sekmé and Set don't have that problem, Atto thought as he returned his attention to them. There are only two of them.

His brother had been generous, giving him holdings as rich and desirable as his own, but split fourteen ways, how rich could it be?

Back on the rugs, Hatula, hair loose and wet at her temples with sweat, had joined the young men's dance. She whooped and stomped with gusto, breasts hopping happily in her gaudy gauze, wrinkled cheeks and hands in stark and primitively humorous contrast to the smooth young flesh around her. The men called her Boopoo and other baby names and flirted outrageously, harmlessly, with Atto's second wife.

No replacement for the first, but Atto had never meant her to be. Of course, he was fond of her and she was practically seismic in bed, the hungriest woman he'd ever met, but he hadn't married her for love.

Atto wasn't angry with Dand Ubit for tacitly giving royal sanction to opinions and schemes he'd already held for years. Not at all. He was furious that deformed runt had seen so far into his heart. It was like breaking bread with a tapeworm: it fed the secretary's power over him.

The dancers tired and began calling for Set to regale them with a heroic poem. After the requisite show of resistance, Set brought out the triangular-bellied thetl he'd hidden behind him, ambled casually to the center of the rugs, sat splay-kneed with the soles of his bare feet touching, cradled the instrument in this natural bowl, and tuned the three strings while the room grew quiet.

He thought a moment, then slammed into the fast, hard opening chords of "Andalla's Feast," a piece about an ancient Maurheti hero who rode his troops into Tel-mari and destroyed a vast enemy contingent who had killed hundreds of Maurheti women and children and were roasting and eating the corpses.

The men loved it and joined in the alliterative, repetitive choruses, but Atto wondered why Set had chosen such a ghoulish saga for an after-supper serenade. Sekmé's expression was strange, as if she was caught between hysterics and sobs and couldn't sound either. Set's face looked odd, too. Possessed. He no longer tried to imitate sightedness and his blind stare drifted to the second-story gallery above the hall.

"The jo were the singers
They danced around the feast
'Your meat will be your poison
And your victory defeat' . . ."

Atto saw Sekmé excuse herself, yawning as though she was too tired to prolong the fun further, and slip away into the inner shadows of the house. She carried her back and shoulders very straight, as tight as a dress drill for the king.

Atto picked up a half-empty decanter of honey liquor. Something, perhaps a bite of flash-fried eel, floated in it like a dead roach. Atto didn't care. He tipped the decanter to his lips and drained it.

Two hours later when the house was finally quiet, Sekmé was still weeping into the pillows in her darkened bedchamber. Even so, she heard Set tiptoe in and sit down beside her. At times, her hearing was almost as good as his.

"I'm so sorry!" he whispered, stroking her back. "I have no idea why I chose 'Andalla's Feast.' I must be terribly perverse."

"N-no," Sekmé sniffled. "God chose it, not you."

"But, why? You're a faithful servant. Why make the pains of war worse for you?"

Sekmé shook her head and rolled over on her back.

"I don't know, Set. Everything feels wrong."

"It's your grief for your men."

"No—God, I wish I *could* grieve!—but someone, an Eshna refugee, would you believe, asked me something very strange." She sat up. "He asked me what it would be like to live without the fight, without the war between Maurhet and Tel-mari."

Set, to her unease, said nothing.

"It's heretical, isn't it?" she asked. "Just like a Tel-mari to cook up such an idea."

Again, Set was silent. Sekmé put her hands on his face.

"What are you thinking? Please. Tell me."

"Nothing," Set said, and she knew he was lying. "Yes. It's a heresy."

"But, how do *you* feel about it?"

"I'm more concerned about Moom and our uncle."

"Really? Why?"

"I don't think he loves her."

Sekmé dropped her hands in her lap.

"What makes you say that?"

"I don't know. It's just a feeling I get when they're together, but it's a strong one."

"You've always been the sensitive one, Set."

"I could be wrong, too, but . . ." He felt down her arms for her hands and squeezed them. "Be careful, Sekmé."

Sekmé returned the squeeze then lifted his hands to her lips and kissed them.

"And now—" Set grinned. "—I've brought someone to see you."

He clicked his tongue twice and Haru's powerful bulk appeared in the moonlight on the balcony.

"But, I don't need anything," Sekmé said, puzzled and, privately, alarmed.

"Maybe you do," Set said. He kissed her ear and melted away into the dark.

The servant shifted nervously and rubbed his thumbs together.

"Do you—do you have a problem, Haru?"

"Actually, yes, mistress. I hope a small one."

Haru came into the room. He wore only his sleeping wrap around his waist. His enormous chest was bare.

Damn, he's big! Sekmé thought, and her agitation increased—and changed color.

"You were rude to me this afternoon, Mistress Sekmé," he said, the first time he'd openly used her name.

"Yes, and I'm still sorry."

"You needn't be," Haru sighed. "I was flattered, too."

Sekmé swallowed hard and nervously tugged her lower lip as

Haru approached and sank slowly onto the bed at her side. Gently, his power kept in check, he took her hands and rested them on his chest. His skin was very smooth and cool as if he'd just bathed. He smiled.

"You'll have to be my teacher in this," Sekmé whispered as she trailed her shaky fingertips down his chest and stomach to the sleeping wrap.

"There aren't any teachers, Sekmé. Only students."

Atto rolled heavily off Hatula's wet body and groaned. Her answering sigh relieved him. She was finally sated.

"You're a whore," he said, and she giggled.

"Best in Maurhet." She pinched his groin.

"Yow!"

"No regrets, Atto?"

He looked at her.

"What do you mean?"

"That you married me."

"Absolutely not!" He drew her close and gave her a long, twisting kiss. "You're the finest woman in the world."

"Thank you."

"You're welcome."

They lay silent a moment letting the desert breeze through the open window dry their bodies, then Hatula got up and closed the shutters. The breeze was cold.

"Atto, you believe there should be no secrets between husband and wife, don't you?"

"Naturally. It's a great balm to the soul to have a partner one can share everything with."

"I'm glad you think so," she said, pulling back the tangled hair from her face, "because I have a secret I think you should hear."

Atto propped himself up on his elbows.

"What is it?"

"Sekmé and Set . . . they're twins."

Atto tensed.

"You're not serious."

"I am."

"How can that be? I was there when Sekmé was born. She was a single birth."

Hatula carefully began to desnarl her locks with her long painted nails.

"You left too soon," she said.

"I was there a month! Long enough for the entire Firstborn Celebration!"

"But not long enough," she said. "I was still pregnant. Set was born three days after you left."

Atto was on his feet now.

"That's absurd! The birth records—"

"False," Hatula said with inappropriate levity. "Set was very small when he was born. We hid him for a year and he looked like a normal, if large, newborn when he was presented." She laughed hollowly. "I was pretty heavy in those days. I *always* looked pregnant. People accepted our story."

"Our?"

"Osmir is dead, Atto, not forgotten."

"My brother *knew*?"

"Of course. He was their father. He wanted their lives to be as normal as possible."

She crossed the wau-weh skin rug, slid her arms around his waist, and rested her head on his broad chest, so like his long-dead brother's.

"You must admit, my love, they *are* splendid children."

Yes, they were, and he kissed her brow to avoid saying more. All he could think of was some obscure lines in the apocryphal Book of the End Time:

The Dark One's Captain will be shadowed by the mistimed parting of its double, a misbegotten, unholy twin. A birth that is the echo to the Knell of Dissolution. Know this as a sign of the End.

★　★　★

Deep in a wadi of the Hills of Whispers, Wepanu ul-Bahf
threw another branch of thornwood on his fire, yawned, and
scratched his belly. The wau-wehs in the cliffs around him had
been whining all night, their voices tripling with echoes, and
he couldn't sleep.

Something walks the dunes, he thought.

As if cued by this observation, the howling abruptly stopped
and a cloaked and hooded stranger appeared in the orange light
of the fire. For an instant, it seemed that the flame actually
burned around him. The stranger raised a hand in greeting.

"God's blessing on you, friend," he said in a profoundly deep
voice. Wepanu felt it vibrate in his hips.

"And on you," he responded. "Come. Share the fire and
some meat before you continue on your journey."

"I will share your fire," the hooded man said as he settled
easily onto the sand, "but I will not eat."

Wepanu's skin tingled and he caught his breath as the stranger
drew back his hood. His face was as beautiful as a young woman's and seemed to glow from within. He was a walker, one
of the rare jo who took on the appearance of flesh to interact
with people who normally couldn't see them. Their prophecies
were invariably darker and more far-reaching than those of ordinary jo.

"A sleepless night," the stranger said. "God moves forward
and the men of flesh misunderstand."

"That is the Great Truth," Wepanu said evenly, but his
mouth was dry.

"What was untouched has been touched."

"I rejoice," Wepanu said.

"As do we," said the beautiful man, "but the men of flesh
will not. There will be death."

"I grieve."

"Grief is a gift, my friend. Your heart is wise."

Wepanu lowered his head. He was unaccustomed to such tribute.

"I am a small soul whom God has seen fit to fill," he said. "That is all."

"It is enough."

The wau-wehs suddenly resumed howling and Wepanu looked up. His guest was gone.

CHAPTER 7

THE HUNT

Sekmé reassigned Haru to the kitchen as the new sous-chef and, to avoid upsetting the master baker, a touchy woman who considered herself an artist, made him the pastry cook as well, a less senior position. The morning flat-cakes and evening sweets improved dramatically.

She also took him along two days later when she, Set, and Bahé went on a morning hunt for red-chested bitterns in the holdings' backlands.

Set led them. Dressed like the others in bright scarlet hunting blouse and trousers, he picked his way carefully through the forest and into the thickets around the largest of the backlands' artificial lakes.

"Your brother is remarkable," Haru whispered as he followed Sekmé. Only she and Bahé were armed with the long, slim, flexible bows favored for bird hunting. Haru was willing to butcher and skin, but not to commit the initial kill.

"Most people don't even realize he's blind," Sekmé whispered back. "He's like an animal himself, a nocturnal one. You should have seen the look on his face when I explained we wear scarlet only to warn other hunters, that most animals are color-blind. He thought about it for days, even wrote a poem . . ."

Set slowed his pace, so Sekmé slipped the bow from her

shoulder and quietly extracted an arrow from her quiver. It was fletched with dark blue teal feathers, her personal color. Bahé followed suit. His arrows were fletched in white.

"How about a bow for family weapon?" he whispered. "Is that ever done?"

"It has been," Sekmé said as she tested the bowstring, "but you probably should choose a firing weapon, a rifle of some kind. It'd be easier for your descendants to modify."

Bahé nodded gravely. He was a thoughtful man and Sekmé liked him in spite of his occasional lapses in common sense. All he really needed was to be taken seriously. Too bad his father didn't.

"What do you think of the Bezel 917?" he asked.

Sekmé screwed up her face in critical uncertainty.

"Nice weapon, accurate even at long range, but it has a terrible kick after firing. I've seen it knock back men as big as Haru. Not good if you want to get off a second shot before the enemy fires at you."

They were now close to the lake, and the low morning haze still clung to the surface of the water and smelled faintly fishy. Set stopped, his back straight but not rigid, as if he were a dancer preparing to dash onstage. He lifted his hands from his sides, and Sekmé, then Bahé, raised their bows, aiming at a point well above Set's head.

Set brought his hands together with a loud smack and two bitterns, bright red bellies identifying them as males, bolted nearly straight up out of the reeds just ahead of him. They squawked and cried anxiously, heavy wings at first beating laboriously to gain speed, then fluidly to gain height, long legs trailing behind after kicking away the mud.

Bahé released his arrow first, and after racing to within an arm's length of the nearest bird, it dropped.

"Damn! My aim was low."

Sekmé did not comment. Her arrow flew up out over the

lake in the wake of the other bird, who already seemed to have picked up enough speed to escape. However, Sekmé's aim—and more serious draw on the bow—sent the arrow on and it skewered the bittern's long neck. The bird writhed briefly, its head whipping violently from side to side, then went limp and plummeted into the mist-coated lake. They heard, rather than saw, the splash.

"Nice shot!" Bahé cried.

"I'm glad you think so," Sekmé said. "Now, fetch."

Bahé rounded on her in disbelief.

"Who, me?"

"Yes, you."

"But, the water's freezing, Sekmé! Not to mention filthy! Fetch your own damned bird!"

"I'm not the one who put the hounds out of commission," Sekmé countered. "The least you can do is perform their function."

"That elixir always works when I have a hangover!" Bahé's voice began to bend into a whine.

"Well, contrary to what you might have heard, a hound is not the same as a man. Now *fetch*!"

Her soft young cousin, appropriately shamed, put up no more resistance. Grumbling loudly, he stomped and crashed through the reeds in his heavy boots and marched into the lake. His curses doubled in color as the water lapped its way up his trousers.

"You're very hard on him, Sekmé," Haru said, putting his arm around her waist.

"He doesn't have to do a thing I say, Haru. We're both on leave in Maurhet. This little exercise is good for him. He knows as well as I do that he could be transferred to Tel-mari at any time."

Set came back through the brush.

"Bahé huffs and puffs like a wounded grampus, but his stroke is good." He tipped his head then pointed. "There's another

bittern in the brush, somewhere over there, but it's a female. She's clicking to some hatchlings."

"We'll let them be," Sekmé said. "We have to protect the offspring or there will be no more bitterns for future hunts."

"What if we didn't hunt them at all?" Set murmured, but Sekmé didn't hear him. She and Haru were kissing. She broke away with a gasp.

"Bahé's coming back," she said.

"So? What are we hiding from?"

"Gossip."

"You've never cared about gossip," Set said.

"That's because I've never done anything to gossip about," Sekmé replied. "By the way, when do you recite for the king?"

Set shrugged.

"Who can fathom the caprices of royalty?" he asked. "I've been summoned but not given a specific day. It could be tomorrow, a month from now, a year. It's not for the lowly poet to know."

At these words, they heard a distant crack, as if one of the large trees had suddenly lost a branch, and Sekmé snapped her head back sharply, staggered, and nearly fell. Her hand went to her right ear, which felt on fire, and became coated with blood. Set was at her side instantly, feeling about for the hurt.

"Shit, Set! Don't poke it!" she cried.

Bahé, who had been slogging back soaking wet through the reeds, the bittern's neck in his fist so the bird's body swung heavily at his hip and knee, dropped his burden and dashed as quickly as waterlogged clothing and extra weight allowed to where Haru was already stanching Sekmé's bleeding ear with moss and Set was slowly circling them, palms up, head back, nostrils quivering as if he could somehow divine the source of this attack.

"What happened?"

"Don't drip on me, Bahé," Sekmé said irritably. "I've been shot."

Bahé bent over her anyway to see the wound.

"Damn! That was close!" He looked at Haru. "Do you think it was another hunter?"

"I was about to ask *you* that."

"No," Set said, still sniffing. "It was a strange sound. Deeper than a shot from a bird rifle and too metallic, or, well, ring-y . . ."

"Ring-y?" Sekmé blinked curiously at her blind but sensitive brother.

"It wasn't a game rifle, I mean," Set said. "I don't think it was a hunting weapon at all and whoever fired it was a long ways away."

"And still got you," Bahé said, "if that was the intent."

"We need to get back to the house so you can be treated properly," Haru said.

"It's nothing, Haru, just a bloody earlobe, not an eye and— Hey! What are you doing? Put me down! I can walk."

"I know. I *want* to carry you."

"You're a fool," Sekmé grumbled. "A big, beautiful fool, but a fool nevertheless."

"I still think it sounded ring-y," Set said as he trotted along in the wake of Haru's long swift strides.

"Don't forget the bittern, Bahé!" Sekmé called out over her lover's shoulder.

"Kiss my ass!" Bahé cried back, but he still retrieved the dead bird.

Outside the holdings beyond the farthest limit of the backlands, Lokar struggled to get his head and shoulders out of the dune he'd fallen in when the kick from his stolen Bezel 917 knocked him off the holdings' wall. When he finally freed himself, he sneezed and spat to get the sand out of his nose and off his tongue. He already knew, having seen a quick image of the results through the rifle's televiewer a nanosecond before his fall, that he had missed—by a hair.

"May she burn in a slow fire for all eternity!" he snarled.

"My sentiments exactly," came a strange, smooth voice above him.

He rubbed the sand from his yellow eyes. A dark hooded and muffled man on an onager loomed over him with a game rifle aimed at his head. Lokar wanted to see the man's eyes to get a clue what he was dealing with, but they were in shadow.

"You're the long-faced, long-nosed, long-missing Lokar, aren't you?" the man asked.

Lokar snorted.

"You're a mess," the rider said. "Ragged. Filthy. I'll bet you haven't eaten properly in days. Not much of an assassin."

"Why should you care?" Lokar sneered. "Sounds as if her death would make you happy. Does it matter who achieves it?"

"It matters that he's successful," said the rider, "and a weakened man concerned about his own belly is less likely to succeed." The rider tipped up the rifle and relaxed a bit in his saddle. "I can make it easier for you, but you must promise me something."

"What's that?"

"That you don't do the deed in Maurhet. There mustn't be the slightest hint that one of her own people is responsible. You must kill her in Tel-mari with a Tel-mari weapon."

Lokar hacked some sand mud onto the dune.

"Forget it! I'm not going back to that stinking cesspit."

"Would ten thousand paners and all your supplies make the place more attractive?"

Lokar considered a moment and scratched his long thighs meditatively.

"Fifteen . . . and new papers and a safe haven for afterward."

"Sensible. A man who plans for his retirement."

"I just don't want to be 'retired' early."

"Agreed."

Lokar got to his feet and retrieved his Bezel 917, currently useless now that its inner works were caked with sand. He shielded his eyes and studied his anonymous new patron.

"I don't expect you to tell me who you are," he said, "but I'd feel more secure in my work if I had some hint as to where you get your authority."

The rider laughed, a deep, belly mirth that, in a way, answered Lokar's question without words.

"My authority comes from very high and from very near," the man said. "That's all you need to know." He unbuckled a saddlebag, removed a small but heavy pouch, and tossed it to Lokar. Its contents clinked in the fugitive's hands.

"That's five hundred paners," the rider said. "Clean yourself up and meet me in the Grand South Wadi in ten days. We'll talk again then."

"You'll bring the money?"

This time, the rider's laugh sounded harsh and sardonic.

"I'll bring *some* of the money," he said. "I'm not about to be gulled by such a miserable excuse for manhood as yourself." He reined up the onager's head and spurred its side. "However, I do like your style, Lokar. You're reptilian."

The rider trotted off into the expanding midmorning light.

CHAPTER 8

AN ACCIDENT

Because Atto was supervising his own holdings that day, Bahé, feeling a personal affront in this attack on his favorite cousin, took it upon himself to round up his brothers—who were still at Sekmé's house enjoying her hospitality and, like the hounds, nursing alcohol-induced discomforts—and organize a search party for the sniper.

They found nothing. By the time they'd scoured the backlands on their onagers and headed through the gate to search along the outer perimeter, a desert wind had come up, erasing all tracks and traces in the sand that collected at the foot of the wall.

When Atto came home that evening and heard what had happened, he was furious and ready to search the holdings himself, alone, in the dark, until Hatula talked him out of it.

"I'm sure he's gone now," she said, climbing into his lap with something sweet and sticky on a plate. "Here, this will loosen those angry wrinkles in your brow. I wish I'd known that great big young man was a culinary wizard when I purchased his contract. I wouldn't have wasted him in the bath chambers." She sighed. "He's a wonderful excuse to drop by the pantry for a midday snack."

"Don't be a nuisance, Moom." Sekmé grinned from her reclining position on a pile of cushions. She held a cloth soaked in cold vinegar to her ear. "He's working."

"I know! I *adore* watching those hands and arms as he works the dough, don't you?"

"I don't go into the kitchen."

Hatula clicked her tongue.

"What am I going to do with you, Sekmé? Twenty-four years old and yet to have a man."

Sekmé considered enlightening her, but didn't. Haru was probably right that there was no reason to hide their relationship, but something inside shook Sekmé every time she thought about letting her mother or uncle know, and her courage failed her, a new and disturbing experience for the Iron Virgin who, secretly, was neither iron nor a virgin. Not anymore.

So she and Haru kept their love hidden from all but Set. Most nights, Haru stayed late to inspect the kitchen and be sure all was in order, then crept up the east stair to Sekmé's bedchamber where they wrestled joyfully until they fell asleep in a sweaty tangle. In the morning, Set, always an early riser, woke them so Haru could make his getaway, then dozed or chatted with Sekmé side by side as they had as children, except that Set brought his vulpé pelt to finger as they talked. He carried it with him, in hand or pocket, virtually everywhere.

"You've changed me," Sekmé said to Haru one evening after riding her muscular mount into unexpectedly giddy territory. Good sex could also be funny sex.

"In what way?"

"I've always thought of my men as comrades, brothers in a way. Fellow mud rats. All of us doing the necessary dirty work for Maurhet. Their being *men* was almost secondary. Do you understand?"

Haru laughed. "Not really."

"It's not that I didn't lust after some of them, I did, or that I begrudged them their trips to the brothels, I didn't, but I think I underestimated their loneliness, probably because I underestimated my own."

She gazed wistfully into his dark blue eyes.

"They're a long way from home, Haru. A long way from their families, their lovers. It's quite a sacrifice."

"But a noble one."

"I wonder."

"Don't let High Command hear you say that."

"They won't." She threw her leg over his hips. "High Command doesn't fill my bed as beautifully as you do. They deserve my duty, not my confession."

They became so familiar that they could ignore each other during the day with little strain. They hunted three more times with Bahé and the recuperated hounds before he returned to his father's holdings with his brothers. The last thing Bahé said to Set before he left—which was dutifully reported to Sekmé—was, "Perhaps we're wrong about our commander. Maybe we should bring her a lady from the Hidden Garden."

"They're expensive," Set said with perfectly counterfeited seriousness.

"I know, but they're the cleanest and the best. That's what Sekmé deserves."

"Bahé, I think we should let my sister choose her own partner if and when she desires one."

Bahé studied his boots and pouted, which made him look a lot like an unhappy little boy whose candy had been stolen.

"You're right, of course," he said. "As always."

Things carried on for Sekmé, days of oasis squiredom, evenings of erotic education, until the beginning of the second month of her leave when, near dawn, not long before Set's appearance, she woke up on her own with severe cramps and muscle spasms in her back and groin.

At first, she didn't wake Haru. Either she'd eaten something that had sat too long in the heat, or her sporadic moon cycle, usually sparse and barely noticeable, had decided to give her a nasty turn for once to remind her that the patterns of biology applied to her as well as other women.

However, when she started to hemorrhage all over the bed-clothes, she shook Haru.

"Get Set," she said, but at that moment, her brother came through the window.

"What's going on?" he whispered.

"She's bleeding," Haru said.

"Go back to the kitchen," Sekmé told him as a new, sharper spasm shot through her abdomen and she felt nauseous. "Set . . . get Moom."

"I'm not leaving you like this," Haru said.

She put her hand over his mouth.

"You have to, Haru. I'll be all right. Please."

"But—"

"Please." She was feeling faint now. "I know what I'm saying."

Reluctantly, Haru slipped out of the room, Set following to fetch Hatula.

Her masses of hair as tangled as thorntree branches after a dust storm, Hatula looked at the blood on the bed and her daughter's pallor and sent Set to the servants' quarters to bring the holdings' doctor, Revered Ando.

Ando, a fit, wiry older man with a badly sunburned face, arrived with his pouch of tools and wearing only a loin wrap. He'd been asleep.

"Uh-huh." He nodded briskly when he saw Sekmé. "Something more than moon shedding, I think."

"Obviously!" Hatula raked her fingers agitatedly through her snarls. "Help her before she bleeds to death."

Ando gave Hatula an ungrateful frown. He'd practically turned himself inside out to save her sister-in-law, and everyone agreed her death was not his fault, but Hatula, and especially Atto, weren't about to forget as well as forgive.

"She's *not* going to die," he said, and got his probe and cauter-wand from his pouch. "Set? Help me. Get her legs up and hold her still. Talk to her."

Set did better than that. In his sweet, clear voice, he sang her

favorite lullaby as she screamed through the probing and scraping and cauterizing of her torn uterus.

> *"The trees in flower are not as bright*
> *The birds that fly are not as free*
> *The honey never tastes as sweet*
> *As thee, my child, as thee.*
> *A single smile as I hold you close*
> *And I'm the bird who flies so high*
> *A flower, too, that glows so bright.*
> *I taste the sweet immortal life*
> *My baby soft, my honey sweet,*
> *My flower, my bird, my tree."*

Atto and his chamber servants had joined Hatula to watch the bloody operation, but at the first scream, Ando ordered everyone except Set to leave. An hour later, the young man came out with the soiled bedclothes.

"What's happening, laddie?" Atto asked.

"She's very quiet." He'd been crying and sounded congested. "The revered says she's fine."

"I want to hear it from *him*," Hatula said. "I will not have a doctor lying to my son just to shut him up."

"But, she *is*," Set insisted. "She's relaxed now. No more knots." He lowered his head and several new tears dropped into the mess in his arms. "It hurt so much."

The doctor came out smiling.

"Your niece is one strong woman, Atto. The bleeding's stopped and she's resting comfortably. I'll bet she's up and hunting in a couple days."

"But, what caused it?" Atto asked. "Is she—does she have a disease?"

"Oh, God, no!" Ando chuckled. "She's fine. It was a spontaneous abortion."

The word hit Atto like a bolt from God's bow.

"An *abortion*?"

"Now, don't alarm yourself, Atto," Ando said. "No serious damage done. Just a tear in the uterus, easy to repair. She's a healthy young lady and should have plenty of uneventful pregnancies when she wants them. Actually, she considers this little episode a lucky accident. She told me she's not ready for an heir."

Neither are we, Atto thought darkly.

"But, Revered Doctor," he said, "I wasn't even aware she had a lover."

"Do you have a servant named Haru?"

"Yes," Hatula said. "He's our pastry chef."

"Well, I'm willing to bet he was the father." Ando tied up his pouch of instruments. "Part of the time she was delirious and kept calling his name." He laughed. "Those military women! They're a loose breed. I told her to take precautions next time, for her men's sake as well as her own."

The house was very quiet that day. The servants went about on tiptoe on threat of immediate dismissal if anyone woke the mistress.

Set sat at Sekmé's side and didn't eat, didn't move, until the sun set. Only then did he crawl across the fresh bedclothes next to his sister and put his arms around her.

"It's not fair," he whispered into her sleeping ear.

Haru went through his daily chores like a sleepwalker. No one seemed to know anything. The servants had no idea what was going on and no one asked him any specific or leading questions. Apparently, his and Sekmé's secret was still a secret.

However, by nightfall, the need to know how Sekmé was began to prey on him, especially considering no one had ordered supper and his hands were idle. He needed a pretense for going into Sekmé's room and decided that, by now, she had to have something to eat.

"All that blood," he mused. "She needs protein, but something soft, easy to digest. Something sweet . . ."

He would bake his lover a custard, which he would deliver himself, and he went into the pantry to retrieve two large, black-shelled teal eggs from their cool, ceramic crock. He smiled to himself as he turned them over in his huge hands. He'd had to handle Sekmé carefully, too. At first, her excitement had made her lovemaking violent and combative, as though she was at war with the fearful delight brought on by this unfamiliar intimacy. She treated his body as if it was a strange mountainous country to scale and conquer, and he'd leave her bedchamber covered with scratches and bruises. Still, he was a patient man, not particularly sensitive to pain, and he rode it out. Gradually, with a great deal of caressing and soft words, she began to trust him and now she shared her fears, her hopes, her misgivings. Just the other night she'd said the oddest thing.

"Haru, what if I don't live long enough to see Set in his own holdings with his own family?"

"He's a grown man, Sekmé. He'll manage even if he *is* your little brother."

"I know, but he can't always manage what's *behind* him."

A peculiar girl, but that was one of the things he liked about her. She wasn't easy to understand and that made her a challenge.

"What are you doing?"

When Haru spun around, he dropped one of the eggs and it splatted on the pantry's tile floor.

Hatula. She'd combed the snarls from her hair but had not put it up. She resembled some kind of black-maned desert cat on the prowl.

"I—I was making a custard, madam, for—for the mistress."

"That can wait," Hatula said. "I don't think she's hungry right now."

She appeared calm, but Haru could not relax. He'd seen how Hatula's lust landed easily on every male within her sight and it

made him nervous. She seemed the type to get whatever, and whomever, she wanted.

She approached him and her keen eyes did pass over him with interest.

"I should have known her little protestations of indifference were an act," she said. "You're a fine stallion."

Haru felt sick but didn't move, not even to set down the second teal egg.

"Sekmé has had a spontaneous abortion," Hatula said matter-of-factly, "and, in spite of what Revered Ando says, she could have more. I miscarried five times before she and Set were born. I believe it's because their father's genes were damaged by the chemicals he handled in the war. I think this also explains Set's blindness and Sekmé's 'accident' today."

She looked at his hands.

"Put the egg down, Haru. One broken is enough."

He hastily set the egg back in the crock. Hatula began to stroll in a small circle, at every other step inspecting her beaded slipper as if it was new—it wasn't—and she was admiring its novelty.

"Do you love my daughter, Haru?"

"Y-yes, madam. I think so."

"Think *hard*, Haru. She's not someone to toy with."

"Yes, madam."

"If *she* neglected to take precautions, *you* certainly should have remembered."

"Yes, madam. I'm sorry, madam."

"Atto says nothing, but I think he's angry. I'm not sure why since it's none of his business and he wouldn't know how to use protection if all fifteen of his sons demonstrated for him at once."

In spite of himself, Haru smiled. Hatula smiled back.

"I wish you and Sekmé had shared this with me. I want my daughter to be happy and you make her happy. Don't be so greedy with this happiness."

"I won't, madam."

Hatula stopped strolling and took his hands in hers.

"I'm glad." She kissed his knuckles—licked them. "Nice. Very, very nice . . ."

She let him go and swished out of the pantry.

"Lucky for Sekmé I have a strong sense of honor," she said as the last of her hair and silk whipped around the door.

Haru's knees nearly gave way with relief, sending his big body down into the smear of broken egg, but he took a couple of deep breaths to steady himself, cleaned up the mess, and called it a night. He retreated to his room in the servants' quarters with a pot of soft cheese and a small loaf of bread, ate all of both, prepared the list of supplies he'd have to purchase in Kemphor the next day, and went to bed.

Sometime after midnight when even the wau-wehs were asleep, five men came into Haru's bedchamber and attacked him. In complete silence, they bound and gagged him, kicked him in the kidneys, and knocked him out with a rag soaked in something acrid placed over his nose and mouth.

When he awoke hours later, he was unbound and alone . . . and stranded in a desiccated wadi somewhere in the Hills of Whispers. At his side were a large water skin and a canvas bag full of dried fruits and meats.

Perhaps it was the lingering influence of the drug, handicapping his reason so that his intuition could have full sway. No matter. He knew immediately that, bad as his situation was, Sekmé's would be worse.

Sekmé woke at midmorning, and Set, who'd heard her moan, placed his hands gently on her face. They were cool.

"Where's Haru?" she asked.

"Hiding, I think."

"I want to see him." Wincing, Sekmé pushed herself up.

"Sekmé, wait. Moom and Uncle know."

"What?"

"The Revered Ando told them."

Sekmé groaned and rubbed her temples.

"Stupid doctor . . ."

"It may be all right. Moom said she'd talk to him and I know she likes him."

"I want to see him."

"Sekmé, you're weak."

"I want to see him."

She grabbed his hand with a grip that belied her weakness and pulled him after her as she stumbled out of the room. She was woozy, but determined.

"I know Haru, Set. He'll blame himself and I can't have that."

"Do you need *me* along to tell him?"

"Please, Set. I want you with me."

"Why?"

Sekmé didn't know, but when she stumbled into the lavishly tapestried sitting room off Hatula's bedchamber and found her mother and uncle embracing, that shaky sense of alarm went off inside her chest.

"Sekmé!" Atto jumped to his feet. "You shouldn't be out of bed, lassie."

"My love, you're so pale . . ."

"Where's Haru, Moom?"

"Ah!" Atto nodded. "The young man."

"In the kitchen, I'm sure," Hatula said. "Where's he's supposed to be. Now, please, dear . . ."

Sekmé dragged Set out of the room and down the stairs, across the reception hall, and into the kitchen. The staff all but leapt to attention in instinctive reaction to their militarily trained mistress.

"Haru?" she asked.

"We've not seen him, mistress."

"He was supposed to go into Kemphor today," the master chef said, her left eye twitching with its characteristic tic. "Perhaps he got an early start."

"I see. He's due to return? . . ."

"Before dark, I think. He has some baking to finish before supper."

Sekmé looked around at the staring servants—the boy who plucked the poultry was trembling—and realized she'd frightened everyone, relatives and employees alike, for no reason. Suddenly, she felt exhausted . . . and guilty. She lifted the lid of a heavy pot simmering on the grate of the massive wood-burning terra-cotta stove. She sniffed.

"What's this?"

"Vegetable broth, mistress," the chef said. "A simple thing. Our midday meal, if we want it. Servants' food."

The woman's insecurity made Sekmé feel guiltier.

"It smells divine." She grinned at the chef. "If you and your staff can afford the loss of a scoop or two, I'd like to try it."

The chef beamed as though Roon himself had praised her for the success of a twelve-course feast.

"Of course, mistress! I'll serve you myself and bring bread as well!"

"Fine. I'll be in my bedchamber. Set, help me. All this excitement . . ."

Sekmé rested the remainder of the day and mentally rehearsed the comforting, reassuring words she would bathe her lover in when he returned with his imported spices, teas, and exotic desert honeys gathered by the Denneshur.

But darkness came and Haru did not.

"He's probably still haggling with the Denneshur," Atto joked over supper. "I don't think he's as ruthless as you are, lassie."

But Sekmé was anxious.

"What did you say to him, Moom?"

"I reminded him of his responsibility, that's all. Nothing to scare him away, I hope."

The master chef corroborated Hatula's assessment.

"I saw him return to his chamber last night, mistress. He was humming to himself."

But, as the evening passed, Atto was the first to voice a negative possibility.

"Sekmé, I know you don't want to hear this, but it wouldn't be the first time a young man ran off when faced with the harder realities of a relationship."

"He didn't run off."

"No. No, I'm sure he didn't."

"I know him, Uncle."

"Yes, you do."

Set said nothing. He stood on Sekmé's balcony listening to the distant wau-wehs, his beautiful artificial eyes turned blindly to the stars.

Sekmé flopped back wearily on her bed.

"Everything below my waist aches," she said, "even my ankles."

She rolled over and looked up at her brother. His profile, faintly lit by light from the rooms below, was as sad as she felt; his soft lips drooped.

"He didn't run off," she said.

Set shook his head.

"Then why—" She stopped, unable to finish her question. Her throat seemed to have closed in on itself. If she tried to speak now, it would hurt more than anything that had already happened.

"Am . . . I . . . being . . . punished?" she managed to gasp.

Set's lips trembled. He balled up the vulpé fur in his fist, pressed it into his cheek, and did her weeping for her.

CHAPTER 9

MERKUS

From the air, theirs looked like any other refugee cookfire. They made sure of it. The fire, built out of peat and vegetable trash, was small and smoky. They took turns cooking their meat and cabbage, ambling into the ruins as they finished, so that no more than half a dozen of them at a time clustered in the dirty glow. They wore refugees' rags, a few even veiled themselves in black like women, and they laughed and belched and discussed food and theft as though they had nothing more on their minds than the success of the present meal and the strategy for the next.

However, tonight, once they'd eaten and kicked dirt over the coals or let the rain wash it down—fire was not as sacred to them as it was to the Maurheti—they would gather in a hidden underground chamber, the only intact room of the once formidable fortress, collect their weapons, and, at last, slip out single file like a hunting pack of wau-wehs to inflict damage on their desert-born enemies.

Their leader, Merkus, did not stand out in any way from his comrades. Like them, he was dark and bearded. They were orphans, widowers, bereaved lovers, and fathers of dead children, and he, too, had suffered terrible losses. All of them had lines in their foreheads, even the sixteen-year-old, their worn hands

showed broken nails, and many were missing teeth. They were literate, as most Tel-mari were, prayed at sunset, and looked upon failure as miserable, but God's will.

Still, Merkus was different. He had the special cunning, the fatalistic bravery, and the unflinching imagination to focus their resentment and give it shape.

He also had a vision, but this was more difficult for the men to grasp or Merkus to explain since it didn't seem connected to burned buildings, twisted and useless war machines, and bodies rendered completely unrecognizable. The vision created ... puzzlement.

Merkus pulled his iron skewer from the fire and blew delicately on the charred chunk of goat meat. He was cold enough to ignore its resemblance to battle carrion, but sensitive enough to think of it every time he ate. Although he'd never admit it to his men, he hated violence and wished there was some other way to be heard, to stir his people's hopes, to punish the Maurheti.

The promise of punishment had made it easy to recruit his band. It was what they wanted.

"We'll send them to God to answer for their crimes," he'd told them, and they'd waved their fists and chanted his name until it echoed off the smooth and elegant vaults of the underground chamber. In a rare moment of ease in the midst of preparations, he'd walked slowly around those walls with an oilstone lamp, inspecting them closely. When had they been built? Who had had such skill? The stones fit together so snugly he couldn't slip a knife blade between them.

Years ago—it seemed another lifetime—before he was Merkus, he would have taken his questions to his rabam, his teacher. He would have finished his simple bowl of grmysh at the long wooden table with the other young scholars, perhaps dallied a bit afterward talking with friends or brooding over the phrases earlier students had gouged into the much-abused wood with their carving knives—anything to wile away the time, until it was the hour his rabam retired to his cell. Then he would scoop up

his notes, his translations, his careful tracings of obscure marginalia and cryptic decorations, and trot across the college's courtyard under a purple sunset to the faculty's quarters.

Many of the rabam were old men, bent over when they walked as if even then they were reading a difficult text, white beards sometimes brushing their knees. They weren't easy to approach. Their eyes had become hard, opaque with the bitterness they could not express for fear of the Maurheti field government's reprisals. They'd given up truly *feeling* the belief in God's ultimate justice that they, nevertheless, still dutifully recited. Undoubtedly, that was why the Maurheti left the college alone. Frightened old men were no threat.

But *his* rabam had been a relatively young man, only forty-three, with a slim, nervous body and gleaming large wet eyes. His emotions often got the better of him. He wept at his prayers, thundered in his lectures, and laughed heartily at the young scholars' irreverent, even profane, jokes as long as they weren't mean-spirited.

"God laughs, too," he said. "He gave us humor and He cannot give us something He Himself cannot understand."

The future Merkus loved him. Many times he made that quick trot in the purple light to see him alone in his tiny cell with its nearly flat bedroll, its battered urn of sharp, sweet bihn leaf tisane, and its piles, towers, and teetering spires of maps and scrolls and boxes heaped with no discernible order on every free inch of the worn rug. He'd sit cross-legged before his teacher, confound his own papers into the mess of others, and ask his questions.

"Was there ever a time when the Maurheti were not in our land?"

The rabam smiled slowly. He was one of the teachers who still had decent teeth, but he was missing the lower left canine, knocked out in a youthful brawl over the meaning of *chosen*.

"What have you been reading, Ahvrym, to ask such a question?"

The young man, still clean shaven at the time, blushed a deep brick red.

"W-well, I, that is . . ."

The rabam chuckled and handed him a glass of tisane.

"That explains the shadows under your eyes and the yawns in prayer. Those older texts are very difficult to decipher, especially in the young hours of the morning, and rarely loaned to underclassmen. What did you bribe old Khelash with?"

Now Ahvrym smiled.

"Three months of my supper sweets."

The rabam laughed outright. The old librarian was as wide as he was tall.

"Actually," Ahvrym said, half laughing as well, "all I wanted to see was *The Ilha-man Riku*."

The rabam's bushy black brows jumped.

"Really? I thought you preferred the battle epics and mythic travels."

Ahvrym scratched his chest and fidgeted.

"All that fighting and blood gets tiring after a while."

"That's our history, Ahvrym."

"I know, but I wanted to look at something . . ." He shrugged.

The rabam leaned forward and rested his fingertips on Ahvrym's knee.

"You're still very young, my friend," he said gently. "I understand your desire for something . . . broader. Some proof that God is indeed as great as you feel He is and that even the impossible is actually possible, but you must take care when you read those old texts. They refer to things we no longer understand in language that no longer makes sense. It's easy to misinterpret what they say."

"But, Rabam," Ahvrym said, his voice beginning to sound as anguished as he felt, "the *Riku* talks about the *arrival* of the Maurheti in Tel-mari. That must mean that, before then, they weren't here."

The rabam's passionate eyes were steady—and uncomfortably intense.

"That seems the logical conclusion," he said.

"And it says *nothing* about *our* being in Maurhet."

"That's true."

"So, if they weren't here and we weren't there . . . *then there was no war.*"

The rabam calmly turned away to draw himself another glass of tisane. He blew across it. Then, holding it delicately in both hands, he took a small, silent sip.

"At least, according to the *Riku*," he said.

"What do you mean?"

"It's a poem, Ahvrym. Long, but still a poem, and poets hear God's voice in a different way than we do."

"Are you saying it's a lie?"

"Not a lie, but it may be a fiction. Do you know the difference?"

Ahvrym shook his head.

"A lie is an untruth, pure and simple. A fiction, however, while not *real*, may still be *true*. Do you understand?"

"I'm . . . not sure."

The rabam took another sip and set down his glass.

"It's not that important. What is important is that the poet presented the *idea* of Tel-mari without war."

"Yes. He—"

"Or perhaps she."

Ahvrym gaped at him, momentarily speechless.

"Come now, Ahvrym. Women think, too."

"But, poetry?"

"Why not? Those were different times, wealthier times. We had our ladies of leisure then just as the Maurheti have now. I'll bet quite a few dabbled in the literary arts."

Ahvrym had to think about this for a while in order to get it settled securely in his mind, and that gave the rabam time to

rise and light the oilstone lamps hanging on either side of his window arch. It was dark now and a soft, misting rain had started to fall. The pale yellow lamplight picked out the thready streaks just outside the window. He closed the panes and latched them.

Ahvrym sighed.

"Well, whoever the poet was—"

The rabam grinned at him.

"—he said that before the Maurheti came, we lived in Sa'Har and he wanted to go back: 'I will rest my head in the sands of Sa'Har.' "

He looked up at his teacher.

"That's the word I've come to you about," he said. "I can't find its translation anywhere, or, at least, nothing definite."

"There's even a very long and extraordinarily heated symposium on whether it's a place or a state of mind," the rabam said, "or another name for Maurhet! After all, the desert has sand."

"What do *you* think it means?"

The rabam leaned his shoulder against one of his sturdier towers of words and crossed his arms.

"Believe it or not, Ahvrym, I don't want to know."

"Why not?"

"Because then it can be anything, limitless, a word of possibilities." His bright eyes filled with tears and Ahvrym felt the surge of affection that always rose in him whenever he witnessed his teacher overcome by passion.

The rabam stretched out his arms and smiled at the ceiling, or, rather, beyond the ceiling.

"I imagine it's a very good thing, Ahvrym. Don't you?"

Ahvrym, now Merkus, tossed aside his skewer and began to pick his teeth with his pinky nail. He heaved himself to his feet, put up his hood, and with a quick jerk of his head, indicated that it was time to go inside.

The sixteen-year-old, their scrounger and spy, skipped about

lighting the lamps. He was a little simple, but absolutely devoted to Merkus. Besides, he was only a few years younger than Merkus was when the Maurheti changed their minds about the innocuousness of the college and gel-bombed it. The rabam had died in the fire. Some said the officer responsible for that raid had sired the one responsible for the Eshna market-day attack.

Poetry again, Merkus thought. A search for symmetry where there probably isn't any.

He asked the ritual question, the one to stir their fires.

"What is our purpose?"

"To punish the Maurheti and send them to God!" his men roared back.

"And after?"

The words had slipped out of their own accord. They were not part of the ritual and the men stared back at him, blank with confusion.

"We come back and go to sleep," said the simple boy.

The others chuckled uncomfortably.

Merkus was not surprised and certainly not angry. Strife was all any of them had ever known. They literally couldn't conceive of an after.

Really, what *would* happen to them without the Maurheti? Would they become a different people? Or would they turn their inbred skills of aggression on each other once their traditional target was removed? What *was* his vision? A return to a time that may never have been, a mythic mystery from the pages of a text so old that the corners crumbled in his fingers and flew away?

"Very good, young Podhi." The men laughed as he patted the beaming sixteen-year-old's curly head. "We come back and go to sleep."

CHAPTER 10

A NEW THREAT

Once a year, sometimes twice, the Calf "touched" the full moon with its nose, a special configuration called the Suckling, which was considered auspicious and a great excuse for a party. About a month after Field General Am sent Sekmé home on leave, the moon and the Calf came up attached and the general decided to join a group of fellow officers in a Tel-mari tavern near the refugee shantytown, the New Hives, on the outskirts of Eshna.

Am was not a heavy drinker, but he enjoyed the occasional buzz a tumbler of damnation ale could provide, and soon he was singing old desert folk songs and bawdy lays while nostalgic tears fractured his vision and a pleasant, sleepy hum filled his ears with cotton and his joints with melted wax.

As was often the case on a Suckling night, it wasn't long before his comrades turned to a favorite topic: the Calf itself.

"But, gentlemen," said Heb, the portly tech com, "why waste our time arguing when it's quite possible to solve this debate once and for all?"

"How?" asked Undergeneral Farké, a dark and morose man. "Shoot it down?"

"You're not far off." Heb smiled. "With a big enough fuel charge and appropriate structural reinforcements, we could get a Needle up right next to the Calf."

"That would be one monstrous Needle," Squad Liaison Than said. He wiped some drops of damnation ale from his heavy mustache.

"And monstrously expensive," Farké snorted. "I doubt the king's council would approve such a project or the exchequer pay for it!"

"Why not?" Heb asked. "It fires the imagination!"

"Heb, we're not discussing *your* imagination," Than began, and Farké snorted again. "We're discussing Roon's. Now, the king is a proper and reasonably intelligent man but he has a rather, uh, shall we say limited vision? Any concern outside war and women and his interest flags dramatically."

"What about onagers?" Farké inserted.

"I'm not sure he considers them all that different from women," Than said languidly, and Farké released a laugh that got tangled in his nose and became yet another form of snort.

"How would the pilot survive?" Am asked, jumping into a conversation he never would have joined sober. "A pressurized cabin is fine when the air is thin, but what about when there's no air at all?"

"You don't need a pilot," Heb said brightly, obviously cheered by the presence of a new voice. "Use the right trajectory and you can shoot an unmanned Needle right over it."

"And do what?" Farké asked. "Sniff under the Calf's tail? Ask it to pose for a portrait?"

"With the right equipment, whatever we want," Heb said. "We'd finally know what that funny little moonlet really is."

"We already know," Than said. "It's a big soft wedge of sour cheese."

All the officers, except Heb, laughed heartily, and Am ordered another round.

"*I've* seen it, *you've* seen it, we've *all* seen it." Than took his new glass from the tray without even a glance at the Tel-mari server. "No matter the magnification, and I've used night instruments that could pick out the fleas on a wau-weh's ass

halfway to Tel-mari, the Calf's nothing but a big, white, pock-skinned bore. One of God's practical jokes."

"God doesn't joke," Heb said, his voice becoming more insistent, even a bit desperate. Am felt sorry for him. "Nothing that shape can be natural."

"I've been saying that about Dand Ubit for years," Farké interjected.

"Heb—" Than sipped his drink delicately to avoid rewetting his mustache. "—there's four thousand-year-old poetry about the Calf. Are you telling me the *ancients* made it?"

"Maybe."

"Oh, *really,* Heb! The ancients lived in mud brick huts and ate insects!"

"The Calf is as big as Kemphor," Am said gently, sensing his colleague's hurt. "How did they get it up there? Why? It's never done anything but float around."

"Maybe it did something once," Heb said softly, visibly deflated.

"Now, the *moon*," Than said, and rubbed his hands together. "I could understand aiming a Needle at the moon. I'll bet there's all kinds of untold mineral wealth there . . ."

"I'd be happy with a dip in one of the moon lakes," Farké said. "They say lunar water can cure everything."

"Not *your* nose, Farké." Than smirked. "That would take a moon *ocean*."

Am remembered why he didn't usually join these particular officers for libations. Still, it was better than drinking alone in a camp emptied by various parties in town. He ordered yet another round.

Time passed but it wasn't until the owner of the tavern, a squat collaborationist with a patch over his left eye—or sometimes his right—began to look so despairing of their departure that the officers became genuinely concerned about his health and stumbled out through the torn curtain that functioned as the tavern's door.

General Am eyed his companions and shook his head. How could three senior officers, disciplined servants of the Maurheti sacred cause, allow themselves to get into such miserable condition? Of course, that's when he felt the preliminary squeeze of his own abused guts.

His colleagues were piling into their balloon-tired vehicle behind the sober, grumpy-eyed driver, who, until moments before, had been snoring happily behind the wheel.

"Gen-genelmen?" Am said, only briefly puzzled by the alien gargle issuing from his throat. "A moment if you pliss. I need to, to . . ."

And he did. All over his uniform.

"Oh . . . oops," said Heb.

"Am, yer a, a . . . ," Farké began.

"Peasant," Than suggested.

"Eggs-actly."

Am tried to climb aboard with them but they shoved him away.

"No, you don't! You stink!"

"Get a, h'm, oh! A cab! Get a cab, Am."

"Yeah. Tel-mari love a bad smell."

Than pounded the driver on the shoulder with his fist.

"Ow, sir! That hurts!"

"Drive on, Subcom—"

"I'm a *full* com, sir."

"Whatever. Drive."

Am ambled back into the tavern, where the owner groaned, waved his sausage-fingered hands in the air, and cried, "Will I never be rid of you?" Therefore, the drunk general was sheltered from the sudden blast in the street that blew in all the windows and flung both men across the smoky room into the pyramid of bottles the officers had constructed on their table. Their jangling secondary explosion poorly echoed the roar of the first.

Instantly alert, if not sober, Am regained his feet and ran into the street where the officers' vehicle, and the officers, had become an orange bonfire three stories high. The intense heat

cracked the paving stones and melted the ornamental grillwork holding the tavern's swinging sign. The sign itself had vaporized.

Am retreated to the relative safety of the glass-strewn tavern. They hadn't had a vehicle bomb in two years, and drunk or not, Am knew what this explosion meant. They had a new terrorist on their hands.

Within three weeks, seven violent acts were attributed to this new threat known as Merkus—not a real name, but an old Tel-mari word that meant *hidden message*. He, or she, and his band, estimated at about twenty, planted explosives in a Maurheti supply depot, a boarding school now used as a barracks, three more officers' vehicles, and even the cockpit of a Needle undergoing routine maintenance at the South Eshna air base. Each explosion claimed soldiers' lives, and two happened in broad daylight in exposed areas right under the noses of crack teams of security officers.

One of the wounded survivors, a young man with a limited but busy imagination, said, "He must be one of those jo the goat eaters are always on about, sir. We saw nobody."

His words made their way into the refugee markets, and before long, the Tel-mari were whispering about, and swearing by, Merkus's "supernatural" powers. Widows made amulets with his name on them and sold them in the streets, children invented rhymes and songs about his band and played terrorist with stick weapons and paint-filled goat-bladder grenades, and old men claimed that Merkus had single-handedly arranged the corpse curse after the gel-bombing of the Eshna market.

Field General Am, for no other reason that he could discern than that he was the highest ranking witness to the first attack, was assigned the task of tracking Merkus down and executing him. It was a distasteful assignment, made even more distasteful when, before he could formulate any strategy, Dand Ubit visited him in his oversize hut and suggested a strategy of his own that had his superiors' stamp of approval.

"It's a bad idea," Am said. "I refuse to be part of it."

"You can't refuse." Dand Ubit rocked on his tiny heels, hands clasped behind his back so he looked even more like an egg on toothpicks.

"I certainly can." Am crossed his arms. "It's only a recommendation."

"A strong one. From very high up."

"A recommendation, nevertheless. Not an order. Commander Sekmé is a combat officer, Secretary, not an intelligence ferret."

Dand Ubit smiled weakly—patronizingly, in Am's opinion—and stopped rocking.

"You're fond of her, aren't you, Am?" His hum was especially unpleasant.

"I respect her, Secretary, and admire her ability."

"But, you do admit she's a lively and interesting young officer—I mean, surrounded as she is by nothing but men." His smile wiggled. "Surely you're not immune to her appeal, Am? A feisty young hen among the roosters and you so long away from your wife?"

In spite of his efforts to remain cold and decorous, Am's temperature rose dramatically.

"Your implications are unfair, Secretary."

"My apologies, of course, but it has been a long time, hasn't it? You've served over thirty years. Retirement is right around the corner. With your daughter a full com spec in the southern borders, you must look forward to passing on that hoary old family side arm of yours."

Am remained silent. Outside, the rain rattled on. Only a native could prefer this wretched damp to the clean, hard heat of the Maurhet desert and even they got testy and quarrelsome during the late weeks of the monsoon.

Dand Ubit tottered over to Am's camp bed and unceremoniously plopped onto the smooth blankets. He casually drew up his tiny right boot and muddied that careful smoothness.

"Things have heated up recently, Am," he sighed. "This

Merkus business—if it isn't taken care of soon, your retirement may have to be postponed. We can't spare anyone as long as this new annoyance keeps exciting the Tel-mari."

"I'll appeal to High Command," Am said quietly.

"Yes, you could do that—" Dand brought up his other boot and proceeded to stretch out on the camp bed. "—but I don't think they'll be disposed to help you, what with your refusal to help *them*."

"That's blackmail, Secretary."

"That's war, Am." Dand Ubit began to pick off clumps of loam from his left boot, his spindly leg held up and back with unexpected flexibility to reach his hand. The clumps fell on the bed.

"War is a young man's game, Am," he said. "Face it. In your heart you're already on the road to your lovely seaside holdings and your lovely sea-scented wife. H'm . . ." He inspected the boot a long moment, and the rain briefly reclaimed its sonic dominance.

Am tried to imagine the extent of his young commander's fury if she knew what High Command had in mind for her. He couldn't.

"Is she a jealous woman, Am?" Dand Ubit asked suddenly.

"Sekmé?"

"No. Your wife."

Three days later, the low-slung, open-cabbed dress vehicle passed through the gates of Sekmé's desert holdings.

Am removed his dust goggles. A small family of oryx trotted briskly out of the vehicle's path and the cool scent of mingled flowers breathed over him.

He shivered. Dry and decongested for the first time in three years and he still shivered. This was a beautifully kept estate, but ill-omened. He didn't need some mystic's imaginary little sprite to tell him.

First thing to do when I retire, he thought, visualizing his wife in her flowing garments, is take a holiday in the Hills of Whispers. Just her and me, the onagers, a Denneshur tent, and a jar of fermenting honey. I want everything to be simple, to be . . .

He struggled for the word and was shocked when it came.

. . . clean.

A young man in a shimmering blue and red ankle-length dressing robe, probably alerted by a servant that a military vehicle was headed up the drive, waited for him at the top of the steps. He looked so much like Sekmé that Am concluded he was her brother, Set, the poet.

He has a disability of some kind, Am thought, but I'll be damned if I remember what it is.

Set seemed to be watching the vehicle closely, eyebrows drawn down a little as though he was somewhat dubious about it. Once the driver set it in idle and got out, Set's attention shifted to him, although he appeared to be following the driver's boots rather than the driver as he crunched through the gravel around to Am's side. Set cocked his head like a listening wau-weh as Am disembarked, and finally turned his eyes on the general.

Odd fellow, but not disabled in any way I can see, Am considered.

He mounted the steps and offered his hand. Set didn't take it. He held his hands behind his back and stared at the general's face.

"Well met before God," Am said, thinking a more old-fashioned greeting would appeal to this tense young man.

Set pursed his lips in an uncertain crooked line.

Is he mute? Am wondered. But, he's a poet who recites his work to the thetl. He can't be mute, or deaf.

Am offered his hand again.

"I'm Field General Am," he said, "your sister's commanding officer."

Set instantly relaxed, brought out both hands, and sandwiched Am's between them. His grin was extraordinary.

"Of course! How foolish of me! I'm Sekmé's brother, Set. Excuse me, but may I read your face?"

Ah, now I remember! He's blind.

"Certainly."

Set's touch was very delicate, searching fingertips quickly memorizing features, texture, age . . . and personality?

Set lowered his hands, apparently satisfied.

"What brings you to our holdings, sir?"

"I have Sekmé's new orders."

The young man's handsome face fell. Am now saw that the eyes were artificial. Interesting. He moved them quite naturally.

"So soon? It's only been a couple months."

"There's new trouble in Tel-mari that High Command feels your sister should handle."

"No one else?"

"Why? Is she unwell?"

"Oh, no!" Set said, widening those inert sight organs. "At least, not now. She was, in a way, I suppose, but . . ." Flustered, he shoved back the long loose sleeves of his robe, which promptly slipped back down again.

"She's fine," he said. "Just tired. She's resting."

"May I see her?"

"Of course! I'll take you to her."

"Are you sure?" Am certainly wasn't. His guide was not only blind, but noticeably distraught as well.

"This is too important for a servant," Set said, and gently took Am's hand.

As they crossed the exquisite rugs of the front hall—this family was wealthier than Am had thought—they met a vigorous, bearded man who was coming from the game parlor.

"Uncle Atto!" Set cried. "General Am is here to see Sekmé."

Am distrusted the man on sight—for no good reason. The handclasp with the big, hearty paw was firm and friendly, the voice warm and courteous, the eyes bright with good humor.

"God do you grace," Atto said elegantly. "I'm sure Sekmé will be delighted to see you. She's been a bit depressed lately."

"I doubt it," Am said. "I have her new orders."

Atto became sober.

"Already? H'm . . . I'd hoped she'd be able to stay longer, but, alas, God's servants get little rest."

There it is, Am thought. His eyes. They haven't lost any merriment. Set's eyes don't even work and they still changed at the news.

"I'd introduce you to my wife, Sekmé's mother," Atto said as he led the way up the stairs to the bedchambers, "but she's gone to town for some trifle or other . . ."

Am bristled again. Guilty fantasies notwithstanding, *he* adored his wife and would never joke about her foibles behind her back.

"Sekmé?" Atto called as they entered a bedchamber full of cool afternoon shadows. "Your commanding officer is here."

Propped up on a small hill of pillows, her head and shoulders silhouetted against the golden rust of the Hills of Whispers visible beyond her open window, Sekmé seemed unsure whether to jump up and salute him, or stay where she was. She was wrapped in furs, but her shoulders and arms were bare. Perhaps, under her covers, she was naked, which, Am couldn't deny, stirred and disconcerted him.

"At your ease, Commander," he said quickly to settle the embarrassment for himself as much as for her. "No need to stand on ceremony. I'm unexpected."

"I wish I could say I was happily surprised," she said, "but I don't think you're here for my comfort."

"I need to speak with you privately, Commander."

She nodded wearily.

"Set, could you take the general to the prayer room? I'll be there in a minute."

Back to the ground floor they trooped, Atto bringing up the rear with garrulous good cheer.

"How go our efforts in Tel-mari? Has the monsoon abated yet? My eldest, Bahé, is due for a tour in-country. Do you know him? An eager young solder, tough as leather and ready for anything. He's aching for combat. Perhaps you could put in a good word with High Command? It'd be a shame to waste such God-given blood lust on simple base duty here in Maurhet . . ."

Am was glad when Atto excused himself at the prayer room and left Set to poke up the small flame in the hearth. Like most well-to-do families, Sekmé's kept the flame burning year-round in imitation of the sacred eternal fire in the Palace Dome.

"It isn't true," Set said softly once Atto was out of earshot. He stabbed the lightning bolt–shaped poker—symbol of God—into the coals.

"What isn't?" Am asked.

"Bahé isn't eager for battle. He's afraid of it."

"That's normal."

"Then why isn't Sekmé afraid of it?"

"I think she is."

"No." Set put aside the poker. The flame rippled its liquid light over his face and glinted off the sea green inlays of his eyes. "She doesn't fear battle. She fears the outcome, the consequences."

"So do I."

Set turned toward him, features glowing as if from the God fire and not a simple prayer hearth.

"Why don't we stop it?" he asked. "Just put down our weapons and stop? Bring on the New Unity. No scripture states clearly how it is to come about. Why don't we make it now? Ourselves?"

Am smiled sadly to himself. Poets. Blind to the monotonous horrors of real life. Eyes full of stars.

"Might as well try to shift the tides or rearrange the seasons," he sighed. "Set, if we put down our weapons as you suggest, the Tel-mari would slaughter us. I think you're saying this because you're angry with me for coming to take away your sister."

"Of course I am," Set said simply, "but I'm completely serious."

"I see that, but, take it from an old veteran, we won't see the New Unity in our lifetime or in quite a few lifetimes to come."

"We could."

Set's words had an air of finality that ended all conversation until Sekmé, dressed in her fatigues, entered the prayer room.

"It must be an emergency," she said, "or you wouldn't have come in person."

"High Command thinks so."

Set got up and slipped silently out of the prayer room. Am waited until he guessed the young man could no longer hear them then closed the chamber's latticework doors. Given the doors' lacy pattern of holes, conversation would not stay inside the chamber, but they added a sense of privacy and the starlike design of firelight in the now-dark house would warn servants not to enter.

"Interesting man, your brother," Am said. "A lot like you." He smiled at her, but did not get a smile in return, so he became serious. "You look thin, Sekmé."

"I had a spontaneous abortion."

This stopped him cold. He had no idea how to react to the news. Should he press her for details since the mission required a healthy operative? Or simply voice his condolences?

"Are you all right?" he asked.

"I will be. What are the orders?"

Very well. If she didn't want to belabor the issue, neither would he. He pulled the sealed letter from his shirt pocket.

"I told them you were a combat officer—" He handed her the letter, and she tore the seal with her fingernail. "—but they insist you perform a covert task this time."

Sekmé drew close to the fire for the light and read silently. He watched her expression darken until she reached the fatal word.

"Yansha!" she cried. "They want me to pose as a *yansha*?"

"High Command believes only a woman can get close enough to Merkus and his men to learn anything substantial, and a yansha, well . . ."

"I will not prostitute myself for High Command!"

Sekmé wadded up the letter and flung it in the fire. Since it was made of a special resin-treated fiber expressly for ease of destruction, the letter vaporized on the embers almost immediately.

"You don't have to," Am said as reassuringly as he could. "Not all yanshas are prostitutes. You could advertise strictly as an entertainer."

Sekmé laughed bitterly.

"That's hardly better! I can't dance, I don't play an instrument, and sing? Might as well strangle a sow for all the melody you'll get out of *my* throat! Set has the beautiful tongue, not me."

"Then go as a gaming yansha," Am said. "I don't care what the regulations say, I've never met an officer who didn't gamble in every style, Maurheti or Tel-mari."

Sekmé frowned at the fire.

"Uh, you do gamble, don't you, Commander?"

"I don't gamble," she muttered, "I cheat."

"Even better."

"I don't know." She wandered over to the lattice door and peeked through the holes. "There's something strange about this. Off, somehow."

"They're frustrated, Sekmé. Merkus gets into places even I don't have clearance for. He has caused more trouble in a shorter space of time than any terrorist since Akmi Saulaud."

Sekmé slowly poked her finger in and out of the lattice holes. Am waited. With her reputation, if Sekmé wanted to contest the orders, she'd probably get a hearing, but Am knew High Command would not back down. Still, the commander would have registered her displeasure and stalled the mission's implementation, which might force them to modify the orders in some way.

But Sekmé shrugged.

"All right," she said.

"I'm glad to hear it."

"Might as well. There's no reason to stay here anymore."

"Did the, uh . . . did he run off?"

"Disappeared," Sekmé said with emphasis. "He wasn't the type to run away."

Am nodded. Whatever she wished to believe.

"When do we leave?"

"Tomorrow morning, Commander. I'll come by at first light."

"No. You and your driver will stay here tonight."

The no-refusal-will-be-tolerated tone of her invitation was true to Maurheti custom and Am, naturally, accepted. He hadn't even bothered to contact the officers' enclave in Kemphor; they were a dull bunch anyway, homeside watch curs, lazy and spoiled. The bedchamber Set led him to was cool and spacious and stocked with more soft and fragrant things than he could possibly use or deserve.

Even so, he slept badly. Sekmé was right. There was something wrong about this mission, something more than its inherent distastefulness, and there was nothing he could do. She'd have to handle it in her own way.

He finally relaxed.

"She's been through worse," he mumbled into his pillows.

Lokar had set up camp in one of the coastside wadis of the Hills of Whispers, not far, and yet invisible, from the Nawset Highway. With the first of the hooded rider's payments, he'd outfitted himself with a Denneshur desert bed—which was something like a thick rug stitched into a tube and lined with wau-weh pup fur—cooking supplies, food, water, a wanderer's long black cloak, a young gelded onager, and a small but satisfying amount of his favorite drug purchased from a Kemphor art dealer. Those high-class intellectuals had the best illegal goods.

Lokar rolled up his trouser leg, found a good vein in his ankle,

stabbed it with the sharp-nosed pipette, and gently squeezed the bladder at the other end. The thin yellow liquid moved into the vein, swelling it briefly, and, a moment later, the gentle, almost female caress slid up his limbs and made him feel soft inside, loose and comfortable.

"You're disgusting," came a deep voice above him.

He looked up. The hooded rider had returned and somehow snuck up on him. Ah! No wonder. The onager was shoeless and its hooves had been thickly wrapped in dressed oryx hide— a much quieter surface in the dunes. A good Denneshur trick, although the hooded rider was no nomadic tribesman.

"As long as I get the job done," Lokar said, "why would you care?"

"You'd better get started," the rider said. "Sekmé leaves for Tel-mari at dawn."

"Then an onager won't do. I'll need transport."

"Bribe someone." The rider looked over Lokar's camp. "Where's your weapon?"

"I'll get it in Tel-mari. No point in getting arrested at the border for smuggling."

"What about your drugs?"

Lokar grinned nastily, exposing his long teeth and most of his gums.

"There's smuggling," he said, "and there's *smuggling*."

"You're disgusting."

"You're redundant. By the way, what's Sekmé's mission, if I may ask?"

The hooded rider turned his muffle-footed mount's head and began to trot off into the darkness.

"You'll find out soon enough," he said. "It will appeal to your sense of degradation."

If he hadn't felt so fine and comfortable in his pharmaceutically altered state, Lokar might have hurled a rock at him. Or an insult. Whichever might have hurt more.

*   *   *

When dawn came, so did Bahé, trotting half-asleep up the drive after a predawn summons from Sekmé to see her before she left. It was a good thing the onager had been born in Sekmé's holdings and knew the way, or her cousin, up late the night before at a party in Atto's holdings, might not have made it. At the foot of the steps, he slid off his mount and kept going until his soft derriere bumped on the hard gravel.

"Get up, soldier," he told himself, and turned onto his knees, wincing as the sharp pebbles bit into them.

"Get up, soldier!"

Bahé bolted to his feet. That last command, sharp, clear, and businesslike, had been real. Field General Am stood on the stair.

"Good morning," he said firmly, but with a smile in his eyes.

"G'morning, sir," Bahé answered, trying to brush the wrinkles from his knees.

"What brings you here in such somnolent shape, son?"

"Somno—what?"

"He's my cousin Bahé, General." Sekmé came out, crisp and fresh in her fatigues, her weapon tucked under her arm as she pulled on a pair of dark leather gloves against the early morning chill. "I called him on a personal matter."

She came down the steps and stood unusually close to Bahé.

"I want you to do something for me, cousin," she said quietly.

"Now?" When Bahé was tired, he whined.

"Yes." She took his hand and pressed the rifle into it. His fingers gripped convulsively. He was now wide awake.

"Wh-what are you—"

"My mission's a little different this time, Bahé. I can carry a knife, but not a rifle. Therefore, will you take care of it until I return?"

"But, this is your *family* weapon, Sekmé!"

"All the more reason I need someone trustworthy like you." She put her hand on her cousin's shoulder. "Care for it as if it was *your* family weapon."

Bahé blinked rapidly at Sekmé. No one had trusted him

with much of anything before and now his cousin, his *famous* cousin, the Lucky Lassie, the Iron Virgin, had chosen him to . . .

"I'm honored."

"Yes. Handle it well."

Bahé lowered his eyes.

"Don't get killed," he whispered.

If Sekmé heard him, she didn't show it. She glanced up at the house where Set was framed in a high window, fingering the vulpé pelt, blind eyes searching for his sister. She whistled to him and he grinned and waved.

"All right," she said to Am and the driver. "We can leave."

The officers climbed into the open vehicle, the driver eased it in a tight circle, crunching over the gravel, and they bounced off down the drive.

Bahé looked at the weapon in his hands, its well-oiled magazine, its antique electrum inlay, and wondered how many lives it had shortened. He tried to imagine himself using it in combat. Would that, finally, make his father proud of him?

"Stop staring at it as if it was a wild animal, boy, and lock it in the hunters' room with the other firearms. You're not strong enough to use such a weapon."

Atto had appeared on the steps.

Bahé sagged and glanced up at Set's window. At least *he* was still here.

Deeper inland, leagues beyond the first line of hills, shivering in a wadi that still lay in shadows, Haru carefully felt about inside the canvas bag of food and tried to calculate how long it would last. He was not reassured. A much smaller man might live on this portion for a week or two if he was sedentary, but Haru? In the desert? Trying to get home?

The sun finally made it over the eastern cliffs and washed the western walls in a bright, hard yellow glare. A small white star approached through that glare, growing larger and sharper until

it shot over the wadi, its scream racing after it—a Needle from Maurhet on its way to the war in Tel-mari. Technically, the pilot could have found him, but the pilot wasn't looking.

Haru curled up in the sand with his meager provisions and tried to hate Sekmé, but it required too much effort, too much energy, and he gave up.

CHAPTER 11

FERRET

The black piece of cloth fit snugly over the bridge of Sekmé's nose and across her cheekbones and draped loose down over the lower part of her face, her neck, and her bosom. She carefully slid her left hand in under the edge and lifted the veil just enough to let her right hand, which held a spoonful of soup, slip under toward her mouth.

"Excellent, Commander," the intelligence liaison officer said in his delicate, almost shy voice. "You've done it at last."

"Why do I have to do it at all?" Sekmé grumbled. "I thought women didn't eat in public."

"*Respectable* women don't eat in public," the officer reminded her. "You're a yansha."

He had a sweet smile considering his features, not to mention 75 percent of his body, were horribly pitted and scarred from a galca accident at a munitions depot. Although he was very lucky—the caustic gel hadn't crippled or blinded him, and the skin grafts had taken well—he could no longer lead a platoon. The men couldn't bear to look at him and he no longer had the will for leadership. Still, a firstborn was a firstborn and he had to serve if he could, so he'd found his way into intelligence, preparing "ferrets" for their missions although he couldn't go on any missions himself. His ruined face would be too easy to recognize.

Sekmé took another spoonful and spilled it on the veil.

"Damn!"

"In Tel-mari, Commander. Remember?"

Sekmé's gray green eyes glared at him over the veil and she swore again, much more colorfully, in Tel-mari.

"Not bad." The officer nodded. "Real yansha nastiness. Even your accent is better when you're angry."

Sekmé tore off the veil, flung it aside, and got up from the table.

"What are you doing?"

"Not hungry anymore."

She pulled up the hood of her long, black, cumbersome wool robe, unlatched the window of the tenement, climbed out, and pulled herself up onto the roof to sulk in the drizzle. Below, in the alley, a slat-ribbed onager grazed in the garbage.

"Commander, please!" The officer almost raised his voice. "You're risking exposure."

"Relax, Zoad. This neighborhood is virtually deserted, courtesy of yours truly."

She drew up her knees and looked out over what remained of the nearby buildings' roofs. She'd been back in Tel-mari only a couple weeks and already it felt as if she'd never been home, never met Haru, never shared her anxieties with Set. She was the commander once again: sober, efficient, no-nonsense, alone.

Still, something was different. She'd noticed it the minute the Needle she was flying reentered the heavy, perpetual cloud cover of Tel-mari. A weariness. Not of body—she'd recovered her energy quickly once she'd gotten her orders and needed it. Not of spirit—she was as committed to the sacred cause as she'd ever been. The Tel-mari remained for her the clever lost race, the forsaken who needed to be watched, corralled, and punished if their weakness for heeding the wiles of the Not-God got the better of them.

So, what was it? She wasn't sure. A sense of tedium, perhaps. A restlessness and impatience with the *methods* of the mission, all these less-than-decisive actions that only kept the Tel-mari in

check for short periods of time and scratched the scabs of their resentment. Why not test the full sinews of the Maurheti force and break Tel-mari resistance once and for all?

Sekmé shuddered and pulled the loose loop of her hood tighter.

What a hideous idea! They'd have to slaughter each and every last one of the Tel-mari to end their resistance. *That* much carnage, no matter at whose expense, was unthinkable, a violation of Nature itself. No matter how benighted their souls, they were living creatures who had not asked to be born, had not asked to be cursed. They did not deserve extinction.

What kind of rift in the fabric of Things as They Must Be would extinction bring? Sekmé couldn't imagine, but the question terrified her on a level so deep, so hidden, it felt like the soul of Not-God itself. God was He That Is and extinction was the greatest of all Is Nots.

Sekmé remembered this sacred grammar and the way it tripped from the lips of that funny little priest who came at the end of every month for years after her father's death to instruct her and her brother in the more esoteric aspects of faith.

"It's funny," Set had said, half laughing, "like a game."

"It's not a game," the priest said.

He was very short, though not a dwarf, and had a head like a flattened loaf of bread resting on a cake plate, which was really the wide stiff collar flaring out under his chin and above his narrow neck.

"But, it sounds like you're playing with the words," Set insisted. "I play with words, too, but yours are funnier."

The little priest's heavy head turned red, but he did not lose his temper. "Perhaps you have a better way of clarifying God's nature?"

"Yes," Set said with conviction, which startled even Sekmé, who was used to his original and often daring ways of assembling reality without the aid of sight.

"Then, will you enlighten us?" the priest asked.

Set was about fourteen at the time, as thin and light-footed as a spider, but much giddier. He couldn't speak without grinning and rarely grinned without laughing, and sometimes he would deliberately flick his artificial eyes askew just to shock people out of their stiffness. He did it now and Sekmé grinned.

"Set! Please!" the scandalized cleric cried.

"But, this is what it's about," Set said. "I can't see. The part of my mind that would unscramble light if I got any, unscrambles nothing. It sleeps, it gets small, it wastes away without work. My eyes see nothing—but I'm not blind."

"But . . . you are," the priest said, rumpling up his low forehead.

"No. I can't *see*—my eyes don't work—and yet I *see* my world. I touch it, I smell it, I taste it, I hear it—Oh! I hear it most of all! A wonderful world! Full of space and shape and weight and heat. I have a picture of it in my mind. I *see* it."

The priest's forehead relaxed. "Yeeees," he said slowly, "I think I understand. Sight without actually seeing."

"That's God," Set said.

"Then, what is Not-God?"

"Not-God is what my *eyes* see."

The priest clapped his hands together triumphantly. "Then you do understand! Not-God is quite an evil thing, isn't it?"

Set squinted at the priest and became pensive. "No . . . not really," he said. "It just *is* . . . in an *is-not* sort of way."

Sekmé smiled at the memory. She missed Set. Curiously, as the days passed, she thought more and more about him and less and less about the lost Haru. Maybe this was because she'd known the muscular young man with the big, beautiful hands only a couple months whereas she'd known and loved Set her entire life.

A few squares of yellow light kindled in the walls of the nearly empty sector, a handful of windows announcing the presence of a handful of stragglers perhaps too bewildered by what had

happened to their lives, their city, their world, to leave it without losing their identity and sanity entirely.

Haru had been a light that came and went. She had hoped her love would mean more and was dismayed at its dwindling. Not that she thought ill of him, never that, but she'd wanted him to touch her more deeply, transform her.

"Into what?" she asked aloud.

"Commander?"

The intel-liaison was still waiting.

"Aren't you getting cold, Commander?"

"No. Actually, it's a rather pleasant—"

She stiffened and the chill shooting down her back clipped her words before they became a lie. She'd heard something, something very small, perhaps something no more meaningful than a bit of plaster finally breaking loose and falling into the alley. Even so, she got the impression, not for the first time, that she was being watched. She stretched her legs and dangled them out over the eaves.

"Well, now that you mention it, it is getting nippy . . ."

She eased herself back down from the roof and, with a short swing on the tile-lined rain gutter, jumped back into the room.

Three buildings away, hidden in the yellow light of one of those anonymous windows, Lokar lowered his weapon, a Tel-mari sniper's rifle expertly cobbled out of stolen Maurheti components.

Too far—and not a clear shot what with the shapeless bulk of that cloak.

Why she was dressed in Tel-mari rags was beyond him.

A few days later, Sekmé's appearance—and it had to be Sekmé; no other woman he knew had that aggressive stride—confused him even more.

"Oh, this is too interesting." He smiled and uncocked his rifle. "Too interesting by far."

Lokar had positioned himself much closer to Sekmé's tenement, on the roof walk of what had once been a rooming house for well-to-do widows, and could see his enemy when she left the tenement. With a few short parting words to a man whose face, well, didn't make sense, she shouldered a soft, checkered sling pouch and sauntered away down the alley . . . in the black-embroidered, calf-length red robe, black boots, red hooded cloak, and fringed black veil of—

"A *yansha*! May God shower Himself in glory, for we share the same sense of humor!"

Killing could wait. Lokar trotted along the roof walk where lonely women once took the air together and shared their sorrow, jumped the short distance to the rotting tenement building next door, and followed Sekmé until she turned into a street that still had traffic: people on foot, in carts, leading onagers—people too lost to pay attention to Sekmé's red flag.

Lokar pulled a small ampule from his pocket, snapped it in half, and squeezed the sugary, drug-saturated jelly onto his tongue. He savored the buzz.

"Well, she's headed for the New Hives," he muttered, "that's certain. That sling pouch has the diamond pattern of a gaming yansha. You need players for games."

It'd be amusing to watch her at work, if he could find a way to do so without being noticed, and perhaps this mission of hers, whatever it was, could make his own much easier. Most of the assault and murder victims among the Tel-mari were women—and almost half of those were yanshas. Rarely did anyone in the occupation government investigate a yansha's death. Their lives were worth little, to the Tel-mari as well as the Maurheti.

"Hell . . . I might be able to kill her *publicly* and get away with it."

But that wasn't his style. Too much mess to clean up afterward.

He looked at the sky. Sniffed. It smelled like a new storm.

"Time to find new lodgings geared to the living rather than the dead."

He turned up his collar and trotted back to the widow's walk.

Sekmé quickly realized two things as she moved among the refugees of the New Hives of Eshna. First, a yansha was the only kind of Tel-mari female she could possibly have impersonated. The cloaked-and-veiled she encountered moved carefully, in a manner so naturally wary that it had to be an inbred, life-long habit. At the same time, their words, although soft, were direct without being confrontational, insistent without pressure, and, in the younger, single women, charming without seduction.

The veiled ones haggled over vegetables, goat cheese, and swamp greens with a patient diffidence that undercut the vendors' sweet talk—and their prices—so efficiently, it left Sekmé breathless.

They are *good*, she thought. I should hover by and take notes.

But she couldn't hover because of the second thing she'd realized: proper social behavior did not apply to her. Whereas most of the men and boys were polite, if gently flirtatious, with the veiled ones in black, they were bluntly sexual, or hostile, with her.

"Hey, yansha! Come home with me and we'll play some very *special* games."

"Get away, she-goat! This is a *respectable* shop."

"Sweet red jenny, would you like a sour red jack? I'll fit snug and warm in your stall."

Sekmé laughed. She hadn't heard such a ludicrous invitation since a new attaché of hers, a boy barely sixteen, had scrambled his intelligence with his first bottle of damnation ale.

However, this man, a thick-limbed fellow in a butcher's leather apron, was not drunk and he did not appreciate her mirth. He grabbed her arm as she passed and yanked her close. Sekmé gasped; his breath was terrible.

"Little red *bitch*," he breathed, and gave her a shake.

"Games only, lover," she said through clenched teeth. Did this man eat nothing but manure?

"Not today," he snarled back, and grabbed her breast.

"*That* is not for sale!"

Sekmé smacked his hand away. A crowd was gathering, but if Sekmé had been naive enough to expect help, she would have been disappointed. As it was, she was merely disgusted. The men watched as if at a sporting event, as if her status as a gaming yansha included street boxing. The women turned away.

"What about this?" the butcher sneered, and shoved his hand into her crotch.

She slapped him hard and jumped back. She had to be careful not to get too violent too quickly. That would not be proper yansha behavior, although she yearned to break his jaw with her fist.

"I'm afraid not." She quickly snatched a bright yellow square of cloth from her tight red sleeve and waved it at him. "However, I'll be reasonable. If you can get this pretty little yellow square from me, you get me, too."

The butcher rubbed his chin and licked his lips. He swung his big hand at the square, and Sekmé whipped it away with a coquettish smirk.

"One for me," she said.

He tried again, this time catching the corner of the bit of cloth. He tugged. Nothing. Her grip was tight.

"Is that the best you can do?" she taunted.

The butcher tightened his fist, pulled as hard as he could, and nearly lost his balance when he achieved the square . . . but it was green.

"Wh-what?"

Sekmé laughed again, and this time, she was not alone.

"Very good, friend," she said, "but I did say a *yellow* square. Perhaps your luck will be better with a yansha who likes your stench, butcher."

The butcher was not the kind to enjoy being the butt of a joke. His confusion became fury more quickly than Sekmé, who rather expected it, nevertheless anticipated. When he lunged at her, he caught her breasts in a painful double-fisted squeeze, and she screamed, a sound so rare to her ears it seemed to come from someone else.

The butcher suddenly released her and threw his arms over his head in self-defense. An older man with a full white beard and sparse hairline had started beating him vigorously across the back with a thick walking stick.

"Ruffian!" he cried, and whacked him again. "Coward! She may be a yansha, but she's a *woman*! How dare you!"

He smacked some more, and the butcher retreated and ran off down a side alley, whoops and hollers in his wake. Apparently, the only thing funnier than watching a yansha humiliate a big, brutish man, was watching a much older, smaller man do it.

But the graybeard took no pleasure in victory. In fact, he ignored their audience completely, put his hand on Sekmé's shoulder—he was her equal in height—and looked her closely in the eye with concern.

"Are you all right, sister?" he asked.

"Come on, grandpa!" another man cried. "Why do you care? She's a yansha!"

Again, the man ignored everyone not directly in his line of vision. Sekmé was struck by the intelligence of the black eyes in the age-bleached face.

"Yes. I'm fine."

"Indeed? I'm sure that hurt a great deal."

Sekmé stared at him. Where did this compassion come from? From what she understood, the crowd's indifference was more consistent with yansha experience.

The man apparently realized it himself, because he added, "I have a daughter about your age. I would go mad if some hooligan handled her the way that goat killer handled you."

He meant it and Sekmé was intrigued. Daughter or no daughter, why would one of the Not-God's children behave so, well . . . of God?

Nevertheless, she had a role to play.

"Don't do me any favors, old man."

He actually looked hurt.

"No? So young and already so hard?" He shrugged. "Very well. No favors. How about employment instead?"

"You're not my type."

"God, no! Not that! You're a gaming yansha. I run a small inn not far from here. Business is slow. If you'll ply your trade there, it'll draw more paying customers. In exchange, I'll give you room and board."

"You'll want a percentage, I'm sure."

"Not at all," said the man, who, Sekmé began to realize, was not as old as his white hair suggested. "The extra business—drinks downed, food eaten, rooms rented to sleep it off—that will be enough."

Sekmé was skeptical on several levels.

"Are you sure? What if I don't bring in any business?"

"If that's the case, you wouldn't want to stay, would you?"

True enough. No use prolonging an unprofitable situation. This was exactly the kind of "in" into the refugee city's life she was looking for, a base of operations from which she could engage in her ferreting.

"All right," she said, "on one condition."

The man's left brow rose a little, but not enough to suggest mistrust or displeasure.

"I'm a gaming yansha," she said. "Period. No other kinds of entertainment are to be expected or asked for by you or any of your customers."

"Agreed."

He held out his arm. His robe was quite old-fashioned and the full sleeve hung nearly all the way down to the mud.

"This way, my dear."

Sekmé hoisted her checkered pouch up onto her shoulder and fell in step with the man and his walking stick.

"My name is Hemsha," he said. "My daughter Bekka and I came to the New Hives after the Eshna market attack."

"So did I," Sekmé said, a beat late. She had to wait for her lungs to reinflate.

"My wife died in the attack," Hemsha continued, "and I lost my old tavern."

"Forgive me, Hemsha, but you really don't look or act like an innkeeper."

Hemsha smiled, obviously touched. Sekmé guessed he had once been very handsome.

"I was a teacher twelve years go—before the *first* Eshna attack," he said, "but there's not much call anymore for professors of philosophy, so Bekka and I are innkeepers."

"Practical."

"Not yet. That's why I'm taking this business risk."

Sekmé grinned, and hoped he could tell in spite of the veil.

"I'll try not to disappoint you."

"You haven't yet." Hemsha gave her a sideways glance. "That was a clever trick you played on the butcher."

"Thank you."

"But, tell me, where does a yansha get hold of a galcloth?"

Sekmé's spine stiffened. She hadn't expected a Tel-mari to know what a galcloth was, let alone that it was not standard yansha equipment. She'd used the galcloth to polish her knife.

"Well," she stalled, "times are hard. Sometimes I have to swallow my pride and let the Maurheti in on the games. One of their younger officers, I think he liked me. He gave it to me as a gift." She took a breath to give herself more thinking time for invention.

"I thought it was pretty," she said. "I liked how it changed color when exposed to light."

"My dear," Hemsha sighed, "they use galcloths to clean and lubricate their weapons."

"Really? Huh. Interesting."

"You shouldn't find it interesting," Hemsha said with gentle intensity, as though instructing a child on a point of morality. "No woman should. It's unclean. *All* of their war machine, down to the buttons on their uniforms, is unclean."

"I have to make a living." Sekmé pouted. "And they have the money."

"Fine. Take their trade and their money, if you must," he conceded sadly, "but don't accept their gifts."

They walked on in silence. A couple boys, ragged and malnourished, ran by chasing a filthy ball and, as they passed Sekmé, made kissing noises and quick snatches at her skirt. Hemsha swatted them away with his stick.

"You're unusually gallant." Sekmé smiled.

"I'm a father." Hemsha ran his fingers through his beard the way a man might stroke a pet. He squinted thoughtfully. "Do you mind if I ask you a personal question?"

"Not if you don't expect me to answer."

"Fair enough." He stamped his stick on the broken paving stones to scare off a goat that had wandered into their path. The animal jumped, bleated, then trotted away, famine-swelled belly swinging from side to side.

"You're quite young to be a gaming yansha," he said. "I thought women in your position turned to gaming later in their careers when, well, when their, um . . ."

"When their looks faded?"

"Mm-h'm."

Hemsha must have thought that since yanshas relied so much on sexual trade, it might be offensive to bring up the inevitable loss of their "marketability." Such delicacy was absurd—and quite charming.

"Ah, Hemsha," Sekmé sighed, suddenly visited by the old grief for her father, "I'm not as young as you think."

CHAPTER 12

THE RECİTATİON

A little over a month after Sekmé's departure, Set received the long-anticipated summons to give a recitation for the king . . . and Bahé got his orders to report to Tel-mari. In a case of uncanny coincidence, the former was to be held the night before the latter.

Atto could barely contain his pleasure.

"My nephew and son go to meet their destinies under the same moon!" he crowed to Hatula as Set, guardedly gratified, and Bahé, openly depressed, looked on. "God showers his blessing on us! You are both to be men."

"I thought I already was," Set quipped sotto voice to Bahé.

"Maybe *you* are, cousin," Bahé whispered back, "but I'm just the fat disappointment."

"Better than having your manhood pickled in a jar in the hunters' room," Set said, a none-too-friendly reference to Atto's on-reserve but unused military shrapnel rifle. As a landed second son without younger siblings but with a large family, Atto had never had to serve.

"I don't want to go, Set."

"I know. I don't *want* you to go."

"No offense, but, right now, I envy you your eyes."

"None taken."

Atto was still in high spirits when Set, in his best robes, the

red ones embroidered with a gold and purple mating-flame pattern, and Bahé, in a new, too-tight uniform, joined him that last star-glutted evening in the balloon-tired troop transport vehicle. Bahé drove—it was the same vehicle he'd use in the morning to get to the air base—in absolute silence as his father's happiness spilled out of him like froth from under the lid of a boiling kettle.

"Since the beginning of time," he said, "we Maurheti have been God's vigilant forces against the eternally greedy minions of Not-God—"

Set couldn't believe he was actually related by blood to this cliché-spewing bore.

"—and as long as our firstborn confront this task with all their hearts, all their souls, God will ultimately triumph."

"Hope it's tomorrow," Bahé muttered.

Atto snapped his head in his son's direction. Instead of his previous near-giddy pride, an active coldness clawed out from his gaze and gripped Bahé so tightly he nearly swerved off the black ribbon of the Nawset Highway.

"If any other son had uttered such a wish, I might have echoed 'may it be so,' but I know you, Bahé."

The young man shivered and tightened his concentration on the road ahead.

"*You* are a coward," Atto continued, "and your wish is merely for *yourself.*"

He spat out this last word with a hiss, and Bahé's body tensed even harder.

"Ever since you were a child, you wanted things sweet and easy. Obstacles were to be avoided, buried under fat and foolishness rather than faced and conquered."

Bahé said nothing. He'd become part of the vehicle's driveshaft.

"You don't even have the nerve to contradict me!" Atto returned his furious gaze to the dark desert and bright city ahead of him.

Seated behind them in the canvas-covered cab, Set hugged his thetl close to his chest, and the vulpé pelt under his robe flattened its softness against his skin.

You can have my eyes, he thought. Nothing is right, Bahé. *You* should stay and *I* should be with my sister.

He thought of the stars he couldn't see and how Sekmé had described them to him: "Pinpricks in the black. Distant hot windows of the city of the universe."

The city of the universe. Sometimes, when he imagined stars, he imagined them *literally* as windows, windows with the faces of people looking out of them, all kinds of people.

And sometimes he imagined one of the people undoing the latch, opening the window, and jumping out.

The Palace Dome was floodlit from the ramparts of the surrounding curtain wall so that, no matter how bright the city's active nightlife, the Dome was still brighter, a smooth, gleaming mound of gold against a purple black night. Its glare blotted out the constellations and forced people who lived in flats nearby to close their slatted blinds if they wanted to sleep. Those who didn't could sit out on their narrow balconies, sip sweet tisane, and read by its light.

Bahé felt like a dune beetle when he got out of the vehicle and looked up at the Dome. A crushed dune beetle. This golden glare personified the state, the state religion, God himself when you considered it was surmounted by the Divine Bolt.

Set must have felt the same way although he couldn't see it.

"It's hot," he said, and turned his blind eyes away as if they were being burned.

"Funny," Bahé murmured, "I was thinking how *cold* it was . . ."

Kerz, the same giant chamberlain who'd brought Wepanu to Roon, led the trio down the torchlit corridors to the Room of the Sacred Fire.

"This is magnificent," Atto said as he strode broadly, pur-

posefully ahead as if he, not Set, were being honored. "Extraordinary artistry."

"Are the walls painted?" Set asked.

"Sculpted and inlaid," Kerz said.

"Then, perhaps, after my recitation, I can explore them?"

"Explore?"

"Touch them."

"Why?" Kerz laughed. "Are you blind?"

"Yes."

Set didn't need to be told that the man was embarrassed. The way people held themselves changed the heat and the charge of the air around them, and this chamberlain's presence was so large that, frankly, Set doubted he needed to speak to give orders.

"Well . . . I suppose so," Kerz said, then tried to cover his discomfort with a joke. "It's not as if you can cart any of it away with you."

Servants had arranged cushions in a circle around the eternal flame for Atto, Set, Bahé, Roon's six wives, Kerz, Roon himself—on a special raised stool whose cushion was embroidered with gold—and the royal household secretary.

Dand Ubit was the only one already seated. He nodded and smiled at Atto when he entered the lofty, black-floored chamber. Atto smiled back.

Bahé recognized the secretary from the previous year's Royal Birthday Parade and his skin crawled. There was something deformed about the man that had nothing to do with his egg-shaped body or tiny feet, but Bahé couldn't define what it was, and when Atto introduced him he did his best to be cordial on the chance he was being unnecessarily unfair.

"Yes, sir. It is an honor to meet you." He grasped the man's forearm and let his mind wander out of the conversation to where Set, with his uncanny inner sonar, had cut a direct path to the queens and was charming them with his self-deprecating

wit—especially effervescent around lovely women—and good looks.

"No, but truly! Let me search your face and braids and I can tell you your age and the color of your hair."

Naturally, he underguessed all of the handsome, but middle-aged, women's years by at least a decade and conveniently failed to sense any white threads in their black locks. Guessing the black was easy: everyone knew the queens were sisters of the Bahr clan, an ancient family that had never had a blonde.

A couple young servants, boys really, padded softly barefoot among them with bowls of brine-soaked root slices, honey-sticky nuts, and pickled sour berries. This mixture of salt and sour, sweet and vinegary, was to remind the guests of the complexity of life and prepare them for the poetic main course, after which a buffet would function as psychological dessert.

After nodding and smiling as pleasantly as he could at the creepy, buzz-voiced secretary, Bahé was starving, a sure sign of his misery.

Come on, king, he thought. Make an appearance so we can get this over with.

At last, Roon appeared. Grinning handsomely, he approached Atto and embraced him as a friend.

"What's he wearing, Bahé?" Set whispered. He'd left the ladies when Roon's imminent arrival was announced, but not before receiving six enthusiastic busses on his cheeks.

"A uniform. He always wears a uniform."

"Even for poetry? How dull."

Now Roon clasped Bahé's hand firmly, warmly—something he hadn't expected.

"I understand you're about to begin your sacred career." The king smiled. "I envy you, young Bahé."

Bahé blinked at him in disbelief.

"Few people realize, Bahé, that being king can be a very tedious job. At times I must flatter the unworthy, cajole the insufferable, and entertain the unscrupulous in order to protect the

interests of my people. Political life runs contrary to every true, pure, manly impulse, but it's the price we in power must pay for orderly government—isn't it, Dand?"

The secretary, who had returned to his cushion and not risen at the king's entrance, nodded with a knowing air of fellow suffering.

"It's not like being a soldier," Roon continued. "*That's* a *real* life. Honest, active, and in direct service to the divine law of checks and balances. Danger doesn't masquerade on the battle-field, Bahé. It doesn't smile one minute and poison you the next. It is what it is."

He patted Bahé's shoulder with a paternal but distant air of approval. Bahé wasn't sure the king's eyes, although focused on him, actually saw him.

"Be glad, young man! You'll never feel more alive than when the gel bombs are falling and the fires are licking at your boots."

For the life of him, Bahé couldn't tell if the king was serious or somehow making fun of him. In response to these apparently genuine expressions of goodwill, all he could do was grimace and grunt.

Set, however, always sensitive to the moods of those who had power over him, and never particularly awed by the pretensions of men who, after all, in *his* eyes, were equal in splendor if not in aura, picked up the king's hints of sarcasm and, when it came his turn to be greeted, decided to be playful.

"Ah, our young bard!" Roon said. "I've looked forward to a recitation for some time."

"I've grown old waiting to give it," Set pouted. "I almost have a beard."

Set heard the scandalized gasps—how dare he be so irreverent before the king?—but they meant nothing because Roon himself grinned.

"*Almost,* eh?" He chuckled, game for a joke. "What would help you *achieve* this beard?"

"Ah, well . . ." Set waved his hand with feigned melancholy.

"Nothing now that I've learned your majesty has the ability to quench the fires of *six*."

This "defeat" of a slim young poet's manhood in an imaginary contest with his own tickled Roon, who laughed heartily and put his arm around Set's shoulders.

"You're quite the wild dog, Set! A real howl in the desert. I like that."

"Thank you. I do, too."

The king looked over at Atto.

"Too bad this lad can't serve, Atto. He'd made an excellent officer."

Set could imagine Bahé's discomfort. In his mind's eye, he saw his unhappy cousin melt into a pool of soft pudding that people walked through and swore at for soiling their slippers.

"May I read your face, Majesty?" he asked. "I know it's a bold question, but all of your other subjects gaze on you without fear. Why not one whose fingers serve as eyes?"

Set heard the chamberlain take a quick step forward and stop, presumably halted by a glance from Roon.

"Yes, of course, bard Set. 'Look' at me if you like."

Set had not planned on reading the king's face. If someone had asked him about it only an hour before, he would have claimed it wasn't necessary, that he didn't need to "know" the king.

But, now he did. Urgently. As if a life would soon depend on it. As if someone small and invisible sat on his shoulder urging him to do so.

Carefully, lightly, he placed his fingertips on the monarch's cheeks and moved them down into his beard, the smooth, warm, slightly oily flesh giving way to a well-trimmed, stiff mat of hair not unlike that in an onager's tail. Dense, black undoubtedly, probably difficult to cut. A musk scent.

True pride. Male and sure. Some vanity, but not excessive. Not, in itself, a warning.

He passed his fingers over the king's lips; they quivered a moment then tightened into a small smile. A bit of embarrassed

amusement at this intimacy from another man. A little patronizing, but not threatened. Superior to it.

The ears now. Good shape. Surprisingly cool to the touch. No unusual twitch of involuntary interest. Organs for ordinary use. The ears of a sighted man. The lies and misdirections were collected, deciphered, put in disdain, but—and this disturbed Set—not rejected. Rather, they were given an extra turn, defined, deflected, and reused in new ways. There were no surprises for these ears, no true horror or ecstasy.

Set's fingers slipped a bit at the temples—the king's hair was dressed with scented oil and some had run down—then passed over the brow. A good, broad brow but not high in spite of the beginnings of recession in the hairline. A bit of sweat. The king's blood ran hot under the skin. He would be the first to undress and would stay naked through the night, inclined to repeat and repeat, as much to cool himself as cool his ardor. Selfish—even inflexible. His wives would have to put up with it or, stuck in his heat, he'd lash out. Impatient.

The nose was excellent, aquiline and strong, the true feature of his royal blood, a legacy. Good, clear, easy breath. Roon had a sound constitution, health, and athleticism. Arrogance. Perhaps not as sensitive to the failings of others as he should be.

At last, Set held his breath and delicately placed his fingers on the king's eyes. The lids closed. He felt the twitch underneath of the wakeful vision searching the corners. Looking for a focus. Focusing everywhere.

This was normal. What wasn't was their tendency to fix—and fix not straight ahead but to the side. When that happened, Set felt a small jolt, as if he'd reached for his metal-stringed thetl after scuffing his feet on the carpet.

Duplicity. As policy. At the expense of others.

Suppressing the tremble, Set drew back his hands.

"Well?" Roon asked, and for the first time, Set heard the stone in his silk.

"I feel ugly, Majesty," Set replied, on one level quite true.

The king laughed gently, sympathetically. He was vain enough to be generous about it.

"Oh, come now, son! You flatter me and slander yourself."

"Not at all," Set replied in a low, flat tone.

"Well, enough of this." Roon gestured to the others. "Let's hear your epic before the evening loses its youth."

They arranged themselves around the flame. Atto sat between the king and Dand Ubit. A trio of wives sat both at the king's left and the secretary's right. Set lowered himself between Kerz—whom he'd begun to think of as the king's pet, minus the spike-studded collar—and Bahé, who sagged forward a little. Bahé's tight new uniform pulled unflatteringly at his fleshy thighs when he crossed his legs.

To concentrate on his tuning, Set slowed his breathing, the better to hear nothing but the instrument and the verses in his mind, but it wasn't easy. He was troubled. The heat from the eternal flame, the one all private prayer-room fires echoed in miniature, seemed to lick right up his skin.

He lifted his face. Before him, as clear as true, physical vision, he saw a group of people sitting in a circle around a transparent orange pillar of curious fire, fire that did not burn. They were looking at him, eyes unblinking, their hands at rest in their laps, faces both calm and sad—waiting.

They were utterly beautiful. More beautiful than any image he had ever conjured from the information at his fingertips. They were graceful beyond graceful—and as silent as death.

Set was not afraid. He returned their stare and continued to tune his instrument. When ready, he began to pluck the spare accompaniment to his new epic poem, *The Fall of Eshna,* composed soon after Sekmé's anguished description of the arranged corpses in the marketplace.

Not every epic gloried in a victory. Some of the greatest contained verses full of doubt, horror, and bitterness. Even so, Set knew it would be a controversial choice. He'd decided in the back of the vehicle while listening to Atto berate his son

that he *wanted* controversy tonight, before the king, in front of the flame.

And now, with a divine audience, controversy was *required*. They had to hear it because they already knew the words. Hearing would give the words life and set them walking.

Bahé stared miserably at the fire as the epic unfolded. This was the longest, most harrowing two and a half hours he'd endured in his life. The words were going to kill him before he ever got to Tel-mari, and there was absolutely nothing he could do about it because the words were sacred and intoxicating. He was afraid he'd pull apart in bloody shreds if he moved, the situation seemed that dire. The words flew about the room like knives, grazing his skin, barely missing vital organs. Each blade had a tiny picture caught in its reflection, a picture that became gigantic when you looked at it more closely, gigantic and terrible, full of blood, and spitting ashes.

If I cut off my thumbs tonight, Bahé thought, I might bleed to death, but I won't have to go into that awful place. I won't have to see this.

But, he *was* seeing it, and for two and a half hours, he hated Set.

The epic stopped eventually and his cousin, who'd rocked gently as he plucked his instrument, more engine than person, blinked the way a sighted man would coming out of a trance, although, in his case, he seemed to be readjusting to *darkness* after having been awake. He set the thetl down and looked at it curiously as if he could see it and was surprised at its behavior. The others sat in silence, uncomfortably unsure whether to praise or condemn their recent experience.

The king broke the silence gently.

"Before I was crowned," he said softly, "like any other first-born, I, too, served in Tel-mari." He scratched his cheek, nails rasping a little against the beard, his gaze directed at the fire.

"I don't spend much energy remembering," he added, "except for the good times, the victories, the friendships. I set aside

the, uh, darker moments, as we all do, and leave them for God.
Only He understands their purpose and He takes responsibility."

He turned to Set.

"I'm not sure even He could accept this," he said.

Set shook his head slowly. He had said his piece for the evening and would defend nothing. Roon sighed.

"Congratulations, young bard," he said. "You've an incomparable gift. God bless you . . . and pity us."

To recover from the beautiful terror of the poem, the queens
and Bahé got quietly to their feet and headed for the buffet of
salted fish, onager tail soup, thornwood tree spirits in hollowed-
out melon rinds, and nut meats in spiced oil—all native dishes—
being served in a smaller, more intimate chamber off the main
hall. Set marked the heavy sound of Bahé's retreating boots and
the soft rustle and scuff of the ladies' garments and slippers with
a mixture of dismay and relief. Dismay because he knew Bahé
would overeat to soothe his nerves, relief because, ironically, with
this overconsumption he'd finally be able to enjoy himself and
chat with the queens.

For his own part, Set still wanted to read the walls and he approached Kerz for assistance.

"Well, Mr. Set," the big chamberlain said in new, unmistakably deferential tones—Set believed the man was now afraid of
him—"most of the calligraphy in here is on the Dome's ceiling
out of reach."

"What about the corridors?"

"Still pretty high up."

Set took him by the hand and smiled.

"You're a large man. We'll manage."

They left the fire hall behind and, once in the corridors, Set
instructed the chamberlain to crouch down so he could step up
onto his shoulders.

"I don't know, Mr. Set." Kerz clicked his tongue skeptically.

"I'll be safe," Set said. "I have excellent balance and you have excellent strength. Just hold my ankles tightly and we'll be fine."

Still hemming and hawing dubiously, Kerz nevertheless crouched down, and Set climbed onto his shoulders with practiced ease. Kerz gripped Set's ankles as tightly as if he were the one in danger of falling, then slowly stood up.

"Excellent!" Set placed his hands on the carved and inlaid walls.

For a while, only Set's whispered mouthings of the words, briefly punctuated with commands to Kerz to shuffle a little farther down the corridor, broke the echoey silence. Then the chamberlain cleared his throat.

"You've, um, you've done this before?"

"My sister used to hoist me up on her shoulders when we went hunting about the sea cliff for tern eggs."

"*She* carried *you*?"

"I have faster fingers," Set explained, "the better to steal from the nests before getting pecked to death."

"I admire the commander . . . your sister."

"She's an admirable person."

"I lost all of my brothers in the Eshna market raid," Kerz said. "There were four of them." He chuckled bitterly. "Never understood why all of them, not just the eldest, decided to serve."

Set paused in his reading, fingertips poised on a gerund.

"I'm sorry. Does that mean you're going to drop me now?"

"No. I *admire* your sister, remember? She contacted my parents herself. As I understand it, she hadn't even taken the time to bathe or eat before she reached all of her men's next of kin."

Set let his fingers trail slowly down the polished stone until his hands dropped to his sides. He didn't know what to say.

"She had her duty," Kerz continued. "Still, another officer might have assigned the task to a subcom. It's a miserable job."

Set waited. The chamberlain, his perch, was not yet finished.

"Anyway, I wanted to thank you for your poem. We were

insane without bodies to grieve over. Now, I at least know why we couldn't have them; the destruction was too great. It helps."

"You should thank Sekmé," Set said, and a strange metallic bitterness filled his mouth as he considered the irony of such gratitude. "Those were her images. It was her raid."

"No, it wasn't."

Set reeled to the left and almost lost his footing.

"What do you mean? She told me it was her plan."

"No, it wasn't."

Set felt dizzy.

"Please . . . please put me down."

The chamberlain released Set's ankles, reached up his legs, and helped him sit on his shoulders. Then he lifted the poet and set him on the floor.

"It couldn't have been her idea," Kerz said. "High Command never would have authorized that kind of blitz unless the idea came from very high up, perhaps as high as the king."

"Are—are you sure?"

"Of course, I'm sure." Kerz squeezed Set's arm reassuringly. "Your sister's a remarkable woman but she *is* a woman and High Command isn't about to give her *that* much authority even if most of us think she deserves it."

"You do? Why?"

"Well, she always puts her men's needs first no matter what and they like having her around." Kerz cleared his throat, a little awkwardly. "It's hard to explain, really, but she's special to them. They get nervous when she's not with them, like maybe that's when a Needle will crash during reconnaissance or the hamjis will blow up a transport vehicle. They believe that as long as Commander Sekmé keeps coming through in one piece, they will, too."

Dear God! Is that what the men really think of Sekmé? Set wondered.

He remembered the deep, guttural grinding of his sister's horror, her racking sobs, the shudder in her body as though her

muscles had separated from her bones and were frantically trying to reestablish their grip. Lokar's treachery notwithstanding, everything Sekmé had said, everything he had felt when he held her, attested to her profound, and genuine, sense of guilt. The raid was hers, all hers, conceived and executed exactly as she had planned . . . except for the disastrous denouement. High Command's approval of the plan—now *that* was suspicious. They must have realized the risk involved—but that was a separate mystery, the mystery of why they'd given such a young officer her head when she might lose it. The raid was Sekmé's.

But the men don't believe it, Set thought. She even contacted their families, offered herself up for their righteous punishment, for blood feud—she practically begged to be chastised—and her men left her alone. She was the lodestone for their morale and presumed pure.

Was Sekmé aware of the power she had? More importantly, was *High Command*?

Set felt very warm all of a sudden and a bit shaky, as if he had a fever.

"I think I'd like to explore the walls on my own now," he said.

"But, you can't reach the words."

"It doesn't matter. I like the feel of the stone and how open and cool the space is."

"You're not hungry?"

"If you are, go on. I can't get lost, can I?"

"No. Most of the chambers are locked and you'll eventually make your way back to where you started. It's a circle."

"Thank you. Then let me wander."

"That's a quote from an old song, isn't it? 'Then let me wander where I must, in the sand or in the dust.' "

Set grinned.

"Kerz, I thought I had you figured out, but you proved me wrong. You're a soldier and a scholar."

"You must come to my house sometime, bard Set. I'm sure my wife would love it."

Set waited until the chamberlain's boots turned out of the corridor and, by that change of direction, disappeared into silence. Then he set off down the middle of the corridor, relying on his sensitivity to the proximity of objects, to enjoy the soft echoes of his own slippers. The sound helped him feel the height and space of the corridor, even its curving, vaulted shape. He liked its emptiness, its smoothness. Moving through it was not unlike swimming, something he was pretty skillful at, although he rarely searched too deeply in the lakes or pools of the holdings; depths greater than the length of his own body disturbed his sense of direction and made him melancholy.

Sekmé was a magnificent swimmer with extraordinary lung capacity. She used to pull him through the water as he lay on his back, gently tugging him by his arms. She could swim backward—at least, that was how it seemed to Set—and they moved hand in hand across the lake or pool, effortlessly. At times, it felt so marvelous he'd embarrass himself. He really was far too sensitive to erotic stimulation. Sekmé never cared.

"Sails are trimmed," she would tease.

Set missed her terribly, and try as he might, he couldn't ignore the anxious fear that every day she fought in Tel-mari might be her last.

Set froze. He'd heard voices, familiar if muffled, from somewhere ahead of him. His heart beat almost too loudly for him to pinpoint the speakers' location, but after a minute or two, he decided they were in a chamber a few paces to his right and that the door was, luckily, only partway open.

"That must have been a shock, Atto. I always thought Commander Sekmé preferred women."

"So did I, Majesty. Needless to say, I got rid of the young man that night."

Set cautiously tiptoed back away from the chamber, but not so far that he couldn't overhear. Roon sounded cordial, if not particularly warm, and Atto . . . it was difficult to say. He seemed

both pleased and agitated, as if the memory of Sekmé's miscarriage continued to disturb him.

"I can't tell you, Majesty, how grateful I am to you and Secretary Dand for this mission you devised for Sekmé."

"She should be well into her role by now."

"As a *yansha*! Sheer brilliance."

"Yes. That was my idea."

Set shuddered. The king was proud of himself.

"Majesty, I doubt very much she'll survive such a mission."

"Thank you. Balance must be maintained. She was getting, shall we say, out of hand?"

"Mm, and, if for some reason Merkus and his hoard *don't* kill her—"

"What?" Roon interrupted, his voice colder. "Atto, your lack of faith disappoints me."

"Oh, no, no, Majesty! I'm sure it'll work. It's a marvelous plan, but Sekmé is . . ." Atto's voice trailed away.

Set held his breath and became rigid with concentration.

"Majesty," Atto murmured, "sometimes I think Sekmé is the incarnation of the Dark One's Captain."

There was a long silence before Roon responded in equally hushed tones.

"With bard Set as her unholy twin?" he asked.

"He *is* her twin, Majesty." Outside in the shadows, Set bit his fist to keep from crying out. "As an extra measure of insurance, I hired Lokar to follow and assassinate her."

"*Lokar?*" Roon snarled. "That reptile? I thought he was dead!"

"His kind dies many deaths, Majesty," Atto sighed. "The important thing is that Lokar wants Sekmé dead even more than we do. Why not let scum take the blame for curative evils?"

Bahé was the only one left at the buffet table. The queens, pleasant and polite as they were, had withdrawn from the field

as the young officer, with the grim appetite of a man convinced death was near, laid waste to the buffet from savories to sweets almost without pause, without breath.

He stopped when he saw Set slink uncertainly into the chamber, vulpé pelt clutched in nervous fingers. Set carried the napkin-sized pelt everywhere, but usually tucked it inside his clothing next to his chest. He didn't knead it like this in public unless he was upset about something.

"Set?" Bahé put down his plate and quickly stepped over to the poet. Set's face was ashen. "What's wrong?"

His cousin merely shook his head.

"Look, Set, you're obviously ill. I'll ask the chamberlain to find my father—he and the king went off somewhere together to talk—and we can go home."

Set nodded, then without ceremony, sat down hard on the floor, his head in his hands. A couple of the younger queens fluttered up to him with goblets of wine for him to sip and silk scarves dipped in water to place on his forehead. The older queens circled the patient and his nurses, clucking their concern. The density of their perfume sent the young man into a full swoon.

Seeing Set's plight, Bahé forgot his diffidence, elbowed his way through the oversolicitous queens and, grunting through the sudden protests of his lower back, picked up his cousin and carried him out of the palace. By the time Atto joined them, Bahé was already at the wheel of the vehicle and a groggy, but conscious, Set sat at his side. In spite of this, Atto was not about to ride in the canvas-tented cab, so all three of them crowded up front in silence as the desert miles passed beneath them on the way back to the holdings.

Once or twice, Bahé glanced at Set and it seemed Set had something urgent to tell him, but couldn't. Not with Atto present. When they got to the holdings, Set couldn't say anything there, either, because the servant who came out to greet them carried him away to a bath and bed.

"Poor laddie," Atto said. "That recitation took a lot out of him. It's almost as if he fought the battle himself."

"What would you know about that?" Bahé spluttered, shocking both his father and himself. "You never fought a day in your life, *second son!*"

Atto stared at him. Bahé was panting as hard as a runner who'd just completed a race through the dunes.

The older man said nothing but slowly, deliberately, consciously, the recognition of Bahé as son, as man, as living being, drained from his eyes until the young officer was facing a completely indifferent stranger.

Atto turned his back on Bahé and walked up the steps into the house.

Hatula could not get what she wanted out of her husband that night and it damaged her sleep. She kept tossing and turning, too hot, too cold, on the verge of grabbing Atto and insisting, only to hold back in confusion before his icy, uncommunicative bulk.

"But, Atto! Did the recitation go well? What's wrong with Set? Didn't the king like his epic? Please! Tell me what's wrong."

"Go to sleep."

"I'm your *wife*, Atto." She knelt at his side so that the long snakes of her hair hung down over her face and brushed his bare back. "There are no secrets between us. Come, love. Let me at least work the tension out of your body."

"Leave me alone."

Near dawn, she gave up trying to sleep. She got out of bed, went to the window, and began to brush and braid her hair. The stars were still out but she could feel the change, almost smell the approaching light.

Below, the shadowy shape of Bahé's military vehicle waited at the foot of the stairs to take her nephew to the air base where he'd climb into a Needle and fly himself to Tel-mari.

Poor Bahé! Bad enough to make him go at all, she thought, let alone insist he take himself.

She watched the darkness pale to a sooty blue and the vehicle's contours took on more definition and solidity.

I should adopt Atto's children, she thought, at least Bahé. There are too many of them to live well on divisions of his holdings. Sekmé could claim him as a brother and give him some of her holdings, too. Sad boy. I don't think he has enough steel in him to make his own way.

She laced her fingers in her hair and pulled them through to divide it for the braids. She was rapidly plaiting the first one closest to her face when she saw a quick, silent shadow dart out of the haze, lift a corner of the vehicle's canvas, and slip underneath.

The shadow was Set. His nimble yet cautious grace, informed by senses other than the common, could not be confused with anyone else's.

Hatula slowly lowered her hands. She looked back at Atto, his sleep-slowed breathing gently raising and lowering the furs draped over his body.

Something was very wrong. She should shake her husband awake and insist he explain it, insist he stop Set from acting on whatever desperate impulse made him stow away in Bahé's vehicle.

But—she didn't. Not entirely sure why she didn't, Hatula instead withdrew into the gloom of the room and crept under the bedclothes, careful not to touch her husband.

A few minutes later, Bahé, gloved and booted, emerged from the house and crunched across the gravel. He carried Sekmé's weapon, retrieved from the case in the hunters' room.

He stopped before getting into the vehicle to look at the oil-cartridge flare rifle in the new light of day. He turned it in his hands, studying the electrum inlay of the stock, which gleamed even at this young hour. Its pattern was based on the ancient

calligraphy for *God*, stylized and abstracted into elegant arabesques that danced seamlessly around the wood. In places, the metal was worn to a very fine sliver of brightness, but, remarkably, it remained complete. Centuries old, God's name continued to claim the tool of death.

Bahé still didn't know if he had the nerve to use it, to add his puny name to its history while its current owner, he hoped, still lived, but he'd be damned if he'd leave it in Atto's custody. Sekmé had entrusted it to *him*, Bahé, and he would rather it sank with his corpse into the swamps of Tel-mari than give his father the sterile satisfaction of a trophy.

He set the weapon in the rifle ring beside the driver's seat, aware that, for the first time, he was riding armed, and started the engine.

He took one last look at the house. He'd considered waking his aunt to say good-bye, but that would have wakened her husband. As for Set, well, he didn't think it would be fair to disturb him. If he had something important to tell him, he could use the box.

He swung the vehicle around in the drive and eased it past the gardens and out the gate into the desert.

At the air base, Bahé gave the job of unloading his things from the vehicle and putting them on the Needle to a couple of staff liaison officers while he went to see the base general to get his transfer papers in order.

"God above!" one said as he slid the long canvas bag from the back of the vehicle. "What's he got in this damned thing? A dead body?"

"Food, probably." The other chuckled as he helped hoist the bag into the Needle. "I wouldn't be surprised if he packed an entire side of smoked oryx."

"Blech! My mother makes that. I hate it."

Set had to bite his tongue to keep from yelping when the bag banged into the hold—and his head banged against the hard metal of the Needle's belly.

This was, by far, the most dangerous thing he'd ever done, and when he heard the squealing whine of the hold's door being slipped back into position followed by the hiss of the automatic seal, he was overcome with anxiety.

What am I doing? Am I insane? I've never been out of Maurhet! I don't know anything about Eshna! I'm *blind*, for God's sake! What makes me think I could find Sekmé even if someone volunteered to lead me through the streets? There are *millions* of people in that city . . .

When he heard someone getting into the separate cockpit section of this very long, lean aircraft, a more immediate fear gripped him.

What if the hold isn't heated? What if it isn't *pressurized*?

He gulped and tried to hold himself completely still as he strained for a mechanical clue, a noise that would answer his questions—and he heard something he'd been too agitated to notice before.

Clucking. There were cages of live barn pullets in the hold and they required heat and pressure to stay alive. Nothing nastier, and less palatable, than dead pullets lying in their own broken lung blood for five hours.

Ah, how wonderful! Set thought. I've become as one with the livestock.

His amused relief was cut short by a metallic howl that ripped into his head. It was soon joined by a roar so deep it seemed to come from the bowels of the Undivine's den itself. Set wriggled about frantically in the bag to get his hands up to cover his ears, but the combination of howl and roar still grabbed his body and all but slammed it up and down in the hold.

Then something did smack him down, as if the sky had collapsed on top of him. The Needle had taken off—straight up—and the immense force of the sudden lift squashed him flat.

The pullets continued to cluck contentedly. Set decided the birds were so unbelievably stupid that they couldn't even regis-

ter imminent death. He was certain his ribcage was going to give way.

However, just when he thought he heard his bones cracking, the monstrous pressure ceased and his body sprang away from the floor in rebound, slammed against the roof of the hold, then flew back toward the tail—along with a cage that also hadn't been tied down—and crashed into the wall.

The Needle had kicked in its forward thrust.

Set lay still a moment, conscious, albeit barely, and listened as the aircraft settled into its cruising speed. Equilibrium was gradually restored and his ears, ringing mightily, popped.

"Oooooooh!"

He heard something click, a hiss, and the quality of sound changed in the hold. He heard the muttering of the live air-to-land communicator and the soft, steady beep of the automatic pilot.

"Ah, damn those lazy idiots!"

Bahé's voice. Bahé's boots stamping into the hold. Bahé's hand righting first the unsecured cage, with its dead pullet, and then his canvas bag.

"What the—?"

Set felt the snaps pull open. Heard his cousin's gasp and then his horrified cry.

"Set! What are you doing here? Are you hurt? God almighty, you could have been killed!"

"I—I think I'm fine. Bruised, though."

"Are you *insane?*" Bahé's hands were all over him, searching for blood and broken bones. Miraculously, they found neither.

"Maybe, but I *had* to come, Bahé. I *had* to."

"The hell you did! Set, I'm so mad I could wring your neck, but I'm going to take you back to the base so the general can do it for me!"

"No!" Set found his cousin's shirt front and clutched it in his fists. Bahé tried to pry them off. "I have to warn Sekmé! She's in danger!"

"She's always in danger, stupid! That's her job."

"But, they've betrayed her, Bahé! This isn't a mission she's on. It's a trap!"

Bahé stopped trying to release himself from his cousin. He was very quiet. Set wasn't even sure he could hear him breathing.

"A trap, Bahé," he repeated. "I overheard the king and Uncle talking about it."

Bahé shifted a little in his crouch. Set took it as permission to explain, and he did. When he was done, he let go of Bahé's shirt and heard the young officer get up and return to the cockpit. However, he didn't hear the hold door close behind him.

"Bahé?"

No answer.

"Bahé, I know I can find her," he lied. "All I need is a Telmari cloak. I know the language. Sekmé used to share her lessons with me when she was a cadet."

Still no answer.

"Will you help me, Bahé?"

Now Set heard something soft, ragged, partly strangled. Bahé was crying. Set scrambled the rest of the way out of the canvas bag and crawled painfully to the cockpit door.

"Will you?"

He heard Bahé sniff, then sigh deeply.

"You're crazy, Set," he whispered.

"I know."

Set carefully sat back on his heels and listened to the tiny symphony of instrument chatter in the cockpit, the small beep and clicks, the steady, muted conversation from the communicator, and felt a sharp thrill of excitement. They were airborne! He was flying!

"Bahé," he asked shyly, hoping that his smile wasn't too distorted by the sore swelling he felt around his nose and mouth, "what—what does it look like outside? Is everything smaller?"

"No," Bahé replied. "Bigger. *We* just got smaller."

CHAPTER 13

YAПSHA

Because Hemsha was her father, Bekka could take off her veil before him when she was at home as long as no other men were present. Sekmé, however, had to wait until the old man retired for the night. Once he finally had, long after the tavern was closed and the few overnight guests had disappeared into their rooms, his daughter studied Sekmé's naked visage curiously.

"What?" Sekmé asked, suddenly worried that something about her face or cropped hair gave away the sand in her blood. "Do I have food in my teeth?"

"No," Bekka said. "You're prettier than I expected for someone who's had such a hard life."

Sekmé snorted skeptically. Bekka had undoubtedly had a much harder life than the one the scar-faced intelligence officer had cooked up for the reluctant commander, but she was more beautiful than any of the women Sekmé had ever seen, Maurheti or Tel-mari. For one thing, Bekka's skin had a luminous, transparent quality, possibly the result of being covered and veiled virtually her entire life. Her eyes were large, very dark, and tipped up at the corners like a cat's. They always seemed to be watching the world with a sad and knowing, but gentle, amusement. Her mouth was full, perhaps a little too full, but

Sekmé felt that if Bekka ever married—a source of great hope and anguish on Hemsha's part—her husband would not protest.

Best of all, Bekka had a fabulous cataract of silky black curls that flowed down her back to her hips. It swung gently at every step and made Hatula's infamous "snakes" resemble serpents in earnest.

What a waste that, most of the time, no one can see it, Sekmé mused.

"I appreciate your father's taking me in," she said as she tasted the grmysh Bekka set before her. It was almost . . . not bad. "For all he knows, I could be a murderer."

"Papa's always been very generous."

Bekka joined her at the table. They had the tavern room to themselves, and she had swept away the rubbish, scraped the trenchers, put up the bottles, and wrapped the leftover meats in oiled paper and squirreled them away in the pantry. Life at the inn may have been primitive, but it was tidy.

The weak yellow light of a streetlamp came through the thick roundels of the ancient arched window. Bekka augmented it with a goat-tallow taper.

"But, why is he generous?" Sekmé asked. "It doesn't make sense. Not in the New Hives."

"It keeps him alive," Bekka said. Her fingers absently toyed with her hair. "Bitterness would destroy him."

"Forgive me for asking, but, how old *is* your father?"

"Fifty-four."

"But, the hair, the beard . . ."

"Oh, the white is new." Bekka's feline gaze drifted toward the candle and locked onto it. "In the first battle of Eshna, Papa lost his school and my brother disappeared. If it hadn't been for my mother's steadfastness, Papa would have killed himself." She paused and her eyes became wet. "When he lost my mother in the second raid, he tried to."

"I'm sorry," Sekmé said. She didn't have to pretend it.

"He lost all of his hair," Bekka said, "everywhere. Even his

eyebrows. When it grew back—and his beard grew back very quickly—it was white."

"Did you go crazy, too?"

Bekka smiled softly, and again, Sekmé marveled at the waste caused by the veil.

"No. One of us had to remain strong and my father, well, he's still a philosopher."

"What about your brother?"

"Nobody's seen him since the first raid twelve years ago."

Sekmé knew almost as much about the first raid as she did of her own, casually referred to as the second. After all, the *first* raid was her father's. God's terrible symmetry was everywhere.

"I, um, I have a brother . . . somewhere," Sekmé said.

"You do?"

Bekka smiled at her and Sekmé felt like swamp mud. She was deceiving Bekka with the truth to gain a false friendship the woman obviously considered genuine.

The Maurheti priests said that the Tel-mari were born without souls, but Sekmé doubted they'd ever met such a beautiful, earnest creature. If they had, would they still deny her a piece of divinity?

"He's a poet," Sekmé said.

Bekka's smile widened.

"He's blind."

Bekka's face fell.

"But, you'd never know it," Sekmé added quickly. "He's so quick and perceptive. Why, he used to lead *me* when it was dark."

This pleased Bekka.

"It's amazing, isn't it?" she asked. "How well we adjust to misfortune if we have faith! God rains His blessings."

God doesn't "rain" anything, Sekmé thought sourly. Belief in that wet Tel-mari demiurge certainly hasn't done this poor girl a damned bit of good.

"Yes, He does," she replied.

★ ★ ★

Her life with Bekka and Hemsha fell into a routine. No matter how early Sekmé rose, and she was used to dawn patrols, Bekka was already up preparing root soup and flatbread for the handful of guests who had spent the night. Once these were fed and sent on their way, Bekka woke her father, fed him, and heated water for his bath on the wood-, coal-, and rubbish-burning hearth—Tel-mari families in the New Hives could not be particular about fuel—while Sekmé hiked up a steep, narrow, nearby lane to a sheltered community well where the women bathed their children and each other and beat their laundry on the ruins of a short stone wall.

Several things about this women-only watering spot intrigued Sekmé. The first was that, at the well, all were equal. Refugees who, judging by the style of their hair and fineness of their robes, had once been well off mingled sociably with ragged street women and their belly-bloated babies. They took note of Sekmé as a newcomer, but otherwise showed no misgivings or prejudice toward her red yansha garb or strangely shorn coiffure. They let her bathe and collect a bucket of water in peace. Occasionally, one of the mothers asked her to mind the children for her while she bathed—a discomfiting task since Sekmé did not feel she had any facility with children. Still, she tried to be philosophical about her assignment and the children tended to be well behaved, more interested in splashing in the water than in hurting others or themselves.

They have no idea they're wretched, Sekmé observed, or that their future is meaningless. All they know is the fun or pain of the moment.

She expected to pity them—the damned *were* to be pitied—but was startled to discover herself envying their play, their simplicity . . . their innocence.

The other intriguing thing about the well was the well itself. Not the aquifer; Tel-mari was so saturated that springs and wells popped up just about anywhere, even in the heart of a heavily

overbuilt and overpopulated city. No, it was the ledge around the well, the catch basin, and the ruins the women slapped the babies' nappies on. All were constructed of very fine, hard stone that had to have been mined deep in the forested interior and carted to Eshna—no mean feat considering the size of some of the blocks: at least as wide and tall as a transport vehicle. The well had to date back to Eshna's ancient beginnings when, according to Tel-mari myth, these homunculi of the Not-God were wealthy, even nominally sophisticated.

On the other hand, some Maurheti experts claimed that the work was not Tel-mari at all, but Maurheti—that this wet land had once been part of the old kingdom before the Tel-mari barbarians came out of the northern forests to sack and plunder in the name of their false deity.

Sekmé ran her finger over the stone and felt the worn brows and depressions of indecipherable symbols, a handful of markings too battered and forgotten to speak. She'd heard the explanations of the ruins her entire life but, confronted with this lovely example of the real thing, she wasn't sure she could believe any of them. The well did not seem Tel-mari *or* Maurheti. If anything, the symbols looked vaguely Denneshur, like those chipped carefully into cave walls in the Hills of Whispers—but even this didn't fit. The Denneshur claimed their name, from *Den-ah-shura*, meant *skeptic* and that, from the beginning of world time, they had refused to side with either Tel-mari or Maurhet and had rejected their cultures of cities and roads.

Sekmé frowned and looked back at the women as they chatted, gossiped, and laughed softly over their morning chores. The Denneshur always made a point of referring to things as happening in "world time," as if there could have been a time before creation, a time before Time.

That wasn't possible, of course. God created time and the world simultaneously. There was no before—only God, and He was timeless.

Having completed her morning ablutions, Sekmé returned

to the tavern for her share of the communal meal, and afterward, while Bekka went to the sprawling, haphazard market, a much more disorganized source of goods and foodstuffs than the market Sekmé had gel-bombed, she reconnoitered under the pretense that she was looking for a little street trade, a round or two of quick, back-alley gambling that would supplement her evening games at the tavern. She hoped that, during these excursions and games, someone might let a word loose, a hint drop, a name or a quickly hushed reference escape, that would give her a clue to the location of Merkus's den. She had a strong feeling that many of the refugees knew exactly where the terrorist and his henchmen were hiding, but that they'd tacitly agreed to bury the knowledge so deeply that even a generous share of Sekmé's portable stash of damnation ale couldn't float it to the surface.

Instead, she heard a lot of other things, often in great detail, that she wasn't sure she wanted to hear: how cruel the Maurheti were to their Tel-mari workforce, which Maurheti officer was raping which Tel-mari refugee's wife in exchange for food and warmer clothing, whose children had died, and which drugs provided the best kick into oblivion.

Once or twice, their complaints hit close to home and Sekmé had to fight every instinct for self-defense to retain her pose of detachment and war-numbed fatalism.

"Field General Am is all right, as far as it goes," a toothless bottle peddler lisped. His wares were attached to his cloak by loops of string, and he clinked and clattered wherever he went. "I mean, he disciplines his men pretty harshly if they get rough with our women or torture our animals or tease our children. I saw him beat an underofficer with his belt for spitting on a serving girl who wouldn't take her veil off."

How does he know that? Sekmé wondered as she gathered up the knucklebones for another throw. That incident had happened in camp at an officers' banquet.

"Still, he's no friend of Tel-mari," a young, weedy comrade added. "He ordered the market raid. Ha! Fifteen. I win."

"No, he didn't," the peddler said. "I heard High Command did."

"And I heard Roon himself approved it whoever ordered it because a Tel-mari cheated a friend of his over the price of a quintet of onagers. Shit! These bones must be weighted."

They were, but Sekmé didn't flutter an eyelash. She was listening too intently. She never did learn why her idea of gel-bombing the Eshna market had been so quickly approved, and the order had indeed issued directly from High Command—very unusual for them, as was this ferret mission of hers.

Sekmé nodded grimly at the men as if affirming their assessments of Maurheti bureaucratic skullduggery, but she was really taking notes.

There's a breached seam in security, that's certain, she thought. *I wonder where?*

"Ah, Maurheti," she said as if the word was bitter. "Who knows why they do what they do? That's twelve. Dealer wins."

"I hate this game," the bottle peddler muttered before adding, "I think the Maurheti like the feel of power, the crunch of the beetle underfoot, and, now and then, they get bored with merely telling us how to run our lives and decide to take a few of them away."

"A woman did it, you know."

All of the players, and Sekmé, turned to this new voice, the deep voice of a powerfully built, broken-nosed man who was leaning against the alley wall and biting his ragged thumbnail.

"I'm not surprised," the skinny young player said. "They're an ungodly race."

We're ungodly? Sekmé thought, outraged in spite of her determination to beat back judgment whenever she was plying her trade.

"She's a commander," the broken-nosed man continued, "a

girl named Sekmé. The Maurheti call her the Iron Lady, or Iron Virgin, but not to her face."

The bottle peddler snickered darkly then winked at Sekmé.

"What do you know, yansha? Never occurred to me that your sisters had exchanged an innate violence for profitable coupling."

Sekmé shrugged. She had to avoid showing offense.

"Anything to advance the cause of civilization," she said, and the players threw back their heads and guffawed.

"Spot me in, sister," the broken-nosed man said. "You've a good flavor, even dry."

"And dry we stay, understand, colt?"

"Whatever you say."

In the late afternoon, Sekmé returned to the tavern with her as yet unhelpful information, ate a bit of whatever Bekka was cooking for the evening's trade, and prepared herself for the crowds of laughing, drinking, swearing, cheating, brawling, gorging, yelling, pinching—and paying—gamblers.

It was miserable work: weighting the bones, palming tiles, ghost-shuffling cards—all to keep her advantage while fending off advances, laughing at bad jokes, and tasting—and secretly discarding—tankard after tankard to appear neighborly and a good mark.

She hated it most of all when Maurheti soldiers showed up to play because it usually meant there would be a fight, often bloody. Even if there wasn't any open violence, the damage done to the cheerful, rough tone of the evening was usually irreparable.

Sekmé had rarely gone into Eshna in her liberty time. She preferred to explore outlying villages and hunt in the marshes rather than dive into the human misery of the Hives, Old or New, but her men did it all the time out of a need to release their various war-induced tensions.

Now she saw the forms of that release. Maurheti soldiers on leave were boorish thugs. The best of them bought a girl, yan-

sha or not, and got drunk with her as fast as he could until he was weeping his loneliness and vomiting his bitterness into her cleavage. The more ambitious roamed the streets in bands to find a victim to torment—elderly man, young boy, older woman, it rarely mattered—first with verbal abuse, then physical. Sekmé knew about this kind of crime, but had had no idea how widespread it was, apparently because most of the victims were too frightened and distrustful of Maurheti authority to report it. In ten days, three beatings occurred right outside Hemsha's inn in spite of his holy threats and active walking stick.

And all of the soldiers cheated, flagrantly. Sekmé could not protest too loudly or they might choose her for their evening's back-alley sport. Yanshas were favorite targets because their "goods" were readily available and, therefore, considered more vile than anything taken by force. The officers liked to punish them.

Sekmé could see what really motivated these military marauders. She saw it in their eyes and was deeply familiar with it. It sat on the Anti-Insurgency Forces like a curse and had to be conquered, bled away, or released before it destroyed your sanity. It was the horrible knowledge that you were in an alien place, doing something destructive, surrounded by people who hated you, and that you could die any minute in any number of gruesome ways. No amount of righteous sermonizing could chase it away. The soldiers came into the tavern with cloudy, barely animated expressions and, after a little whoring, boozing, and battery, left as miserable as they'd entered—but with clearer eyes.

Sometimes, after the tavern closed, Sekmé climbed out onto the roof, as she had when training with the faceless officer, and looked at the stars while sorting out her many layers of distress.

She would insist on a new leave policy, she decided. The men needed more visits home more often. Also, she would petition High Command for more military police in Eshna to

keep an eye on those soldiers who decided to go into town for entertainment. Maybe these changes would alleviate some of the tension on both sides.

"Or, maybe not," she sighed. "This is the way it's always been. The tide going one way or the other as balance dictates. The Tel-mari will take their own cruel revenge someday, I'm sure."

She studied the moon, a pale orange drum in the night, and its misshapen "baby," the Calf. The Calf was slowly passing beneath its parent, out of synch until the next Suckling.

The Calf was a strange bit of cosmic flotsam. Long and slim, it trotted around the world, lapping the moon several times as the larger body ambled through its phases. Like all pilots, Sekmé had once turned her Needle's sights on the Calf and had been startled by the regularity of its surface. It looked like a wedge hacked out of a chalk mountain with a monstrous adze. Since the recon run was routine, Sekmé had let her imagination wander over the Calf's peculiarly clean edges and strangely even whiteness. She'd let herself wonder why this asteroid was the way it was and had even entertained the idea that it wasn't a moon bit at all.

"All right, then, genius, what *would* it be?" she asked herself as she sat on the roof of the tavern. "Set would have a *thousand* answers for that one! Maybe God dropped His boot knife and forgot to pick it up. Or maybe He left it there as a practical joke. Something to tease us."

She felt for the knife in her own boot. Still there. Nice to know, considering she still felt she was being watched.

"Seshi? Are you out there?"

Of course, it could just be her conscience glowering at her through her confusion. Even blister worms and sand mites, hardly masters of souls, were wards of God's protection. Why couldn't humble, well-behaved Tel-mari be? Why were they, in particular, damned?

"Seshi? It's getting cold. I smell rain."

Had they chosen their fate? Why be damned if you'd done nothing? Maybe they *did* have souls . . . or at least some of them.

"Seshi, please!"

God forgive me! All those corpses . . .

Bekka poked her head, veilless, out Sekmé's window and looked up at the brooding yansha.

"Seshi, if you catch a chill, you won't be able to work and I'll have to nurse you, which will make me very grumpy."

Her tone was firm but playful and Sekmé, finally remembering that, in her yansha disguise, *she* was Seshi, removed her veil and smiled at her.

"Bekka, you're such a mother pieduck! I'll be in in a minute."

Goodnight, Calf, she thought with one last glance at the weird moonlet, whatever you are.

Lokar considered picking off his target while she bathed in the secluded well, but the roofline above it was too exposed, and whether he was successful or not, one of the other women might see him. This would raise an inconvenient hue and cry that would alert the menfolk who had a nasty habit of killing any male who had spied on their unclad females. Such uncouth brutes! After all, most of these women were pretty hideous undressed: baggy-breasted, sow-bellied, and wobble-thighed. How anyone could find them attractive and want to mate with them was a mystery he was grateful he couldn't fathom.

Sekmé, at least, was slim, but Lokar's lust was to see those clean limbs torn from her body, her small breasts ripped away, and her head chopped off with a very dull blade. Her alley games puzzled him and did not give him an opportunity for murder. Lokar guessed she was sniffing out information for some future action, but had no idea what information these smelly refugees could impart. They were lice on the world body.

Ah, well. He was the most patient assassin in the world. His time would come.

In the street below, he saw the broken-nosed man pause briefly outside the dark inn and look it over before moving on. He did this every evening as if making sure all was secure for the night. Lokar chuckled silently. Miserable fool! Probably worried about the safety of the liquor inside. Maurheti or Telmari, it didn't matter. Lokar prided himself in recognizing the need in all of its guises.

"Take care, brother," he whispered as he popped open another capsule of comfort. "Take very great care."

CHAPTER 14

ALLEY POET

"Set didn't have a chance to visit his poet and singer friends in Kemphor before the recitation," Hatula explained the morning after her son's departure. "Bahé offered to take him back before he headed for the base. He didn't tell you?"

Atto, strolling the balcony as he surveyed the morning rush of servants from quarters to house before breakfast, grunted. This seemed plausible. You could expect Bahé to be absent-minded. But Set?

"Perhaps Set was too nervous about the recitation to bring up his wish to stay in town," he mused, "and he was ill afterward."

"I'm sure that's it." Hatula gathered up her skirts and fluttered busily out of the bedchamber, on her way to supervise the holdings' morning cycle of chores.

"How long does Set usually stay with these friends of his?" Atto called after her.

"Oh, maybe a few days. Maybe a few weeks."

"A few *weeks*?"

"He's a grown man, Atto. He can do what he wants."

Perhaps, Atto thought, perhaps not. Had the eloquent terror of the epic been a purely voluntary creation? Or had the Spirit of Negation had a hand in it?

Once, he would have laughed at himself for such superstitious paranoia. Once.

"Let me know when he returns, Hatula, if I miss him."

Bahé carried the canvas bag from the Needle over his shoulder. When necessary, he could count on a considerable core of strength under his extra flesh, and it was crucial that no one else handle his already brutalized cousin.

"What's in the bag, Subcom? Supper?"

"Get out of my way, soldier, before I drop it on your head."

He took Set into his new—new to him anyway—private tent and helped him out of the bag and into a scavenged set of Tel-mari rags that had once belonged to a scullery servant. Set grinned through the entire process, which annoyed Bahé.

"Set, what you're doing is *dangerous*."

"I know," Set said, "but I can't help thinking how wonderful an adventure it is, too. I've never traveled so far."

"I should still toss you back into the next Needle home—"

"But you won't," Set said softly, seriously. "Sekmé is important to you, too. You have her weapon."

Bahé sighed. Once Set decided on something, he couldn't be dissuaded. Bahé pulled up the hood on Set's cloak, arranged it, then stood back to assess his work.

"How do I look?" Set asked—in Tel-mari.

Bahé twitched. Even though Set's accent was flawless, the language sounded wrong on his lips.

"You look like a raggedy beggar with a big blue and purple welt under your left eye," Bahé responded, also in Tel-mari. He had to get used to it. "Don't make your eyes follow my voice. Try to let them wander so you look, well, blind. You'll blend in better."

"Are many refugees blind?" Set sounded dismayed, as if he actually pitied the Tel-mari.

"You won't be unusual."

Bahé then explained how to find the highway and follow it into the city.

"I wish I could drive you in, but Field General Am wants me to start working with his communications officer this afternoon."

He smiled sadly at his cousin. Handsome, clever, quick—everything Bahé had always envied and now the last person in the world he wanted to trade places with.

"Don't get killed, Set. That would really make me angry."

"All right, I won't."

The Tel-mari "dry" season had begun, which meant it rained about every third day. This was still far from dry enough to set the mud, so Set high-stepped through a thick, sticky porridge pungent with life's leavings: manure, rotten food, the natural, loamy mineral smell of the soil itself, the sick, sweetish funk of dead animals.

Except for the difficulty of transit, which heated him to a sweat under his woolen rags, Set didn't mind the mud. Its stench moved him by telling him of the basic fertility of the land hidden under the teeming misery of its people. No wonder all those wonderfully perfumed flowers in the holdings' gardens came from this place! If he were a plant, he'd live here, too. Rich soil, rain—

An overripe purbet fruit bounced off a passing cart and hit him in the face.

—fertilizer. Yes, I could be a plant here, Set thought.

Not easy to be a person, though. In the steady refugee traffic in and out of Eshna, Set smelled, heard, felt, and even tasted what Sekmé had once described: the sour aura of animal stress even in the children, a weary undertone of bitter fatalism, and the flat, overcooked savor of malnourishment, illness, and discontent.

At the same time, something nearly as strong, if harder to discern, moved among the Tel-mari like the lowest thrum on a thetl. It was in the rustle of a veiled one who casually, expertly,

picked up her tired, whining child and cooed to it soothingly. It was in the crisp bark of a vendor who, although he'd been calling his wares for hours, still wasn't hoarse.

"Fiiiiine young caaaaapon! Chicks and breeeeeders! Fiiiiine young caaaapon!"

It was in the deep, complex meatiness of a well-made pot of stew bubbling in a quiet corner of the market. Set shyly begged for some and was rewarded with a chipped crock of oily, but surprisingly tasty grmysh.

And it definitely sang in the low chuckle, short *ha!*, muffled giggle, and sudden long, loose rocking laughter of wry humor.

The Tel-mari had been conquered, but not defeated. Ragged, quarrelsome, desperate, and reduced to animal pettiness, they held on to an identity, a spirit unbroken in the face of millions of deaths. This spirit had founded a New Hives only a couple months after the death of the Old. It had lined up the ranks of the slaughtered to curse their killers. It was alive, virulent—immortal.

Set drew back up against a wall with his crock of mulled goat organs and wept.

It was true! He'd known it all along. The Tel-mari were complete, real people; they had souls!

Just like me! he thought.

"There now, boy, don't cry," said the woman who'd given him the stew. Judging by her voice, she was a heavy-bosomed matron who breathed campfire smoke all day. "I know it's hard at times, but we have to bear up. We're alive, aren't we? That's God's gift."

"I'm not used to begging," Set said. "I wish I had some way to pay you for your kindness."

"Never mind," the woman said tenderly. Set felt her big flat hand pass over his head. "We have to help each other along. Tomorrow, it may be me begging from you."

"What's your name, mistress?"

"Betshira, my little blind man. Betshira the grmysh seller."

Set pinched his brows together in concentration.

"Betshira . . . Betshira . . ."

"Yes, I'm rather fond of the name." She chuckled. "Kinda used to it, you know?"

Set carefully put his crock on the ground, tucked his hands into his sleeves, smiled, and recited the poem he'd composed on the spot.

> *"Betshira, Betshira,*
> *The lady with the spoon,*
> *Can warm the body, warm the soul,*
> *By day or light of moon.*
> *Bring your empty belly,*
> *Perhaps a coin or two,*
> *She'll leave you fed and merry*
> *With lovely Eshna stew."*

Not much, Set had to admit, but serviceable on such short notice in a foreign language, and the grmysh seller was delighted. With a high cry, she clapped those big hands of hers together then clamped them around Set's shoulders and gave him a squeeze that reawakened his body's memory of the Needle's takeoff.

"Aren't you sweet!" she cried. "What a lovely little verse! You're the most darling little man! I could squeeze you forever!"

Set hoped she meant that metaphorically. He was beginning to feel dizzy from lack of air.

"How do you do that? Make up a verse just like that?"

"I don't know," Set wheezed when Betshira released him. "It's a gift . . . from God."

His last two words pleased her more than the ditty because this time when she squeezed him she sobbed into his ear and stroked him all over as if he were a prodigal pet.

"You remind me of my dear little Ipuy," she said. "He was a good boy, a very good boy, and those demons killed him!"

"God defend us from disasters, Betshira!" came a man's voice from somewhere outside their clinch. Set was too busy being mauled to discern the direction. "What are you doing to that poor blind boy?"

"He's wonderful, Ramil! He's a poet!"

That was how Set became a fixture among the street people of Eshna. Instead of singing for his supper, he made up poems for the people who fed him, shared their straw and rubbish lean-tos, and rushed him into the back alleys when the bands of dead-eyed Maurheti soldiers went looking for the helpless.

"I'm trying to find my sister," he told them, and pretending to be a deeply ashamed yet loyal brother, added under his breath yet loud enough to hear, "she's a yansha."

"Mm," they said, sometimes with a knowing cluck. "Can't really blame the girl. Still, it's an evil life."

"I've read her face with my fingers," Set said. "I know her walk and her smell. Her hair is short and straight. Eyes the same color as . . . as mine. Her mouth is like mine but with a smaller upper lip. Nose the same. She has a bold step like a man's."

He felt them thinking about this as they warmed their hands around a campfire of broken sticks. He sensed their quiet nods, heard the faint, considering scratch of nails through stubble.

"Does she have as nice a voice as yours?" a young woman asked. She sounded barely more than a girl, but had told Set she was a widow who'd given birth to a dead son.

"Yes, but she can't sing." Set grinned and wrinkled his nose. "Can't carry a tune."

"Then she's either slutting or she's a gaming yansha," a man's bass boomed.

"Oh, never a slut," Set said, his heart squeezing painfully.

"Then a gaming yansha."

"Yes . . . yes, that's right."

"How old?"

"Twenty-four."

The man grunted.

"Shouldn't be too hard to find," he said. "Anyone that young already gaming will stand out."

Set felt the faint steam of the man's breath and smelled a rotten tooth. The man was leaning close to him.

"What's your name, son?"

"Set."

"Sounds foreign."

"It might be," Set said. "I don't remember my father."

"Well, don't worry. I'm not particular about blood purity."

"Thank you."

"What's your sister's name?"

"I don't know. I mean—I don't think she's using her real name anymore."

The man grunted again. Much of his verbal expression came through the back of his throat or the front of his nose. *Hrum* and *snort*.

"It doesn't matter much anyway," he said. "Before the last raid, I was a tale dancer."

"A tale dancer? Is that like being a poet?"

"Hell, no! It's a kind of low-level spy. I didn't have any loyalties. I'd track down anything for anyone if the price was right. If your sister is anywhere in Eshna, I'll find her, although it may take a little time."

"I hope that's all it takes," Set said. "I have a feeling she doesn't have much more than a *little* time."

"I'll keep my eyes and ears open."

Set reached out his hand and rested it on the man's cheek. The man flinched, but didn't pull away, and Set's fingers searched his broad features, thick, broken nose, and tangled beard.

"You said that before the last raid, you had no loyalties. Do you now?"

"Yes."

"To whom?"

"To myself . . . and anyone who kills Maurheti soldiers."

"Like Merkus?" asked the girl.

"Merkus doesn't exist," the man said, then, slyly, "or maybe he's right behind you."

The girl must have looked. Set heard her rustle.

"You're teasing me."

"Yes, unfortunately . . ."

Later, when the young widow took Set into the relative dryness of her box and canvas "house," she took his hands and led them up under her veil.

"I haven't looked in a glass for three years," she whispered. "Am I very thin?"

"Thin . . . but beautiful."

"Really?"

"Yes."

She moved his hands down to her throat. He felt her swallow, and the tiny intermittent bump of her pulse came faster.

"When my husband died, I wanted to die, too."

"I'm glad you didn't."

"I don't think I could live if I were blind. How do you manage?"

"Being blind teaches your other senses to pay attention," Set said, fingers slipping down into her robe. "You learn to see in other ways."

"So, you've become very sensitive."

Set stopped his explorations, suddenly ashamed. He shouldn't take advantage of her loneliness like this.

"Perhaps I should go . . ."

"No! Please." Her girl's voice turned plaintive. "Sometimes I think I'm going to disappear, that I'm not real anymore. No one touches me, not nicely anyway, but now, when you—" Her voice caught on her tears. "You're gentle. It makes me feel like I'm still alive in the world."

Set spent the nights thereafter in her arms, which did not make him feel virtuous, but did make him feel useful.

★ ★ ★

Wepanu ul-Bahf squatted beside his small smoky fire and listened to the voices in the wind outside as they brushed past the mouth of the cave. They were muttering blood, catastrophe, change.

He glanced up at the vault of the cave. As she had in the Great Dome, the wau-weh–snouted jo flitted about in the unstable light, examining the ancient symbols carved in, stamped on, and sometimes painted over the stone.

"This one," she said, pointing to a starlike shape, "is homeless. It wanders full of weeping songs and desert wind. This one—" She pointed to a shape similar to a large, many-petaled flower. "—is mountains and rivers, famine, festival, and silence."

She darted across the cave, her transparent body flickering like one of the dancing sparks from the fire, and stopped at a third symbol.

"This one, like a stark, leafless tree, holds self-hatred in its branches, denial, vinegar, streets of fire, and spices."

She pressed her hands over the fourth and fifth symbols: a divided circle and a thin crescent.

"These were confounded," she said, "confused, and produced the sins of the world in the name of blessedness."

Wepanu squinted. He had superb eyesight for a man his age, but the smoky firelight left much to be desired.

"That one," he said, raising his lean black arm to point to the one she covered with her transparent right hand. "The crescent. It looks Tel-mari."

"Not anymore," the jo said. "All of these gods died during the journey, although their names lasted for centuries without them."

Wepanu nodded.

"We of the desert—"

"Only you knew the truth," the jo said. "Only you knew it was time to find a *new* god, the *real* God."

"We're still looking."

"Better looking than standing still."

A distant wau-weh barked twice, followed by the long, low, pitiful wail of something Wepanu could not identify. He glanced back toward the desert darkness. Another walker? He turned to the jo, but she'd disappeared. In her wake, the cave smelled of freshly baked bread. She'd been tasting someone else's dreams again.

Wepanu poked at the fire and frowned.

"The jo had better tell me who it is soon," he muttered, "or the sand will claim another corpse."

CHAPTER 15

THE WEDDING

A friend of my sister-in-law's palm reader actually met him once and says he's very handsome, but very serious. His eyes are full of ghosts."

"He's a fantasy. All these attacks? Must be half a dozen groups at least. It's a story to put the swine off the trail."

"No, I've never met him, but I'd like to. He's one of God's servants, a righteous man driven to extreme measures by circumstances beyond any mortal's endurance. I feel I understand him."

"I think he and his men were living in the old sewer lines, but they've moved on."

"I don't care what people think. He's a murderer and God does not sanction murder, no matter how vile the victim."

After weeks as a yansha, during which she became adept at fleecing her marks without stirring even the vaguest suspicions, mastered climbing in rubble to pick over old clues without catching her long, loose skirts on anything, and conquered eating soup while wearing a veil, Sekmé still had no better information on Merkus than rumor, hearsay, and tall tales. She was exceedingly frustrated.

On the other hand, she and Bekka had become close, at least as close as a devout veiled one and a street entertainer could.

Sekmé's favorite time of day was after closing, after Hemsha had retired, when both she and Bekka could take off their veils, put their bare feet in a common tub of hot, salted water, and chat over tiny cups of damnation ale.

"Papa would take a switch to me if he knew I was drinking this," Bekka said.

"Why? Aren't you allowed a little alcohol now and then?"

"Of course, but we're depleting the tavern's stock."

"Ah! The philosopher has a tight fist, does he?"

"It's a myth that thinkers have no common sense," Bekka said.

"Not where I come from," Sekmé retorted, remembering her teachers—and her brother. Set was clever, but sometimes reckless.

"Where *do* you come from?" Bekka asked. "You haven't told me much about your past."

Sekmé looked into those lovely dark eyes and sighed. Apart from her mother, she'd never had a close female friend, had never been aware of the need, and she wished she could unburden herself, unlock the door to those secrets she couldn't even share with Set.

She wriggled her toes in the steaming tub and her foot brushed against Bekka's. Right now, in this damp, mildew- and cabbage-scented, candlelit kitchen, her mission seemed absurd, but she had to stick to her half-truths or she might, through no fault of her hosts, get herself, and them, killed.

"I grew up on a farm with my brother," she said, "one of the last ones commandeered by the Maurheti."

"What did you grow? Mang? Yarprin? Were there animals?"

"Yes. All of that and birds, too."

"It must have been wonderful."

Sekmé shrugged as if the farm's loss was too painful to discuss. In truth, she felt a bit homesick.

"What was your mother like, Seshi?"

"She's still alive, I think. She's bigger than I am."

"You mean heavier?"

"Don't let *her* hear you say that!"

Bekka giggled and splashed a little.

"My mother was tiny," she said. "She had a neat, tidy little body like a doll. My father and brother adored her. So did I."

She studied her feet for a while. Her memories were as melancholy as Sekmé's and for the same reason: war.

"Someday, I'd like to be as good a mother as she was."

Sekmé reached out and stroked Bekka's hair. It seemed a natural, soothing thing to do, as if Bekka was her daughter.

"How about you?" Bekka asked. "Do you want children someday?"

It was only after Sekmé emphatically answered "never" that she realized it was supposed to have been a rhetorical question. Bekka blanched and her soft mouth opened in an *oh!* of dismay.

"But, what if things were different, Seshi? What if you weren't a yansha?"

"But, I am."

"But, if you *weren't*? Try to imagine it."

This wasn't the first time a Tel-mari had asked Sekmé to imagine the impossible, which it would be if her role was true.

Should she stick to it now and say that things *would* be different if she was not a yansha? Part of her role was to follow cultural expectations.

"No. Not even if I wasn't a yansha."

For once, no playacting. She was sharing a foot soak with this woman.

"I'm not the same kind of person as you, Bekka. I like children, but I don't want to raise them. Maybe I'm selfish—"

This opening up, this confession—it was too seductive . . . and too dangerous. Time to change direction.

"—I don't know, but I *have* thought it would be nice to have woman friends."

"You don't have any?"

"In my profession, most of your conversations and confidences are with men."

Bekka's brows lifted, rounding her feline eyes. "I thought yanshas kept together in sisterhoods."

She was right. Once again, Sekmé had fallen under the spell of honesty and answered as herself.

"I struck out on my own," she said diffidently, looking away from Bekka's face. "Perhaps my situation is unusual."

"So is your not wanting children."

Someone banged the flat of their palm on the tavern door and both Bekka and Sekmé deftly redid their veils. Bekka also stepped out of the tub into her slippers. Sekmé was about to follow, but Bekka waved her back.

"I'm mistress," she said. "You're a guest."

She hurried into the front room. There were muffled words at the door, a cry of pleasure from Bekka, and the door swung open. Three people, a man and two women, all talking at once, spilled loudly into the tavern.

"Such happy news!" Bekka cried.

"The best!" said the man.

"We want you and your father there." A young woman's voice.

"Not just there, but we want you to provide the food and drink." An older woman.

"But how?" Bekka asked. "You and Momer—"

"Don't say another word," the man, Momer, said. "A daughter gets married only once. I *can* afford it."

Sekmé took her feet out of the tub and tracked water to the kitchen doorway. She poked her head into the room. "A wedding?"

Momer, a thickset fellow in the usual refugee rags, but with unusually surprised-looking hair and a missing right arm, squinted at the newcomer, saw the red garments, noticed the black and white diamond-patterned pouch slumped in the corner, and announced, "With entertainment!"

His daughter, the bride-to-be—which surprised Sekmé, con-

sidering the young woman's tremendous obesity; she knew some men preferred large women, but this was ridiculous—made a clipped cry of shock.

"Papa! She's a *yansha*!" She looked Sekmé up and down and yipped again. "She's *barefoot*, Papa!"

These Tel-mari and their hypocrisy toward female flesh! Sekmé was about to bite back and tell this surveillance blimp masquerading as a girl that it was vastly more important how a woman's body was treated than how much showed, when Hemsha, in his mashed-heeled slippers, clumped down the inn's stairs to find out what was going on.

"Momer! What did I hear you say about 'affording' our services for Anyk's wedding?"

"Hemsha, I didn't mean to imply that you were too expensive—"

"Don't be absurd, man!" Hemsha sounded gruff and irritable, but his eyes were twinkling and he played with his beard, lacing his fingers through it and braiding wayward strands—his habit when pondering something amusing. Sekmé had seen it often, usually before a witty barb aimed at herself.

"You can't *possibly* pay for it!" Hemsha said with finality.

Momer's face fell so far it altered proportion from wide and florid to narrow and livid.

"B-but, H-Hemsha . . ." He sounded near tears.

"Not another word, fool! Your money is worthless here." Hemsha paused a moment, then added, as if an afterthought, "It's my and Bekka's *gift*. Gaming yansha included."

Sekmé finally noticed Momer's wife because she screamed, ran to Hemsha, and began to kiss his hands, lifting just enough veil to become downright slobbery about it. Before then, her emaciated, bent, and shrouded body had been so still and silent she'd been, for all intents and purposes, invisible.

"Come now," Hemsha said gently, embarrassed, "that's enough, Peera."

He pulled away, but was not revolted. Sekmé would have been. Peera's hands and wrists, presumably her entire body, were covered with weeping sores, the final rot phase of a wasting disease.

"Sit, everyone!" Hemsha started to bring chairs down off the central table. "You, too, Seshi. This calls for libations!"

It also called for a special Tel-mari tradition: a toast competition. Each person, beginning with Hemsha, the host, had to toast the bride in ever increasing elaborateness, and drunkenness, until some vaguely defined point of absurdity when everyone decided to stop.

They didn't reach that point until dawn when Hemsha said, "May God rain the fruits of the heavens and bounty of the seas on you, lovely Anyk, on your brave and daring husband-to-be, Umash, on your many, many sons- and daughters-to-be, whose health is the great and sacred work of God's joy, and all of your kin and cousins, friends and associates, and may the onagers of the mountains and the goats of the leas dance and couple for joy and bear foals and kids that bray and bleat your fame to the spirits of our ancestors and their forefathers who gather on the Calf of the Moon to ululate and jubilate in the fortune of their children, the flower and honey of Tel-mari, the briar blossom and suckling piglets of the Divine—"

"Oh . . . God!" Momer groaned from the drunken heap he'd made of himself in the middle of the tavern floor. Arms and legs akimbo, he'd somehow managed to upend Bekka's and Sekmé's foot-soak tub over his head. "Suckling piglets, Hemsha?" he asked. "What, in the name of all that's holy, are you talking about?"

Hemsha burped, shrugged . . . passed out.

Sekmé helped Bekka, who'd only had two small cups of liquor but was very dizzy, upstairs to her bedroom. She undressed her and put her in bed.

As Sekmé was leaving, she heard Bekka start to weep. She returned to the bed and knelt next to her.

"What's wrong, Bekka?"

"Seshi, I'll never be married and have children! Oh! I want children so much!"

"Shh! Don't be silly. You're a wonderful person and very beautiful. There must be dozens of young men who'd be thrilled and honored to marry you."

Bekka shook her head and rolled aside so Sekmé couldn't see her cry.

"Why not, Bekka? Please tell me. I'm good at secrets." She put her hand on Bekka's shoulder then stroked her hair. "We're friends, aren't we? Friends share their pain."

"You won't be my friend if I tell you."

"Of *course* I will. Please trust me."

Bekka's weeping stopped, but she still wouldn't look at Sekmé.

"I—I'm unclean."

"Unclean?"

"I've already had a baby."

Sekmé kept stroking Bekka's hair and considered carefully what to say that wouldn't give away her Maurheti upbringing—Maurheti bastards were automatically adopted by the mother and her family and granted a portion of any holdings—and yet would provide comfort.

"Well, that just narrows your choices. The baby?"

"Stillborn."

"I see." Sekmé moved her hand from Bekka's hair to her cheek. "Bekka, it was a sin, yes—yanshas know a lot about sin—but even sinners deserve forgiveness and love."

But Bekka began to weep again and folded her body in, fetus-like.

"You don't understand," she whimpered. "The man who raped me was *Maurheti*. The stain can never be forgiven."

Sekmé chewed the inside of her mouth raw to keep from saying all of the furious expletives that rushed to her lips. How could Bekka blame herself for someone else's cruelty?

"Your father loves you," she managed to croak.

"Papa is one of the blessed in the flesh." Bekka sniffed. "He's better than most people."

"*I* love you."

"You're a woman."

For her reply, Sekmé pulled Bekka over, turned her tear-puffy face toward her in spite of Bekka's feeble protests and kinked-up body, and kissed her—a soft melt on those overfull lips, almost as if she were kissing the image of a saint.

When Sekmé sat back, Bekka was staring at her, not with horror, but with puzzled sadness. Sekmé was pleased. She thought she'd frightened this haunted young beauty, but Bekka was not threatened and that . . . satisfied. All she had wanted to do was honor the grace of another kind of woman, one who fought her battles quietly, privately, within the confines of a veil.

Sekmé got up from Bekka's bed and withdrew.

The amount of preparation that went into a traditional Tel-mari wedding would have been impossible for the refugees to accomplish if it wasn't for the Tel-mari belief that a wedding was, above all, a public rite, not a private party. As a result, twenty families and dozens of unattached acquaintances contributed goods and services as their gifts to the couple. Perhaps the gigantic Anyk and her much smaller Umash wouldn't have much more as newlyweds than they'd had as single friends, but the celebration would be lavish enough to brand the mark of matrimony on their impoverished heads for all eternity.

The night before the wedding, Bekka took a break from her marathon baking and her brewing of a special wedding ale made from mang peel to paint Anyk's face.

Sekmé had been helping haul rubbish out of the ruined courtyard behind the inn and setting up long tables for the banquet, but she came up to watch this distinctly female ritual.

The dye was made out of boiled fen widow flowers. Bekka dipped a fine brush into the blackish-purple ink, and starting at

the top center point just under the hairline, she began to limn delicate filigree, stylized flowers, and magic symbols on Anyk's large, fleshy face. She prayed softly under her breath as she worked and, whenever she mentioned God, stopped to let Anyk kiss her fingertips and hold her palm up.

Sekmé remembered the gesture. The refugee who'd repaired her weapon after the Eshna raid had used it. The Tel-mari God didn't require this tribute every time he was mentioned—just at moments of deep emotion. Here, it was piety before sacramental bliss. Then, in the Old Hives, it had been annoyed exasperation.

Sekmé smiled. That crazy refugee. Where was he now?

"I've always wondered," she said, as if the matrimonial face painting was not a completely new experience for her, "what those symbols mean."

"Which ones?" Bekka interrupted her painting and her prayers.

"The broken circles."

She pointed to the disks, one on each rounded cheekbone, both with a double-curved line dividing them in half, the left half painted dark, the right left empty. The sinuous break reminded her of God's Thunderbolt, an odd association for a symbol on a Tel-mari's face.

"I'm not sure," Bekka said. "It's one of our oldest sacred symbols."

"Some say it means the marriage of opposites," Anyk ventured.

Sitting placidly at the foot of Bekka's bed, dreamily contemplating the mysteries of her coming "night of screams," she resembled some kind of soft, benign land form. Sekmé would have considered miniature trees growing from her shoulders a surreal, but appropriate, embellishment.

"Perhaps your father knows, Bekka."

"Perhaps. I should ask him."

She painted the phases of the moon in a continuous circle down and around Anyk's forehead, to her jaw, her chin, and

back up the other side to the moon in full. On the swell of the chin, she painted a long, horizontal triangle, its sharpest point aimed to Anyk's right.

"That is the Calf," Bekka said.

Interesting, Sekmé thought. To the unaided eye, it's not clearly a triangle. You need the sights of a Needle to see that.

Actually, the symbol for the Calf looked a great deal *like* a Needle.

When Bekka was done decorating Anyk's face, the heavy young woman redid her veil.

"Not to come off until my husband tears it off," she giggled, her ponderous body jiggling happily.

Broken circles, torn veils, screams in the wedding bed, and pointed asteroids piercing the night. Even the soulless feel the Great Division, Sekmé thought. Perhaps they feel it even more than we do. At least we're on the same side God is.

Sekmé watched Bekka and Anyk embrace and coo to each other in happy tenderness, convinced of their own God's grace.

The morning of the wedding was chillier than usual, the sky a frozen ashy purple and threatening. When Sekmé returned from her ablutions Bekka was at the doorway talking to the broken-nosed refugee.

The man had become one of Sekmé's regular customers. He was an honest gambler and Sekmé respected him, but she was suspicious of this dawn appearance by a man who was usually active at night. She became downright alarmed when she saw the heavy, sooty bag he handed Bekka. She hurried to them.

"*Oilstones?*" she whispered to Bekka with a furious glance at the broken-nosed man who merely yawned. "If the Maurheti catch you with them, they'll arrest your father on suspicion of anarchism."

Bekka gently put her fingertips to Sekmé's lips, an instantly effective silencer. "They're for the wedding, Seshi, not home-

made explosives." She smiled, another highly potent way to melt Sekmé's distress. "Weddings need light and these are brighter than candles."

She took the broken-nosed man's hand in thanks. He nodded brusquely and marched off.

"Not even the Maurheti would break up a wedding," Bekka said.

Sekmé wasn't so sure, but it wasn't up to her to protect Bekka, however much she wanted to. Her desire was ruining her determination to remain neutral.

First a kiss, now this! I'd better hear something about Merkus soon, or I'll have to abandon the mission as hopelessly corrupted.

The guests began to arrive at midday, dozens of veiled ones with their burly, bearded spouses and overexcited, ragged children who ran up and down the stairs of the inn and took premature pokes at the pots of food set out on tables in the courtyard. Young as they were, some less than seven years old, the boys flirted with Sekmé—although she doubted they understood what their gestures meant—and the girls shied away from her as if her shaky moral status were somehow contagious.

The women avoided her, too. Many were the same ones who gossiped at her side and let her watch their children at the bathing well. The only difference was the presence of the men.

The men gathered around Hemsha and his liquor, but although they eagerly took overflowing tankards, none of them drank a drop. Not yet. Not before the rite itself.

The rite began when a flock of young women, including an out-of-breath and sweating Anyk, rushed in from the street, screaming, closely pursued by the bridegroom and a group of his friends. The women fluttered about the tavern, circling in a swirl of black, their fists lashing out at every male within reach, then fled up the stairs to the bedchambers. The young men followed, deliberately pounding their boots at each step and roaring to sound more dangerous.

The bomb-weakened structure shook as the hunted and the hunters raced around the rooms above the wedding guests' heads—a piece of plaster came loose and broke on Sekmé's shoulder—then, at a great howl of victory, accompanied by an even greater mass shriek of theatrical terror, everyone pounded back downstairs, Umash and six of his friends leading the way with the struggling mass of Anyk in their arms.

By now the guests were waiting in a large circle in the court-yard, and as the young men paraded about with their protesting catch, the guests clapped in time and cried, "Blood! Blood! Blood!"

Umash drew a short saber from a scabbard on his belt. The weapon, nearly semicircular in its curve with a hilt barnacled in red, green, and blue gems, utterly belied the intense poverty of its owner. With a visceral shock, Sekmé realized that the Tel-mari, like the Maurheti, must have passed down such relics for generations, preferring to starve rather than sell them.

As his friends held Anyk tightly, Umash pushed back her sleeve, exposing her pale, fleshy forearm. She shrieked and fought harder, but with the cries of "Blood!" reaching a ringing cre-scendo, the groom flicked the blade across her arm, nicking a thin, clean line of red.

The cries stopped. In fact, the crowd seemed to have turned to stone the minute crimson appeared on Anyk's skin. Everyone—man, woman, child, even bride—stared at the tiny beads of blood collecting at what was, after all, a superficial, and symbolic, wound.

Umash, a pale young man with a thin beard and the large eyes of chronic hunger, slowly lowered his weapon and, with-out removing his gaze from Anyk's arm, pushed back his own sleeve and cut his own flesh.

Foolish, Sekmé thought. He's so anemic even this loss could make him faint.

He didn't. He bent over Anyk and kissed her arm. The

blood marked his lip. Then he held his own wound to Anyk's mouth and she licked it.

"Who is the hunter, who is prey?" the bridegroom asked in an archaic, traditional dialect. "I have taken thy blood and thou hast taken mine. We are of one blood, one flesh."

The young men set Anyk on her feet and withdrew. She touched Umash's cheek.

"Who is master? Who is slave?" she said. "Neither walks in chains, neither beats the other with rods, neither puts the other before God in his heart but walks side by side in God's wake."

"I serve," said Umash.

"I serve," said Anyk.

"Submit to God!" the crowd shouted, and fell silent again.

In a feat of strength that must have been dictated by emotion and belief, the starving bridegroom put his thin arms around his bride and lifted her. Staggering under the weight, he moved through the silent circle back into the inn, heaved himself up the steps to the second story, and disappeared into the bridal bedchamber Sekmé and Bekka had prepared with fresh linens, flower petals, and bowls of dry, fragrant mang fruit.

Sekmé shook her head. If you believed hard enough that your God could help you, did that make your God real? Or you? Both ideas were heretical in a God/Not-God cosmos, but both seemed possible as Sekmé weighed the evidence of Umash's devotion.

Hemsha stepped into the center of the hushed circle of guests with a large bottle of Bekka's wedding brew, held it up high, and, with the others, waited.

A minute. Five. Sekmé scratched her ear. Umash's second task was, in a way, as difficult as his first.

Finally, as hoped, Anyk screamed, and Hemsha smashed the bottle of brew on the ground.

Umash and Anyk were married—and the livid sky burst open. The rain fell in sheets.

"Anyk!" Peera cried in her ruined squeal of a voice to her absent daughter, "look at the blessings! You and Umash will have many, many babies!"

"God help us," Sekmé muttered as she rushed past with a great steaming pot of grmysh.

All of the tables and their mounds of provisions had to be brought inside the tavern, but the celebration proper remained outside. There people danced with their plates of food and tankards of wedding ale and kicked up the mud and fell in puddles and stood on each others' shoulders and laughed in the rain. At one point, over 150 guests crowded into the tavern and courtyard, and what with the wet and the mud, they quickly began to resemble one another—anonymous mud people.

Sekmé kept a fast and serious dice game going with twenty men at the back table in the tavern, and several times she had to stop the action to rinse the mud from the dice by dunking them in her tankard of ale. After an hour of play, she gave up on ever drinking it.

Out in the street in front of the inn, the guests' children, skirts and robed tied up above their knees, ran slippery footraces that deteriorated into mud-sliding competitions, each boy and prepubescent girl, as yet unveiled, skidding along on their heels, hips, or bellies and measuring the distance.

Three feral goats, tired of being in the rain, trotted boldly through the open tavern door and headed straight for the kitchen where they kicked over a boiling kettle of root soup, scalding themselves, then raced blindly through the tavern, knocking over several guests, and galloped up the stairs to the bedchambers. Hemsha, Momer, and Sekmé, their feet hopelessly slick with caked-on glop, scrambled after them. After chasing two of the goats back downstairs and into the street, they lost the third when the confused animal jumped up on a bed, leapt out the window, and fell into a great silty puddle that had formed in the mud of the courtyard. It sank rapidly, bleating desperately, into the sucking ooze.

All in all, it was a wonderful wedding, or was until a Maur-heti military police patrol of five men came by in the wee hours of the night.

These men were supposed to keep order. They were sup-posed to round up the marauding bands of soldiers who were looking for mischief. However, Sekmé knew the minute they entered the tavern and looked around, thumbs hooked in the belts of their long, hooded, rain-repellent slickcoats, that this was not their plan tonight. They took silent note of the stolen oilstones burning gaily in broken cups and orphaned saucers set about the room and Sekmé realized she had to distract them.

"Gentlemen? A game?" she asked in Maurheti, laying on a thick Tel-mari accent and jingling her swollen coin pouch.

The biggest man turned to her, pushed back his hood, and Sekmé's stomach seemed to drop out of her. She knew him: Commander Boas, an excellent officer, but a bully who liked to humiliate the weakest of his men in front of the others. Luckily, because of Sekmé's veil, he didn't recognize her. He smiled a cold, close-mouthed smile, dark eyes narrowing, and rubbed his chin.

"I smell something, men," he said, and his partners chuckled. One of them took a guest's tankard from him and pushed him away. The Tel-mari slipped in the mud and dropped back onto the wet tiles.

"Yes, I smell something sweet," Boas repeated as he shoved his way through the quieting crowd to Sekmé's game table. "Something sweet and sticky—like rotten meat."

The men laughed again. Good thing they couldn't see how hard Sekmé's jaw was set behind the veil.

"Gaming only, honey-tongue," she said in syrupy tones. She rattled the dice in her hand. "Care to 'sweeten' my purse?"

"Oh, yes, indeed!"

Sekmé put her fists on her hips and tilted her head, hoping her considerable anger looked at least partially "fake." The men were armed and touchy.

"Bad boy," she said, offering the dice. "Mommy will have to beat you."

Boas snatched the proffered dice and threw them. All three landed five up.

"God's perfection," she announced. "House wins."

Boas smacked his hand down over the dice and leaned across the table, thrusting his face into Sekmé's.

"Who said I was playing?" He grinned without mirth.

"If you're not," Sekmé said evenly, "you'll have to withdraw. These men—" She indicated the Tel-mari guests. "—were in the middle of a game."

"What 'men'?" Boas smirked with a long glance around the room. "There aren't any men here. Only goats and little girls."

"Play or withdraw. I don't care either way."

Boas lifted his hand, plunged it into his slickcoat pocket, and brought out a fistful of Maurheti paners.

"Roll, sister."

The Tel-mari guests shrank back like soft-bodied crustaceans into their shells. Covered with mud, they blended into the walls, and Sekmé had the illusion she was alone with Boas and his men, playing an evil game for a deadly prize. This time, she'd better not cheat. Military police provided the official records of what happened in the streets of Eshna, and the death of a yan-sha barely deserved mention, let alone explanation.

At first, luck was with Boas and he grinned and clicked his tongue as the Tel-mari coins stacked up next to his paners. Sekmé could see the idea forming in his head as though she were inside it, how he intended ultimately to claim her as payment for the debt he would put her in.

Then Sekmé began to win. She wasn't cheating, but perhaps God, in His role as the Preserver of Balance, saw fit to tilt fate in the woman's direction for once. Boas's grin faded, replaced by a low boiling. Seven throws in a row went Sekmé's way, then one his. Their respective pots were virtually identical.

"Ah, an elegant balance," Sekmé said, using a sacred version

of the Maurheti word as a subtle way of reminding Boas of his role as policeman, not thug. "I suggest that we end our game here. God has willed stasis."

Maybe it was the yansha's use of a religious term, maybe it was his own basic meanness, but Boas caught Sekmé's hand as she started to gather up her winnings, and twisted her arm around.

"One . . . more . . . throw," he said.

He shoved her back and Sekmé shook out her arm.

Idiot! she thought. As soon as I get back from this miserable mission, your career is over. Damn everything! I hate this hellish veil . . .

"Fine. One. Winner take all."

They pushed their piles of money into the middle of the table.

Boas threw. Six, four, four. Sekmé threw. Six, two, six.

"You cheated!" The cry rushed up out of Boas's chest like a Needle lifting off in the middle of battle.

"No!" Sekmé said.

"She didn't," Hemsha cut in, and startled, Boas swung around, fists ready.

"Who said that?"

"You'd strike a miserable old goat?" Hemsha asked. "Shame on you."

Boas dismissed this remark with a flick of his hand and returned to Sekmé. "You cheated and I want my money back."

"I didn't and you can't have it."

Boas grabbed the edge of the table and heaved it and its contents at Sekmé. She jumped back nimbly.

"You cheated, and as God is my judge, you'll pay me one way or another!"

"Not in this world," she said, a good Maurheti retort—a threat actually, usually followed by a fistfight intended to send the opponent posthaste to that implied next world.

Again, maybe it was the sound of Maurheti prize phrases issuing from a yansha's filthy mouth, but Boas lost control and

lunged at her. With this, the mud people in the shadows came out of their suspended animation.

Boas and his men were five big soldiers, but there were several dozen Tel-mari uncles, cousins, comrades, and hangers-on in the room and they engulfed the Maurheti in a furious storm of fists, boots, and teeth. In minutes, the soldiers found themselves in the street in the rain, chests aching, breath short, noses and lips bleeding, ears ringing, joints wrenched, and nausea rising in the wake of a searing burn in their groins.

"You're a gutsy little woman," the broken-nosed man said. He'd done much of the assault and battery on the Maurheti and had taken a great deal of quiet pride in his work. "Those men could have used their weapons at any time, but your game kept their fury down to a barroom brawl."

"'They might come back and make up for the omission,'" Sekmé said.

"I don't think so," the man said. "They have to report the use of every shot. They could lie, of course, but there were too many witnesses to their humiliation and the story would eventually get back to High Command."

Sekmé stared at him. "How do you know this?"

"Common sense." The broken-nosed man shrugged. "Thank you for the game—the one *before* those serpents showed up. I know you usually cheat, but it's still entertaining."

"You're annoyingly perceptive, friend."

"Don't worry. Your secret's safe with me. I don't care to violate confidences anymore. I've already had a bellyful."

He blew his misshapen nose into his hand. Blew blood. He'd taken some blows, too, and they'd added another bend to his already labyrinthine olfactory organ.

"By the way," he asked, wiping his hand on his robe, "do you have a brother?"

"All men are brothers to yansha," Sekmé replied, not eager to feed this sharp-eyed gargoyle any more personal or professional insights.

"Just curious."

"I know. Very."

He grunted and shuffled off into the rain.

Sekmé watched him melt into the muddy angles of the street. He'd played several games with her, lost every one of them, and yet still had money to play again. She was pretty sure he lived on the street—Bekka had invited him in person instead of sending a boy with the traditional goat parchment and sweetmeats—but he was not like the other homeless wanderers. It was as if he lived among them out of choice, or principle, rather than necessity.

Another odd one, she thought. A cousin to the one who repaired my weapon.

The celebration soon broke up. No one felt like dancing and singing after the fight with the Maurheti military police, and the guests collected their children, first wiping the mud from their faces to confirm their identities, kissed Anyk and her new husband, who'd come down from their marriage bed to see them off, clapped Momer and Hemsha on the back, nodded to the pestilential Peera, and slipped away, in clumps and singles, into the storm. People of the wet, people of the soil, lost in a dying city.

When they were gone and Bekka, too tired to begin cleaning up, had retired to her bedchamber, Sekmé sat at the main table opposite Hemsha, set out two fresh tankards, poured a measure of damnation ale into each from the only bottle not smashed in the fight—and removed her veil to drink it.

"Wh-what are you doing, Seshi? Unveiled? I haven't paid you for that."

"Consider it a gift from someone too exhausted to care anymore."

Sekmé tossed back the liquor, and Hemsha absently reached for his tankard. His fingers brushed it, but didn't grip. He was staring at her. She set down her drink and stared back.

"What happened?" Hemsha whispered. "You were some-one's daughter, once. You had a father."

"My father was killed when I was twelve."

"You must hate them very much."

"Yes, I do."

"Well, the Maurheti can be savages, but, you must remember, they are men, too. Men do these things and men can change."

Sekmé frowned at him. In her fatigue, she couldn't make sense of what he'd said. She'd been speaking of the Tel-mari . . . but now she wasn't sure.

"They . . . I think they killed my son twelve years ago, too," Hemsha said. "Was your loss during the first battle of Eshna?"

"Yes."

"I see." Hemsha sucked in his lower lip and a bit of his beard. The thinker was thinking again.

"If it's any comfort," he said, "I understand that the officer who planned that raid died in it under suspicious circumstances."

Sekmé's mental fog cleared. Hemsha was talking about her father.

"Suspicious? How?"

"I don't know, but many in the Old Hives believed that Maurheti High Command wanted the officer dead and set him up so he couldn't escape."

Sekmé pushed her tankard aside. If she tasted it again, she'd vomit.

"Why would they want to kill one of their own officers?"

Hemsha shook his head, smiled faintly. "I don't know. Perhaps they don't really want to win."

"Win? I don't understand."

"Sometimes, Seshi, when I'm alone in my bedchamber, just before I fall asleep, I have my most unusual ideas." Hemsha began his familiar fingerplay with his facial hair. "It occurred to me not long after this latest raid on Eshna. I don't mind telling you I was quite out of my head; Shella meant everything to me.

Anyway, it occurred to me that the Maurheti are perfectly happy with the way things are or they wouldn't have let the war go on as long as it has. They *want* a perpetual state of tension and animosity. It benefits them."

Sekmé leveled on Hemsha the look she usually reserved for game birds and antelope she was about to slay.

"Hemsha, war isn't a game. *Battles* are won, not war. War is a state of nature. All creatures fight to survive."

"That's what a Maurheti would say."

"Believe me, it doesn't benefit them more than anyone else." Sekmé's voice was so low, it sounded more like Set's than her own.

"Doesn't it?" Hemsha asked. "Without war, the Maurheti would no longer have us as their slaves because, as you know, we'd never submit except by force. How well would they do without us to perform their dirty little jobs for them? Without our lands to steal? Without someone to fight? They'd probably turn on each other like cannibals."

To Sekmé, the silence following this was deadly, full of the demons that had plagued her since that terrible curse in the Eshna marketplace. They laughed at her and danced around her head as jo supposedly did, their red tongues lolling all the way down to their genitals, but she, Sekmé, a woman of action, was paralyzed.

Hemsha patted her hand affectionately and stood up. He stretched, yawned, and scratched his belly.

"Don't stay up too late, my dear. You look tired."

CHAPTER 16
THE SACRİFİCE

S et and his young widow were up very early to watch the
sunrise together. The rain had stopped.

"How do you know dawn has come if you can't see
it?" the widow asked. She rearranged her embrace and nuzzled
his chest.

"I hear it, smell it." He smiled. "The birds tell me and the air
changes. It becomes sweet and crisp, awake."

"It's still too bad you can't see it," she said. "All the colors are
so beautiful."

"I know colors," Set said.

"How? You've been blind from birth."

"There are other ways to know them. Colors have a texture,
did you know? You can smell them. Sometimes, you can even
hear them."

The widow raised herself up to look at Set's face. It was still
too dark to see clearly, but she found his nose and kissed it.

"Tell me how you learned which is which. Maybe you felt
'blue,' but someone had to tell you what it was."

"My sister told me."

Set closed his already darkened eyes and, for a moment,
"saw" Sekmé again.

*"Do you remember my installation, Set? At father's funeral, when I
received the weapon?"*

"*I remember a lot of shouting.*"

"*That was to drive away the defeat and summon the victory, but I remember the colors.*"

"I remember the colors," he repeated to the widow.

"*Red on the weapon. Father's blood,*" Sekmé said in his memory.

"Red," Set recited. "Warm, living, urgent. A smell of iron."

"*The heat of that day in the desert.*"

"White," Set said. "Blazing, pure, dry, and without blemish."

"*The fire when they burned his body.*"

"Orange." Set's voice became distant, dreamy. "Fruit and furnace, dancing before the eyes. It can be sweet or burn."

"*The sea and sky beyond the sea cliffs.*"

"Blue. Like resting on a bluff with a cool breeze in your hair."

"*The thornwood leaves mixed into his ashes.*"

"The vegetable color. Green. Pungent, spicy, cool, sheltering. Nourishing."

"*The cave in the cliffs where we set his chest of ashes.*"

"Brown. Loamy, mineral scent, and rot. Reassuring and repulsive. The place of death and life reborn. Brown holds a secret."

"*The way I felt, Set. The terrible loneliness . . .*"

"Black. The Void. The silence against which all other colors are stronger, louder. The color that is not a color but draws all colors into itself."

"Set?" The widow's voice, not Sekmé's.

"That's me," Set said. "Black."

"Only a poet would cook up such rubbish," a new, very deep, gruff voice interrupted. Set recognized the broken-nosed man.

"What is it?"

"Quit lying about, son. I've found your sister."

"What?!"

"I wasn't sure at first," the man said, "but I am now."

Set sat up and felt about for his robe—and the vulpé pelt.

"Is it dawn yet?" he asked.

"Does it matter?"

"Yes. I want *her* to see *me*."

"It will be by the time we get there."

"Shall I come?" the widow asked. "I want to see your happiness."

"Not this time." Set kissed her. "She may not be glad to see me."

"Why not?"

"I can't tell you. Stay here and wait for me. I won't be long."

Sekmé had peeled off her filthy clothing, rinsed her body in a tub of freezing rainwater, shivered dry, and crawled into bed. It was a couple hours before dawn, and cold and spent, she fell asleep instantly.

Like any classically disciplined officer, Boas attacked just before the sun. He carefully broke a window to the kitchen, climbed inside, crept up the stairs of the inn, found Sekmé's bedchamber—the one with the pile of muddy red yansha rags on the floor—and threw himself on top of her. In the predawn black, Sekmé found herself crushed and muffled under a man who quickly, and expertly, one-handedly threw aside the bedclothes and undid his belt.

"You cheated me," he snarled under his breath as he fought to keep her still, "and now you'll pay."

He'd pinned one of Sekmé's arms back behind her head, and as she struggled, she managed to worm her hand under the bolster and grasp her knife. Boas had wriggled out of his trousers and she could feel the heat of his organ on her thigh. His pressure on her arm lessened—he was paying more attention to his business below—and Sekmé whipped her hand free and cut him. In the dark, she wasn't sure where.

Boas was exceptionally well trained. He didn't yell, but he did fly off Sekmé's bed like water off a hot greased skillet. Sekmé scrambled to her feet, and rocking a little unsteadily on the badly

sprung mattress, pressed herself back against the wall, knife out before her, clutched in her fist.

She listened. She heard labored breathing and the shuffling of heavy boots on the floor. Then, a small snap and hiss and the yellow glow from an oilstone illuminated the bedchamber.

They stared at each other: a Maurheti officer, trousers down to his knees, favoring his left leg because it had a deep gash in the thigh below the hip, and a naked young woman with a knife.

At first, Boas didn't seem to understand his mistake. His stare had the same flat stillness as a surprised antelope's; then Sekmé saw it become agitated like a black pool in which someone has thrown a stone.

"You?!" he whispered.

"Leave now, Boas," she said. "This is High Command's business, not yours."

Boas shook his head.

"No," he said. "No, no, no, no! This can't be true!"

Sekmé's mouth was dry and she licked her lips. She couldn't risk lowering her blade. Not yet.

"Get *out*, Boas. You made a mistake, but it's over. Go quickly."

"Oh, no, Commander. It's *not* over." He slowly retrieved his side arm from his shoulder holster and pulled back the safety with his thumb. "You'll turn me in."

"I won't. Let's just forget anything happened and leave it at that."

A weird half grin distorted Boas's mouth. He was sweating heavily in the cold.

"Think so? Maybe if you were a man, but—"

"Put it down, Boas."

"—since you're a woman—"

"I don't want to hurt you."

"—I doubt you could possibly forget."

She heard the small click inside the weapon, the one heard just before it fires.

The blade left her hand and went straight into Boas's left eye. His hand spasmed and the safety automatically snapped back into place. The weapon fell with a thick-sounding thud. Boas's collapse was curiously quieter, if heavier, as if Sekmé had knocked over a carton of field blankets. A puddle of blood quietly expanded under Boas's face. Sekmé had killed one of her own.

The latch to her door turned and Bekka appeared. Her eyes flicked over Boas's body and up to Sekmé who stood like an uncertain stork on the bed.

"I'm sorry," Sekmé said.

Bekka didn't ask what had happened and Sekmé guessed that, as a victim of rape, the young Tel-mari already knew. Sekmé hopped down from the bed.

"I'll leave at once," she said.

"But, the body—" Bekka pursed her lips as if pondering an especially nasty housekeeping problem. Obviously, she wasn't going to shed a single tear for this man dead in her inn.

"That mud sump in the courtyard," Sekmé said. "It ate a goat readily enough."

Sekmé dressed, and she and Bekka lugged Boas's dead weight down to the rain-sodden courtyard, filled his pockets with stones, and pushed him into the soupy mud. He sank slowly, gloomily, as if his own death depressed him.

Bekka looked at Sekmé's yansha garb and its new layer of filth.

"Come upstairs," she said. "You can't travel as a yansha anymore."

There she gave Sekmé one of her own robes.

"Don't worry, Seshi. No one will say anything even if he floats back up."

"I know. Just another casualty of war."

Bekka stopped arranging Sekmé's veil and studied her eyes closely.

"You knew this man before, didn't you?"

No point in lying now. "Yes."

"Then it's an even greater blessing that he's gone from your life."

Sekmé stared. She couldn't believe the harshness issuing from those soft, overripe lips.

Bekka smiled ironically. "The veiled ones are stronger than you yansha suppose."

"I'm not a yansha."

"I didn't think so," Bekka said calmly. "I never have."

"I'm trying to find Merkus."

Bekka's fine brows knotted in the hardest scowl Sekmé had yet seen in that lovely face.

"Why?"

"I . . . can't tell you."

Bekka looked away, still scowling.

"Bekka, do *you* know where he is?"

The young Tel-mari closed her eyes and sighed deeply, resignedly.

"Papa is so concerned that we take care with our expenses, but he can't even tote up a day's sales without dropping a sum." She opened her eyes. They were full of tears. "That's why *I* keep count and why he never goes to the market. We'd be cheated out of everything. As it is, he never notices the bit of meat here, the measure of salt there. Never notices at all."

"*You* supply Merkus's band?!"

"Only a few things. They scavenge most of their food and there are others, besides me, who bring certain staples."

"That's very dangerous! They're *killers*, Bekka."

"Merkus is my brother, Seshi."

It was as if Bekka had thrown a bucket of ice water at her.

"Your *brother*?"

"Papa thinks he's dead, but he just went away. Papa's school was destroyed and Ahvrym lost his favorite rabam. We've lost so many . . ."

Sekmé grabbed her shoulders. She wanted to shake her for her foolhardiness, but instead asked for information. "Where is he, Bekka?"

"What are you going to do when you find him?"

Those terrible, wonderful feline eyes. Again, Sekmé gave them a piece of the truth.

"His life is in danger, Bekka. The Maurheti are looking for him and they're very close."

Bekka nodded. She expected this.

"I'm supposed to drop off some salt and dried goat meat this morning. You go in my place. One of his men will meet you there."

"Where?"

"It's the ruin of a law court," Bekka said, "not far from the bathing fountain."

She unexpectedly stroked Sekmé's cheek.

"I don't know why you were sent," she whispered, "and I can't ask you to promise, but . . ."

"But what?"

Bekka touched Sekmé's ear.

"For my sake, Seshi, don't hurt him."

"I have to go now," the broken-nosed man said. "Are you sure you'll be all right?"

"Of course," Set said. "I'd know my sister's step anywhere."

"The inn is right across the street. She leaves this way every morning to go to the bathing fountain."

"She always loved baths."

"You may have to wait awhile."

"I don't mind."

But Set didn't have to wait long at all. Soon after the broken-nosed man left him in his hiding place, Set heard Sekmé leave the tavern. It was dawn and her footsteps were strong, quick, with a purpose and a direction.

His heart flying, Set shadowed her. He couldn't see that she was not in yansha dress and that she carried not a bundle of skin oils and sponges, but a sack of salt and dried meat. He couldn't see that this was not a normal morning.

Lokar could. He was dozing off the tail of a particularly fine dose of junk when, right at dawn, Sekmé—no Tel-mari female swaggered like that, not even a yansha—left the inn.

What's this? Lokar wondered. A bit early, aren't we? And what's this black robe about?

Something was afoot. He shouldered his rifle and began to follow along the rooftops.

So intrigued was he by Sekmé's change in routine that he didn't notice the graceful but cautious shadow some paces behind her, stepping carefully as if feeling its way.

The rain would be back soon so Sekmé hurried over the debris that had become such a permanent element of the Eshna cityscape that moss and small wildflowers grew on it.

The bathing fountain at this early hour was deserted. She would have liked to stop for a moment and, well . . . say good-bye, perhaps. Good-bye to the exclusive, female world there. She was returning to the cold, genderless realm of war.

Bekka was right not to ask for a promise. It was unnerving enough to be caught out, recognized as an impostor, and yet protected. Bekka's loyalties, perhaps most Tel-mari women's loyalties, tempered by cruelties and displacements from all directions, were personal. With their children, aging parents, and other cares, few had the luxury to color their feelings with politics. Death wore its own face and robes before them—not a uniform.

Sekmé paused a moment at the top of the hill. The heavy sky seemed to sit only an arm's length above her head.

Should I be doing this? she wondered. I'm a soldier, not an assassin.

She glanced at the ruined roofs below, the centuries of broken masonry coated in fuzzy yellow, black, and green—civilization's corpses—and wiped her lips.

Soldier, assassin—what the hell was the difference?

She moved on. A few hundred steps down the far side of the hill, the road flattened into a terrace. On one side stood the usual scramble of tenements, slapped together as if a giant's toddler had piled them up, haphazard, unstable, careless.

The other side, however, was taken up by a single facade, the wall of a much larger, and considerably more ancient, building. Its bank of long, thin windows, black, empty, and glassless, was at the level of the second or third story. At ground level, the remains of a colonnade and three large doorways presented a mournful image of utter ruin and abandonment. Two of the doors were blocked with rubble. The third had been widened by an explosion, perhaps centuries earlier.

Sekmé stepped through the colonnade, stood in the doorway, and looked in—and up. The interior was open from ground floor to atrium without division, without roof. The clouds passed over this great shell and promised to flood it shortly.

Courthouse? Skeptical, Sekmé entered cautiously. Now was the time to worry about Merkus's minions. She was very exposed here and they'd been expecting Bekka.

She looked about for the logical place, the place she would choose if she were waiting for a delivery. In the eastern wall was a niche with a shell-shaped cornice—an odd choice considering how far this place was from the sea—that suggested a once significant point of interest. A missing statue? A reference for sacred direction? A place for a high official to sit?

Regardless, it seemed the logical place for a sack of salt and meat. A couple dark holes, doors once, in the east wall led to other rooms. Mouths to hiding places. Above, those high windows might hold other snipers' nests.

Sekmé gritted her teeth. She had to pretend she was harmless, unafraid of her "allies." Holding her breath and expecting

at any moment a hail of rifle fire, she marched across the empty stone floor under the angry sky to the niche.

Nothing. Not a stir. Perhaps they wanted her to leave her sack and depart. That would not do. She had to speak to whoever was watching in order to get closer to Merkus.

She set down the sack and backed away slowly, eyes raised to the windows and the broken roofline. For some reason, she felt the watcher, or watchers, would be higher rather than lower.

"Hello?" she called in Tel-mari. "God be with you, I need to speak to Merkus."

Nothing.

"His life is in danger."

"Sekmé!"

Later Sekmé would not be able to recall clearly exactly what happened. She remembered turning at her name in time to see Set dash into the ruins directly at her—and to hear and see the rifle report behind him, fired by someone in the doorway who swore as he fired.

Set's chest blew open and pieces of flesh and shattered bone splattered all over Sekmé as he fell into her arms, shot in the back. The shell itself, deflecting off Set's spine and breastbone, angled up and went through Sekmé's shoulder.

Then, the windows overhead in the eastern wall filled with flames as once hidden men discharged their weapons at a single target: Lokar.

Sekmé's rival danced into the courthouse as the flack and shells hit him and spun him about, stripping pieces of flesh away as he turned. One arm tore off entirely and half of his long face disintegrated as Sekmé watched.

When what was left of Lokar finally fell, the courthouse became silent. Sekmé assumed she'd gone deaf from the racket of the barrage. That was fine. She didn't need, or want, to hear anything again for as long as she lived. She sat on the sack of salt and meat in the niche with her brother's corpse pressed to her breast soaking her, pouring its blood into hers.

A few millennia later, the broken-nosed man, armed with a sniper's rifle, came out of one of the dark mouths beside the niche and stood over her and Set. When she looked up, he took his weapon and hit her in the face with it.

She opened her eyes in the underground chamber that served as Merkus's lair. Stolen Maurheti oilstone lamps hung about the walls, and the air smelled damp, thick, almost muddy. Although she couldn't hear it, she knew it was raining.

Her shoulder hurt badly and the pain reminded her she'd been conscious before this in some other part of the fortress. Above ground. Torchlit. The men had beaten her there, pulled off her boots and battered her feet with sticks. Kicked her. She remembered now, but it was as if she'd been watching rather than suffering this torture. She must be severely injured.

She tried to move her feet, but they were bound. So were her hands. She heard someone approach and saw a man in black, hooded, his face masked with black cloth tied rough and tight the way a bandit does, not elegantly as a woman would with her veil. She could see his eyes, dark, searching—and curious. He crouched beside her, his hands loose on his knees.

She coughed out some blood.

"M-Merkus?"

"Odds or evens, my dear?" he whispered.

Sekmé groaned. God was a comedian.

"I'll grant you these are not ideal circumstances for a reunion," he said, and pulled down the cloth covering his face: same aquiline nose, same black beard, same incongruous intelligence. "I see my men took out their frustrations on you, Sekmé."

He knew her name. That meant he knew her role in the Eshna raid.

"Your men are beasts, Merkus."

"Whose fault is that?" he asked, oddly gentle rather than accusing. "Strip a man of everything dear to him and you *have* cre-

ated a beast." He leaned down close to her face. "They lost their past, thanks to you Maurheti, and cannot imagine a future."

"Imagine," she murmured. "You asked me to do the same thing once." She tried to grin, but had no idea what kind of expression she actually achieved.

"You didn't listen, did you?"

"You're not much of a teacher."

In response, Merkus grabbed Sekmé's wrists and dragged her across the dirt floor to a dark corner of the chamber. He reached down one of the oilstone lamps, held it low to the wall, then turned her head toward it with his boot.

"Can you see this, my dear? Or are your eyes too swollen?"

Sekmé squinted at the faint inscription.

"A crescent moon," she said.

"Yes. It's one of the oldest symbols of our faith. As the moon reflects the sun, so we reflect the spirit of God. However, there's more." He delicately traced his finger around the shape.

"I used to be a scholar of these things," he said. "See how this particular crescent tips back as though asleep? This early symbol didn't just represent the moon, but a woman's body, softly curved and yielding, in ecstasy before the wonder of the heavens." He lowered his hand. "Iss-ter was her name, lady of the trees and rain, all living things, the mountains and waters. She was the world itself, curling around the universe, embracing it as her lover, her child."

He scratched his beard—the way Hemsha would.

"You see," he continued, "God was *female* as well as male in ancient, more animistic times, until your God, with his divisive bolt of death, tore her away from her husband." He took a stone from the dirt floor and scratched a faint curve in the wall, continuing the crescent around until it became . . . the broken circle. "Today this shape represents our submission *to* God," he said, "our need to be humble and yielding before forces greater than man."

He smiled at her; yes, it was similar to Bekka's smile. He was, indeed, her brother.

"Of course," he said, "you and your men are *not* a greater force. We've no need to submit to *you*."

Sekmé merely sniffed. Her nose was running both blood and snot.

Merkus turned back to the inscription. "Iss-ter is a pretty metaphor, don't you think? Primitive, maybe, but still more complex than this simple shape would suggest."

"Your point?"

"Did you expect a terrorist to be a scholar, Commander? Or were you convinced I was a barbarous madman succumbing to a lust for revenge and dragging others into the mayhem with me?"

"Aren't you?"

"Killing repulses me, Sekmé. Surprised? Unfortunately, when you're working with the ignorant—and ignorance, although dangerous, is a curable condition—you must begin at the most basic level. My men understand vengeance, but, in time, will learn."

"Learn *what*?" Sekmé tried to lift her head but gave up when a sharp pain cracked through her neck. "Don't tell me you *know*! That you have a *plan*!"

Merkus's dark eyes became wistful and he slipped his right hand inside his belted robe.

"I'm afraid I don't have time to discuss it with you, my dear," he said. "Suffice it to say that I'm still learning, too."

He withdrew Set's vulpé pelt, its thick, lush white fur stained a deep, blackening crimson. Carefully, without watching his hands, as if to prevent himself from committing an unseemly act, he tucked the fur into Sekmé's rags near her breast.

"The young man . . ."

"My brother."

Merkus nodded wearily. "We'll give him a proper burial. He was innocent."

"He was a poet."

Merkus gazed at her a long moment. It looked as if he pitied her, but that was unlikely. She knew his next move would be her death.

He stood up and held the oilstone lamp over her as if inspecting a side of oryx meat.

"My men wanted to kill you outright," he said, "but I told them I thought you deserved something special."

He bent over a moment to check her bonds—for what, she couldn't tell—then grunted in grim satisfaction. He reached into a pocket and retrieved his four coins.

"Let's see what Fate decides," he said. "Odds, my men slaughter you here. Evens, we throw you bound and gagged into the swamp."

"Oh . . . joy . . ."

Merkus shook the coins—they jingled in his hands—and dropped them.

"Evens," he said. "The swamp it is."

He whistled for his men.

When Merkus's men lifted her, they pulled on her bad shoulder and she fainted at the pain. The breeze through her hair revived her as they stood on the fortress parapet and swung her back and forth.

"Scream, bitch," one of the men said. "Why don't you scream?"

Plenty of time for that in the hereafter, Sekmé thought, and she was suddenly airborne, a heady, almost pleasant moment. No pressure on her wounds.

Then she hit the swamp. It was like breaking through a plate of frozen glass. She sank instantly in the murk, eyes and nostrils quickly filling with slime, her mind beginning to fire sparks behind her eyes. She struggled, but not for long. She was already too weak. In moments, all was stillness and she felt the heat, her life, leaking steadily out of her. The synapse sparks became

larger, softer, like slow bursts of galca seen from above in a Needle. One burst looked like Set and lingered. His eyes were clear and glowing.

"Sa'Har, my beloved twin," he said in a marvelously musical version of his once mortal voice. "I always knew you were beautiful."

"Sa'Har?"

"I've come there, Sekmé. It's calm—the end of conflict."

"Death?"

"It's a word for the living, Sekmé."

"I'm dying, Set."

"No. You must satisfy your duty to others so you can fulfill a *new* duty to yourself."

"I don't understand."

"You will." He slid his slender fingers under her bonds and snapped them like thread.

"I'm afraid, Set."

"Take my hand."

She did and he pulled her swiftly through the water. Her mind went dark.

She came to, coughing and spluttering, when she was hauled roughly out of the swamp onto solid ground. She wiped the slime from her eyes with her free hand and saw she was grasping the tail of a very large bog monitor. She hastily released it. The great lizard snapped its snaggle-fanged jaws at her a couple times to underline its annoyance, then darted back into the swamp and undulated away.

CHAPTER 17

BAHÉ

Bahé hated night reconnaissance more than all other duties in Tel-mari, even more than gutting goats in the mess hall. It was cold, wet, dangerous, and exhausting, but Field General Am, a basically good sort, insisted all of his men do it at least once every few days to "keep their edge."

"Actually, I feel pretty blunt afterward, sir," Bahé admitted.

Am laughed at him. "Cheer up, Subcom! You're tougher than you think."

Being subcom did have its better moments. Bahé got to use the portable communications equipment, the box. The unit was heavy, a big metal chest in a special pack that weighed down his shoulders, but he loved the feeling of high-tech control when he agitated the crystal, aligned the bands, and called up the coms and subcoms of other units, even the base back in Maurhet. He'd made fast electronic friends and was quickly learning the ins and outs of underhanded bargaining for special favors, supplies, and privileges. Just that morning, he'd managed to get a com to divert a couple crates of honey sweets from a base shipment to his unit for a homesick officer's birthday banquet in exchange for the services of one of Eshna's better known pillow yanshas, a woman he hadn't used himself but knew through several of his comrades. He liked these little victories.

But he hated a muddy march. He stayed close to Am, partly

because the general needed quick access to the box, partly because this seasoned officer laughed at his jokes and made him feel safe.

Also, Am hadn't disciplined Bahé when he discovered him holed up in his tiny tent one evening caressing Sekmé's weapon.

"That's the commander's flare rifle," Am had said calmly. "I recognize the scrollwork."

Bahé clutched the weapon tighter.

"She told me to take care of it, sir. I couldn't leave it behind at the holdings."

"Why not?"

Bahé felt hot. He didn't want to air his personal problems with his commanding officer, but Am guessed them anyway.

"Your father?"

"How—how did you know?"

"Odd man, Atto," Am said as, hands clasped behind his back, he toured Bahé's tent. "He smiles from the nose down."

"Yes, sir."

"Doesn't think much of you, does he?"

Bahé looked at his hands and the electrum scrollwork on Sekmé's rifle.

"No, sir."

"H'm . . ."

"I'm not going to use the rifle, General. Sekmé's going to need it again."

Am looked at him. Bahé was surprised how tired the general looked. Grayer, too.

"She inspires a lot of loyalty, doesn't she, Bahé?"

"That's because *she's* loyal, sir."

Am nodded, then pointed at the rifle. "Technically, a soldier carrying someone else's family weapon is subject to a disciplinary lashing."

"Lashing?!"

"I know it's barbaric, but it's an ancient law, religious rather

than military, and, well, there's a lot about religion that doesn't make sense."

"You sound sad, sir."

"Not sad. Bitter. Your cousin . . ." Am clicked his tongue. "I can't help her, Bahé."

"Does she need help, sir?"

"Probably."

Their conversation had died then and Am left the tent.

Now Bahé sniffed in the drizzle, hitched the box up past the pinched point in his back, and trudged after the general. His boots were twice as heavy as usual in their thick casings of mud. The soldiers were near the swamp outside Eshna, a notorious hiding place for criminals and bandits. In the distance, the pale blue and yellow glow of ignis fatuus created the illusion of jo holding a fire ritual or ghosts picking through the mire for their bones.

"It's creepy here, sir."

"Just a swamp, Subcom."

"I know, but it's still creepy."

"What's the matter, Bahé?" the newly promoted Com Dek asked as he joined them, playfully elbowing his subordinate in the ribs. "See any jo playing ball with a skull?"

Bahé suddenly stopped, his mouth open in horror. "No!" he breathed.

"A ghost, then?" When Dek laughed, the freckles around his eyes ran together like ants on candy.

"Almost." Bahé raised his hand. It was shaking.

Am followed the gesture—and swore.

"Damn!"

Am threw down his weapon and ran into the swamp. It was only a few inches deep at this point, but full of algae, and as he splashed, the green flew everywhere. He was soon covered with it, but reached the wraith wavering in the mist, gathered it up in his arms, and stumbled back to his men.

Bahé didn't want to believe his eyes, but had to now that he saw her up close: Sekmé—barefoot, in the remnants of a Telmari robe, bleeding, coated with slime, face swollen, limbs twisted in pain.

Am's face was rock. "Dek, get medical out here. Tell them it's urgent, but don't tell them who it is."

"Sir?"

"You heard me! I want this kept quiet."

Bahé unstrapped the box and set it down so Dek could make his call, but he didn't listen to a word of it. Am had laid Sekmé on the ground and was covering her with a field blanket, a thin sheet of waterproof material made from galca ash. Bahé knelt in the mud next to her. She blinked at him dully. The corners of her eyes were crusted with swamp goo.

"Sekmé! What happened? Who did this?"

"Shh, Bahé!" Am said. "She's in bad shape."

A flicker of comprehension illuminated Sekmé's eyes and she grabbed Bahé's sleeve.

"What? What is it?"

He bent close, but she didn't say anything. Instead, she pulled out the filthy, soaked, and matted vulpé pelt, still dark with Set's blood, and crushed it into his hands.

"Oh . . . no . . ."

Bahé bolted to his feet and ran into the trees to be sick. He kept heaving long after his stomach was empty, wishing he could turn himself inside out.

"I want to die . . ."

They carried Sekmé, wrapped head to foot like a corpse, back to camp and hid her in Am's hut. The general shooed away everyone who was not a medical officer, and Bahé found himself standing in the rain, weeping.

"Get inside, Bahé," Dek said. "You'll catch your death."

"I want to."

"Don't be stupid." Dek pushed the limp and compliant Bahé

back to his tent. "Take off the box, get out of those clothes, and get some sleep. There's nothing you can do."

Once alone, Bahé, always the good boy who did what he was told, unbuckled the box and mechanically began to undress. He stopped when he was down to his undergarments, again desperate with despair.

"I want to die! I want them all to die . . ."

He spied the box on the floor where he'd left it.

Hatula had a right to know everything. Luckily, she was a lighter sleeper than Atto.

The clear purple night over Maurhet glittered with millions of alien suns.

"Do you think there are people up there, Moom?" Set had asked her once as a child. "Do you think they might come here someday?"

"My sweet Set," Hatula had said, hugging him, "the stars are very far away. How would they get here?"

"In a boat," he'd said. "A very big boat."

"How big?"

"As big as the Calf of the Moon."

She'd laughed. Laughed at her fanciful, beautiful son, rare and secret twin to his brilliant, daring sister.

She wished she could laugh at him now, hold him, kiss him, keep him safe.

Hatula closed the lattice doors to the bedroom balcony and moved over to the table that held the box, a box issued to families of firstborn so that urgent messages from Tel-mari could reach them, usually news of death and pain. Sekmé's voice had visited a hundred of these family boxes after the Eshna market raid.

Hatula stroked the crystal, a fine, long chip of magnetized quartz, the heart of the box, then gripped it and snapped it off. She wouldn't be waiting for any more news from Tel-mari.

She looked at the bed. Atto was snoring. If she nudged him, he'd roll onto his side and the sound would stop, but tonight she wanted him on his back.

She crawled across the bedclothes, straddled him, and sat on his belly with a pillow in her hands. He woke and gazed at her, bleary-eyed.

"Hatula?" He yawned then smiled suggestively. "You really want this now?"

"Yes, my love. Now."

She pressed the pillow down over his face. Atto fought wildly, but nothing is stronger than a mother whose children have been attacked.

CHAPTER 18

THE ORPHAN

For several weeks, on Am's orders, Sekmé was a secret patient. None of the doctors who tended her were to tell anyone, especially High Command, who their charge was, and the men were not to mention her name in camp.

"I can't emphasize enough how serious this is," Am said. "Her life *depends* on your absolute cooperation. High Command must not know."

"What about Lokar, sir?" Dek asked.

Sekmé had broken her eerily calm silence long enough to describe the massacre in the courthouse.

"As far as we're concerned," Am said, "he died in the bog months ago."

"And Set?" Bahé whispered hoarsely. He'd lost his voice retching in the woods. It was slow to come back.

"Keep that to yourself for now," Am ordered, but gently. "That would endanger her, too."

Of course, because of the secrecy, the entire unit became intensely interested in Sekmé's condition and needed to discuss it among themselves even if they could not speak her name. They began to refer to her as "the orphan" and took pride in keeping their conversations obtuse.

"Bahé's bunked beside the orphan."

"Again?"

"I took the orphan some liquid sustenance yesterday."

"How'd you get clearance?"

"Three boxes of sweets and a bottle of damnation libation."

"How *is* the orphan?"

"Bad, but growing."

"Goes to show. You just can't kill the orphan."

Am let Bahé move in next to Sekmé the second night when he realized the young man had spent much of the first night outside in the wet. Sharing sleeping quarters with two others made the oversize hut seem unusually crowded, but Am judged it necessary. He'd seen the look in Bahé's eyes in the eyes of other soldiers, soldiers who'd lost friends in battle. It was a dangerous time for the subcom, and the general let regulations sag a bit. He did not assign Bahé any patrols during Sekmé's convalescence and did not insist he eat with the others. As much as possible, he let Bahé stay with his cousin. It seemed therapeutic.

As for the so-called orphan, she seemed to be doing well, at least physically. Once her wounds were dressed, antibiotics and painkillers administered, her feet and ankles wrapped, she slept deeply and healed quickly.

However, her calm, a kind of psychic silence, disturbed the general. She spoke more, but not much. One evening she asked that the vulpé pelt, since cleaned to a caramel tan and in Bahé's keeping, be returned to her. The subcom gave it up reluctantly, but did as he was told.

Another evening, when Bahé at last ventured out to eat with the others, Sekmé discussed her situation with Am.

"I was set up," she whispered without preamble.

The general had been waiting for this, although not eagerly.

"I know." He sat at the foot of the cot. "Bahé told me about a conversation Set overheard in the Dome."

"Yes?"

"Atto played a large role—he hired Lokar—and Dand Ubit got his little rat paws into it as well."

Sekmé blinked slowly at him and he shifted uncomfortably.

"So did the king," she said.

"Don't even whisper it, Commander."

"They set me up the same way they set up my father."

"Hush, Sekmé, please!"

The "orphan" raised her brows at Am's use of her name instead of her rank. The general got up and retreated behind his paper-snow–capped desk.

"Our main concern," he said, "should be deciding what to do now that, contrary to all expectations, you survived."

"We'll go after Merkus," she said simply.

Am narrowed his eyes hard on her.

"I'll lead the raid myself," she added.

"We'd have to get clearance from High Command, Sekmé."

"Why?"

"Well, obviously because . . . because . . ."

"Because nothing," Sekmé said. "High Command has already made it clear they want Merkus taken care of, so we'll take care of him."

"Are you up to it?"

"I will be. I've been on my feet quite a few times the past couple of days. They don't hurt anymore."

"I didn't mean your feet," Am said.

"I know." Sekmé smiled, the first expression other than deadpan self-absorption he'd seen on her since her rescue. It looked strange.

"You'll have to trust me about everything else," she said.

When Sekmé was finally up and about, Bahé delivered her weapon to her and offered to cut her hair.

"It's hanging in your eyes . . . Commander."

She sat on a stool in the middle of Am's hut and stripped to the waist so hair wouldn't get inside her fatigues. Bahé winced when he saw her scars, both old and new, but steeled himself

and began snipping his cousin's fine dark hair. He noticed some strands of gray, which didn't surprise him.

"Sekmé, I don't think I make a very good soldier."

Sekmé didn't respond right away and Bahé wondered if she'd heard him. He was about to repeat his remark when she asked, very calmly, "Why not?"

"I don't handle death well. I keep thinking about it. My death, Set's death, even Lokar's death." He sighed. "I had to help slaughter a goat once for the officers' mess and I threw up."

"That's why you're a communications officer," Sekmé said. "It was the best I could do under the circumstances. You're firstborn, after all."

Bahé stopped snipping.

"*You* arranged for me to be a communications officer?"

"I began lobbying Am over a year ago. I knew you'd be transferred in soon."

"I'm so ashamed."

Sekmé looked back over her shoulder at him. "Why?"

"Because . . . because a man is supposed to be able to face his enemies and fight."

"We all have our strengths, Bahé. From what I understand, you're an ace on the box and a pretty cagey scrounger. Your work counts a lot."

Bahé had to sit down and did so on the floor in Sekmé's fallen scraps of hair.

"If anything happened to you—" Emotion gripped his voice. "—I don't know what I'd do. I'd have no one left."

"You have your brothers at home, your fellow officers here. You have your aunt, too. She's always been fond of you."

"No," Bahé said. "Only you and Set ever understood me."

"That's not true."

"You know it is, Sekmé. Don't pretend to console me."

Sekmé turned on her stool and looked down at Bahé. His face was in his hands.

"Bahé, in ten days the entire unit is going to assist a gel-

bomb raid on Merkus's stronghold. I'd ask Am to let you stay behind, but he needs you and your box."

Bahé spoke from between his fingers. "I know. Don't apologize. It makes it worse."

Sekmé rested her hand on his shoulder a moment, then got up, dressed, and left the hut.

CHAPTER 19

DEPARTURE

I t was a murky dawn, barely distinguishable from night. Only a thin line of pale, greenish-yellow light above the eastern horizon told Merkus that the sun had actually risen.

He and the simple boy Podhi were always the first up, Merkus because his thoughts gave him worry for the day, Podhi because his relative lack of thought made him eager. Podhi liked mornings because they ate their freshest meals then.

Merkus started the cookfire and set a pot of mush to boil. He gave Podhi a stick and told him to keep stirring, slowly so none of it splattered. The boy set to his task with an intense seriousness that gave him the look of a scholar poring over a difficult manuscript.

Merkus smiled. He remembered that hallowed concentration, a concentration focused on the quiet world of philosophy, a man's encounter with the divine at work, things of life and meaning—not killing or destruction.

He wandered away from the fire into the fortress's forecourt where, centuries ago, the poor of the city had huddled with their children and animals while Eshna's aristocracy tried, unsuccessfully, to resist Maurheti invasion.

He stretched and arched his back. Yes, it was a weak dawn, not much to recommend it, but still a dawn. Another chance.

He sniffed. Something was wrong. The air didn't feel right,

as if it were vibrating, stirring its smoky pollution in his nostrils. He glanced back over the fortress to the swamp, to the west.

"Oh . . . God!"

Crouched in the swamp with Am and a hundred of his fellow water rats, chilly muck up to his balls, Bahé watched five Needles shoot out of the west in V formation, Sekmé's in the lead. They screamed over the swamp and dropped their loads on the ruined fortress. The great red glare of the mass of explosions created a second, brighter dawn.

"It's the end of the world!" he breathed.

"For Merkus, anyway," Am said. "Come on, men! We have to stop the stragglers."

Bahé couldn't imagine anything surviving that inferno, but he hitched up the box and plodded on through the goop behind the general.

Four of the Needles reappeared, their job done, and headed back west to the base.

Most, but not all, of Merkus's men were buried in the rubble when the gel bombs hit. Bahé witnessed what happened to the others. When he and his comrades stormed the broken walls, the first thing he saw was ten small bonfires whirling in the forecourt like dust devils. They were ten of Merkus's men, coated with flaming galca, gradually cooking to death. Blood burst through their skin, boiled, then turned to char. Their flesh peeled, caught fire, and blew off with the other ashes. Still they danced, still they lived. They screamed until their throats burned away and didn't stop dancing until some organ—heart, brain, or lungs—exploded or their spines collapsed. Even then, a soldier occasionally had to fire a shell into the crusty, gummy lump that had once been a man's head.

Bahé stood paralyzed and Dek had to grab him and wrestle him into a sheltered corner behind some rubbish.

"Snipers, Bahé! On the upper ramparts." He shook his

unresponsive subordinate. "Do you understand, Bahé? Keep down and protect the box! The general might have to call in another strike."

"I don't think so," Bahé muttered.

"What do you mean?"

Bahé pointed to a far breach in the wall. Most of the soldiers were darting in and out of cover or trying to get into the main body of the fortress to snuff out the last terrorists, but a lone figure at the breach, absolutely exposed but absolutely unconcerned about it, calmly, methodically, took aim at each high-level hiding place and picked off the snipers one by one. A bit of masonry gave way at each flare charge and a man would fall into the forecourt.

"That's uncanny!" Dek said. "It's as if she's shooting woodhens."

"No," Bahé said. "She lets woodhens get away. They're too small."

Merkus scrambled through the underground passageways of the fortress. They were slimy and smelled like aged manure, but one of them led out under the western wall. He just couldn't remember which one.

Podhi was dead. He'd seen him, and untold numbers of his other men, burn. He could hear the last of them taking a stand from the upper ramparts, but knew it was no good. They were finished. The only option now was to save himself.

How had they found him? Had someone betrayed them? Was that possible? All of his men had sworn a holy oath, and the poor, desperate, and ignorant always took their oaths seriously, didn't they?

He banged off the wall in the dark, his soggy oilstone barely flickering, and caromed around a sharp turn. There it was: the tunnel angling up through the foundation, a heavy door wedged into its tail.

Merkus kicked the door with his heel and shoved against it with his shoulder. Slowly, the swollen wood scraped along the stone. A final kick gave him enough inches to squeeze out.

He stood on a mud- and moss-covered ledge about twenty feet above the swamp, which was deep and full of bog monitors. To his left, the ledge ran back around to the forecourt where the Maurheti were still busy with their slaughter. To his right, the ledge led along the western wall then sloped down to a spit of relatively dry land that led through the swamp to freedom. He headed that way.

However, before he could reach the ancient ramp, someone dropped from the wall above him and blocked his path. She aimed her flare rifle at his nose.

"Ah . . . this explains a great deal," he said.

"Get out your coins," Sekmé said in a low, cold voice. Even with death close enough to sniff, Merkus had to admire his foe's remarkable recuperative powers. She looked splendid.

"I lost them."

"No, you have them. You always do."

"But—"

She cocked the weapon. Merkus pulled out the four coins of Fate.

"We'll let chance decide for *you* this time," Sekmé said. "Evens, you die."

"Look, I don't see why we can't—"

"Toss the coins."

"I mean, after all we've been through—"

The barrel of the weapon jutted up under his nostrils.

"Toss . . . the . . . coins."

Merkus's hand trembled—for once, irony failed to amuse him—but he held the coins out from his side and let them drop to the moss and mud.

Two birds. Two feathers. Evens.

Without lowering her weapon, Sekmé carefully turned each

coin over with the sharp tip of her boot. On the back of the birds were . . . birds. On the back of the feathers, feathers. They were double-sided coins.

"Twice you helped me," she said. "Twice you gave me a chance to survive. Why?"

Merkus tugged nervously on his beard and grinned. He was still shaking.

"Uh . . . because you're beautiful?"

Sekmé shook her head.

"All right," Merkus capitulated. "I wanted to see if I could do it."

"Do what?"

"Refrain from destroying my enemy, resist the expected violence." He looked heavenward for a moment, hands spread wide in supplication. "I thought, if I could let you go, it would mean it was possible to live without killing and, perhaps, without war."

He lowered his hands and looked at Sekmé. She hadn't moved. Her rifle was still aimed at his face. However, something in her eyes . . .

Sekmé suddenly flipped the rifle around in her hands and, grasping the barrel, swung it as hard as she could against the fortress wall. The stock shattered on the stone and the firing mechanism broke away. She picked up this heart of the weapon and flung it into the swamp.

Merkus inched away from her, convinced she was mad.

"Wh-what are you doing?" he asked.

"Killing my rifle," she said. "When the last of a direct line of descent has died without heir, the family weapon is destroyed."

"Oh." He watched her gather the pieces of barrel and stock and stick them upright in the moss in a circle. "I'm not sure I understand. Why are you doing this?"

"My orders were to destroy Merkus," she said, "and I've ruined everything that *was* him: his supplies, his weapons, his hiding place. His men are dead or scattered. Merkus was never

your real name and nothing of him is left. You are no longer Merkus and . . . I am no longer myself." She stood up and brushed her gloved hands together to remove the moss.

"Ahvrym killed me."

"You deserved to die," he said softly. "I should hate you."

"Yes . . . probably," she said vaguely as if talking to herself. Then she drew herself up with an air of decision. "But now I'm leaving their war. I want no part of it."

"God bless us both!"

"Of course, it could be a mistake." She scratched her ear— the one missing its lobe. "By leaving the war, I may perpetuate it. They wanted me dead because I was effective."

"Believe me, this is the better way," Merkus said feelingly. "Who knows? Your choice is so shocking, it might catch on."

"It's a very strange path."

"Where will you go now that you're 'dead'?"

Sekmé reached inside her water-resistant jacket and pulled out the stained vulpé pelt. She fingered it thoughtfully and looked toward the morning. The thin, white, jagged line of the White Mountains glowed on the horizon.

"East," she said. "What about you?"

He smiled. "I'll toss the coins. Surprise myself."

Sekmé pulled off her glove and offered her hand. He grasped it firmly.

"You're a bastard, Ahvrym," she said.

"Thank you."

"One bit of advice: Don't underestimate the women. They're one of your greatest strengths."

"I'll remember that."

They parted and the former Merkus ran down the ledge to the spit of land.

He looked back once. Sekmé was gone.

The Maurheti found the remains of Sekmé's flare rifle a couple hours later.

"She must be dead. Someone killed her weapon for her." Am crouched beside the circle of debris.

"A Tel-mari, sir?" Dek asked. "That doesn't make sense. It was a perfectly good flare rifle."

"Nevertheless, none of us—"

"She did it herself," Bahé said suddenly. His eyes, focused intently on the circle, were unnaturally bright, as if he had a high fever.

"Impossible, Subcom."

"I'm sure of it, General."

"How?"

"I just am."

The general put his hand on Bahé's forehead. Cold. The fever was not in his body.

"All right, Subcom, I believe you."

The electrum filigree had separated from the stock in a single piece and was wedged upright in the moss near Am's knee. He wiggled it free.

"I know that, as her cousin, you're not direct descent, but I think she would have liked you to have this to embellish your own family weapon."

He held out the piece of electrum. Bahé barely glanced at it.

"I don't want it," he said.

CHAPTER 20

POSSİBİLİTİES

Even with careful conservation, Haru's food lasted only fifteen days, his water twenty-six. After that, he caught an old, lame wau-weh and wrung its neck. The nourishment and moisture from its raw flesh kept him going another day and a half.

He'd never paid much attention before to how cold it got in the desert at night. He'd always had plenty of coverlets and braziers of slow-burning oilstones to ward off the chill. Now he had nothing but the clothes on his back. Some nights he found shelter in a small cave in the wadis, but he kept wandering, trying to find the way back, and sometimes that found him at nightfall with no shelter at all.

He knew how to build a fire—he was a cook, after all—but there was very little fuel. Thornwood burned poorly and smoked, and he didn't know the first thing about finding oilstone deposits, although the wadis had hundreds of them hidden in their wrinkles.

On the thirtieth day, he discovered a brackish pool. He drank from it anyway and, for the next three days, was so ill with stomach cramps that he couldn't move, not even to get out of the midday sun that broiled his skin and threatened to poach his brain.

By the thirty-sixth day, he began to think seriously of death,

having done his best to ignore it until then. The hallucinations started. He thought he saw Sekmé, naked in a bath of sand, cleansing herself with ashes. His mother, over a decade dead, made an appearance and, as she had in life, scolded him for the carelessness that had landed him in this predicament.

"What excuse do you have *this* time?" she asked, calloused fists on her skinny hips.

"I fell in love."

"Nonsense! You ate too many nuts."

"What?"

"Indigestion like yours needs a strong purgative. I suggest you cut out your stomach."

"What?!"

She vanished.

Now, as he lay incapacitated the morning of the fortieth day, he thought he heard a hard instrument beating on the rock. He opened his eyes. An ancient naked man with strangely smooth coal black skin was pounding the ground with a heavy staff. Even though the sun was already hot, he seemed tireless. The rhythm never flagged.

Haru heard something crack, as if a block of ice in the cold pantry had settled, and a small fountain of warm, dirty red water spurted from the ground. In seconds, it ran clear and the ancient man held a battered cookpot under the flow.

Haru's tongue was thick and dry in his mouth, and his throat hurt when he spoke.

"Did . . . you . . . get water . . . out of stone?"

"Don't be a fool." The man also filled a water skin. "Sometimes a layer of lime blocks a spring. I broke it open."

Skin full, the man finally carried the battered pot of water to Haru and lifted his head so he could drink.

"Sip it, boy, *sip*! You'll spit it up and die anyway if you don't go slowly, not a good idea in such terrible and wondrous times. The *possibilities*, Haru! Sa'Har has never been so close."

Haru stopped drinking.

"How do you know my name?"

"You told me."

"When?"

"Just now."

"No, I didn—"

He stopped, thunderstruck. There was some kind of creature sitting on the man's shoulder. It looked like a tiny naked girl of glass with a wau-weh's head and three red eyes, one on the tip of her snout.

"What . . . is . . . *that?*"

The man grinned, a broad crescent of big yellow teeth. "Well, Haru, *that* is proof that *you* have possibilities, too. Can you make oryx stew?"

"Huh?"

"Am I not speaking loud enough? I said, can you make oryx stew?"

"I . . . yes."

"Good! You can stay with me, then."

"But, I have to get back home!"

Wepanu ul-Bahf grasped his staff and straightened.

"Be honest with yourself, Haru. *This* is your home, now."

"I can't live in the desert! I don't know how!"

Wepanu nodded as if he'd heard this objection many times and was thoroughly sick of it.

"No," he said, and his dark eyes flashed. "Not *yet.*"

PART TWO

Dissolution and Convergence

CHAPTER 21

THE WHİTE MOUNTAİNS

S ekmé had her boots, her water-resistant fatigues, her heavy, hooded slickcoat, a couple oilstones, and her knife—not much, but enough to live off the land. She'd grown up with Tel-mari plants in the holdings, pruned, tamed, and artificially forced, to be sure, but they were the same as the wild flora; she knew their nutritional and medicinal properties. She knew how to find potable water and how to build temporary shelters and fires. After all, she was a well-trained combat officer even if she no longer had a war to fight.

That was what disturbed her more than issues of survival in the wet, rocky Tel-mari interior. Apart from a vague desire to see the legendary mountains where Set's vulpé pelt had come from, she had no plans, conceived of no future, and didn't know if she'd ever be able—or want—to return home. By smashing her flare rifle and letting Merkus go, she'd effectively erased her identity. She was No One—which was not as liberating a condition as it sounded.

Although the great forests lay to the north rather than to the east where she was headed, many of the same trees arched over her, including the massive-trunked tavals with their wide crowns

of tangled branches covered with thumbnail-sized olive green leaves, and the more slender ruchas with their pale, papery bark and flat, hand-shaped emerald leaves. These stood among the cracked granite boulders and outcroppings, mossy streams running between their half-exposed roots, as proud and silent as any grove in the dark stands of the north.

Sekmé appreciated this more open country. It was easier terrain for tracking small animals, and she fashioned snares and a bow and arrows from branches and fibers stripped from saplings. She didn't catch anything the first two days, but found a large rock mink rustling and squeaking in her trap on the third. Its flesh was greasy and gamy, but edible. She scraped its tiny pelt with her knife and, using more plant fibers, stitched a quiver for her arrows.

At night, she would find a sheltered corner, outcropping, or a cave in the rocks and gather together two piles of the driest twigs and leaves she could find—one inside to sleep on, one just outside to burn. It was cold and damp at night, and those rare times the stars appeared from behind the clouds they wore frosty halos as if trapped in the fog of their celestial breath.

She preferred dawn when her body shivered awake and hunger stimulated her mind and body to real, essential activities, work that was clear, defined, and important. Self-preservation had a way of distracting one from more upsetting metaphysical questions.

Sunset was more difficult. The yellow and orange of her fire complemented the pink and lavender phosphorescence of the snow on the progressively nearer White Mountains. Bed piled up for the night, a rodent of some kind digesting uneasily in her belly, Sekmé squatted by the flames and tortured her soul, poking it with the sharp skewers of guilt, grief, and loneliness.

Why am I doing this? she wondered. I'm no ascetic; I'm a soldier! Maybe I let Merkus—Ahvrym—go because I owed him. That doesn't mean I'm a traitor, does it?

Ah, but desertion did. It was a terrible crime and completely against her nature. She'd never given up on anything in her life.

She looked up at the Calf, a dim, lumbering ghost as often as not wandering the night without its later-rising parent, and felt a heavy lump of guilt and regret collect at the base of her throat.

That's me, she thought. I'm an empty shell, an automaton someone wound up and set in motion toward nowhere.

But this empty-shelled automaton wept itself to sleep every night thinking of Set.

After ten days of steady, uphill walking, Sekmé reached a grassy plateau at the base of the foothills. It was drier here and the grass was full of whirring, transparent-bodied locusts. Curiously, small rodents were scarce, so Sekmé caught a few dozen of the locusts and fried them in some taval nut fat on one of the larger rucha leaves.

The fried insects were surprisingly tasty and filling, but that night she had a series of baffling nightmares. In the most vivid, she was a man, apparently a Denneshur tribesman, because he had their dark brown skin, but he didn't wear the usual coin- and embroidery-embellished robes. Instead, he wore a peculiar, loose-fitting set of white fatigues. He was trying to put out the fire consuming his house by holding up a large, heavy tube that spit jets of water on the flames.

The house itself was the oddest part of the dream. It didn't resemble any house Sekmé had ever seen. Not only did it stand on stilts like an acrobat, it was shaped like a flattened egg resting on its side. It seemed to be made out of opaque glass.

When Sekmé awoke, she vomited up her poorly digested meal, a peculiar, noxious green mess that, in her sickened state, seemed mobile, even alive, wriggling on the cave floor. She lay back with her eyes closed and remembered a Denneshur folktale about a man who built a boat to sail to heaven but instead arrived in hell. Before he could escape, the demons burned his boat. It was a parable about the futility of man's ambition, but there

were things about the dream that did not fit the folktale. Its extreme specificity, for one. Not only could she see every hair of the man's stubbled chin and every bolt and joint of the house, er, boat's stilts, but she could see writing on the boat, every letter clean, clear, precise—but unreadable. It was an entirely foreign alphabet.

Also, the dream's mood contradicted the parable's horror. The man did not think he was in hell, and indeed, the landscape was lush and moist like Tel-mari rather than barren and fiery like the Pit. Still, with her intimate knowledge of the miseries found in the fecund wet, Sekmé would have been perfectly willing to grant the man a damp hell if he hadn't been so calm and resigned about his task. He seemed less interested in saving the boat than in making sure the fire didn't spread to anything else.

Where the parable suggested "Dear God! I'll never get home!" the dream offered "Now there's no turning back," a very different thing.

Perhaps the horror came later, Sekmé thought, then shivered and sat up. What an awful idea! Not recognizing hell until it was too late to do anything about it.

That day she saw the animal she'd been looking for in a thorny thicket under a small grove of unfamiliar white-trunked trees with round crimson leaves. With that luxurious coat, it could only be a vulpé. She watched it sneak and trot and pounce at rodents for a long time. Its behavior, and build, resembled a wau-weh's although it was half the size. It also had a shorter snout and smaller ears, probably to conserve heat in this drier, colder climate. And that incredible, glowing pelt was quite unlike the tan, yellow, or black wau-weh coat even if it wasn't entirely white. The legs and feet, tip of the bushy tail, and face were black.

Sekmé crept closer while the vulpé was busily biting the head off a vole. She briefly considered killing the vulpé for its fur and meat. Wau-weh flesh was edible, why not vulpé? How-

ever, her hands shook when she took aim and she realized she could never destroy a creature so closely associated with Set. She lowered her bow and sighed.

The vulpé heard her and, dropping its kill, did something no wau-weh ever had: it ran up a tree and perched on a branch to look at her, tail switching nervously, teeth bared as though grinning. She half expected it to speak.

"Don't worry, little brother," she said. "God intervened on your behalf and made me harmless."

To vulpés anyway. The next evening she killed a wild onager.

She'd covered a lot of ground that day, most of it uphill, and watched the trees shrink to hardy shrubs and mosses, felt the air become even colder, and heard the wind pick up force through the narrowing valleys and gathering canyons. She had reached the White Mountains and, at dusk, passed the remnants of a small, ancient glacier, pink and purple in the sunset, and its trash: a ten-mile moraine of dark, loose boulders and granite she decided not to cross.

I need warmer clothing, she thought, and at the last light, as if served up on a platter, a shaggy onager appeared, a large male with a white nose, drinking from a small glacial lake not far from a series of small caves. Dinner, coat, and shelter, all in one fortuitous bend of the trail.

Sekmé crouched slowly, retrieved an arrow from her mink-skin quiver, and drew back her bow. It was a very long shot in near darkness and she was bone tired from her wanderings, but, handed such a blessing, it was her duty to try.

She released the arrow, it disappeared briefly in the gloom, and the onager's head jerked back. It was hit in the neck. Sekmé worried the wound wasn't mortal and the animal would run away, but its knees suddenly buckled and it fell, kicking and writhing beside the pool. Either she'd severed a major nerve or hit an artery. She jogged up and, careful to avoid the flailing hooves, began to gut it while it was still alive. The onager coughed, rolled its eyes back in its head, and stopped moving.

By the time Sekmé finished removing the intestines, it was too dark to see what she was doing. She lit an oilstone and realized the onager was too big to drag in one piece to the caves and she was too tired to continue her butchering. Besides, the temperature had dropped alarmingly with the sun. Her hands, face, and feet were already tingling.

She took only the time necessary to gather some moss and fallen leaves for her bed and fire and carry them to a cave where, once set up, she dropped into a dead sleep. She wasn't particularly concerned about predators destroying her kill. She hadn't seen any tracks. In fact, the only predators she'd seen were some swine-faced white bats and the vulpé, both too small to do much damage.

That night it snowed. In the morning, her onager was gone.

It must have disappeared just before dawn, because its depression in the new snow had not been filled by recent flakes and the hard bare ground was still red with blood. The onager's entrails, which Sekmé had tossed aside hoping that any scavengers might prefer them to the heavy, half-frozen carcass, were also missing.

A wave of unease prickled under Sekmé's skin as she studied the snow. Only one set of tracks led from the site: the soft hoof marks of an unshod onager. There were no other animal tracks and no evidence of men at all. It was as if the dead onager had gathered in its guts, gotten up, and walked away.

Sekmé rejected this idea as fantasy. Obviously, someone had stolen her kill.

"Damn them!"

She kicked her heel repeatedly into the frozen, bloody ground. She was cruelly cold and hungry this morning and had so counted on the onager's meat and hairy hide that she succumbed to the dangerous fury she'd been beating back ever since her convalescence in the "orphanage." Without even stopping to ask herself who the thief could be, she snatched up her few

implements and stalked out after him with only one purpose in mind: to claim what was hers.

Luckily, the snow had stopped, or she would have lost the trail. As it was, the tracks looked fresh, crisp, and well defined. Still, whenever the canyon widened or the trail fell before her and she got a look ahead, she saw no one. At every turn, it was as if she'd just missed catching sight of her unknown foe by a fraction of a minute. It was enormously frustrating.

At midday, the canyon gave out on a wide plateau of pure, perennial white. Beyond it lay the icebound, jagged teeth of the White Mountains. The tracks headed right across the plateau, straight for them. No rider in sight.

Because of the earlier heat of her anger, Sekmé only now began to feel the cold—and she was losing her ability to feel anything. She barely sensed the ground as she walked. Only the jolt, a short wave of aching pressure through her legs at each step, reassured her that her feet were not yet frozen.

I should turn back, she thought as cold numbed her frustration as well as her body, but it seemed an abstract option. She'd been right about the hazards of outrage, but it no longer seemed important.

It took most of the afternoon to reach the towering, forbidding granite cliffs. By then, her feet and hands were dead weights, and icicles had gathered on the hood of her jacket, the coagulated evidence of her labored breathing.

The tracks entered a narrow-mouthed canyon. Sekmé stopped and scanned the cliff walls above her. This would be an excellent place for an ambush, although the walls of the cliffs were prohibitively sheer.

Well, I'm going to die anyway, she thought. At least it'll be in active pursuit of a goal. Ha! As if I had a goal! I don't have anything, not even a dead onager.

The narrow passage was only about a mile long. At that point it spread out and Sekmé came to a stark, empty chimney

of featureless rock, the remains of an extinct volcano. Its broad, flat floor, blanketed in a thick layer of snow, supported no life whatsoever and the curving cliff walls reached to the sky without break. There wasn't enough footing for a goat. Dusk had already fallen, tinting everything in this silent canyon a chill, thin indigo.

As Sekmé entered this circle of nothingness, her breath came faster and shorter, not from cold, but fear. She felt as if she was back in the roofless courthouse where Set died.

"Gentle Divinity," she whispered, "perhaps You meant all along for me to perish in such a place and are trying again. If so, be swift. I do not want to linger."

Halfway across the crater, the single line of tracks disappeared—utterly. It was as if the phantom rider and his mount had suddenly levitated into the air and out of the box canyon.

"I don't understand," Sekmé whispered. "I . . . don't understand."

Then, in the darkening cliff walls, stars began to appear—at least, something resembling stars. At first, only one or two—Sekmé rubbed her eyes thinking they were products of her failing perception—then they began to double, quadruple, quintuple their number, sparking at an almost exponential rate until, with a final splash of fire, the entire stone chimney, from floor to ragged lip, glowed with tiny flames.

Sekmé stepped back and spun around, then stepped back again in confusion. She was surrounded by this rockbound galaxy—or audience. The tiny lights buzzed faintly in the frigid stillness, as if their energy was shorting in the snow, but the closer she listened, the more convinced she became that the buzzing was voices.

"It is too dangerous! The flesh has broken one of us already."

"We must. The man of flesh needs the story."

"*This* flesh? This flesh is a well of distemper!"

"We have no choice. Its kin-flesh has gone dark."

Sekmé strung her bow, fingers almost too numb to grasp the arrow she'd made of a sapling shoot.

"Who are you?" she cried, and turned right, left, ready to fire at the first star that moved from its place.

The buzzing stopped. Sekmé licked her cold, chapped lips, but her tongue was too parched to wet them.

"Who *are* you?" she cried again. "Come out where I can see you!"

She heard the thud of hoofbeats in the snow behind her. It echoed off the cliff walls and magnified the number of her enemies. Into the canyon came twelve riders in white heading toward her.

Sekmé's trust in reality shuddered and skittered away into the darkness of her lost hope. *White riders?*

"I've gone insane," she whispered. "Why are you doing this, Divine One? I asked not to linger . . ."

The riders came close, their shaggy onagers panting steam and frost, and rode in a circle around her. She aimed her bow at one muffled rider, then another. They moved too quickly to get a proper bead.

Then they stopped and Sekmé could have picked off any one of them she chose, but she hesitated. The riders were silent and anonymous. All she could see were their bright red eyes, like smoldering coals, peering through the thick fur lining of their parkas, eyes shaped like wau-weh eyes, narrow at the corners. She became confused and let her bow go slack.

"*What* are you?"

One of the riders, a bit taller than the others and more heavily built in the chest and shoulders, pushed back his hood with his white gloved hand. Sekmé gasped. He was beautiful, ageless—a man with long, loose white hair whose inhuman eyes in his ice-pale, unlined face were full of a sadness and pity that seemed thousands of years old. He spurred his mount a few steps toward her and Sekmé reraised her bow.

"I don't want to hurt you," she said sincerely, "but I will if I have to."

The rider glanced at his comrades as if to reiterate the hopelessness of the situation, but they kept their eyes forward, minds apparently made up. He groaned—Sekmé heard it: a deep, falling rumble like a retreating thunderstorm or distant avalanche—then pulled up his hood, heeled his onager's flanks, and pounded through the drifts full speed toward her, kicking up a cloud of ice dust that all but obscured his onager's legs.

Sekmé tried to run, but her nearly frozen feet couldn't respond and she tripped, trapping herself in a shallow coffin of snow she had no time to scramble from. She lifted her head just in time to see the onager's hooves, almost upon her, suddenly dig down hard in the snow, bracing the animal and bringing it to an abrupt, and violent, halt. The rider, feet already free of the stirrups, jettisoned from the saddle and flew headfirst right at Sekmé.

She opened her mouth to scream, but stopped when the expected blow—the terrible ripping crack of ribs, the snap of her neck like the familiar pop from the kitchen that used to make her shudder before family banquets—became something else altogether.

She was a hole in the ground, a yawning pit that swallowed rider, dusk, sky, everything. She felt no pain, no violence. Instead, she lost the sense of her skin, the knowledge of her bones. Her body became incoherent to her consciousness then disappeared completely. She could have been miles wide or smaller than a gnat; it was impossible to tell and she was too awash in startled curiosity to care. Something had taken her, flung itself astride her, and all decisions, all sensations, all interpretations of inner and outer stimuli, were out of her hands—for now.

Even so, reduced and refracted, she knew she was alive. That would become important when whatever rode her decided to rest and let her see what else had fallen in.

CHAPTER 22

WATER

Bahé had stopped eating. When it was time for mess, he stayed in his tent and drank. General Am thought the young man was drowning his sorrows with damnation ale, until he took the bottle out of Bahé's hands and tasted it: water.

"You can't live on water alone, Bahé."

"I'm fine," he said.

Am knew otherwise. Now and then, he woke up in the middle of the night to relieve himself and saw the oilstone lantern still lit in the young man's tent. Bahé wasn't sleeping, either.

"I'm sending you home on leave."

"I'm fine, sir."

"That's an order, Subcom. I'll not have my men harming themselves when there's plenty of harm outside to deal with."

Dek helped Bahé pack.

"God, I envy you!" he said. "It's gotten really weird around here lately. Everyone's in a bad mood and wants to go home. I'm overdue for a leave myself, but Am never gets down far enough in that pile on his desk to find the records. I bet your family will be happy to see you."

"I don't know," Bahé said. "Their box is down."

"They don't know you're coming? Great! It'll be a wonderful surprise."

"I don't know."

"Well, fine. None of us can see the future, can we? Remember to bring me some dried fruit, Bahé. You'll do that for me, won't you? I'd *kill* for some dried fruit."

Bahé nodded vaguely. Dek slapped his shoulder with hearty camaraderie.

"You're one of the best, Bahé! A man among men."

Am wanted another officer to go with him to make sure he arrived safely, and there were plenty of volunteers, but Bahé refused to leave unless they trusted him to go alone.

"I can throw you in a cell for this, Bahé."

"All right."

Am's shoulders drooped. He didn't want to arrest the shell-shocked boy—just get him to listen to reason.

"It's for your own safety, son."

"I know where I'm going, sir. I don't need a chaperone."

Am threatened other punishments, none of which he intended to carry out, but Bahé wouldn't budge. In the end, he climbed into the cockpit of the Needle alone.

Am and the other officers were completely unaware that Atto's son had armed the Needle with gel bombs.

Haru, in a secondhand Denneshur robe and hood, looked up from his morning cookfire and pot of oryx stew when the Needle flew over. For some reason, this sighting gave him a sick, dizzy feeling.

"Wepanu?"

"Hush, Haru," the naked seer said from his crouch near the fire. He hadn't looked up. "Some things are fated."

"But . . ."

"But nothing. The wheel turns. There is change. Accept it."

"I'm frightened, Wepanu."

"Of course. The hand of God is a fearsome thing."

★ ★ ★

Hatula saw the Needle, too, from her balcony. She'd convinced the revered Ando—whose cheerful nonchalance did not extend to examining corpses—that Atto had died of a heart attack. She now lived as a semirecluse in her shadowy chambers, waiting for Bahé to come home to what were, she supposed, *his* holdings.

Her nephews, once they'd gotten over their father's death, abandoned Atto's holdings to stay with Hatula, to protect her, they said, but she knew they were frightened boys who needed a parent—any parent. She let them do as they liked. When Bahé returned, he could adopt the paternal role as baron. These things no longer concerned her.

However, when she saw the Needle flash over the holdings, followed by its lingering scream, she knew, as certainly as if he'd told her, that Bahé was not coming home. She drew on a long blue cloak and, without telling anyone, crept out the back of the house, snuck out of the holdings, and went for a barefoot walk in the desert.

The guards on Kemphor's city walls paid little attention to the Needle as it shot across the midday glare and out over the ocean. Half a dozen of the aircraft did so daily to decelerate before the sharp turn that headed them back to the desert air base. The guards' weapons stayed at rest across their shoulders, their hands hooked loosely over barrel and stock.

The Needle roared as it slowed, turned, and came back. No one noticed the unusual angle of its course until it was directly over the desalination plants at the base of the sea cliffs—and dropped a load of gel bombs on them.

The explosion was heard as far as Haru's cookfire. The desalination process involved many volatile, galca-based chemicals as well as charcoal to purify the turgid sea water. The guards on the Kemphor ramparts nearly fell off into the sand and gaped in astonishment as the Needle raced inland. They saw it make

another turn just shy of the Hills of Whispers, readying for another pass.

This gave the guards time to shake themselves out of shock, and when the Needle flew over Kemphor again, it was met by a hail of caustic flares, acid bullets, and short-range rockets. The Needle's tail blew off and the craft began a spiraling roll into the ocean. Nevertheless, it righted itself long enough to drop the last of its gel bombs on the remaining buildings of the desalination plants.

At the sound of the first explosion, Roon and Kerz raced up to the balcony of one of the palace towers, followed some minutes later by a wheezing Dand Ubit. The secretary arrived in time to witness the second bombing and the Needle's long, curling, smoky dive into the sea.

The king gripped the balcony's decorative iron rail until his knuckles whitened, and he chewed his lower lip.

"Kerz," he said in a low, tight voice, "get hold of General Am in Tel-mari. I want to know who that was and why."

The big chamberlain ran back down the tower.

It took some time for Dand Ubit to catch his breath, but when he did, he joined Roon at the railing.

"Regardless of why, Your Majesty," he said, "you know what the outcome will be."

The king nodded. In his mind's eye he could already see the leaves dropping from the trees of the holdings and the grasses turning brown and brittle.

CHAPTER 23

THE RAID

Pain returned first. Pain and disorientation. She was back in the flesh, or at least the memory of it, and it was not her flesh. The world spun around her in a shrill, acrid, smoky roar. The Needle had been struck from behind—how? with what stolen weapon?—and lost its tail, its balance.

I'm falling! I'm falling!

The thought voice was not Sekmé's, but a man's, and at first, she refused to recognize it. She would not have it be so. But the man's hands, which he beat bloody on the instruments, were the same ones that had lifted her high and sat her on broad, solid shoulders. They were the same ones that had crept like mice into Hatula's braids and teasingly picked their lacings apart. They were the ones that, with Set's listening fingers resting on top, had shown her blind brother how to knot a bird snare, brush out an onager's mane, and clean the bony pond fish for outdoor roasting. They were Osmir's hands—they were her father's.

She felt the strength and fury that propelled these hands and the searing ache when they struck metal. The instruments were frozen, fused together by burning, leaking fuel. The eject would not respond.

He threw his head back and nearly broke his teeth clenching

them. His legs had begun to burn, and in spite of the chaos, he'd not been spared the knowledge.

I'm dying!

Words left him as the animal terror of burning to death overcame human reason. Images ran together on top of each other like leaves blown into a corner by an autumn gust. He was wrestling with his brother, quickly besting him with a surprise twist of his shoulder. He was reading in the hall of the Academy in the middle of the night, his nervous preexam exhaustion making the glow of the long rows of oilstone lamps first sharpen to pins of fire then bleed into cottony blurs of gold then collapse and expand again and again in time with his anxious pulse. Hatula was laughing. He'd let his children pull him to the ground, pin him so they could yank off his leather slippers and tickle his feet.

I'm dying . . .

Sekmé was suddenly pulled from Osmir's senses and thrust directly into the fibrillating heart of the Needle's controls. There, amid the blue and orange fireworks of shorting circuits, melting foil, and smoldering insulation, she saw the isolated cluster of wire and connections that controlled the release of the clamps and the short burst of compressed air that would free the pilot's seat of the Needle. Fire had not yet reached the cluster, but the coiled bundle that should have fed it power from the Needle's backup cell, a cube swathed in fireproof batting, was missing. Not disconnected—missing. No base mechanic could have failed to notice such an omission.

And no mechanic *had*, Sekmé realized. Her father's Needle had been sabotaged.

She could change nothing. All she could do was relive, with agonizing directness, what had already happened as if she herself had been there. She was a kind of bodiless consciousness, weaving in and out of an experience as her rider's will had long ago dictated. She could choose nothing, not the memory, not the *level* of the memory.

Mercifully, memory of the Needle's demise broke apart into glittering, indecipherable shards before she could experience the moment of her father's death. Instead, Eshna's ruins seemed to rebuild themselves, shattered stone leaping up from the pyre and reclasping fragments of concrete before pulling itself back into place on a wall or tower. The dead reattached their limbs and ran back into houses that retrieved the foul vomit of an explosion, inhaled it.

The images reshuffled, flipped around; she sat in another man's mind, a man sitting on a cold stone floor in the weak yellow glow of a nearly spent oilstone by his knee, surrounded by shabby, teetering piles of books and scrolls.

A lean nervousness coursed through this man and kept him alert, curious, sleepless. He followed the ancient text in his lap with his index finger, from right to left, line after obscure line:

> *But they returned in time*
> *And rode out of the empty lands*
> *To fall upon Eshenna*
> *As a storm falls on a plain*
> *And sets the grass on fire.*
> *Lament, Eshenna, lament!*
> *For they will claim you as a bride*
> *But treat you like a whore.*

The man sat back and lifted his eyes to the vaulting of the ceiling. Under the stains and calligraphy of mildew, the curving wedges between each rib were painted with vines, fruit, and flowers. Birds with red crests and blue breasts flew among the vines and built painted nests in the corners of the frescoes. No scholar had yet been able to identify these birds, fruit, and vines. They were unknown species—or fanciful inventions.

"What do You see for us?" he murmured in Tel-mari.

He reached into the pocket of his heavy woolen robe and retrieved a pair of silver shears. In an act of sacrilege designed

to be a great sacrifice—a sacred crime—he collected his thick brown beard in his fist and cut it off.

Rolling it carefully into a soft, spongy ball, he placed the hair in a small stone bowl, sprinkled it with fen widow flower extract, and set it on fire with his dying oilstone. The stink of burning hair laced with floral sugar made him dizzy. The floor began to rock gently and ripple as if made liquid by a temblor.

"I see wave after wave," the rabam chanted as he slipped into altered consciousness. "The rise and fall. Time breathes and we dance to its beat. To escape the dance, we must step out of time."

Step out of time? Sekmé realized she didn't understand and couldn't because she was no longer the rabam. She saw the outline of his heat, a mobile reddish glow, as she drew away, out a window, into the soft furry chill of dawn. As if caught in a sudden gust, she careened down into the slow blue shadows of the courtyard and smacked into—and knew—a new flesh. A young man. Beardless. Excited and confused to the point of bursting by the words he carried wrapped in linen under his arm as he ran. A good strong heart pumping with hope and terror, the skin of his cheeks and forehead flushed dark red, slapped by the cold damp.

Bless Khelash's insatiable belly! A purloined joint of roasted goat, hastily, greasily stowed in a wide sleeve—Ahvrym would never wear that robe again!—and the librarian had given him access to documents so old, so fragile, they weren't to be touched except with fine silken gloves and the Grand Ra'Habam's permission. His own father, the rector, couldn't get permission because he had a reputation for absentminded slovenliness: he had dirty hands.

But Ahvrym had seen the texts, touched them, and what he had read! He had to tell his rabam, had to ask him to explain it.

It was a simple thing, really, what was once known as a family-line poem, a poem that told the stories of the writer's ancestors, often in colorfully inflated language. Still, these po-

ems always contained kernels of truth, no matter how exaggerated, and in the text tucked under his arm Ahvrym had found buried in the obscure and ornate elegies to long-dead noblemen and merchants a reference to a "first father" who "rose up from Sa'Har" to help build "the city in stone." Several things about these words raised chills on the back of Ahvrym's neck, not the least of which was the common, vulgate text used. Normally, when a poet mentioned a holy place or a mythic location, the vulgate suddenly switched to a court term to point out the location's special status. Not so here. The poet used the vulgate for *Sa'Har* as if it were a real place inhabited by real people. His reference to a city in stone also excited Ahvrym. Could that be a reference to Old Eshna, the beautiful—and enigmatic—ruins that were constructed of finely worked stone?

Finally, the term *first father*—it was a very odd phrase in Telmari, clumsy even, with an almost tribal feeling. Even so, the poet used it several times in reference to this ancestor, unselfconsciously. However, the idea of a first father—of a first *anything*, especially first*born*—was extremely common in *Maurheti* poetry, especially in family-line poetry, a form both cultures shared.

Perhaps they shared much more than a literary form. Perhaps this poem contained traces, however tenuous, of a shared past, even a shared ancestry, that coincided with the coming from the fabled land of Sa'Har. Maybe it was only crazy speculation, but Ahvrym couldn't dismiss the idea without seeing his rabam first. His rabam would cast a cooler, calmer eye on the text.

"If we . . . share a past," he gasped as he stopped to adjust his delicate parcel, "that would mean . . . we were brothers . . . and the war . . . was not . . ."

He looked up. In the lightening sky he saw five pink stars hovering in a line over the uneven black bulk of the city below the school. They floated strangely, as if adjusting to each other's location, carefully keeping the distance between them equal.

And they were growing—rapidly.

Unnerved, Ahvrym anxiously clutched the parcel to his chest. He heard the brittle crackle of desiccated fibers.

"Rab . . . Rab . . ." He couldn't find his voice until the "stars" were close enough to find theirs—and his scream could not compete.

"Rabam!"

The metal spheres spewed out of the Needles like shit pellets from a goat and landed everywhere. The entire city seemed to ignite at once with a chemical fire so intense it immediately spawned a high, harsh wind that carried embers and globs of burning galca to those buildings not directly hit by the bombs. Ahvrym, alone in an open space, watched the infernal burn ooze down the walls like magma, and the school collapsed around him. Stone, glass, metal—shredded, melted, and flaming—flew at him as if hurled by blind giants who knew he was there but couldn't quite figure out where.

He lost the manuscript, dropped it in the first wave of heat, and saw the linen napkin take flight, twist about in a flame tornado, and evaporate. He never saw the destruction of the scroll itself. It had rendered to dust before the package unwrapped itself.

He ran toward the burning building where his rabam was dying, but instinct foiled desire and turned him away before he put his hands on the sizzling latch of the toppling door. It took over his legs even as he begged them to take him to death, too, and guided him through Old Eshna, burning Eshna, to the chaotic outer sectors full of frightened people, panicked animals, and smoke that tasted like oil, ash, and copper.

"Leave me alone! Leave me alone!" he screamed, although no one, least of all himself, could hear it in the confusion. Was he screaming at the Maurheti pilots? The nearly blinded bodies that knocked into him and grabbed at his hood? Or did he scream at that duplicitous poet who'd offered a hint of hope?

A knot of ragged women, pressing their veils tightly over their noses in an attempt to make them filters against the ash,

pointed to the sky. One of the Needles, its tail burning, tumbled from the clouds, barely missed the upper floor of a guild meeting hall, dropped over the swamp, and fell into the trees. A great globe of orange rolled out over them, turning them to cinder fingers.

Instead of cheering his enemy's demise, Ahvrym sat in the ashes and wept as if he'd lost his only brother.

Sekmé knew the weight and slump of his shoulders, the constriction of his belly and groin, and the quick, thoughtless reflexes of his terror. He was a creature wild with survival savagery, adrenaline-shaken and vicious—and yet he wept. Why?

No answer. She lost her contact and was pulled from this time. These were finished things, expired experience. The riding will kicked her along. It had other lives to give her, other histories to return.

CHAPTER 24

THE JO

At first, Haru tried to ignore the tiny, transparent naked girl with the dog snout, but she kept following him around and staring at him with her red eyes. She'd perch on a broken rock and watch him cook for Wepanu or hover over him in the dark cave while they were preparing to sleep. She would swim in the hidden springs and ride backward on the old seer's shoulder so she could keep an eye, or three, on the big young man bringing up the rear.

Finally, he couldn't stand the scrutiny anymore. He and Wepanu had set up camp for the evening in a steep wadi and the older man had gone off to meditate on a nearby bluff overlooking the hills. Haru and the jo stayed behind. Haru smoothed a place for the fire and was unloading his burden of salvaged twigs when the jo decided to sit on his head. Her all but weightless presence tickled like eczema. He dropped the wood and swatted at her.

"Get off! Why can't you leave me alone?"

"We love the ones who see us, man of flesh," she said in her high, squeaky voice.

She flitted over to a stunted thornwood tree and sat on a branch.

"I didn't ask to see you."

"Suffering changes the senses," she said. "You no longer see or hear as you did. Rejoice! You have access to great wisdom."

"From a jo?" He snorted contemptuously. "Everyone knows you're liars."

"Only those who can't see say we lie. We know many things."

"Nothing important, I'll bet. Now, if you'll excuse me, I have a fire to build."

"Wepanu listens to us."

"Wepanu's a prophet." Haru took a piece of oilstone he'd retrieved from a deposit the old man had shown him and struck it against a stone. A yellow spark fell into the twigs, which caught fire. "Prophets listen to everything and pick out the good bits. Wepanu will let anyone natter on if he thinks something might come of it."

"Wepanu is wise, Haru," the jo said. "We were here when you first came."

"Then you saw my kidnappers." Haru took the water skin and filled the small cookpot to make soup. They always ate lightly after Wepanu meditated. "Why don't you follow *them*? Give them boils or something."

"When you were new, life was difficult. You knew little about this world."

"You could have helped me, you know. Shown me where water was, anything, but no. You remained invisible and—"

"But you did learn and we watched your numbers increase. We watched you build your city in stone, and your pride grew until you forgot the vows you had brought with you and began to quarrel."

"Wait a minute." Haru turned from his soup and eyed the jo suspiciously. "What are you talking about?"

"Not *Haru*, man of flesh!"

The jo took off from the thornwood tree and flew up to the solitary black silhouette on the bluff.

"Wait!" Haru cried. "When was this? Come back!"

He kicked the dust. Wasn't that the way it always turned out? All this time he'd been trying to get that tiny bitch to stop pestering him and now that he *did* want to talk . . .

"Damn jo! Nothing but fables and nonsense."

So why was he more afraid now than he'd been the day the ill-fated Needle with its mad pilot flew overhead on its way to bomb Kemphor? Why did everything around him, sand, rock, darkening sky, suddenly look completely alien, as if he were seeing the world for the first time?

Haru left the cookpot simmering on the fire and hiked up the rocks to where the naked seer sat cross-legged in the last of the day's light. The jo was nowhere to be seen.

Haru hesitated. He'd never interrupted Wepanu's meditations before and didn't know if he should. It might anger the old man. He decided to wait and sat next to him, but Wepanu opened his eyes and looked at him, not angrily, but not happily either.

"Yes, Haru?"

The young man coughed. Talking about the jo embarrassed him.

"The jo, um, why do they call us *men of flesh*? Why not just *men* or *people*?"

"It's to distinguish themselves from us," Wepanu said. "They're people, too."

"I thought they were spirits."

"What is a spirit?"

Haru stared at the seer. His question was serious.

"You know."

"No, I don't, Haru. Tell me."

"Well, it's a being. A piece of the divine."

"We're all pieces of the divine, Haru . . . and *we* tell lies, don't we?"

Haru blushed hotly. So—she'd told him.

"Yes, I know." The young man rubbed his forehead. This

would be more complicated than he'd expected. "But, I mean, *we* eat, sleep, breathe. We're *alive*."

"So are the jo."

"Do they eat? What do they breathe?"

Wepanu unfolded his legs and stretched them out in the sun. He yawned.

"Haru, just because a being does not consume the same things we do does not mean it does not live."

"The jo . . . *consume?*"

"Of course. Everything consumes. As we consume material things, things of physical substance, they consume nonmaterial, nonphysical things."

"Like what?"

"*Think,* Haru. What things are nonphysical?"

Wepanu's tone stung Haru. The old man was always reminding him to "Think! Think!" as if he would otherwise revert to a brutish, instinctive life.

"All right, then," he said, a little irritably, "what does *God* consume?"

"Himself, of course." Wepanu smiled; his large, stained teeth looked orange in the late sunset. "God consumes Himself to re-create Himself."

Chastened, Haru grasped a handful of dirt and let it fall through his fingers.

"So, everything dies," he murmured, "even God."

Wepanu shook his head. "Everything *lives*. Even God. Ultimately, matter *is* energy, energy *is* matter, and death isn't a permanence. It's a process that happens constantly. Your yesterday self is dead and your today self will be dead tomorrow." Wepanu closed his eyes and straightened his back. "Really, this is a worthless concern, Haru. If you would stop clinging to what you have and mourning what you've lost, you'd agree with me and get back to making the soup like a *useful* cook."

"The jo said something else," Haru mumbled. "Something I didn't understand."

"A riddle?"

"Well, no. Something about men breaking a vow and . . ."

Wepanu opened his eyes again but his gaze was far away. His meditations usually rejuvenated him, but this evening he looked tired and old in spite of his preternaturally smooth black skin.

"Death changes the jo, too," he said, "but their life passages are much longer than ours. For them, it was only yesterday when man appeared on the world."

"They were here at the Great Division?"

"If you insist on calling it that." Wepanu sighed. "But the men of flesh, the blind ones who eat solid foods, had already been here several generations before they fell into disunity."

Haru felt that odd sense of dislocation again, the feeling that nothing, not even his own body, was familiar.

"That can't be," he said.

"Why not? The Tel-mari believe in a Time Before. They call it Sa'Har."

"That's a folktale, Wepanu. It's not real."

The old man shrugged and recrossed his legs.

"A pond can't hold the ocean," he said.

"What's that supposed to mean?"

"Get back to the soup, Haru, and make sure it hasn't boiled away or we'll both be growling tonight."

CHAPTER 25

DEK

The great tanks and cisterns outside Kemphor, the ones that were supposed to provide the city and holdings with enough emergency water for several months, went dry in a matter of weeks. No one had realized how thirsty those foreign-born inland crops—or four million people—could be. Scouts combed the nearby Hills of Whispers for springs, wells were dug at likely places, and portable desalination equipment was issued to different quarters of the city and the holdings, but the drought was too extensive to respond to such meager remedies.

"How long will it take to rebuild the desalination plants?" Roon asked Dand Ubit in the cool, shadowy isolation of the palace library.

"Working day and night under ideal conditions, at least a year."

"A *year?*"

"Under ideal conditions," the secretary droned. "In reality, it's not just a matter of the buildings themselves. Machinery must be reforged and chemicals redistilled." Dand's moon face puckered a little. "Unfortunately, Majesty, much of this kind of restoration requires the use of—"

"Fresh water."

"Exactly. Mixing concretes, tempering metals, steam—"

"Not to mention keeping the workers from dying of heat prostration."

"Oh. Yes. That, too."

Roon frowned at the secretary. The man was such a toad.

"Might I make a suggestion, Majesty?"

"Yes. I'm entertaining even ludicrous ones these days."

"Well . . ." Dand rocked back and forth on his toes and heels, which, considering the puniness of his feet, created a rather short, frenetic wobble. "Tel-mari is very wet."

"And the sun is hot. Get beyond the obvious, Dand."

"Why not bring in water from there, Majesty? The military governorate can redirect some of the current labor force and, ahem, 'recruit' more for the project. Also, considering the growing desiccation of the holdings, we can shift our attention from importing woods and ore to importing foodstuffs."

"What would the labor force eat?"

"Less." Dand Ubit smiled unpleasantly. "They're Tel-mari. Not of God."

"If they resist?"

The secretary spread his waxy hands as if the answer were elementary. "Shoot them. Fewer bellies."

Nasty—but logical. Roon had to concede that Dand Ubit's scheme was the most workable he'd yet heard.

"I'll issue the orders but leave your final suggestion to individual commanding officers' discretion," the king said. He shook his head. "Who would have thought a single deranged soldier could bring about such disasters? What was going on in his mind?"

"Who knows, Majesty? As you said, he was deranged."

"But even the mad have their reasons, Dand, whether we understand them or not."

Some weeks later, Com Dek pondered the same question as he and a small platoon roamed the filthy streets of the New

Hives press-ganging anyone they could find—they'd already collected quite a motley selection of middle-aged matrons, elderly men, and skinny children—for extra shifts at a nearby slaughterhouse. The drought in Maurhet, having killed the flora, now claimed responsibility for the alarming mortality of the fauna, too. Kemphor was rationing meat.

"Bahé was a gentle, almost passive man," he told his subcom, a weedy little recruit fresh from Maurhet named Gost. "He hated the violence here. He's the last person I would have expected to attack his homeland."

Gost was not as strong as his troubled predecessor and had some difficulty carrying the heavy communications box—he kept shifting it about and hitching it up and sighing his discomfort—but he didn't openly complain. Dek had the feeling the recruit admired him and wanted to impress him with his stoic manliness, which made him uneasy. He didn't feel like a role model.

"He just snapped, sir," Gost said in a voice still breaking out of boyhood. "I overheard General Am on the box the other day and—"

"You're not supposed to eavesdrop, Subcom."

"No, sir, but he was discussing Bahé with someone in High Command and said he thought his behavior had to do with grief for his cousins."

"That's probably true, Gost."

"But, that's so—forgive me, sir, but that's cowardly."

Dek shot a sharp look at his underling.

"In what way?"

"We've all lost family, sir. It's part of our fate as God's soldiers."

"You never knew Commander Sekmé or her brother, Subcom. If you had, you might understand our grief a little better."

"*Our* grief, sir?"

"Forget it, Gost. Let's check down this street."

The boy was too green to know any better. In Tel-mari only a few days, how could he know that his new comrades were quieter than usual, more sullen and reluctant to perform their

duties especially now that they included harassing and killing refugees who hadn't broken any law? He couldn't know that fewer games of chance went on in camp, more damnation ale was consumed, fewer good-natured pranks were pulled, and more serious brawls were fought than at any other time in Dek's—or Am's—memory.

"Morale is really limping, Com Dek," the general had muttered one sopping evening after the mess officer had discovered another com had hung himself in the cold locker among the naked pullets and flayed onager pieces. "We're turning our weapons on ourselves."

Dek remembered that creepy little memorial made of the broken bits of Sekmé's family weapon.

"A firstborn's role is always clear," he said to himself. "You're a cadet, a soldier, an officer, then, if you're lucky, retired and pensioned. If you renounce that, what are you?"

"Sir?"

"Nothing, Gost. What about that tavern over there?"

The platoon and its cowed retinue of refugees gathered outside Hemsha's tavern, and Gost banged on the door with his freckled fist.

"Open up! Maurheti patrol."

"We're closed," Hemsha's voice replied from within. "Come back tonight. We're having a two-drinks-for-the-price-of-one special."

Dek approached the door.

"We're not here to drink," he said. "We're recruiting labor. By order of the military governorate, I must insist that all occupants of this dwelling present themselves for assessment."

The door opened wide enough for Hemsha to poke his grizzled head out. He glanced at the patrol and their charges.

"Women and children?" he said. "You should be ashamed of yourselves."

"Emergency measures," Dek said. "All able-bodied natives are to be assessed."

"For what?"

"In this case, slaughterhouse duty."

Hemsha scowled with grand offense. "You must be joking! My daughter and I have never done that kind of work in our lives."

"Papa? Who is it?" Bekka's voice came over his shoulder.

"Just some very misguided young boys, my dear. Pay no attention."

Gost grabbed Hemsha by the beard and yanked him out from behind the tavern door into the street. He shoved him into the mud.

"Boys, eh?" He cocked his rifle at Hemsha's head.

Bekka screamed. "Papa!"

"Back off, Gost!" Dek snapped. "He's no use if you shoot him."

"I'm no use to *you*, regardless," Hemsha said as he began to pick himself up. "I refuse to help you in your war."

Gost cracked him across the skull with the rifle and Hemsha dropped back down, a wide gash over his left eye bleeding profusely. Bekka darted out of the tavern and grabbed Gost's jacket. He pressed his hand over her face and pushed her away, and she slammed back hard against the tavern wall.

"I told you to back off, Gost!" Dek cried, annoyed that he might actually have to follow through on his threat somehow.

"He's a subversive, sir!" Gost replied. "We're supposed to kill subversives."

"I don't care! Back off or . . . or you're on report!"

The color drained out of the subcom's face.

"*On report?* He's a Tel-mari!"

The honeymoon's over, Dek thought. Oh, well. Probably better this way. More real.

"Listen to me, soldier," he growled. "I've given you an order. Follow it or you'll wish *you* were Tel-mari."

Gost hesitated and Dek pointedly unclasped the flap on his side arm's holster.

"Be practical, Subcom. I know what our orders are, but we can't just kill them for sport."

Gost arched his brows—Dek would never forget this venomous look of defiant contempt—and proceeded to kick Hemsha repeatedly in the kidneys.

Dek drew his side arm and fired. He didn't even give the action his full attention. Gost tripped back over Hemsha and fell against the tavern wall next to Bekka before sliding slowly to the ground, the hole in his head leaving a red streak on the masonry.

Bekka stared at the body the way one would stare at a dead bog monitor—still afraid, but fascinated—then she dropped to her knees beside her father and anxiously opened the collar of his robe with her slender fingers. She had nothing handy to wipe the blood from his eyes, so she pulled off her veil and stroked them carefully with it before parting his eyelids with her fingertips. She put her ear to his lips, listened to his chest, and finally sat back on her heels, all tension drained from her body. Hemsha had successfully escaped giving aid and comfort to the enemy.

Dek looked back at the platoon and the captive Tel-mari. They were waiting for him to speak, act—define the business of the next moment. He'd never seen such a mass of blank faces.

He turned to Bekka.

"Get up, miss."

Bekka didn't move. Dek cocked his side arm again and pressed its barrel against her temple.

"Get up, miss. It's time to work."

Bekka raised her head slowly and gazed up at him. Her expression was smooth, utterly calm, resigned, and her large, luminous feline eyes were steady. Her full lips didn't tremble.

Dek's hand did. She was the most beautiful woman he'd ever seen, and to his enormous discomfort, in the middle of his stern, official behavior, he found himself wanting to apologize for his boorishness—and his overabundant freckles.

"Please, miss. My orders . . ."

Bekka remained where she was. Her opinion of his orders was clear.

A strange sensation overcame Dek, as if his nostrils had filled with the foul odor of rotten fish and that odor had emanated from his own body. This was dirty. Dishonorable. Unnatural.

In seconds, Dek became an atheist.

He withdrew his side arm.

Behind him, the Tel-mari captives, in one motion, sat down in the street. The Maurheti platoon looked at them in dismay but, after Dek's confusing behavior, didn't seem to know what to do.

Dek undid Gost's shoulder harness, lifted the box, and strapped it on his own back. He tried not to look at Bekka anymore and instead turned to his men.

"Let's go," he said.

"What about the prisoners, sir?" a thirty-year veteran sergeant of foot asked.

"We'll tell the general this neighborhood is abandoned."

"And—and Gost?"

"His body won't be here long," Dek said with a quick, nervous glance at the silent Tel-mari. "He, um, he deserted."

The sergeant of foot stepped forward and spoke softly, his warm breath in Dek's face. "Am won't believe us, Com."

"Probably not," Dek whispered back, "but that's my problem, isn't it?"

The platoon withdrew, leaving behind a peculiar gathering of men, women, and children sitting in the muddy street. How long they were there, no one knew, but by evening both Gost's and Hemsha's bodies were gone, the street was empty, and a new legend was passing mouth to mouth among the Eshna refugees.

Ten days later, another patrol brought thirty Tel-mari—again, mostly women and children and the elderly—to the slaughterhouse. They threatened them, beat several, even killed a child, but not one refugee lifted a finger to butcher the bleating goats

and screaming onagers. Instead, they sat on the blood-slick killing floor, folded their hands in their laps, and began to pray, silently. They made no sound at all, not even when they were beaten.

When a week later the female labor force at a large plant that refined sugar from pomap roots refused to get out of bed even when denied food and access to the latrines, the Maurheti knew they had an epidemic.

"Did I hear correctly, Dand? They're not fighting back?"

Roon stood on the edge of the sea cliffs with a retinue of officials, ministers, and private contractors surveying the clearing away of debris from the ruined desalination plants below. The crisp salt air mingled with the harsh, dirty smoke of the great rock breakers and haulers below, and the king's eyes smarted behind his tinted visor. His unstable secretary had to stand sideways and lean into the gust or risk being knocked off his tiny feet.

"No, Majesty," Dand said, cupping his hands around his drone so it could be heard and not blown away. "They sit down and do nothing."

"Even when beaten?"

"Well, a few fight then, but not many." The secretary dabbed his watering eyes with a fine silk handkerchief. "They don't fight, they don't work. I think, Majesty, their will is finally broken."

"I'm not so sure," Roon said.

He watched the rock breakers crawling over the uneven ground on caterpillar treads like tiny mollusks that clung to the coral at low tide, and he felt a new wave of foreboding. Perhaps if Dand had a wife or two, he would understand how truly *willful* such "passive" opposition could be and that there was no good way to respond. If you ignored it, by definition you lost. Your wishes remained unfulfilled. If you tried to force compliance, you lost the moral upper hand and became a bully, attacking a nonaggressive victim.

One of his ministers, a gaunt, lugubrious man in a flapping dark green coat, handed him the final contract from one of the private construction executives. Roon winced at the sum, but signed it anyway.

The Tel-mari had never simply sat back and done nothing before. Perhaps this behavior was a momentary aberration and they'd return to their accustomed belligerence, which Maurhet knew how to handle. A reassuring idea if he could believe it, but the signs were bad. Daily the field generals in Tel-mari pestered him for instructions, and he couldn't stall them forever.

He forced a confident smile.

"We needn't worry, Dand," he said. "Someone's brat will bite someone and this noncompliance fad will fall as quickly as it has risen."

"I hope so, Majesty."

"Now, to matters closer to home." Roon turned to his domestic minister, a retired base general whose entire body, from eyelids to chin to breasts to buttocks, seemed to sag more from depression than years or weight.

Roon sighed.

"Out with it, Hetra. This kind of news only festers if it isn't dealt with at once."

The rock breakers crawled on, burning up more fuel, coughing up more smoke, using up more of their increasingly limited time before something other than rock—Roon cared not to speculate what—broke.

A couple turns of the Calf later, Am sat in his cavernous camp hut with a confidential communiqué from his wife. The desert was reclaiming their holdings and she'd had to let the servants go. She could no longer provide for them. However, she'd kept the Denneshur stable boy and a few animals and personal belongings and was heading for their smaller, remote "retirement" holdings by the sea. The stable boy had promised to help her dig a well and establish a garden of native plants.

"There has been trouble in the city," she wrote. "Granary lootings and large, unruly protests, mostly about the rationing. It disheartens me to see how fragile our sense of community is when faced with a community-wide crisis. So far, it's been quiet in the holdings, but I refuse to sit by and wait for the inevitable. When you can, my love, please join me. We will become true children of the desert.

"Hatula's nephews have stopped searching for her and have scattered, some to their father's holdings, others to Kemphor, others God knows where. I think she knew what was coming. Her family was always unusually sensitive."

Am folded the communiqué and tapped it against his lip. Dek had delivered it that morning along with a missive from High Command authorizing—in other words, quietly insisting—that the "water reclamation project" be expanded inland to the outlying villages.

Villages less likely to be contaminated by this new passive defiance, Am thought, but they'll hear about it soon enough.

He'd heard the original legend from a Tel-mari prostitute— even he occasionally needed the succor of a surrogate wife—and what she'd said about the soldiers involved sounded suspicious, especially considering Dek's odd report about the empty neighborhood in a part of the New Hives Am knew very well was one of the most densely populated in Eshna.

Conclusion? Dek was lying—and yet Am would not confront him. It had to have been a strange moment, staring into the eyes of a woman who'd been elevated in the legend to "an angel in the flesh, a new saint for the oppressed and dispossessed." She must have been extraordinary to turn the intentions of a smart, able soldier like Dek.

Am had met his share of extraordinary women, too, the most extraordinary thing about them being their undeniable femaleness in the face of other traits traditionally considered male. It put the lie to every theory about gender-specific behavior. The most practical-minded person he'd ever known? His lovely and

loving wife. The most promising and, frankly, professional officer? Sekmé the . . . disturbing.

On the other side of the coin, who had been the most intu-
itive and emotional person he'd ever met? Probably Sekmé's
sibling, the bard Set.

"And who's the most depressed? Me."

One more season in this mud-banked asylum would ruin
him. He'd have to retire before he was fully pensioned.

"Given the situation in Kemphor, I doubt I'll be pensioned
in any case."

What to do? Get out while the going was good, as his wife
had done? Or wait and do his duty as a good general should?

Depends on what I'm waiting for, he thought.

Dek came into the hut.

"The transport and water tank vehicles are ready, General."

"Fine. High Command wanted us to act with due haste and
I think we have."

"Yes, sir."

"So, tell me, Dek. Was she beautiful?"

"Who, sir?"

"The Tel-mari who sat down."

Dek looked like a cornered oryx frozen in Am's sights, but
he was nothing if not stouthearted.

"Yes," he said simply.

"I see. What if she'd been ugly?"

Dek was silent a long moment, and his answer, when it
came, barely broke that silence. "I . . . don't know."

"God forgive us then," Am said. "We're beasts."

CHAPTER 26

THE VİLLAGE

At the southern edge of the Great Northern Forest lay a medium-sized woodcutters' village. Once a year, when the rains abated, a Maurheti military representative, usually an officer approaching retirement, and three or four raw recruits drove up the rutted road in their balloon-tired transport vehicle to pick up the village's tax: a load of trimmed taval tree logs and a dozen cases of the special sour syrup the village distilled from the trees' sap. The officers were polite enough and usually in a hurry to get back to Eshna, and considering their take was less than a tenth of what the villagers sold to their own countrymen, their visits were regarded as a minor evil, along the lines of having the village doctor scale your teeth.

However, when the headman rode back into the village after his monthly run to Eshna for medicines, salt, and gossip, he had grim news.

"It's true," he said to the gathered villagers as he dismounted his lead onager and began to untie the bulging saddlebags and bundles from the three pack animals. "The Maurheti are expanding their forced labor program into the outlying villages."

"Is this because of the drought?"

The headman glowered at the burly woodcutter. For a newcomer, he certainly wielded the saws and axes well, but he was

too inquisitive, too interested in the workings of war and government, to be the former carpenter he claimed to be.

"That's only part of it, Ahvrym. They're having trouble getting the city refugees to work for them."

He then related the new legend and described the burgeoning rash of protests it had inspired.

"Why don't the Maurheti retaliate?" Ahvrym asked.

"They do," the headman said. "Dozens have been beaten and several killed."

"But, that's nothing," Ahvrym said. "I've known the Maurheti to lay waste to entire cities over much less."

"What can I tell you, Ahvrym? I'm not a mind reader. The Maurheti have never made any sense. Maybe they're saving up their revenge and will butcher us all."

"Or maybe their will is weakening," Ahvrym said pensively.

"Nonsense! The Maurheti are here for good and they'll be *here*, in this village, in a matter of days."

"Shall we sit down like the refugees did?" a woman in a rusty brown robe and veil asked.

"Please, everyone!" the harried headman cried. "I need to think! Ahvrym, why don't you distribute everyone's supplies? I have to be alone for a while."

The headman strode off stiffly to his stone cabin with the beautifully carved wooden trim and shut himself inside with a bang.

"He shouldn't do so much riding with his bad back," Ahvrym said.

The villagers encircled the newcomer.

"What'll we do, Ahvrym?"

You're asking *me*? he thought. Do I have *leader* tattooed on my brow? Seems, once again, God recruits where He must . . .

He scanned the treetops. They swayed gently over the village, but high above them, the ragged clouds raced angrily. The air smelled nervous, full of iron and ice.

"There's a large storm coming," he said. "The Maurheti hate traveling in storms. They'll be cold and exhausted when they get here."

"And trigger-happy," said another, older woodcutter.

"Maybe, maybe not," Ahvrym said. He fingered his beard. "We have to prepare for a number of possibilities." His lips spread into a grin. "Including one they'd never think of . . ."

In the first, predominantly agrarian village, the Tel-mari were terrified of the Maurheti soldiers and complied immediately with orders to load the transport vehicles with food-stuffs and carry bucket after bucket of water from the nearby lake to fill the tank vehicles. Am's men didn't have to fire a shot, and the general left a minimal contingent behind to oversee the work.

Things went differently at the second, somewhat larger village. Here, the people were miners and not as easily frightened. They fought back with rocks, oilstone firebottles, and a few small arms. The Maurheti killed about 200 villagers, and the remaining 300 surrendered.

Am left a larger detail behind to watch the miners.

The third village, the woodcutters' hamlet, was more difficult to reach. Although nowhere near as steep as the White Mountains, the terrain was rocky, and the bad road, in places overgrown or washed out, hindered their progress. To make matters worse, about halfway there, the storm that had been threatening for two days broke at last—an especially cold and unpleasant high-country squall. If it wasn't blowing hard enough to force a vehicle to skate sideways in the rust-colored soup that had once been a road, it battered it with hailstones the size of teal eggs. Six men were badly injured, and Am had to sacrifice a transport vehicle so they could be taken back to the camp near Eshna.

As a result, when the Maurheti reached the village at a dusk that didn't look much different from midnight, they were cold,

wet, miserably tired, and dangerously irritable. They looked ready to break things and Am almost despaired of maintaining order. Their vehicles bounced into the center of town in the driving rain and the soldiers leapt out and headed for the modest wood and thatch homes.

But—something was wrong. Although the windows of every house were lit from within by the familiar orange glow of locally salvaged, low-grade oilstone, no one was home. Instead, the soldiers tracked mud over the well-swept stone floors of the houses and encountered tables set with bowls and utensils for supper, bottles of homemade beer at each plate, kettles of soup simmering on the hearth, baskets of nuts and breads on the sideboards, and, in the bedchambers, fresh linens on the rusk and conifer needle mattresses.

Naturally, the soldiers expected a trick and they tore apart three of the houses looking for hidden saboteurs, booby traps— something. They found nothing.

"They're gone, General," Com Dek said. "What do we do?"

Am stared at the food laid out on the table in the largest house of the village, undoubtedly the headman's, and heard his body's plaintive plea, until now suppressed, begging for warmth, sustenance, and rest.

"I suppose it could be an ambush," he said. "Set up a three-shift watch for the night and, well . . ." He picked up a bottle of beer. "Eat something and get some sleep."

Confused and unsure, but too tired to resist, the men divided themselves up for the watch and moved in. It wasn't long before Am, who had the headman's cabin all to himself, could hear the laughter of his men weaving in and out of the rain as they got drunk on Tel-mari backcountry brew.

He sat at the head of the table and drummed his fingers. The villagers couldn't have been gone long, or the oilstones and fires would have burned out.

Not that we can follow any tracks in this downpour, he mused. Clever bastards. I wonder what they have planned?

"Good evening, Field General."

Am nearly jumped out of his skin. How could he have missed the man, a shadow sitting in shadows? He must have been crippled by his exhaustion.

He grabbed his side arm.

"Please!" the man said, rising and stepping into the light. "I'm alone and unarmed. Killing me would be ungracious."

What kind of Tel-mari spoke like that? As if he were a Maurheti squire in the comfort of his own holdings?

"Who are you?" Am asked without lowering his weapon.

The man made a small bow. He didn't exhibit the least fear at being a target at point-blank range.

"I am Ahvrym," he said. "Ambassador, so to speak, of the people who live here."

"Where are they?"

"Not far. Warm and dry. They know these woods well and have merely taken up temporary lodgings while you and your men refresh yourselves."

"Very generous," Am said, but it didn't sound as sarcastic as he'd intended.

"Yes, isn't it?" Ahvrym smiled.

There was something curiously familiar about this burly, bearded, hawk-nosed lunatic, Am thought. "Once we've 're-freshed' ourselves, as you put it, what then?"

"Why, then you go away. The people come back, sweep the floors, and life goes on as if you'd never come."

"You must be insane."

"Am I?" Ahvrym's dark eyes filled with a cunning gleam. "You came here for wood, yes, but you mainly came here for laborers. As you can see, I'm the only man here. If you want wood, you'll have to cut it yourselves. As for water, your *real* need, open your tanks to the sky. God has decided to be generous."

As if for emphasis, a great flare of lightning and boom of thunder ripped overhead.

"We'll wait you out," Am said.

Ahvrym sighed skeptically. "A bad idea, General," he said. "You see, the goods we set out are all there is. Everything else was carried away to the holiday cottages."

"We'll find them."

"They'll see you coming and move on. They're woodsmen, General. They have shelters all over these hills, most so well camouflaged you'd die of old age before you found them."

Ahvrym pulled out a chair, sat down next to Am, and worked the clay stopper out of a bottle of beer.

"Of course, you could give in to vengeance and destroy the village—" He tipped the bottle back for a hearty swig. "—but they'll just rebuild."

He wiped his mouth with the back of his hand and used his sleeve to carefully mop the bits of foam from his beard.

"So, you see, no matter what you do, their labor will continue to be directed toward their own benefit, not yours."

"Why did *you* stay?" Am asked. "If what you say is true, everything would happen as expected whether you'd told us or not."

"Ah, you've touched on one of my personal weaknesses." Ahvrym grinned. "I've always enjoyed the dramatic gesture, even when it's been utterly foolhardy." He set down his beer. "As perhaps you can tell, General, I'm an outsider, a refugee from Eshna. I know a bit more about survival in the midst of war than these villagers do, and I offered my assistance. I've seen a great deal of death in my time, as I'm sure you have, and, well, this plan is something of an experiment and I could not resist discussing it with a man of perception even if he is a participant in that very experiment."

Now Am thought he knew what was familiar about this man. "An officer of mine once described a Tel-mari terrorist who loved nothing better than to hear himself talk. He, too, had a scholar's command of Maurheti."

To his credit, Ahvrym didn't flinch. "Indeed? Must have been an excellent fellow in spite of his profession."

"I couldn't say. During our last encounter with this man, both he and my officer disappeared."

Ahvrym raised his eyebrows in excellent imitation of ingenuousness.

"God give us grace! You don't suppose they went off together, do you?"

"I think he killed her."

Although he still didn't register any alarm, Ahvrym fell silent. He casually took up his beer and finished it before responding. "That's not true," he said.

"I don't believe you."

"The truth doesn't change just because one denies it."

"There's quite a price on your head."

"I don't doubt it. Is it higher for me alive or dead?"

"Dead."

Ahvrym nodded and fingered his beard. "So, you'll kill me."

"Yes, but I'll have to do it secretly and dispose of your body where no one can find it. We can't afford any more Tel-mari martyrs."

"How can you claim your reward if there aren't any witnesses?"

"I'm not interested in the reward," Am said. "I'm doing this for Sekmé."

As Am expected, the night's second watch was heavily composed of the nearly dead drunk. When he steered the wrist-shackled Ahvrym out of the cabin with a poke of his side arm, only the rain greeted them. Dek was asleep standing up outside the door, and the officer who should have been guarding the lead transport vehicle was nowhere to be seen.

Am herded his captive to the vehicle and settled him into the seat beside the driver's. Then he tied Ahvrym's ankles together.

"You're very complacent," Am observed.

"But not cooperative," Ahvrym countered. "I'm another laborer whose labor will not benefit you."

With his man secure, Am climbed into the vehicle, started it up, and headed into the rain-drenched woods above the village.

For nearly two hours, the general negotiated the tricky turns and avoided the fallen brush of the woodcutters' road.

Ahvrym fidgeted.

"How far do you intend to take me?" he asked. "It seems we've passed dozens of suitable places to lose my corpse."

"I know what I'm looking for."

"Perhaps you'd care to enlighten me?"

"Where did Sekmé go?"

Ahvrym stared at Am closely. "You *believe* me?"

"Where did she go?"

"The truth? I don't know. However, I guarantee you she was hale and lucid when we parted company." Ahvrym smiled curiously. "You seem to care a little too much about your commander. She did desert, after all."

Am didn't reply. He reached over Ahvrym and unlatched the passenger door. At the next rut, it swung open and banged against the side of the vehicle.

"General, I'm soon to become *permanently* wet. Why subject me to the weather now?"

The vehicle was passing a shallow ravine full of weeds, a ravine much less impressive than many they had encountered on their drive. Am patted Ahvrym's shoulder with apparent, and confusing, affection—then pushed him out of the vehicle.

Ahvrym landed in the weeds, rolled half a dozen times, and got caught in the prickly branches of a wasp nettle. Although it left him scraped, bruised, and muddy, this little tumble was far from fatal.

Above him, he heard the balloon-tired transport vehicle shift gears, turn around, and head back down to the village.

Ahvrym spent the rest of that stormy night shredding the rope that bound his ankles and banging the wrist shackles on a rock. Near dawn, they, and the storm, gave up.

"I'm not sure how, my dear," he whispered, "but I think you saved my life again."

He climbed out of the ravine and headed north, deeper into the forest.

CHAPTER 27

THE CALF

Sekmé retained her curiosity and it bred questions rather than answers. As time unspooled, the impressions, the memories, ran together, at times forward, at times back, at times simultaneously. Apparently, this was how the rider experienced reality. Not that the "flesh" thought only in purely linear terms, but this "mind" was more loosely constructed, more fluid . . . and covered a great deal more ground. Great woodlands literally rippled as trees shrank back to saplings and toppled giants righted themselves and readorned their branches with leaves. Grassland fires retreated in a mad scramble across the plateaus and leapt up into the bolts of lightning that had spawned them. The Calf raced around the sky backward, as if unable to find its stall, and the moon panted in and out, swelling and shrinking through countless rounds of months, years, decades.

Occasionally, the pace slowed and something, perhaps only an instant, played out in real, forward time, although Sekmé didn't understand why, as those events seemed completely unconnected to one another.

A band of men, Maurheti as best she could tell—their language was rough and unintelligible—rode down out of a ridge of steep rocky mountains in the middle of the night into a Telmari village. They burned the houses and kidnapped the women,

whom they carried over their saddles like bundles of meat back to their mountain hideaways. One of the women, very pale, turned her head, and her cheek caught the light of the moon just long enough for Sekmé to see an ornamental scar in the shape of a thunderbolt—the Maurheti symbol for God.

Sekmé was puzzled. Had she misidentified the bandits? Who were these people?

A young girl, barely in puberty, unmistakably Tel-mari, drew water at another village's well and daydreamed about a tall young man in the hamlet over the hill. The girl meant nothing to Sekmé, but there was something familiar about the boy, something in his pout. Unfortunately, the image didn't last more than a breath and she was drawn away, back further into the centuries.

A very old woman dying in a cool, beautiful room with walls of creamy stone veined with orange and rust that curled like petrified clouds, remembered how, as a small girl, she'd listened to her great-aunt describe the people who had founded the "city in stone."

"Before they came, they used to bow in God's direction, but now people live so far from God they don't know where He is anymore. They raise their palms to Him instead, hoping He'll find their need and fill it."

"But, isn't God everywhere?" the once-little girl asked.

"Yes, but our eyes have become narrow, child. We have trouble seeing Him at all, let alone in one direction. Only the pure see Him everywhere."

"Am I pure, Aunt?"

"Only the dead are pure, Niece."

Rivers flooded or evaporated into gullies of hard, cracked clay. People died or came to life, and Sekmé, her consciousness fatigued by the changes, lost track of which were Tel-mari, which Maurheti. Their dress and manner became strange, foreign, their customs tangled and obscure. She no longer understood any of their language—only their thoughts.

Abruptly, the ride came to a halt in the life and flesh of

someone she recognized: the dark-skinned man in white fatigues from her locust-inflicted dream. He trembled with the
exhilaration of a deeply felt conviction he was sharing with a
large group of people of all ages and every description—all of
whom wore the same white fatigues. They listened with wide
eyes, twitching lips, and involuntary cries of ecstatic pain. They
listened with belief. He was preaching to the converted.

"God told us the truth," he said in a full-chested booming
voice. "He told us many times in many ways that we would
understand, but we became too infatuated with the *ways* He
told us, the *forms* of His speech, and we failed to hear the common truths beneath them. When the *form* of a truth becomes
more real than the truth itself, then man divides himself, sets
himself apart based on the *form* he trusts, and seeks to destroy
those he does not."

Sekmé understood what the dark-skinned man said, although
his language was unintelligible to the point of gibberish, full of
curious open vowels and aspirated, guttural consonants.

The dark man sweated with the heat of his passion; large drops
ran unheeded down his forehead into his rapidly blinking eyes.
His belief in God filled him to overflowing, although he had
never seen the Divine Source of his belief. He didn't need to.

What *did* he see? God's new future: His people gathered in a
wide but, in Sekmé's opinion, typical high-country meadow.
What was strange was the dark man's assessment of this meadow
as an unspoiled paradise of eye-dazzling greens, yellows, and
blues he'd never seen before, an uninhabited wilderness overflowing with God's bounty—when quite clearly this meadow
lay in Tel-mari. Perhaps enthusiasm had loosened his sanity and
mingled metaphor with reality. Sekmé tried to catch some of
those sparks of associative thought and memory that were the
background noise of anyone's consciousness, but the man was
absorbed, body and soul, in the moment. All psychic noise and
chatter had been interrupted. True ecstasy did not allow for
distraction.

"Now pray, my family," the dark man cried. "Turn to God in thankfulness and supplication. Make the beauty of your many colors and many songs blend in a harmony of praise!"

When the people began to pray, the white-fatigued illusion of sectarian unity dissolved into genial diversity. Some people prayed standing with their palms out. Others covered their faces or folded their hands together. A few chanted phrases and rocked back and forth, while still others sat on the ground, backs erect, and droned long, deep syllables that joined the chants and whispered devotions to create a single rolling hum.

The dark man himself prayed by kneeling in the grass and touching his forehead to the ground.

The worshipers' words, already strange to Sekmé's inner ear, became even more peculiar when the rider suddenly cut her loose of the dark man and sent her spinning into the multitudes, passing through many—sips of hope, bites of fear, the taste of exhaustion—and batting off others like the tiny sliver-thin winged night witches that hovered around oilstone lamps.

One man stood apart from the others, and his appearance arrested her flight. He looked so much like the hamlet swain the village girl had pined for that Sekmé could have sworn he was the mature version. However, this worshiper did not share the same *millennium*, let alone the same cluster of sodden hills. He was an ancestor—by too many generations to count.

Even so, as with the boy, Sekmé seemed to know him. Her manipulator held her hovering before him a long time. A strongly built, almost stocky body, perhaps fifty years old, a handsome, squarish face, fair, as if unused to sunlight, large, exotically tilted green eyes, a fine, aquiline nose—the whole framed by a full head of thick black curls. She felt all of this was familiar but could not recall how—except for the mouth. It frightened her with its relaxed, carelessly sensual pout, the full lower lip that pushed the upper forward. She knew this pout. Unfortunately, the rider wrenched her away before she could find its name and, once again, deposited her in the mind of the dark-

skinned man, this time without the familiar landscape of Telmari to orient her . . . him.

The man stood in an enormous, gleaming white cavern filled with strange gems and oddly smooth formations—cubes, cones, tubes—that must have been carved in crystal. The cavern was as big as Kemphor and the air inside was as dry, but it was dustless and free of oilstone-based pollution. The cavern hummed softly, like an exceptionally large Needle.

No! The image of the Needle made it clear now. This wasn't a cavern; it was a machine, an immense machine. The walls were coated metals, the gems lights of many colors.

The man was content. He looked out at the empty machine from a platform that floated free, and felt a proud wistfulness. The *Exodus* had done its job and would be put to sleep. In all likelihood, it would never reawake.

He heard a small chime, familiar and friendly, echo through the empty shell of what had been his home for many, many years. It had taken decades to reach this haven so like the one he'd left and now he had only an hour to join the others. An hour to say good-bye to one life, and hello to another: a life built on trust and brotherhood.

He said something and the platform glided gently through the machine, a finely polished magic carpet piloted by nothing and powered by nothing—nothing Sekmé's mind could see or understand. It crossed the expanse of the machine as if soaring through a vast white canyon lined with terraces, each pierced with hundreds of caves, an entire cliff city of metal and crystal and strange, unknown softnesses that bound the pieces together in an elegant whole. Below, instead of a river, stretched a string of great white and transparent domes, each the size of the Palace Dome, the transparent ones shielding gardens of feathery trees in warm baths of steam. Above, instead of the sky, lights imitated stars of red, gold, green, and blue.

The platform reached the far end of the machine and the man stepped off onto a terrace with a specially enlarged cave

mouth, circled in gold, that led to a tunnel: the way to exodus from *Exodus*.

But, before heading down the tunnel, the dark-skinned man strolled along the terrace, hands comfortably tucked into the pockets of his shiny, insulated silver suit, to a great panel in the machine's hull. He spoke again and the panel slid up sound-lessly, revealing an enormous window.

Sekmé's share of consciousness recoiled in terror. No land, no trees, no sky—nothing! Instead, the bright disk of a gigantic unknown green, tan, and blue world filled the view.

And yet, the tan edge near the blue, there, just left of center— had she seen it before? Perhaps years ago—or years to come— perhaps from above? And closer?

The man turned his head slowly away from the window as if his neck was also mechanical, a swivel, and at his side, with that soft, provocative pout, stood—

"Set!" Sekmé screamed. "Set! Tell me what it means! Set!"

The connection broke and the centuries tumbled away like shards of glass. Sekmé, in her own flesh, began to cough and sneeze violently. Hundreds of unseen others somewhere above her joined in with high-pitched squeaks and whistles and the beating of naked wings. The ground was cold, hard, vaguely damp, and stinking, and each spine-wrenching hack echoed over and over around her. She couldn't see. Something thick and throbbing was working its way laboriously out of her nose and throat. She shook her head trying to dislodge it.

"Set! S-S-Set! I . . . c-can't breathe!"

Her final spasm cracked her body like a furious snake. Her vision cleared and something as pale as smoke, almost as insub-stantial, streamed out of her chest and nostrils and collected in a low greenish cloud on the cave floor before her. She now knew where she was: a large, irregular, bitterly cold cavern weakly lit by an oilstone fire and . . . and whatever that thing was she'd heaved out of herself.

As if to oblige her and negate her repugnance, the cloud re-

solved itself into the form of the ethereal rider who had galloped into her soul. He lay shaking, wheezing hard, his red eyes dull and staring at the cave's vault. Sekmé followed his stare. She could barely see them, but she recognized them: hundreds, perhaps thousands of those pig-snouted white bats that flitted over the high country. They, and their guano, explained the cavern's stench.

Sekmé crawled to the traumatized rider and looked down into his face. He seemed fairly solid, but she could see the cracks in the cave floor beneath him—*through* him.

"Have you . . . lied to me?" Her voice scratched, as if from disuse. She cleared her throat. "Have you *lied* to me?"

The rider's eyes shifted listlessly her way.

"Man of flesh," he gasped, "full of light. To taste is to be sated without diminishing the source—"

"Answer me!"

"—but to return the light is to perish."

He seemed about to faint and Sekmé tried to slap him, but her hand passed through his face, a sensation like sweeping her fingers through boiling pudding. She snapped them away and they cooled instantly.

What had happened to her glove?

She leaned closer, almost nose to nose.

"The Calf?" she whispered.

"Let me die."

"Not before you answer my questions!" she cried, and tears leapt into her vision.

"I . . . already . . . have . . ."

The rider shuddered and his eyes closed. His wheezing rattled one more time, caught on something that sounded wet, and his body collapsed, a dissolution so sudden Sekmé uttered an involuntary shriek and fell back. The rider's substance emitted a faint sizzling sigh as it melted into a greenish smudge of phosphorescence—then quietly disappeared.

Sekmé rested her hands on the spot where the rider had

died, and wept a long time. They had been intimate, profoundly so, in a way she could not explain, and yet she didn't know who—or even what—he was.

But Set knew. Set knew all of it. He'd always known.

She stroked the unyielding stone and whispered, as a kind of elegy, a fragment from one of her brother's lyrics:

> *"For I am a rider of the sands*
> *A follower of many skies;*
> *A sailor in the night*
> *Who fell to a strange, strange sea . . ."*

A snort from the shadows ended her keening and brought her back to the situation at hand. Not far from where the rider had lain stood his onager: a big shaggy jack saddled and haltered in leather and silver tooled with a well-known and ancient Denneshur pattern of stylized flames. Sekmé got to her feet and approached him cautiously.

"Shh, easy . . . easy now . . ."

The onager's ears twisted her way, but he didn't shy. Sekmé was briefly startled by the beast's red eyes, but that could have been the oilstone light shining in its dilated pupils.

She touched its back. Solid. It was a real onager.

"Good boy . . ."

She stroked its withers, then her hand stopped. The onager had a white nose, exactly like the blaze on the onager she'd killed and gutted—and lost. She studied its eyes again, but if the onager was inhabited by a rider of its own, it didn't let on.

The entrance to the cave lay a bit farther along, deeper in the shadows. It was barely big enough for Sekmé to crawl through, let alone wide enough to admit an onager, and when she poked her head and shoulders outside into the mountain cold, squinting into the night blizzard to get her bearings, she discovered that the entrance was halfway up the sheer side of the box canyon.

"I don't remember scaling that. How long have I been here?"

She pulled back into the cave and performed a more thorough search of her surroundings.

Her bow and quiver lay near the fire, and the arrows were scattered about as if she'd taken them one by one and flung them aside. The tip of each one was crusted with dried blood. She glanced again at the quiet hosts rustling on the ceiling and decided not to invest any more time trying to identify her prey. Besides, there was other evidence she'd been living in the cave for some time: oilstone tar and dust piled thickly under the freshly burning stones, the sorry condition of her clothing— not to mention the loss of her gloves, the funk of her own body. Whether she'd been aware of her actions *at the time*, she couldn't remember them now. She had others' memories instead.

So did the cave. She found dozens of pyramidal piles of oilstones tucked into every corner, a stash big enough for quite a few people to wait out a long, cold winter. Who had put them there? How long ago?

Sekmé felt a sudden rush of vertigo and dropped down next to the fire until it subsided. Then she picked up one of the oilstones and fingered it, running her thumb over its clean edges, smudging her palm on a broken one. This tiny piece of the mineral world, humble and innocent in itself, could warm the body, light a room . . . destroy everything. It depended on the choice its handler made. At the moment, she felt very much like the oilstone.

I guess I've always been a tool, she thought, certainly not to my credit. But what am I supposed to do now? What do I do with all these? . . .

The images rushed in on her again and she rubbed her aching temples. This was not the place to explore the issue. It was too harsh and demanded too much of her already overtaxed mind and body. She had to find lower, warmer ground.

She blew into her stiff hands to loosen them, then got up

and gathered as many of the oilstones as she could stuff into the onager's saddlebags. She retrieved her bow and arrows and held her breath as she swung up onto the strange animal's back. He didn't flinch.

Maybe the onager *was* a host, as she had been, to a being that maintained it—an impressive trick if it was indeed the same one she'd disemboweled—but it was tractable and that was all she wanted.

"All right then," she said as she fixed a bit of oilstone to one of her arrows, lit it, and held it aloft, "do you know a way out that's large enough for both of us?"

The onager perked up its ears, nickered gently, and began to descend into the long, winding darkness of the cavern.

CHAPTER 28

FİRE

The first fires, in the heart of Kemphor, were isolated acts of frustration aimed at merchants of foodstuffs and other necessities who'd been too "correct" in following the government's rationing policies. These were easily doused with bladders—heavy sealed pouches of chemicals dropped from round-bellied "short-stitch" Needles—and dumps of sea water.

However, when frustration became desperation, it aimed its thirst and hunger at the holdings, and the destruction quickly escalated beyond the flabby Kemphor peacekeepers' capabilities. Roon called in assistance from the air base—a terrible mistake. The military, trained to discipline a race many of them did not consider real people, was deeply uncomfortable turning weapons on brothers, cousins, fathers, and children, and the soldiers and airmen acted more ruthlessly than required. A couple dozen looters from the city, mostly women looking for food for their babies, were strafed with acid pellets as they ran across a holdings' dried-out grainfields. In retaliation, a second group of looters, mostly young men, burned the estate with industrial galca stolen from a failed ironworks. When the military caught up with the looters, they destroyed the entire suburb of Kemphor where they'd hidden.

Meanwhile, with the convoy of tank vehicles carrying water

from Tel-mari reduced to a trickle due to increased noncompliance from the native workforce, the king faced a dilemma he believed none of his predecessors ever had: a need to escalate on two different fronts at the same time. To make matters worse, a dispute had disrupted progress at the desalination plant construction site, a dispute over, of all things, water—not its lack, but its overabundance. The workers demanded greater protection against getting swept off the rocks into the sea, but management refused to provide it, claiming that the installation of safety rigging would hold up construction. In the end, construction was held up anyway.

"The Division is out of balance," Dand Ubit said, his humming voice barely crossing the expanse of the empty Dome room.

"A graceful way of characterizing catastrophe," Roon said. He stood next to the sacred fire and contemplated its quiet, gas-fed flame. "Since the Tel-mari insist on this passive aggression of theirs and we're getting little out anyway, perhaps we should bring some of the troops home to help restore order here."

"Your majesty forgets my previous suggestion." The secretary tottered closer—uncomfortably close in Roon's opinion—and joined the king in contemplating the fire.

"I do not," Roon said. "The generals have had that option from the beginning."

"Don't make it an option," Dand hummed. "Make it an order. In fact, if I may be so bold—" He dared to rest his pale, carefully manicured hand on the king's arm. "—perhaps it is time to 'cleanse the field' as prophesied in the Book of the End Time."

These words all but clotted Roon's blood, but he turned only the slightest bit away from the secretary, just enough to disengage his arm from the man's fingers.

"Majesty, listen to me." Dand leaned forward to close this new gap. "Atto was a fool, but in this he was quite correct. His niece was the Scourge of Not-God. Everything that has come to pass was set in motion by her abnormally swift rise in rank

and subsequent desertion. She 'turned the point of the sword inward,' " he quoted.

"You're insane," Roon said in quiet, stiff tones, hoping the secretary would take the hint. But Dand did not withdraw.

"You know it's true, Majesty. Perhaps you think that no one has that kind of power, and I would agree with you under normal circumstances. But, consider the woman's lineage, the peculiarities of her birth."

Roon gave the secretary an ugly glare. "How dare you?" he snarled. "Set was a *poet!*"

"A delicate topic, I know, Majesty, but the boy was the most ingenious part of the Unholy One's plan. Don't you see? Something good and beautiful designed to blunt our perceptions and lull us into trust. How could such a fine officer, with such a gifted brother, be the tool of our destruction? Ah, but even *you* saw the need for her death. Unfortunately, we didn't comprehend the puissance of the forces marshaled against us."

The king's brows tightened over his burning eyes. "If you think this attempt at eloquence blunts the horror of what you're suggesting," he said, "think again. You're talking *millions* of lives."

Dand leaned back and the sacred fire's glow dyed his moon face orange.

"If we truly finish our task in Tel-mari, Majesty, our own people, now too restive and thirsty to tend to their accustomed business, can move in to claim the land and water."

"What of your precious 'balance,' Dand?"

The secretary's smile split his face like a wound.

"This is the End Time, Majesty," he said fervently. "The Time of Convergence. We spill from the scales into the hands of God."

Wepanu and Haru continued to roam the Hills of Whispers from wadi to ridge to wadi without a plan. Sometimes they slept in caves, sometimes under the stars, and a few times, Wepanu traveled through the night and the young cook followed,

eyes so heavy he was certain he'd walked half of their journey asleep. Once in a while they came upon a band of Denneshur tribesmen who greeted Wepanu with low bows of respect and gave him gossip and supplies without asking for anything in return. They always invited him to stay with them, and always included Haru in the invitation, probably assuming he was the old man's disciple, but Wepanu invariably refused and walked on.

"Wepanu, do you have to live in the desert to be a prophet?"

Haru was setting up camp again at sundown and the old man was scanning the nearby cliff with that familiar, special squint he used when looking for a good place to meditate.

"No, of course not."

"Then why do you?"

"I like it." Wepanu grinned at Haru. "I like its honesty."

"I always thought the desert was mysterious," Haru said.

The dog-faced jo sat on the handle of the cookpot as he diced in a bitter artru root. He was used to her now and even asked her occasional questions, which, as usual, she answered in riddles.

"You confuse demeanor with substance," Wepanu said. "An aloof man may, in reality, be very direct in his needs, whereas a chatty one might be hiding a great deal." He pointed with his staff to a depression high on the cliff nearby. "That is where I'm going this evening," he said. "What about you?"

"As soon as I've started the soup I'll find a place." Haru had taken up meditation, too—there was little to do in the desert *but* contemplate one's thoughts—and had worked up to half an hour of genuine inner quiet, although he hadn't yet learned anything profound about the universe and was beginning to wonder if that was the point.

"Remember to force nothing, hold nothing, expect nothing," Wepanu said as his withered but wiry legs propelled him up the cliff. "When they come, they come."

This last bit was new.

"They?"

But Wepanu had disappeared around a turn in the rock.

Haru looked at the jo and shrugged. She opened her mouth and let her long tongue flap loosely out over her teeth, panting as a comfortable dog might at its master's hearth.

Once the soup was simmering steadily, Haru tightened the belt of his robe, put up his hood, and went out to find his own meditation spot. Unlike Wepanu, he thought the sunset too distracting and chose a cool, sandy place in a vertical crease of a pillar of rust-colored stone. He smoothed the sand, settled down comfortably, crossed his legs, and closed his eyes. The quiet of the desert dropped around him and he began to listen to his own breathing—after a few minutes, his heartbeat.

However, not long into his meditation, his eyes snapped open. The jo hovered before his nose.

"What?"

She snorted and flitted away, back to the camp. Concentration broken, Haru decided to check on the soup before trying again. He didn't want to admit that the pesky little sprite had set off a small alarm in his consciousness.

The alarm made sense, though, when he reached the camp. Their cookpot was gone.

Haru knew immediately that the thieves weren't Denneshur. The clear set of tracks had been made by hard-heeled boots, not soft Denneshur slippers or sandals.

More curious than angry and trusting that his physique remained imposing enough to command respect, Haru muffled his face and followed the tracks to a nearby cleft in the rocks, where he startled a group of young people: three men and two women. The women screamed, the lad holding the cookpot dropped it, spilling its contents on his brother, and the eldest aimed a hunting bow at him.

Haru was not in the least afraid. The bow trembled violently in the young man's hands—he couldn't have hit the side of the royal palace at ten paces—and all of them looked pretty miserable: gaunt, sunburned, ragged, and frightened. Besides, in spite

of their wretched condition, he recognized them. The young men, barely out of boyhood, were three of Sekmé's cousins and the girls were servants from her holdings.

He uncovered his face.

"Haru!" the heavier girl, Tiu the laundress, cried.

"God all knowing!" the cousin with the bow said as he lowered the weapon with a jerk, his muscles giving out in his relief. "We thought you were dead!"

"I think that's what Atto wanted, Bross," Haru said softly.

"God's joke is on him, then," the youngest cousin, Amet, said bitterly.

"What do you mean?"

"You don't know?" asked the second girl, a petite chambermaid named Zeffa.

"Know what?"

They told him about Atto's death, Bahé's act of suicidal destruction, and the withering of the holdings.

Haru squatted silently beside them as though listening to tales from a legendary past. He did feel some satisfaction at hearing of Atto's death and some pain when he heard how looters from the city, driven out by the drought-induced famine, had targeted Atto's holdings—and the cousins themselves—for their first forays because they wanted revenge against Bahé. Still, Haru was surprised how little he actually felt for the place he'd once called home.

Where does a man store his sense of place and kinship? he wondered. And where did mine go?

Zeffa smoothed back her hair, as if this primping could somehow restore looks eaten away by hunger and scorched by naked sun.

"You look good, Haru," she said.

"You look like a Denneshur!" the middle cousin, a once fleshy, now bony boy named Nehro, exclaimed.

"It suits you," Bross added. "Is that how you did it? Did you go 'desert' on us, Haru?"

Haru didn't think the situation was very funny. "What happened to Sekmé?" he asked.

The five glanced at each other, embarrassed. The chambermaid stopped trying to arrange her hair and chewed on it instead. Bross coughed nervously.

"No one really knows," he said. "She went on a secret mission and nobody heard from her for months."

"Not even her general," Nehro said.

"Then one of the airmen stationed at the base—"

"—he ran into a scullery servant in Kemphor—"

"—said that she'd surfaced and led a big air strike near Eshna—"

"—he couldn't give any details. He wasn't supposed to know—"

"—and she disappeared during the battle."

Haru blinked. "*Disappeared? Is that what he said? Not killed? Wounded?*"

"No. Disappeared."

"Set went looking for her," Tiu whispered.

The others tried to hush her, as if she was breaking a solemn oath.

"Well, he'd want to know," she said defiantly, but her voice shook. "The airman said that when Sekmé finally made it back to her unit, she . . ."

The laundress couldn't continue so Bross did. "She told Bahé Set had been killed."

Haru didn't ask how. It wasn't important. What was important was how things had sifted out of a mix long in the making.

He remembered how Sekmé, in the lazy conversation after lovemaking, had discussed her men in a tone of curiosity and concern that bespoke a need to understand them, as if they were part of an extended family. He remembered her closeness to her brother and how, as her lover, he'd been secretly jealous of it in spite of his affection for the moon-burned poet.

He also remembered how badly the soft-bellied Bahé needed

a rudder, and that the young man had done everything Sekmé told him to do, even swim out in a scum-slicked pond to retrieve a dead bittern. She had been his commander in more ways than one.

The hairs on his neck crawled. Bahé was an extreme example, but what of the others? The rank and file who had toasted her at the banquet and told stories about her as if she were a folk legend? "Disappeared" could be much more dangerous than killed outright.

He glanced up. In the back of the cleft, hovering quietly so she could observe them, the jo shone like a tiny star. As he watched, she reconfigured her face, pushing the dog snout in and replacing the third eye in the middle of her forehead. She was not smiling.

"What are you staring at, Haru?" Zeffa asked.

"You've gone 'desert,' all right," Amet said. "Quiet and spooky."

Haru got to his feet. "You need food and water."

"Do you have more?"

"The desert does," Wepanu declared, suddenly before them. He stood with his staff held at a commanding angle and seemed to enjoy the stupefied expressions that greeted his nakedness.

"Haru, fetch our things," he said. "We'll camp here tonight . . . with the children."

When Dek brought him the encrypted message, Am asked him to stay while he decoded it.

"Such a high-level message at this time makes me uncomfortable, Com Dek. Wait a bit. Have a seat."

The young man unshouldered his weapon and squatted on the floor of the hut since, apart from the general's chair and camp bed, there was no seat. Outside, the low, lonely growl of a new storm, followed seconds later by the shy early patter of rain on the canvas, accompanied Am's reading. By the time he was done, the rain had picked up to its familiar, steady

percussion. The storm front, broad and bovine, could last for weeks.

Am slowly folded the message into a tiny square, which he turned over and over in his hands.

"What does it say, sir?"

"In a minute, Com."

Dek shifted uncomfortably. The general did not sound like himself. He had the voice of an old man.

"Dek, what are the rumors about Sekmé?"

"Sir?"

"Why do the men think she deserted? Don't worry, son, this is a personal request. Your answer stops with me."

"Uh, well, they think she left because High Command mis-used her or set her up and . . ." He licked his lips nervously. "General, most of us have those moments, you know? When we feel like parts of a machine and not . . . alive. This made it worse."

Am nodded and, to Dek's surprise, sat on the floor next to him. Dek was eye to eye with a man now, not his commanding officer, a man exhausted to the base of his soul.

"How worse, Dek?" Am asked softly. "Tell me."

"Well, for the commander, of all people, to give up—"

"She didn't give up, Dek. She wouldn't have made it back across the swamp if she had."

"Then, why did she leave, sir?" Dek asked, hurt creeping into his voice in spite of himself. "We suffer, too, and we haven't left."

The general looked at the floor and smiled briefly, as though a distant pleasure had tried to move from one corner of his memory to another without being noticed but had accidentally caught a ray of sunlight on its skirt.

"I think Sekmé left for the same reason I'm going to disobey this order, Com."

He handed the folded square to the freckled young man and waited for him to read it. He seemed to know, and was satisfied, when all the heat seemed to drain out of Dek's body.

"My God, sir!" the com whispered as he shakily handed the paper back to Am. "Is—is this the End Time?"

The general chuckled, hardly the kind of sound Dek expected under the circumstances.

"Look around, son. Is the sky still above? Is the mud still below?"

Dek squinted at him suspiciously. "Um . . . yes."

"Is it still raining?"

"Yes."

"Then the only thing ending that I can see is the way we've been doing things." Am got to his feet, picked up the oilstone lamp from his hopelessly overloaded desk, and burned the order in its flame. "I'm tired of the war, Dek, sick of everything to do with it, and I'm beginning to think God is sick of it, too."

"Then what do we do, sir?"

The general turned from the desk and stood over Dek. For a moment, the young com felt he was under more than human scrutiny.

"You have the box, Com," he said in a low, disturbingly even tone. "Why don't you discuss it with your comrades as I've discussed it with you? In confidence as equals?"

Dek lowered his head and shook it slowly in disbelief. "I don't know, sir. This whole business makes me feel itchy all over."

"Good! I leave it up to you and the dictates of your heart. Speaking of which . . ." Am studied the young man sideways, and Dek cringed. "Do you remember where the woman lives? The one who sat down first?"

"No," Dek answered—far too quickly.

"Also good."

By the next morning, General Am had vanished. It was impossible that no one, not a single guard, servant, late-returning officer, or early-departing prostitute, had seen him, and it was

impossible that he hadn't left a trace, but the impossible was supposed to become possible in the End Time.

Dek sneaked away three days later and headed into Eshna. Several people saw him go and a yansha helped him dress in Tel-mari robes after a farewell bout of "naked mercy." No one reported him because no one cared. Desertion was becoming common among the Maurheti.

Even so, Bekka did not trust the request for sanctuary whispered through the tavern door.

"We are a house in mourning," she said. "Leave us in peace."

"Please!" Dek begged, all but weeping. "You need me! The Maurheti have orders to destroy the city and burn the villages."

"They've done that before," Bekka said. "Their violence is nothing new."

"This time it is! We . . . they are to slaughter every Tel-mari man, woman, and child. *Every one!*"

Bekka was silent and Dek wondered if she'd left him there, begging to no one.

"They won't do that," she finally murmured.

"Not all of them, no," Dek agreed, "but some of the generals are fanatics and will try. You need me to help you escape."

"In my own country?"

Dek sank to his knees and rested his hands on the rain-softened wood of the door.

"Please, miss. It's ugly everywhere but with you."

She was silent again. Then, very slowly, the door creaked open. Her large, black, feline eyes glowed from the darkness.

"You are the world's greatest fool," she said. "Come in before you get hurt."

CHAPTER 29

THE CİTY

Initially, Ahvrym had headed north because the Maurheti were in the south. This remained his reasoning after the weird general shunted him out of that hideous balloon-tired monster into the shallow ravine. South was dangerous.

Now, however, weeks later, he wasn't sure, partly because he no longer knew which way was south, or north for that matter. The trees of the Great Northern Forest had closed in around him, confusing the trail, which shrank in on itself and began to run about the hills, in and out of the massive trunks, in disoriented panic. Ahvrym considered turning back but realized that trying to retrace his steps on such a trail would be just as difficult as laying new ones on the route ahead. Both would be treks into unfamiliar territory.

"A trail usually leads *somewhere*," he told himself. "At least, I hope so."

Being lost was a little like being a child again the first time his father, Hemsha the scholar, let him run free in the university. All the corridors and dark stairways and courtyards full of overgrown vines and pale, bearded students, all of it strange and, perhaps, frightening with damp and hush and the bleary-eyed gleam of disapproval, failed to upset him because he knew his father would find him eventually. Lost isn't lost if someone is going to find you.

Why did he feel the same way now? Who was going to find him in *these* towering corridors? Among *these* gigantic columns and *these* tiny, unseen, wild eyes of disapproval?

An inland hind stepped gingerly out of the trees ahead of him, caught a glimpse of his shadow in its huge wet eyes, and bounded heavily back into the brush, a brief streak of tawny yellow that soon disappeared.

"You're a crazy man, Ahvrym," he told himself. "Adrift in the wilderness and you feel like singing!"

So, he did—the crudest, most unsingable drinking ditty he could think of. After all, who would stop him? Singing lightened his step and he strode in time, swinging his hands as he walked up this latest hill.

When he reached the top, he stopped abruptly and the forest's natural quiet quickly swallowed his song. His feet had felt the change almost before he saw it.

Paved. The trail had widened and was now paved—paved not with stones but with fine, if cracked, concrete, the kind reserved for large, important buildings, not ordinary roadwork.

Ahvrym knelt down to touch it with his fingers, and his back shuddered with cold anxiety.

Paved. In the God's-honest middle of nowhere.

"Divine Heart preserve me!" he whispered. "I've entered the other side of the world . . ."

Cracked as it was and host to a colony of thriving weeds and grasses, the paved road was much easier to follow, not only because the surface was more regular, but because it moved forward with fewer twists or lapses of memory—as if it *did* know where it was going. Ahvrym followed, thinking he should be ready for anything, a forgotten aqueduct, perhaps, or—heaven forfend!—a secret in-country Maurheti outpost.

The road headed into new terrain, no less wooded, but rockier, a landscape of rifts and ravines, split boulders and narrow canyons hung with strange tangled vines whose tendrils, dozens of yards long, when they found the rare shafts of light

that fingered down into the sheltered shade, exploded into gar-
lands of yellow, orange, and purple flowers. Narrow waterfalls
snaked down the sides of the canyons and lost their way in the
foliage only to emerge below to form dark pools in the gloom
of the elbowing cliffs. White moths as large as fans dipped in
and out of the rifts, and small birds with red crests and blue
breasts hid in the vines and trilled a quick four-tone song to each
other.

Ahvrym was enchanted by this upland jungle. It almost
seemed a place from his dreams, a place of legend, a place he
might have read about in an ancient romance bartered out of
hiding by a succulent tidbit from the kitchen, and he might
have picked up his wandering pace to keep time with his spirits
if he hadn't turned a sharp angle in the ravine and come across
something that almost made him retreat: burn. Although the
vegetation was lush, long recovered from whatever holocaust
had taken place, the rocks and cliffs were heavily streaked and
coated with the thick, ugly tarlike substance. Where burn still
coated patches of ground, nothing grew. It was everywhere. Acres
of it.

Ahvrym's heart sank. The road would take him to a dead
place. What was the point of that? He'd seen plenty of death.

Still, he went on, perhaps driven by the fact that the burn
had accumulated in the distant past—it was so ancient it had
hardened to an almost glossy sheen—and the bulk of the living
forest had forgotten it. Or, perhaps he was still intrigued by the
use of fine concrete for a highway. In any case, he expected ruins of some sort.

At about midday, the road narrowed and became blocked by
a dense thicket that had joined its thorns, like clawed fingers,
across the pavement. It snagged on Ahvrym's woolen robes but
gave way with a few hearty swipes of his knife. When he
emerged on the other side, he saw a long, bright gash in the dark
walls before him, a gash that revealed the first view of some-

thing so fantastic, he refused to believe his vision until he passed through the shadows and came into a wide, sunlit clearing.

It was a city, and for a moment, Ahvrym couldn't take another step. He thought he knew a lot about cities, especially ruined ones, but this was unlike any urban place he had ever seen or imagined.

"It's carved in the cliffs!" he gasped. "It's a city in stone!"

Charred, gutted, and splattered with burn, heavily draped with vines and softened by hardy, rock-clinging gray-green weeds, the rock still proclaimed its ancient identity. For miles in every direction, from floor to dizzying rim, the cliffs were carved into cracked columns, broken pediments, headless turrets, and crumbling, curling stairways. Row after row of ruined basilicas, blind corridors, abandoned suites, deserted flats, and pitted, sheltered walkways stacked up on each other, bridged natural rifts and clefts, and jutted out with chipped gables, naked terraces, shattered cornices, and the remains of elaborate ornamentation in unknown patterns—all carved directly from the living rock. Enhancing the natural whorls of rose and ocher and lavender and peach, the split, scorched, and twisted leavings of metal railings and inlay continued their centuries-long oxidation and melted in bloody tears down the stone, a bittersweet complement to the burn.

The scale of the place, the amount of labor involved in its creation—and its destruction—was inconceivable. Head back, mouth agape, Ahvrym followed the road, which was now part of a network of avenues, and passed lane after lane of broken-angled, gap-toothed, smashed, and rattled masonry, all of it stained with rain and rot and inconceivable masses of thick, black, fossilized burn.

Ahvrym glanced away to collect his thoughts and saw a tree glowing in full afternoon sunlight, growing up through what must have once been the bottom of a cistern. The basin was made of the same fine concrete as the road and was almost completely

painted with a deep coat of burn, but a seed had found a clean spot to send up a sprout.

Sprout! The tree was enormous, a fully mature taval like all the other giants of the Great Northern Forest. It had to be at least 5,000 years old.

Ahvrym shuddered from what he assumed was horror only to realize, somewhat confusedly, that it was excitement. His curiosity had resurfaced.

"A ruined city, yes," he murmured, "but a very *ancient* city."

He had none of the proper tools or reference works with him, he had virtually nothing at all, but he kept exploring the city with a question: *who?* It was important. Was *this*, and not Eshna, the city in stone referred to in the family-line poem he'd read as a scholar? If so, then whoever had built this city and whoever had destroyed it . . . oh, better not to speculate. Still, it was very tempting, what with the flowers and birds that recalled the frescoes on the ceilings of the long-vanished school and the ludicrously literal incarnation of a city *in* stone.

As he continued his wanderings, the city's essential muteness and strangeness crept into him. The sun went down and dusk quickly filled the canyons. With darkness, a cold wind blew in from the north and came rushing down the passes, whistling and moaning through the black, empty windows and other openings in the cliff city, as if the people were still there, lamenting the condition of their home.

Ahvrym believed in many things including lost souls, souls that had misplaced their identity or mistaken a dead end in the afterworld for a highway to paradise, and he was not at all pleased when the night suddenly came awake with these mournful wails and sighs. Although it might have been a bit more comfortable inside one of the empty chambers out of the wind, he made his fire in the open, in the cold, and watched through the hours— just in case.

"It's an interesting place," he told himself. "Even so, I don't think I want to stay."

He decided to leave in the morning, head south a ways and perhaps east, but when the sun finally filled the clearings with enough light to see by, he couldn't remember the way back. Every lonely avenue, every blasted lane, seemed the same. The windows and archways, caught in eternal gaping surprise, looked as anonymous as cells, not one of them offering an irregularity he recognized.

He supposed he should have marked his trail, but how? He had three oilstones, a pocketful of dried berries and raw nuts, and a knife. There was nothing he could do but keep moving and hope he somehow stumbled onto the way out.

Resigned, he walked for hours, oblivious to the passage of time, overwhelmed with depression and a vague, difficult-to-name dread.

I wish I was a poet, he thought. Perhaps then I could predict the future from these entrails, summon ghosts without getting eaten by them.

The sun was setting again, tinging every intact surface pink, when he reached what looked like the cavernous mouth of an underground aqueduct. Perfectly round and three times as tall as a man, it opened out of the cliff onto a stone watercourse, or canal, now nearly dry except for an anemic trickle from some- where far up inside the mountain. The canal skirted the road and headed for a vast, shallow basin at the center of one of the larger, more symmetrical clearings. Perhaps the basin had func- tioned as a place to water animals, Ahvrym didn't know—it was now choked with ragged vegetation—but when he passed the aqueduct's mouth, he thought he heard an onager's half-braying whinny echoing deep within the cliff.

No more eager to meet the soul of a lost animal than that of a lost man, Ahvrym immediately ducked behind a fallen piece of a decorated pediment and drew his knife.

He heard nothing more for a long time. Then, faintly at first, growing steadily louder and closer, he heard the regular hard thump of an unshod onager's hooves on stone. His body tensed

for the coming encounter although he realized, with a sick clutching in his throat, that a knife probably wouldn't make much of a mark on a ghost.

Another whinny and what looked like a large—and convincingly live—jack sauntered out of the round darkness, nostrils flaring at the sudden open air and light, ears flicking with interest at the birdsong above. Ahvrym's knife hand dropped to his side. He didn't care anymore about onager ghosts, it was the rider on the onager's back that almost stopped his heart.

He recognized her instantly in spite of her rags and filth and almost called out her name, but the expression on her face when she emerged into the light and saw the city for the first time stopped him. He understood the wonder as well as the hint of horror, but the double take, as if she'd *expected* to find the city—but not here—intrigued him.

He stepped out from behind the chunk of pediment—and they stared at each other, for the moment completely speechless, until Sekmé, blinking as if coming out of a reverie, gently urged the onager forward, stopped at Ahvrym's side, and dismounted. She gazed up at the city with an unfathomable expression, then shook her head slowly. The evening had deepened to lavender.

"It looks like Kemphor," she said.

"It looks like Eshna," he replied.

Sekmé nodded slightly, pulled a couple oilstones from her pocket, and struck them together. She handed one to Ahvrym without looking at him, almost shyly. As the daylight failed, the benign yellow glow of the oilstones illuminated their faces.

"Do your people know these ruins are here?" Ahvrym asked.

Sekmé's attention seemed to drift briefly.

"Yes . . . no! I mean I don't think you could see this from the air. The cliffs hide it and the vines . . ."

She gestured vaguely, uncertainly. Ahvrym wasn't sure he agreed, but he had no incentive to argue with her.

"I was looking for the proper place to camp for the night when I heard your onager. He *is* a rather imposing—and hairy—specimen, isn't he?"

Sekmé paid no attention to his comments about her mount.

"Over there," she said, pointing, "that larger structure with the columns, the one that looks like a temple. It seems fairly unscathed. Maybe we could camp in there. The wood around here is pretty green, but it should burn."

"Much as I agree with your line of thinking," Ahvrym said, inwardly alarmed at the idea of actually *entering* one of the city's dwellings, "the idea of burning *anything* seems—"

"I know, but it's getting cold."

Ahvrym looked at her and his reluctance faded. Her teeth were chattering. They gathered what fuel they could wrest from the overrun basin and moved, onager and all, into the cave of the cliff building's ground floor. Inside, the floor was flooded with runoff from a seasonal stream that issued from under the foundation. It had become a shallow weed- and algae-choked pond.

Sekmé held up her oilstone and scanned the ceiling. Tangles of creepers and the pale, furry nests of spiders nearly obliterated what had once been a field of gilded interlocking coffers.

"We could go upstairs," Ahvrym suggested.

"I don't trust it." Sekmé frowned. "Those creepers have rooted in the stone and broken it up. The entire ceiling might collapse."

Ahvrym held out his own stone to the darkness.

"I think I see another room back there." He pointed. "It's up a step. Maybe it's dry."

Sekmé promptly waded out across the murky indoor pond to investigate, leading the onager behind her. Her oilstone soon became the only visible sign of her presence, although Ahvrym heard the shaggy beast's heavy splashing.

"You're right," she said. "Keep close to the wall. It's not as wet."

Ahvrym did so, slipping a little on algae, and soon they stood in a long, barrel-vaulted chamber. The damp air had guaranteed a good living for fungus in and around the extensive network of cracks in the decorative plaster, but the floor was dry.

"Why is that here?" Sekmé murmured to herself.

"What?"

She pointed to a shallow raised ring of cut stone in the middle of the room. "A sacred hearth."

"Like Kemphor?"

"Damned close."

They dumped their load of green twigs, dry moss, and leaves into the circle and coaxed a smoky fire from it. The onager edged up to the heat and Sekmé offered the animal some moss—which it ignored. She looked at the beast closely, surprised or, rather, suspicious, but tossed the moss into the fire.

"I was . . . told there was a city here," she said. "I didn't believe it."

"Our earliest writings refer to one," Ahvrym told her. "A 'city in stone' they call it, or 'the City of Many Tongues.' "

"Meaning?"

Ahvrym shrugged. "Maybe many things. *Tongues* could mean voices, a populous place, or a place with many different opinions. It could also be synonymous with *mouths*. A lot of people to feed."

"Yes," Sekmé said pensively. "This city is big enough for two Kemphors."

"Or Eshnas."

"I—I might have said once that this was a Maurheti city, proof that we'd long ago held the interior, but, then, who gelbombed it?"

Ahvrym nodded. "Not our style. Still, the hearth—"

"Who ever made *anything* like this?" Sekmé interrupted. "It's not built, it's *carved!*"

"No Tel-mari."

"No Maurheti, either."

They fell silent and watched the limping flames of their hissing fire.

"Do you like dried bat meat?" Sekmé asked.

"I hate it," Ahvrym said.

"So do I. Let's have some."

She unstrapped one of the pouches hanging across the onager's back, opened it, and handed Ahvrym a couple leathery strips before retrieving two for herself. They stood side by side at the fire and ate in silence, partly because they didn't have anything to say, partly because the dried meat was so tough and chewy it required all of their concentration and jaw power to consume.

What has happened to her? Ahvrym wondered. She seems healthy enough, if a bit frayed around the edges, but her face . . . it's as haunted as this city.

After finishing a piece of bat jerky, Ahvrym rescued a singed branch from the fire, pressed his burning and, therefore, softened oilstone onto the tip, and turned to explore the darkness. As he'd hoped, Sekmé's curiosity was piqued and she followed. The yellow light of their oilstones rolled up the walls and was swallowed by the vaulted darkness above, while their shadows, long and sharp below, fanned away into nothingness overhead. It was a huge room.

At first, Ahvrym found nothing at all, let alone anything interesting. The walls were too stained and damaged. Undaunted, he held his torch higher, toward the plaster that was above the creeping damp. And there he found something.

"Praise the Great God! Can you see any of this, Sekmé?"

Sekmé held her torch near his.

"Do you see the symbols?" he asked excitedly.

She squinted: a star, a multipetaled flower, a crescent moon, a cross, and the strange, two-toned broken circle.

"Ancient Tel-mari ancestor signs!" Ahvrym cried triumphantly.

"Not just Tel-mari," Sekmé said softly. "Those symbols are carved all over the caves in the Hills of Whispers. The Denneshur say they're sacred."

"They are."

"What do they mean?"

"No one is sure." Ahvrym passed the torch slowly from sign to sign. "The elder rabami believe they represent different early tribes."

"Tribes? *Tribes* built this city?"

"*Tribe* is a term of art, my dear. It's a group of people who have something in common: ancestors, a belief system, culture. It doesn't mean they're hunters living in caves."

"Why are they grouped together?"

"Perhaps the tribes considered themselves parts of a larger, all-encompassing tribe."

Sekmé frowned darkly, but not from skepticism. He could see her trying desperately to piece something together.

"Ahvrym . . . these symbols are in the *desert*, too."

"So you said." He sighed. "Ours? Yours? It's a mystery. Still, the crescent and the broken circle . . ." His voice trailed away.

"What?"

Ahvrym's answer was to dash into the darkness toward the far wall, the light from his oilstone dancing wildly.

"Ahvrym! Don't run in the dark!" Sekmé ran after him. "You don't know what else might have crawled in looking for shelter!"

He didn't care. His makeshift torch had illuminated a tiny corner of a find so spectacular that he didn't quite believe it even when he stood before it. He had to touch it to be certain.

The far wall, composed of a hard pink stone that did not seem part of the natural cliff, had been polished to a high gloss, and the fungi and algae had been unable to cling to it. As a result, compared to the rest of the room, the wall was almost as smooth and clean as the day it had been finished. However, the most remarkable thing about its surface was the vast design carefully chiseled

into it and inlaid with a bright white unoxidized metal Ahvrym could not identify. The design, a precise but strange outline of several complicated shapes labeled with short lines of fine script, filled the wall except for five large blocks of inlaid text beneath it, each headed by one of the ancestor symbols.

Sekmé hissed in her breath when she caught up with Ahvrym, and stared at the design with something like alarm.

"Wait!"

She ran back to the dimly glowing hearth. Ahvrym heard some small nickerings of curiosity from the onager, then Sekmé returned lugging one of her saddlebags. She upended it at Ahvrym's feet, dumping a dozen high-grade oilstones on the ground.

"Sekmé?"

"Another mystery," she said. "An unintentional gift from the past."

Over the next hour, they broke and ignited the oilstones and, once they were softened, stuck them about the wall to light the images, Sekmé flinging some of them high and hard so they'd adhere above the top of the design. This done, they stepped back to assess their find.

"It's beautiful!" Ahvrym sighed.

"It's a map," Sekmé said. She pointed to several places with her torch. "These are islands. This looks like a very long river, and over here, there's a large inland sea." She lowered her torch. She looked distinctly troubled.

"I did some aerial surveying when I was a cadet," she said. "We learned how, in case we had to identify lesser-known parts of Tel-mari from a Needle. I mapped the coast of Maurhet all the way south to the Salt Barrens."

"Ah! And where is that coastline on *this* map?" Ahvrym asked. "It's remarkable to see one's world from such a vast perspective."

Sekmé slowly paced the length of the wall. To Ahvrym, she seemed reluctant to study the map too closely.

"It isn't there," she concluded in a soft voice.

"What?"

"There are a lot of places that look something like it, but . . . no." She gave him a tense and unconvincing smile. "Who knows how these people got their information? All of this—" She waved the torch over a nearby duet of linked continents. "—is *completely* unfamiliar."

They fell silent again and Ahvrym inspected the inscriptions more carefully.

"Has it ever occurred to you, Sekmé," he suddenly mused aloud, "that there could be peoples in these unknown places that know nothing of us?"

"That kind of fantasy was my brother's specialty," she said sadly, "not mine."

"But, what if there were? The Denneshur have roamed God knows where, and you, well, I suspect you've covered a fair bit of ground yourself recently. Isn't it conceivable there might be other tribes in even more distant places?"

Sekmé looked pale. The idea frightened her, which puzzled Ahvrym; she was a battle-hardened Maurheti officer. Still, he didn't want to make her uncomfortable, so he turned to the five blocks of text. Four of them might as well have been completely decorative. He couldn't read a single word, although the variety of the script was extraordinary and quite lovely.

However, the text under the crescent, that ancient Tel-mari symbol, did exhibit some familiar elements.

"The same script is on the map," Sekmé said softly. "You can read some of it."

"I can, can I?" Ahvrym asked with a bemused smile. "How do you know that?"

No mistake this time—Sekmé was blushing, deeply.

"You said you were a scholar, didn't you?"

"Yes, but that does not guarantee universal knowledge."

Ahvrym ran his finger up the block to the top line and scanned it closely. Near the far right, he stopped and, unable to control his wonder, whispered a soft blessing.

"God grant us an easy path!" he breathed. "You're right! This! Do you see?"

Sekmé eyed the script.

$$\text{الله}$$

"It's a very old name for God," Ahvrym said. "And here! Something about a great journey to . . . I'm not quite sure . . . to return to the start, or something like that."

"Begin again?"

"Perhaps. The syntax is so archaic it barely makes sense. And here—" His finger moved down a few lines and again passed from right to left. "—it says something about 'a city of brothers joined together in love' and 'the end of strife.' "

Ahvrym stroked the words as if they were alive.

"I think people from all over this map got together to build this wonderful city in stone *cooperatively*," he said at last.

"But, the Great Division . . ." Sekmé sounded deeply unsure. "That kind of cooperation—it isn't supposed to be possible."

"It had to be for quite a while, my dear," Ahvrym said. "This was a very great city. You need centuries for that."

"Still, in the end . . ."

Ahvrym stroked his beard. Something was missing, something vital to their understanding, but he wasn't sure what. He studied the text again, but what little he could decipher seemed to be more optimistic declarations of "brotherhood" and "new beginnings."

Sekmé also studied the map. In the inconstant light and inky shadows, she looked smaller, frailer, lonelier.

"I wish my brother was here," she whispered. "He was always conjuring up that kind of blasphemy because he knew it upset people. Once, he even said—" Her voice stopped. Her eyes had become distant again, lost in an internal landscape.

"Said what, my dear?" Ahvrym asked gently.

Sekmé started, and finished her sentence as if she'd never

broken off. "—that the Maurheti and Tel-mari were really the same people."

"If they lived in this city together for hundreds of years, maybe they were." Ahvrym looked more closely at the map's labeling. "I wonder if they marked the city's location? Odd to name all these islands and yet leave out their own—"

He snatched his hand back as though he'd burned it.

"Ahvrym, stop it!" Sekmé barked in agitation. "Every time you find something new you jump and—and I almost have a seizure!"

"This word, Sekmé! On this land mass near the inland sea." His finger shook.

الصحراء

"Sa'Har!" he whispered.

Sekmé curled her fingers over his trembling hand and pulled it away from the wall. "Stop now . . . please."

"It's true!" he cried. "Sa'Har was a *place*! *A real place!*"

"Ahvrym . . ."

"This is where it began, Sekmé! This city! It's from the Time Before! The people 'rose up' from Sa'Har to build it! They *were* Sa'Har!"

He grabbed her arms and lifted her from the ground in his excitement.

"I always knew it! It *is* possible to live side by side and not wage war! It *is* possible to live 'in Sa'Har'!"

Sekmé squirmed in his arms, her eyes, full of anguish, casting about the darkness for escape.

"Let go of me, Ahvrym," she said in a low, shaky voice.

He did and she slipped quickly back into the darkness.

"Sekmé?"

The flame of her oilstone torch bobbed steadily back to the hearth and was tossed in. The fire flared high for a moment with this sudden infusion of concentrated fuel, silhouetting her dejected crouch, then died back to its red glow.

Ahvrym approached her cautiously. He realized that, in the rush of his emotions, he'd forgotten to find out what had happened since their parting under fire. Did she know about the strange turns the war had taken? Was she on her way back to surrender to that unpredictable and overfond general of hers?

When he crouched next to her, he discovered that she was weeping. In her hands, she kneaded the piece of fur he'd found on her brother's corpse. It was still faintly stained with his blood.

"This isn't Sa'Har," she whispered, tears running out of her nose. She wiped it with the cuff of her slickcoat. "That map isn't of any place we'll ever be able to find."

"Why not, my dear?"

She groaned and covered her eyes.

"I try to understand them, Ahvrym, I try as hard as I can . . ."

"Understand what?"

"Set could and he was blind." Sekmé held out her hands, fingers spread, as though she was trying to frame the space before her. "They should have given their visions to him. I'm useless."

"Whose visions?"

"You believe in jo, Ahvrym, don't you? And walkers?"

"Yes—and I'm beginning to believe in telepathy. How do you know this about me?"

"I . . . never mind. This is more important."

She told him about the white-haired rider and described her visions of the dark-skinned man. Ahvrym held himself rigid until she concluded, then he reached out and touched her hair. It was longer than the last time he'd seen her, but still too short to behave. He tried to tuck some behind her ear, the ear without a lobe, but it slipped out.

"Do you believe these visions, Sekmé?"

"I don't know. Everyone says the jo are liars, but Set was there. To use him in a lie—I don't think they could do that. It would be too cruel."

She palmed the wet from her eyes.

"Maybe I don't *want* to understand, Ahvrym. Maybe it would injure me if I did, and I don't think I have the tolerance for that anymore." She smiled bitterly. "All my life I've done terrible things for supposedly noble reasons, and now this strange rider entrusts *me* with all the memories, all the *histories*, he's eaten for *centuries*. Why? What did he think *I* was going to do with them? I have no moral integrity at all! It doesn't make sense."

"My poor Sekmé!" Ahvrym said tenderly. "I'd rather lose my way in your confusion than march along a certainty. It's much more lively."

Sekmé laughed, the giddiness of ragged nerves, then began to weep again, her body shuddering with exhaustion. "But, if the Calf is a machine, and Sa'Har—"

"It doesn't change the fact that we're two misplaced people shivering in front of a pitiful fire inside a ruined building."

"This is a terrible place, Ahvrym."

"Uncomfortable, certainly. I hate getting lower plant forms caught in my beard."

"No! I mean, if even the people who built this city couldn't make it last, then maybe it's impossible to live together without war. Maybe it's our fate, sooner or later, to kill one another."

"But, Sekmé, they succeeded for such a long time! Doesn't that fire your hope?" He rested his hand on her cheek. "It isn't the fall that defines us, it's the getting up again."

The green in Sekmé's irritated eyes was especially bright when she looked at him.

"How many times do we have to relearn everything before we get it right?" she murmured.

"As many times as we need. Maybe those histories can help."

Ahvrym looked back at the pink wall haloed in burning oil-stone fragments, its strange map and inscriptions glowing as though written in mercury.

"We've lost a great deal, Sekmé, even our myths. This wall

and your visions have made certain of that, but I don't feel afraid. Those 'certainties' were quite a burden."

"But I could use a *little* certainty right now. I feel sick."

"Dampness and bat meat: a vile duo."

He put his arm around her shoulders and drew her close. She let her head rest against his neck.

"Ahvrym?"

"H'm?"

"I want to see where you buried Set."

"I'd be happy to show you, my dear, but I don't know the way back."

"That's not a problem. I'll find the route."

He kissed the crown of her head. She didn't protest.

Is she too tired to care? he wondered. God, if it's Your will, I'd prefer she truly trusted me.

"I'd like to find my sister," he said.

"Bekka."

"Sometime you must explain to me how you ended up being the courier and not her."

Sekmé snuggled closer to his chest and sighed, a long release of bone-deep fatigue. The corner of Set's vulpé pelt poked up from under her collar and tickled his nose.

"No matter where we go, we can't go 'home,' can we, Avhrym?"

"No."

She was silent a long time and became heavy in his arms. Ahvrym thought she'd fallen asleep and was about to shift her gently to the floor when she spoke again in a voice from a dream.

"Very well. We'll wander . . ."

CHAPTER 30

ESHNA

Ahvrym rode quietly in the bright, clear morning while Sekmé, on foot, led the onager through the city in stone and searched for the way out. He watched her scan the road, study the breaks in nearby brush, and follow the birds' bobbing, wheeling flight in and out of the cliffs. At each new branch of canyon, she stopped to listen.

"For water," she explained when Ahvrym asked. "Water running *away* from the city."

"Was that your specialty, my dear? Tracker?"

Sekmé smiled ironically.

"My only specialty seems to be survival in spite of everything—including my own mistakes. My men liked that." She shrugged. "Actually, my father taught me how to track, how to hunt."

"Your father was a soldier, too, wasn't he?"

Sekmé, kneeling on one knee to study what looked like a track in a bit of mud, stiffened.

"He died horribly," she said, very low.

"Many people did."

She looked up over her shoulder at him, her hand shading her eyes. "I'm sorry about your friend."

"My friend?"

"The one with the long brown beard." She got up and brushed the dirt from her pants leg.

"The one? . . ."

"With the beard," Sekmé repeated. "I think my father would have liked him."

She turned the onager's head and began to lead him down a narrower rift where the vines were thicker, the burn thinner.

"My rabam!" Ahvrym whispered, wondering if he sounded as shaken and bloodless as he felt.

"Yes," she said sadly, "I'm very sorry."

He couldn't say another word for a long time, during which the air cooled, became thicker, and clouds collected above the canyon. His nose twitched.

"I smell rain," he said, "and trees."

Sure enough, Sekmé had found the way out of the upland canyon lands back into the greater forest.

"You should join me up here on this splendid beast," Ahvrym said, feeling a surge of relief and renewed optimism. "We'd travel faster."

Sekmé eyed him curiously, her mouth bent at a strange angle.

"Naturally, I'll sit behind you," he said, "so you can navigate."

Still, she hesitated.

"That *is* best, isn't it?" He offered his hand to help her up, but she instead hooked her toe in a ring above the stirrup and pulled herself into the saddle unassisted.

"You're tense, Sekmé. Please relax or the ride will be very uncomfortable." He squeezed her arm amiably. "I have no designs on you, my dear."

"I know," she said softly. "I was only remembering . . ."

The return through the forest was much easier with a keen-eyed scout riding before him, and Ahvrym became loquacious, relating in detail his life among the woodcutters, the onset of passive warfare, and his encounter with General Am. Sekmé let him ramble on, occasionally interjecting a "huh!" or "really?"—

very mild comments considering how strange a turn things in Tel-mari had taken.

"What I don't understand, Ahvrym, is the drought itself."

"I heard that one of your officers went mad and destroyed the, uh . . . those plants where you make salt water fresh. What was his name? Bohé? Béha?"

Sekmé blanched and stopped coaxing the onager up the steep path. The animal halted a moment, as if waiting for her to make up her mind, then plodded forward on his own.

"What is the sea like, Sekmé?" Ahvrym asked, hoping to bring her out of her dark musings. "I've never seen it."

"H'm? Oh. Big. Wet. Are you sure about the desalination plants?"

"I didn't even know what they were until this. Very clever."

"Far too centralized," Sekmé muttered darkly. "Vulnerable."

"Well! Now, perhaps, you should tell me more about your curious experiences in the White Mountains," Ahvrym suggested with forced cheerfulness.

"It's very cold there," Sekmé said curtly, hamstringing the subject for the time being. They rode in silence until they reached the woodcutters' hamlet.

It had been burned to the ground.

"Bastard!" Ahvrym cried as they dismounted. "I thought he was an honorable man! How could he do this after what we said to each other?"

"I don't think he did." Sekmé turned over an ember, still red with heat, with the toe of her boot. "This is recent."

They found no evidence of bodies in the ruins.

"At least they got out," Ahvrym said.

"If they ever came back," Sekmé added.

"Why burn an empty village?"

Sekmé pushed back the filthy hood of her slickcoat and let the light, spitting rain wet her face. She wiped it dry with her sleeve.

"I don't know. Usually the point of a raid is to kill. Unless . . ."

Ahvrym had been crouching in the ashes, poking at the shards of a broken crock. He looked up.

"Unless what?"

"Maybe the orders were very broad," Sekmé said uncertainly, "with unpleasant consequences for any deviation."

"So, you're told 'burn villages' and you do?"

Sekmé kicked her heel angrily against a step that now led nowhere, not so much knocking off the damp ashes as inflicting more damage on the broken leather.

"Let's go, Ahvrym. We're wasting our time."

They headed down out of the forest, camping as necessary off the road under thickets and in hollows, until they reached the Tel-mari swamplands.

Night had fallen and the swamp's evening breath had collected in a low fog that hid both solid ground and soft and reached the onager's knees. As a rule, only those who knew the swamp well, as Ahvrym did, would venture out in it after dark. They were very surprised to catch sight and sound of many small groups of people, all on the move away from Eshna. Now and then they heard a distant yell or scream, even a rifle report, when someone found an unexpected mud sink, invisible tangled root, or sleeping bog monitor.

Incredibly, when they could hear the travelers' conversations, half of them were in Maurheti.

"Refugees and deserters," Ahvrym whispered.

Their pace had slowed and he peered ahead over Sekmé's shoulder into the weeping moss and phantom trees to reset his bearings.

"In great numbers," Sekmé said. "Something has happened."

They decided to keep close to the shore of the main body of the swamp and away from any identifiable trails.

"It doesn't matter who we meet," Ahvrym said philosophically, "it would be unpleasant."

Near the middle of the night, the fog broke up and stars appeared above the swamp. Sekmé looked up at them and realized they'd changed. More to the point: she had.

"Which one do you think it was, Ahvrym?"

"Was what?"

"The old sun?"

"You've decided to believe the jo?"

"I need to believe *something*."

Ahvrym followed her gaze and slowly passed his fingers through his matted beard. "How about the large one to the left of the Winking Children?"

"No. The small one. To the right."

"Why?"

"I don't want to think of us in grand terms ever again."

Their discussion was violently interrupted when two Needles, one right on the tail of the other, shrieked out of the west and raced over the swamp. They banked sharply, rolled, and howled back in a tight, dizzyingly paced circle. The one in the lead suddenly shot straight up, then dove for the slimy water only to pull up at the last second. The other duplicated its every move.

"That's crazy!" Sekmé cried as she fought to rein in the terrified, rearing onager with Ahvrym clutching her hard from behind and all but locking her arms to her side. "Why are they chasing each other?"

In the damp swamp air, the lights lining the hulls of the Needles lit up the surrounding mist as they passed, giving the aircraft pale, greenish auras that melted in their wake like comets' tails. The scream was deafening.

The Needles rolled again and swung back for another pass. This time, the one behind opened fire on the leader with its strafing weapons. A short, rapid line of pink flames cut through the darkness, and a large piece of the leader's left wing ripped away, dangled briefly, and fell, haloed in red sparks, into the swamp. Current danced blue lightning around the hull, and the

craft flipped onto its side. The second Needle, following much too closely, had no time to pull away and ran headlong into the now vertical blade of the damaged wing. Both aircraft split open and exploded in a massive ball of white before raining in fiery splinters into the all-accepting belly of the swamp.

Sekmé and Ahvrym stared at the bubbling, hissing, steaming cauldron of the swamp and observed the casual, yet eager, sinuous approach of at least a dozen bog monitors. The great lizards wasted no time cleaning up after others' misfortunes. They weren't even going to wait for the water to cool down.

Sekmé ran her hand over her brow, leaving behind a dark streak of ash.

"It's happening again, Ahvrym."

Ahvrym spat to his left, his right, and held his palms out to the swamp as if to hide this vision of destruction from his sight and ward off its evil radiation.

"The world's gone mad," he said.

"We'd better find Bekka before the contagion strikes her, too."

"What about Set? I thought you—"

"Set is dead, Ahvrym." Sekmé turned the onager's head toward the trees. "I'm sure he'd understand."

When Dek and Bekka heard the pounding in the bleakest, loneliest hours of the night, they leapt out of bed and hid under it.

"If they break in . . . ," Dek whispered.

"They can't. The door is double bolted."

"They can if they're desperate enough! I told you we should have gone inland."

"I'm not leaving Eshna. It's my home."

"But, Bekka!"

"Bekka!" a deep voice cried from the street below. "If you're there, for the mercy of God, let us in!"

Bekka scrambled out from under the bed.

"Where are you going?" Dek demanded, and forgetting where

he was, lifted his head and banged it on the wooden slats of the bedframe.

"It's my brother!" Bekka said. "He's alive!"

"Wait! I'm coming, too."

"No! He was a *terrorist*, Dek. God knows what has happened to him since they killed his men." She tied on her veil. "Stay here until I know it's safe for you to meet him."

"Is it safe for *you*?"

Bekka quickly crouched down and gave him a fast kiss. "Patience, my love! I won't be long."

When she opened the tavern door, not only was she shocked by the filthy, unkempt mess her brother had become, but she was completely taken off guard by his traveling companion.

"Seshi!"

"As you requested—" Sekmé smiled shyly. "—I didn't hurt him."

Dek, unable to obey Bekka's instructions out of fear for her safety, pushed his head past Bekka's shoulder.

The former Maurheti officers jumped when they saw each other.

"Dek?"

"Commander?"

Ahvrym's thick eyebrows bunched in confusion. "How interesting! Why do I feel like the distant cousin at the wedding?"

No one paid him any attention. Dek stepped outside, barefoot, into the mud, grabbed Sekmé's collar, and stared hard into her face with a mixture of wonder and mistrust.

"Aren't you dead?" he whispered.

"Should I be?"

"My God! This—this adds a new color to everything."

"Perhaps while you're trying to define that hue, you can explain what you're doing in my sister's house, Maurheti," Ahvrym growled.

"Come in and wash first," Bekka said. "You can tether the onager in the court." She turned to her lost brother and her fe-

line eyes narrowed over her veil. "Ahvrym, this man no longer has a country. Neither does Seshi—"

"Sekmé," her brother said.

"—and if you can travel with a former murderer, then I can board one in my house."

"What does father think of all this?" Ahvrym crossed his arms.

"Papa is dead."

This news cut off Ahvrym's outrage at the knees, and at the sight of his devastation, Bekka, never one to cling to anger, softened. She removed her veil.

"As far as I'm concerned—" She offered a hand to each of the new arrivals. "—all of us are family here. War does not enter this inn."

Sekmé had never been so glad of a narrow wooden tub of lukewarm water in her life. All the oils and perfumes of Maurhet couldn't have made the bath sweeter, although she remembered her first sight of Haru in the steam and became sad. She hadn't thought about him for a long time.

While she was musing, Ahvrym, who had bathed at the deserted women's well up the hill, tramped into the kitchen and surprised her, or, rather, himself. Sekmé merely looked up as if expecting a question, whereas Ahvrym turned scarlet and quickly retreated.

"Ahvrym?"

"May I be fried in oil for all eternity!" he mumbled.

"No, I don't think so." Sekmé pensively scooped up some water with a dented tankard and poured it over her hair. "Come in here so we can talk."

Ahvrym crept in, eyes down, like a guilty pupil approaching a stern teacher. It was very funny, but Sekmé couldn't laugh. His embarrassment was genuine, and she knew exactly how painful that was for him. She'd ridden his memory.

"While you were gone, Dek confirmed what you said. My cousin Bahé gel-bombed the desalination plants."

"Your *cousin?*"

"He also told me why there were so many deserters in the swamp."

Ahvrym snuck a quick peek at her, then lowered his eyes again.

"High Command ordered the extermination of *all* Tel-mari." Sekmé poured more water down her back.

"Genocide!" Ahvrym gasped.

"Yes, but many of the generals, not just ordinary soldiers, concluded the order was immoral or something—Dek was pretty evasive about that—and they decided not to obey."

Ahvrym overcame his embarrassment and looked directly at her. "What?!"

Sekmé lifted her wet hands in a gesture of helplessness. "I'm as perplexed as you are, but Dek says the generals were unwilling to attack a people determined not to fight back."

Ahvrym tugged nervously on his beard. "That never stopped the Maurheti before!" he said. "There has to be more to it."

"I agree, but Dek wouldn't tell me."

"You're his commander!"

Sekmé shook her head wearily. "Not anymore! I think Bekka is."

Ahvrym snarled a few scatological curses but otherwise didn't comment. Instead, he stepped into the splash puddles around the tub and crouched next to Sekmé. The tub was narrow, and to sit in it she'd had to fold her knees up to her chest.

"It seems this mutiny broke the Maurheti into two armies," he said. He was looking at her shoulder.

"Looks like. They're fighting each other more than they're fighting the Tel-mari."

"Is this still painful?" Ahvrym pointed to the shiny blue scar on Sekmé's shoulder just below the edge of her clavicle. She looked away.

"Sometimes."

Ahvrym gently pried the tankard from her fingers, filled it

with water, and poured it over her scar. She watched him out of the corner of her eye.

"Bekka will never leave Eshna," he said, "which I think means that Dek will never leave Eshna."

"I think you're right."

He poured another draft over her shoulder.

"Will you leave Eshna?" he asked.

"The more I hear about the drought, the more I worry about my mother."

Ahvrym nodded and, very slowly, poured a third measure of tepid water over her wound.

"May I come with you?"

"Yes."

Ahvrym set the tankard on the floor beside the tub, leaned over Sekmé, and carefully, almost chastely, kissed her shoulder. He stood up and left the kitchen.

When he was gone, Sekmé realized she'd known long before a jo had taken her inside this man's skin that this was going to happen. She'd foreseen it in the steam of a nearly forgotten bath in Maurhet.

I guess Set and I *are* twins, she thought.

Except that Set never would have considered stealing a Needle, and Sekmé was.

CHAPTER 31

KEMPHOR

Night patrols prowled the streets of Kemphor looking for roaming bands of looters. Some of the looters were disgusted former guards and were armed. When armed group met armed group, the temptation to use those arms overwhelmed any lingering sense of brotherhood. Hunger had systematically reduced the focus of loyalty from country to kin to self, and there seemed no way to reverse it.

Those without arms, or knowledge of how to use them, left. Some went north or east into the desert. Some bought places on the small fishing boats that had once procured giant eels and other delicacies for the aristocrats in the holdings. For passage along the coast to questionable safety in barren hills, the fishermen charged as much as two barrels of salted meat or grain.

King Roon kept to his palace and watched the economy, then the city, collapse around him and he felt a helplessness none of his royal upbringing had prepared him for. During the day, he heard the mobs outside crying, screaming, begging him to help, cursing him when he didn't appear. By night, the scattered reports all over the city from family weapons of every make kept him awake.

The enemy of Maurhet had always been the faraway inhabitants of dark, wet Tel-mari. Only a year ago, who would have

believed that complacency would become a worse threat? That the Maurheti belief in an unchanging world would disintegrate?

"We invited it on ourselves," he whispered to himself as he poured two goblets of pale orange mang wine, then tore a small packet of fine powder and sprinkled the contents over them.

His wives sat silently on cushions around the sacred hearth with their small children—princes and princesses of the blood—at their sides. A total of twenty people. Each held a small cup of the same wine.

Roon set the two goblets on a glass table next to the throne and replaced the gold stopper in the decanter, the last of eight such vessels. He settled back into the throne and waited.

In a few minutes, Dand Ubit entered the Dome room. He noticed the queens and royal children around the fire, but registered no unusual surprise.

"I apologize for my tardiness, Majesty," he droned as he minced up to Roon on his inadequate feet. "One of the patrols found a nest of looters squatting in your stables trying to milk the onagers."

"That close to our person, eh?"

Dand was taken aback. It was rare for the king to refer to himself in the royal plural.

"Y-yes, my king, but they have been dealt with."

"No one could ever accuse you of being lax in your policies, Secretary."

Dand eyed Roon uncertainly.

"Is your majesty well?"

"Never better, Dand. Come. Join us in a little evening refreshment. It's a warm night."

It was indeed, so Dand approached the throne and took the goblet the king offered. He waited politely for Roon to taste his first, but the king seemed in no hurry to drink and absently swirled the wine in the goblet.

"We realize now that you were right, Dand."

"About what, Majesty?"

"About this being the End Time and that it was time to 'cleanse the field.' "

The secretary smiled, a tight, self-satisfied little crease. "I merely read the signs, Majesty."

"Yes. Too bad you couldn't read *how* God intended to cleanse the field and of *whom*."

Dand's smile disappeared. "Majesty?"

"A quarter of our troops in Tel-mari have deserted, Dand. Another third keep to camp and refuse to obey orders. The rest spend their time killing each other."

Roon rose to his feet, both hands cradling the bowl of the goblet.

"Here in Kemphor," he continued, "our people despair. Unable to provide for their children, they commit acts of violence in a futile effort to survive. The smarter ones flee the city entirely."

Dand made a weak wave of resignation. "God's design is a great mystery, Your Majesty."

"You didn't think so before." Roon drew closer to the secretary. "We recall you were quite certain about these so-called signs and how we should proceed."

The secretary blanched and tried to take a puny step back, but Roon put his arm around his shoulders and clutched him tight in a cold imitation of affection.

"We believe you placed ultimate blame on Commander Sekmé, calling her the Not-God's Captain."

"She *is* to blame, Majesty!" Dand said, his hum rising to a buzzy squeak. "Everything followed in progression from her actions! Her cousin's madness! The drought! Everything!"

"Dand," Roon murmured with tender condescension, "you're really quite stupid, aren't you? So are we. *We* decided the commander was a threat, but we could have chosen any number of ways to deal with that threat. Instead, at your suggestion, we

chose a course of action that not only did not curb her threat, but led to further mistakes that hastened our catastrophe.

"Bahé? Mad as he was, he could have chosen any number of deaths, but he chose one dictated by our most sacred value—blood loyalty—and he struck where we were least prepared. We didn't even have the imagination to envision such an act."

Roon squeezed the secretary even tighter. Dand's hand shook, spilling some of the wine.

"Shall we go on, Secretary? Who suggested we bring water from Tel-mari and punish any resistance? Who thought genocide a viable solution when that resistance took an unexpected form?"

"P-please, Majesty!" Dand squeaked. "I only advise—"

"Ah, yes, true! Let's not forget *our* role in this disaster. We authorized all of it."

Dand squirmed in the king's embrace.

"I am only one man, Majesty!"

"Yes, and *I* am only one man. Each of us must accept his share of the blame."

"Y-yes, Majesty."

Roon released the secretary, who coughed, took a deep breath, shakily smoothed his clothing, and composed himself.

"I've accepted my share," the king said. "Have you?"

Dand nodded nervously, the expected thing to do. He was obviously hoping the king had vented all he'd intended and would dismiss him.

"We're mere mortals," the king sighed, "flawed and weak before God. Given those flaws, we did our best, didn't we? Perhaps our fate was inevitable, set in motion from the Beginning. Only God can say."

Dand's body relaxed. He nodded again.

"I apologize if I frightened you, Dand," the king said kindly. "Go ahead and drink. You look as if you need it."

The secretary gratefully lifted the orange fluid to his lips and

drank, quickly draining the goblet. He delicately dabbed his temples and upper lip with his sleeve.

"Thank you, Majesty," he said. "I remain forever in—"

A small strangling sound issued from his throat, his eyes bulged to perfect spheres, and his teeth clenched so hard that two of them cracked and split in half. He toppled off his tiny feet and hit the hard black floor, lifeless.

Roon studied the corpse a moment then turned to his wives and children. All of them watched as he raised his goblet.

"You see, my beloved ones?" he said. "The pain is very short."

When Sekmé and Ahvrym reached the air base, it was almost dawn, which made the former commander nervous. She peered through the fire-wire fence.

"We should have come earlier," she said as they dismounted. "Most raids and supply runs begin at dawn."

"I don't see much preparation for either." Ahvrym shouldered his pouch of personal belongings: some food, a spare set of clothing, a beard comb, and four sacred texts his sister had kept for him since his student days.

"I still don't like it, Ahvrym."

She took the reins of the onager and led him behind her as she circled the fence toward the gate. She was glad the beast had never been shod.

"Are we taking the onager with us?" Ahvrym asked.

"Shh! Let me think . . ."

When they reached the gate, they saw a single Needle looming in the gray.

"Only one left," Ahvrym said. "Perhaps others have had the same idea."

"Ahvrym, if you don't shut up, I'll cut off your beard and stuff it down your throat!"

"It's just that I've never flown before, Sekmé."

"So?"

"So, I'm a little . . . anxious."

Sekmé looked at him and he cleared his throat self-consciously.

"Just because one has blown up a number of the things doesn't mean one knows them personally," he said.

Sekmé snickered. "How in the world did *you* become a terrorist?" she asked.

"A grave error in judgment, believe me."

"Stand!" a voice barked behind them. "Move and die!"

Sekmé rolled her eyes. They'd been caught.

"Turn around!" The sentry, a tall, thick-waisted woman with a beautifully inlaid acid-pellet rifle emerged from the morning haze.

Sekmé and Ahvrym obeyed.

"What are you doing here?" the sentry asked in Tel-mari. "Who are you?"

"Refugees, of course," Ahvrym answered in his patrician Maurheti.

"We were looking for food," Sekmé said in Tel-mari.

The sentry squinted at her.

"Why are you dressed like a man?" She looked closer. "You're not veiled!"

"I needed the veil for female purposes," Sekmé said. "One has to improvise these days."

But the sentry was suspicious and cocked her weapon.

"Remove the hood," she said.

"I hope that weapon is in repair, Field Sergeant," Sekmé said as she pushed back her hood. "I wouldn't appreciate an accident."

It was not an idle concern. When the sergeant saw who it was, her arms jerked and she almost discharged the weapon in Sekmé's face. Sekmé gently turned the rifle barrel away with her hand.

"Calm down, Sergeant."

"Commander! You're dead!"

"Why does everyone keep saying that? I'm obviously alive."

"But—?"

"Never mind. It would take too long to explain and I need that Needle."

The sergeant snapped out of her amazement and retrained the weapon on Sekmé.

"I'm sorry, Commander. You're a deserter."

Sekmé detected a lack of enthusiasm under her words. "Do you *want* to shoot me?"

"*Shoot* you?" Ahvrym cried. He tried to wrest the weapon from the sentry's hands.

"Stop it!" Sekmé entered the tussle and grabbed the weapon herself. She pulled open the magazine and shook the pellets out into the mud. "No more of this nonsense! Sergeant, either arrest me or help me." She shoved the weapon back into the sentry's hands.

"Help you?"

"Let us through the gate so this gentleman and I—"

"*Gentleman?*" the sergeant gasped.

"Don't be naive, Sergeant! He's a spy."

"I am?" Ahvrym muttered.

"We need that Needle to get back to Kemphor."

"Kemphor!" The sergeant shook her head. "You don't want to go there, Commander."

"I do."

"Not with my help."

Sekmé scowled, concentrating furiously.

"All right," she said quietly, "I'll tell you the truth." She gave Ahvrym a wide, desperate glance. "This is my lover."

"I am?" Ahvrym mouthed.

"He is?"

"I—I know it's perverse, Sergeant, but—"

"Oh, Commander!" the sergeant breathed.

"—but it happens."

The sergeant nodded, overcome. "I know! Oh . . . I know."

"Then, help me."

The sentry hesitated.

"Please?"

"But . . ."

"Are *you* going to stay in Tel-mari?"

The young woman drew herself up sharply, apparently offended.

"Look," Sekmé said, "I'm not questioning your loyalty, but practicality dictates—"

"The onager," the sentry interrupted.

"What?"

"The onager for the Needle."

Sekmé bit her lip and looked to Ahvrym.

He shrugged. "Practicality dictates."

Ahvrym didn't say a word as Sekmé helped him strap into the copilot's narrow curved seat in the cockpit, but she felt his rigid fear as if she once again inhabited his limbs. She wanted to reassure him, tell him everything would be fine, that he was perfectly safe, but she wasn't sure. When one steals an aircraft, one has little time to inspect it for airworthiness. For all she knew, this Needle had been left at the base because of major mechanical problems, missing parts, or lack of fuel. She was relieved when, at her touch, it shrieked to life.

"Let's hope we can get up and out before we're pursued."

Ahvrym's hands clutched the edge of his seat, nails and knuckles bleached with tension, but he nodded.

The launch was uneventful, a clean, swift, vertical assent without shudder. They cleared the clouds, and morning sunlight flooded the cockpit.

"Excellent!" Sekmé grinned. "Time to put some distance between ourselves and the rain."

Ahvrym looked pained and bit green.

"I'm impressed," Sekmé said. "The first time I went up in a Needle, I vomited before we topped the trees. Take deep, slow breaths. It helps."

Ahvrym didn't move except to close his eyes.

"All right," Sekmé said. "I've done that, too. Hang on for the thrust."

She pushed the lever forward and the Needle shot across the sky. She relaxed. The craft appeared to be in fine repair. She studied the gauges and found they had plenty of fuel.

Ahvrym, however, remained locked in petrified panic. He carefully opened his eyes and peeped out at the sea of clouds beneath them. Sekmé heard something catch in his throat, probably a strangled whimper.

She tapped her index finger on the steering bar. It probably wouldn't help to continue her story of her own maiden flight; the man was sweating a musky funk. Best to leave him alone.

The clouds, first pink, then yellow, brightened to white as the sun rose behind them. In the distance, the tops of storms resembled the broken towers of the ghost city, bent and unstable, but they flattened at the upper reaches of the atmosphere, as though God's invisible scimitar had sheared the air. It was deceptively peaceful.

Slowly, Ahvrym's hands unclenched and he began to take a more considered interest in what was happening around him. He studied Sekmé's hands. They rested easily, assuredly, on the controls.

"Sekmé," he whispered, "do you think your mother is still alive?"

"I don't know."

Ahvrym nodded gently. "How small our circle of concerns becomes . . ."

Sekmé fidgeted slightly. She'd wanted to ask him something since the night in the dead city, something her "ride" hadn't answered. Actually, from the beginning it had never been far from her consciousness and, with the noted exception of darkman dreams, had overrun all other night images.

"Ahvrym, the curse in the Eshna marketplace, the bodies—"

She stopped. The question had suddenly become intolerable.

He was staring at her.

"Don't look at me like that . . ."

"My dear, I can't help it. I don't know what to think." His brow knit. "If I'd known when we met that you had planned the attack, I might have killed you with your own weapon. I was crazy with the horror of it. So, part of me is glad it still gives you pain, and yet . . ."

"Was it your idea?"

His face opened in surprise. "No! Oh, I wanted to help, but, when I bent over the first body, a young girl's . . . I couldn't touch them." He looked at her more closely. "This matters to you, doesn't it? Why?"

"Curious."

"No. There's more."

Sekmé's hands tightened on the steering bar.

"I'm responsible for plenty of atrocities," Ahvrym said.

"I'm aware of that, but I didn't want you to be—"

"The source of your nightmares," he finished.

Sekmé kept her eyes on the gauges, but she sensed the shift, the warming of his attention.

"My dear, I'm—"

"Don't! Please."

"As you wish."

Eventually the clouds thinned away to a fine vapor and vanished. Below them, the sere and stark ridges and curls and rents and scars of the desert rolled by in a light golden haze of heat-raised dust.

Ahvrym pressed his nose against the cockpit's eye—the bubble of heavy crystal.

" 'I will rest my head in the sands of Sa'Har,' " he murmured.

"That—that's from something," Sekmé said. "What is it?"

"Part of a very old poem." Ahvrym pulled back from the eye. "Can one really live in the desert?"

"The Denneshur have lived there for centuries."

"It must be a hard life."

"It is."

"Perhaps, living so close to the skin and bones of things gives one a clearer picture of the truth."

"I don't know about that," Sekmé said skeptically. "The Denneshur see more jo than anyone else."

"I've been thinking about that." Ahvrym began the familiar worrying of his beard. "If we did originally come from . . . another place, then maybe the jo are the *real* people on this world, the native intelligence, and we are *invaders*."

"You sound like my brother!"

"I'm serious, my dear. Maybe we didn't realize our violation because we weren't equipped to see it."

"Not that I agree with you, but that would explain why the jo aren't very forthcoming with answers."

"Exactly! They owe us nothing. Only a chosen few get the benefit of their knowledge."

"*Chosen* few!" Sekmé scoffed. "Try *afflicted* few! Maybe they share that so-called knowledge with those they *hate* the most. Have you considered that?"

Ahvrym smiled cryptically and settled more cozily into his seat.

"Hate isn't the opposite of love. Indifference is."

"One more clever turn of phrase, Ahvrym, and I'll eject you."

"My lips are sealed."

When they cleared the Hills of Whispers and flew out over the Maurhet dunes, they saw the city of Kemphor: instead of a bright, white gleam on the horizon, it was obscured by a thick cloud of black that snaked a long tail inland on the wind.

"That looks familiar," Ahvrym said grimly. "What are those smaller cities below us?"

"The holdings."

"Where your mother is?"

"In one of them, yes, but I'm going to make a pass over Kemphor first."

Ahvrym frowned at the withered trees and scorched grounds of the estate beneath them.

"Might as well," he mumbled.

Sekmé dipped the nose of the Needle and it pierced the fabric of the smoke over Kemphor, and they got their first close look at the Maurheti capital.

"My God!"

"It looks like Eshna, Sekmé."

"No . . . no, it doesn't."

At least a hundred buildings, including the palace, were burning. The Great Dome had collapsed like a massive eggshell, its gold-coated masonry smothering the sacred flame. When she dropped the Needle lower and eased her speed, Sekmé saw panicked looters in the debris fighting over sacks of grain and clothing from the royal stores, while crates of bullion and jewels were broken open with bayonets only to be kicked over and abandoned in disgust. Two water-tank transports collided in the chaos, and the looters immediately boarded them to get at their precious cargo.

Everywhere buildings had been gutted by gel bombs, and fresh burn sizzled in the wounds, continuing its caustic consumption even where the fires had died down. Without Eshna's brand of precipitation, Kemphor could burn and smoke for weeks.

Neither Sekmé nor Ahvrym had to say what both were thinking. This must have been what it was like to watch the city in stone die; it was happening again. Sekmé pulled the Needle up out of the smoke, and they flew past the blackened carcasses of the desalination plants and made a wide, smooth arc over the sea.

As his side of the aircraft dipped toward the sparkling expanse of calm, indifferent blue, Ahvrym gasped and pressed his palms together in homage.

"How beautiful!"

CHAPTER 32

SANDS

The lake where Sekmé had hunted bitterns had been drained and lay barren and cracked in the midday heat like an old man's hands. She set the Needle down in it, and as they walked across toward the house, their boots crushed the tiny bones of unfortunate fish and desiccated amphibians. Not a single flower or leaf remained on the trees, and native weeds with long, thick roots, sharp, brittle spines, and musky, animal scents had overrun the withered grasses and herbs. There was evidence of bonfires everywhere.

The stables, animal pens, and servants' quarters were empty. Dune flies bred unchecked in dry onager dung, and looters had smashed all of the servants' furniture and crockery.

Ahvrym watched Sekmé with concern. He wished she'd say something, a curse perhaps, even if she aimed it at him. Her silence as she searched the grounds of the estate unnerved him. It was as if she'd destroyed the place herself, on orders from High Command, and was merely inspecting the damage. However, she repeatedly raised her hand to her chest where he knew she'd hidden the vulpé fur. It seemed a ritualistic gesture, a form of self-benediction. Ahvrym doubted she could keep her composure intact much longer.

"I begin to regret the heavy insulation of my native garb," he said, wiping his brow for emphasis. The desert heat was as hard

as a fist. "What about you, Sekmé? That robe was designed to warm an aging man's thin blood."

She blinked at him, uncomprehending.

"Perhaps it's time to look in the house?" he hinted. "I'm sure it's cooler inside."

Sekmé looked up at the mansion. It was intact but showed evidence of vandalism and neglect. Several of the balconies were broken, and someone had painted the word *Unborn*—another epithet for the Not-God—in red over the main entrance.

She sighed and reluctantly led the way up the rubble- and sand-strewn steps.

She's afraid, Ahvrym thought. *She doesn't really want to find her mother.*

The entrance hall, prayer room, hunters' room, pantry, kitchen—all had been stripped, perhaps to fuel those "purifying" bonfires. Not a single rug, goblet, sack of grain, weapon, oilstone, or stick of furniture remained—only those things that could not readily be carted away: the decorative tiles, the stone flooring, the patterns etched in the walls and ceiling.

Thousands of years from now, Ahvrym wondered, *will anyone be able to read* these *inscriptions?*

Sekmé was already halfway to the second story. Ahvrym sprinted after her.

"Much cooler, don't you think? Less glare, too," he said, more out of a need to break the silence than to convey anything she didn't already know. She ignored him.

The rooms of the second story had also been stripped, although a few of the bedchambers, including Sekmé's, still held their low beds. Sekmé's even retained some of the bedclothes, although they were yellow with the dust that had blown in through the window.

Ahvrym stepped out onto the balcony and looked at the ramparts of the Hills of Whispers rising from the soft curves of the Maurhet dunes to the east.

"Was this your view while you were growing up?" he asked.

Sekmé, who sat at the foot of the dusty bed, watched him but did not answer.

"Remarkable," he said. "I think I understand you better now."

He stepped back inside and sat next to her.

"Your mother is gone, Sekmé."

Sekmé removed the vulpé pelt from her parka and stared at it.

"When I was very small," she said, "no more than three, Set and I were asleep together in this bed and my mother came in. It was before dawn. She shook us awake and told us to come quickly. I was afraid because she was in her sleeping shift and her hair was loose around her face. She hadn't braided it. I was sure something terrible had happened."

She stroked the fur gently as if it was still alive and she didn't want to startle it.

"Set was whimpering, so she carried him. I remember how dark it was and how still. Not even the servants were up."

Ahvrym couldn't watch her pet a dead skin any longer and he rested his hand on hers to stop it.

"She took us outside to the steps. All of us barefoot and it was freezing! It can be very cold before the sun rises."

"Really? I thought the desert was always hot."

"The desert is always a surprise," Sekmé said. "It surprised *me* that morning because, without any warning, it produced my father."

She smiled, a funny half crook full of nostalgia he'd never seen before.

"He had just stepped out of his vehicle and his hair was all blown about and full of dust, but he was grinning so broadly you could see it in the dark. He ran up the steps, grabbed all of us in one embrace, and danced us around and around in the cold."

She slipped her hand out from under Ahvrym's, carefully

folded the vulpé fur, and set it aside. She gazed at it one last time, then looked into Ahvrym's eyes.

"That's my oldest memory," she whispered, leaning close until her right cheek almost touched his. "All of it . . . gone."

"Sekmé, man's war with himself began so long ago we don't even know which world it started on. Their children came here to get away from it and flourished a long time before they broke faith again. Do you understand faith, Sekmé?" Ahvrym closed the gap so that not only their cheeks touched, but their foreheads as well.

"No single person establishes a faith and no single person can destroy it," he said. "If we've failed again, we've failed together, and not because one young woman decided she wanted to be a person instead of a soldier."

Sekmé sank her face in his beard and sobbed. When her hands searched out the throat under the whiskers and caressed it, Ahvrym cradled her in his arms and lay back with her in the desert grit on the bed.

He removed her clothes slowly, as if they were bandages.

CHAPTER 33

FLİGHT

Haru opened his eyes. He'd been meditating in the afternoon shade of a thornwood tree, trying to gain insight into how to protect his and Wepanu's little tribe of refugees. It hadn't done much more than clarify their problems. Every day, more and more desperate people from Kemphor wandered into the desert. Some were mad with privation, others armed, and their little band had to keep moving to stay out of the way. They'd had little rest in weeks.

Haru stretched. After traipsing all over the Hills of Whispers with Wepanu, he was used to this kind of life, but the refugees were not. The three boys—he couldn't think of them as men—were eager but didn't have an ounce of common sense between them. One even ate some thornwood berries without blanching them first and nearly shit his life away. It was hard to believe they were Sekmé's kin. The girls, with their servant backgrounds, were more practical but not very strong, and they tended to push themselves to exhaustion, impeding their progress.

"We have to leave the Hills of Whispers," Haru had recently told the old seer late one evening after they'd camped in a sheltered hollow and the "children" had fallen into a dead sleep. "We need a place to settle. Somewhere safe."

Wepanu pouted.

"I don't mean *you* need a place to settle," Haru added quickly. "Wandering is your way, but these refugees aren't Denneshur. They need to catch their breath and consider the future. They need stability."

The seer still looked unhappy, but his brow softened. Haru held his palm out to him, the universal gesture of request.

"Please, Wepanu. The wandering is killing them."

The old man nodded and scratched his groin. "I know, Haru. I know they're suffering, but the jo have told me to wait."

"Wait for what?"

As an answer, Wepanu curled up on the ground next to the cookfire and closed his eyes.

"It won't be long," he murmured.

"*What* won't be?"

But the jo had appeared in the hollow and shushed Haru by pinching his nostrils together with her tiny hands. He hated when she did that.

Haru got up, brushed off the sand, and scanned the nearby sunset-edged promontory to see if Wepanu was still deep in his own devotions. He wasn't. Haru decided he'd better find the others and start roasting the oryx they'd killed that morning. The fire would be ready now.

He smiled to himself. They'd almost lost the oryx on the narrow trail out of the ravine when that Needle flew over. The refugees were still so traumatized by their memories of fires in the holdings that they'd panicked and dropped the carcass. Luckily, Haru had caught hold of one of the horns and hefted the beast back up onto the trail before it fell over the edge. He still had his strength.

When he reached the fire, the others, except Wepanu, were waiting for him.

Good! They haven't tried to skin the oryx themselves, Haru thought. At least they're beginning to learn what it is they *don't* know.

However, before he could start teaching them the proper way to dress and spit the meat, a low whine rose in the sky from the west followed by a familiar howl.

"Not another one!" Bross cried, and the girls screamed.

"Calm down!" Haru said. "It's not after a puny little band of refugees."

The Needle flew out of the sunset glare unusually slowly, which was why they'd heard it before they saw it, and for a moment, even Haru wondered if it wasn't looking for them, but it passed over the wadi and disappeared into the hills.

"See?" He smiled. "We don't need to worry about—"

"Wait!" Zeffa the chambermaid said. "What's that sound?"

"They've seen us!" Nehro cried. "It's coming back!"

The young refugees fled for the cliffs to hide among the rocks.

Haru watched the Needle reappear over the wadi, moving even slower than before as if sniffing out something on the ground. It circled once then came to a hovering stop in plain view of the tiny camp and its fire of red coals.

In spite of the refugees' horror stories, Haru didn't feel the need to run. In fact, he was strangely excited. Somehow, he knew that not only was he not in any danger, but the Needle signaled a change, the arrival of something new. When the craft slowly began its descent, he held up his arm as a shield against the whirling dust and walked out to meet it.

The Needle settled gently in the sand and its engines' scream gradually subsided to a thick groan and stopped. The dust cleared and Haru lowered his arm as the panel in the craft's belly opened, a small service ladder extended, and two people climbed down.

The man was dark, bearded, and barrel-chested—undoubtedly Tel-mari, which puzzled Haru, especially considering that the other person, dressed in salvaged castoffs from her brother's ruined room, was Sekmé.

He stared at her, unable to put his feelings into words. She stared back.

"It's been a long time, Sekmé," he said pointedly.

She understood and nodded. He was grateful for the regret in her eyes.

"This young man," the Tel-mari said to her. "You share history with him?"

"Yes."

The bearded man had his arm around Sekmé's waist and the way they looked at each other told Haru there was a trust between them that he'd never known with her. They might have come from very different places, but they had a great deal in common.

The Tel-mari bowed formally, one hand placed over his heart.

"My name is Ahvrym," he said.

Haru had to decide. How he greeted this enemy, this usurper, would affect everything. The children had come out of hiding and were running toward them.

He could tell Sekmé knew what he was thinking. Her green eyes were steady and yet not as he remembered them. She'd suffered and been changed by it. There was a circumspect quality in her otherwise direct expression that wasn't the result of a diminishment in courage, but an expansion in perspective. Curiously, this change made her look more like her brother.

Then her eyes, startled, flicked past his shoulder. She'd seen the jo. The relationship between them shifted instantly and he felt an enormous sense of relief.

Haru extended his hand to the Tel-mari and smiled.

"My name is Haru," he said, then added the traditional Denneshur coda. "Our fire waits to warm you."

The refugees panted up in a small cloud of dust.

"Sekmé? It *is* you!"

For a few chaotic minutes, Sekmé's remaining cousins assaulted her with embraces and a rapid onslaught of questions they didn't wait to have answered.

"How-are-you-we-thought-you-were-dead-you-look-wonderful!"

"Where-have-you-been-I-thought-we'd-never-see-you-

again-have-you-heard-what-happened-to-the-holdings-it's-a-disaster!"

"What-happened-has-the-army-fallen-apart-we've-been-living-here-with-Haru-isn't-it-amazing-he's-alive-too!"

Haru noticed Wepanu, who must have come while they were fussing over Sekmé, walking slowly around and under the hot aircraft, his dark face full of bemused amazement.

"Who's this, Sekmé?" Tiu asked.

"Ahvrym. A friend."

"Ahvrym?" Bross's excitement cooled. "A Tel-mari?"

"Displaced, to be sure." Ahvrym bowed.

Bross was aghast. "He's not of God, Sekmé!"

With a flash of her old, martial prowess, Sekmé grabbed her cousin by the belt and yanked him to her side. She smiled—all teeth.

"The war is *over*, Bross," she said softly.

"It is?"

"For us it is."

She let him go.

"If you say so, Sekmé," Bross shrugged, "but I don't think the others know."

She turned to Haru. "What others?"

"The Hills of Whispers are full of refugees, Sekmé." He saw Wepanu poke his staff up through the Needle's belly panel. "It's become dangerous."

"What are you going to do?"

"I don't know. We've been running all over the desert like fugitives."

She glanced at the others and quickly appraised their condition with a look of dismay.

"It'll only get worse," she said. "Kemphor has fallen. We saw the Dome burn."

"Sekmé," Ahvrym cut in, "who's that naked fellow by the Needle?"

"What?" She spun around, then giggled. "Oh, dear! He certainly is 'as the innocent,' isn't he?"

"That's Wepanu ul-Bahf," Haru said.

"The seer?" Sekmé looked at the old man with new interest.

"I don't think he's seen a Needle this close before," Haru added.

Wepanu began to climb into the aircraft.

"Oh, no!" Ahvrym said. "I'd better stop him."

Sekmé dropped her hand on his arm. "Don't. He'll be all right. He can't get into the cockpit. Let him play."

"Sekmé," Ahvrym said slowly as an idea gradually blossomed, "how much fuel is left in the Needle?"

"Almost three-quarters. We carried very little. Why?"

"How—how far could we go?"

Sekmé's lips parted in the dawn of revelation.

"That depends." She gazed warmly at Ahvrym. In the fading light, his features were indistinct except for the intelligent brilliance of his eyes. "Where do you want to go?"

Ahvrym moved close and cupped his fingers around her face.

"What lies south of the Salt Barrens?" he whispered.

"I don't know."

"Shall we toss a coin?"

"We'd lose it in the sand." Sekmé grinned. "Besides, we already know what it would say, don't we?"

The moon and the Calf rose together that night as the Needle lifted out of the wadi and over the cliffs. In the cockpit, Sekmé adjusted her night viewers and offered Ahvrym a pair.

"No," he declined. "I'd rather see the stars in their natural colors." He chuckled softly. "That old man is unique, isn't he?"

"When we've reached cruise, I'll bring him up here. I promised."

She considered a moment, then unbuckled her viewers and set them aside.

"I'd like to see the stars, too," she said.

"You don't need them?"

"Not really. Not until we're about to land."

She checked Ahvrym's restraint belts one more time—stroked his beard.

"I hope this experiment works," she said. "I don't think even the Denneshur have gone that far south."

"It will." Ahvrym smiled up at the Calf. "We've already gained Sa'Har."

Sekmé pushed the thrust forward and the Needle leapt across the southern reaches of the Hills of Whispers toward an unknown land.

ABOUT THE AUTHOR

KATIE WAITMAN works as a secretary for a number of law professors. She is currently working on a sequel to a second novel in the world of *The Merro Tree*, her first book.